Great Expectations

How to Order:

Quantity discounts are available from the publisher, Prima Publishing, P.O. Box 1260DP, Rocklin, CA 95677; telephone (916) 624-5718. On your letterhead include information concerning the intended use of the books and the number of books you wish to purchase.

U.S. Bookstores and Libraries: Please submit all orders to St. Martin's Press, 175 Fifth Avenue, New York, NY 10010; telephone (212) 674-5151.

Great Expectations

*The San Francisco 49ers
and the Quest for the "Three-peat"*

Dennis Pottenger

Prima Publishing
P.O. Box 1260DP
Rocklin, CA 95677
(916) 624-5718

Typography by Janet Hansen, Alphatype
Production by Carol Dondrea, Bookman Productions
Editing by Steve Bailey
Interior design by Judith Levinson, Bookman Productions
Jacket design by The Dunlavey Studio
Jacket photograph © by Jeff Bayer

Grateful acknowledgment is made to Dr. Harry Edwards for permission to use excerpts from his book *The Struggle That Must Be* (New York: Macmillan Publishing Company, 1980).

Many of the designations used by manufacturers and sellers to distinguish their products are claimed as trademarks. Where those designations appear in this book and Prima Publishing was aware of a trademark claim, the designations have been printed in initial capital letters (for example, Spiderman, Nike, and PowerBurst).

Prima Publishing
Rocklin, CA

Library of Congress Cataloging-in-Publication Data

Pottenger, Dennis.
Great expectations : the San Francisco 49ers and the quest
  for "three-peat" / by Dennis Pottenger.
      p.   cm.
    ISBN 1-55958-100-X :
    1. San Francisco 49ers (Football team)   I. Title.
GV956.S3P67   1991
796.332'64'097961—dc20   91-7654
                                                                CIP

91 92 93 94   RRD   10 9 8 7 6 5 4 3 2 1

Printed in the United States of America

For Annette, who helped me believe

Put out into deep water
—Luke 5:4, New Testament

Notes on Text

One of the major literary devices featured in *Great Expectations* is the use of italics. The device is used to take the reader into the thoughts and feelings of the person in the passage—to not only capture the emotion of the moment and provide narrative drama but also to reflect and reveal the personality of the individual involved. In virtually every instance where italics are used, the thoughts and feelings attributed result directly from interviews by the author. In some cases, material used in italics is not a verbatim quotation, but a statement based on a direct quotation. In these instances, the spirit of the quotation remains true.

Virtually every direct quotation used in *Great Expectations* was tape-recorded by the author. Other direct quotations—such as the events in the 49er locker room described in Chapter Seven—were recorded in handwritten notes by the author.

In several cases, the dialogue in this book results from memories of the people involved. Because some quotations are based on memory, they may reflect the spirit of the conversation or quotation but may not be verbatim.

Direct quotations from members of the 49ers' organization that originally appeared elsewhere are used frequently in *Great Expectations*. In most cases, the reporter who originally recorded the quotation is acknowledged in the passage where the quotation appears.

Only one name has been changed. At the request of Jamie Williams, the name of his friend who appears in Chapter Four has been changed to protect that person's true identity. All other characters are real.

Contents

Preface

George Seifert finishes his dinner and begins to pace.

It's a quarter to 6 in the evening, Saturday, July 28, day four of the San Francisco 49ers' summer training camp at Sierra College in Rocklin, California. Seifert, the 50-year-old head coach of the two-time defending world champions of professional football, is dressed in beige pants, a brown short-sleeved shirt, and customary brown topsiders without socks. At the front of the cafeteria, Seifert moves slowly along one side of a rectangular table loaded with food. Past the apples, grapes, and bananas. Past the slices of ham and turkey. Past the mayo and the mustard and the 10 kinds of bread.

Back now up by the fruit, Seifert plucks two grapes from their stems, eats one, turns to his left, and wanders down the other side of the table. He eats another grape. George Seifert is not hungry. And he's not having dessert. He's killing time. Because he knows that in a few minutes, he will walk to his right and enter a place he knows will be quite unpleasant tonight.

The press room.

Because the press room is where the reporters are.

And because, only four days into the 1990 National Football League season, the Niners are in trouble.

When the reporters—about a dozen in all—are seated expectantly before him, George Seifert hunches his shoulders forward and gets down to the business of explaining how, after only four days, his football team is coming apart at the seams. How, just six months after San Francisco beat up on the Denver Broncos to become the first NFL team in a decade to win back-to-back Super Bowls, the dream of winning three in a row—Three-peat—is fast becoming less a matter of beating the Rams or the Giants or the Raiders than it is just putting enough healthy bodies on the field.

Most of the trouble—not only in Rocklin but also in Austin, Texas; Florham Park, New Jersey; West De Pere, Wisconsin; and almost every training camp in the NFL—involves money. Six starters from the Seifert team that went to the top of the world in New Orleans are holding out for better contracts. Linebacker Charles Haley. Safety Chet Brooks. Defensive end Kevin Fagan. Center Jesse Sapolu. Guard Guy McIntyre. And tackle Harris Barton. Two Pro Bowl players. Two All-Maddens. One All-Pro. One All-Rookie. All starters. All no-shows.

Unfortunately for Seifert, contract squabbles are not his only worries. The offensive line is in chaos. Neither the starting center, Jesse Sapolu, nor the starting left guard, Guy McIntyre, is in camp. No one knows when they will be. In addition, both backup centers have bad knees and can't play. And one rookie, center Dean Caliguire, is still hobbling around on the ankle he broke during his senior year at the University of Pittsburgh. It all means that Harris Barton, San Francisco's most versatile offensive lineman, will have to waste time filling in for Sapolu at center instead of learning his new position, right guard. *When* he gets into camp.

If all of this isn't enough to render George Seifert's nerves as raw as a pulled hamstring, there's a topper—which, to Seifert, chafes even more than having a dozen reporters watch him eat breakfast. Last night, Jeff Bregel, a fourth-year offensive lineman from USC, announced his retirement. In 1987, when San Francisco picked Bregel in the second round of the college draft, the 49ers' coaches had hoped—indeed, expected—that the young man, an Academic All-American and a finalist for the Outland Trophy as college football's outstanding interior lineman in his senior year, would evolve into a dominant force on the Niner offensive line for six, eight years—for most of the decade to come. But Bregel sometimes forgot who and when he was supposed to block, and the coaches would yank him from the game, yell at him, give him his assignment again, and then, after a while, they'd send him in for one more try.

Not anymore, George Seifert said to the reporters in the press room. Bregel had walked in and told John McVay, San Francisco's vice-president of football administration, that he'd had enough. That he was through. Just like that.

Then it happened. A question that led to an answer that was more than just an answer—a question that was a picture, a symbol, of a whole season—and one writer's dream—all in a few words.

"Coach," one reporter asked Seifert, "how much of an effect do you think all of these things—the holdouts, the injuries, the retirements, the talk of Three-peat—will have on the season?" Seifert crinkled his mouth into a tense pucker and focused his gray, bird-of-prey eyes out the window at the burnt red sun falling through the heat and haze in the distance.

"There are always going to be disruptions," Seifert said, wringing his hands so tightly under the table that his fingertips turned white. "Through the course of camp, and during the course of the season, we have to work with the players [who] are on hand and stay involved with our football. That's what we're here for. . . . These are all veteran players who have been a part of our program for some time. We look forward to them coming back and being a part of this club again. . . . Just because they are involved in contract negotiations, and in some cases will miss some time in camp, I don't believe [that] will distract us from our ultimate goal. . . . We all have great expectations."

Great expectations. Two words that had come to me on a golf course, out of nowhere, one day a few months before. Two words that shook me awake inside. Two words that told me I was *supposed* to write this book.

When George Seifert finished his sentence, he did something that I couldn't explain then and can't explain now. He looked right at me. Turned his head from his right all the way around to his left. To Seifert, I must have looked odd—even for a reporter. Here's this guy he's never met before grinning stupidly with all of his teeth showing at the head coach of the two-time defending champions of professional football. A proud, intense man who has so many problems on his mind right now but has somehow summoned the patience to face reporters and has great expectations for a team and a season that are making him nervous as hell right now.

And yet there I was, grinning stupidly, with all of my teeth showing, at George Seifert, the head coach of the two-time defending world champions of professional football, in front of all of the reporters in the press room at Sierra College. Seifert must have wondered what the hell was wrong with me.

There was nothing wrong with me.

His team had great expectations.

So did I.

On the last Sunday night in January 1990, I watched what the Niners did to the Broncos in the New Orleans Superdome. It was right there on CBS. Look at it. Montana to Rice. Montana to Taylor. Fifty-five to 10. By halftime, when San Francisco led 27–3, some of the reporters already had 30 inches written. Denver was dead.

What I remembered most, though, in the days and weeks after the game, wasn't the final score. It wasn't Joe

Montana's five touchdown passes—a Super Bowl record. And it wasn't that after the game was over the entire 49er team stood in the locker room chanting "THREE-PEAT! THREE-PEAT!" What clung to me, what tugged at me somewhere inside, had nothing to do with any of those things.

It had to do with Ronnie Lott.

The morning after the game, on the front page of the *Sacramento Bee,* reporter S. L. Price wrote about the curious scene that had unfolded in front of Lott's locker after the game. Lott stood, Price wrote, "in the bowels of the Louisiana Superdome . . . surrounded by dozens of microphones and notepads and looking about as excited as someone shopping for dog food. . . . He smiled rarely. He spoke in a monotone. He was asked why he didn't seem excited. He said, 'It doesn't really matter.' "

The most lopsided Super Bowl win in league history; San Francisco's fourth NFL title in Lott's nine seasons in pro ball; the first club to win consecutive Super Bowls since Bradshaw and Swann and the Steel Curtain 10 years ago; a six-month journey of effort, sacrifice, and pain that had just ended in glorious total triumph—and yet "it doesn't really matter"? I didn't understand. How, I puzzled, could Ronnie Lott achieve so much and yet be so humble? How could he stand at the very crest of his world overlooking every man in his profession—overlooking most every man in *sport*—and yet speak so softly of what he and his 49er teammates had just done?

A reporter asked Lott to explain. "The reason it doesn't matter is that we try to take things in stride," Lott said. "We're all excited because we won, but we're very humble about winning this one and we'll be humble about winning any future ones. Because we know how hard it is to get here. For us to sit here and be cocky or boisterous or get big-headed—by no means are we going to be that way."

It was then that I knew I had to meet Ronnie Lott.

Eight months later, I did. I quit my job as a staff writer for the city magazine in Sacramento and said goodbye to my wife for five months. It was time for my dream—this book—to begin.

When it all started, my head and heart were both stuffed full of questions. There was so much I wanted to know. About football. About the organization. About the people. What, I wondered, was the magic that keeps Ronnie Lott and Joe Montana hungry for more after achieving all there is to achieve in the NFL? How do Lott, Montana, and Jerry Rice use that magic to keep themselves focused on football in a time of big money, big egos, and big distractions? What was the Taj? Who were Spiderman, Captain America, and Venus Fly Trap? Who were Kid Flash, the Assassin, and Professor X? Who was the Prince? Who was the King? And who was Doc? And just what kind of people get up almost every day for six months to try to do something great? Something that no one else has ever done before?

Deep down, my list of questions could be wrapped inside a single, almost intangible image. What is the one quality, the *master* key, that opens doors for Lott, Montana, and the rest of the Niners? What is the human combination that allows them passage out of the dark, cold, and cynical world of professional football into the grand ballroom of greatness?

In my quest for the answer, I was searching for something deeper than Joe to Jerry for six. Something bigger than six-figure endorsements and deferred bonuses. Something better than fame and fortune and football. I wanted to see, touch, and feel the pulse of the most successful professional sports franchise in America.

I wanted to know *everything*.

During the year that I spent working on this book, I straggled down hundreds of paths. I got doors slammed in my face. I got phones hung up in my ear. I watched people care for each other. I watched people hurt for each other. I saw people feel so helpless they cried. I saw people feel so confident they giggled. I saw how pressure and strain and exhaustion change people. And I saw how *nothing* changes people.

As for me, I got frustrated. I got scared. I got in arguments. I felt lonely. I cried. I laughed. I hurt. I doubted myself. I doubted others. I doubted life. I faced people who didn't trust me. I faced people who didn't want to trust me. And I faced people who never would trust me.

Between the smothering heat of Rocklin in July and the shivering Santa Clara winds in December were times when I felt lost and tired and convinced that I was never going to find my way out of the mess I'd gotten myself into. But I never quit. I finished what I started. As I was about to learn, that's what having great expectations is all about.

Prologue

"ARE YOU READY FOR SOME *FOOT-BALL?!!*"

It's an hour and a half before kickoff at Candlestick on a Monday night early in December. Inside the San Francisco 49ers' locker room, Joe Montana is singing for Harris Barton. It's tradition. Before every Monday night football game, Montana gets in front of his uptight offensive lineman and belts out the line from Hank Williams Jr.'s theme song for ABC television's "Monday Night Football." Barton, San Francisco's 280-pound right guard, sits hulking over the little wooden stool in front of his locker. As usual, Barton is as tight as a coiled spring. He wishes Joe Montana would just shut up and let him brood. If Montana's howling question is tradition, so is Harris Barton's answer. He smiles weakly. Then he speaks.

"Get out of my face," he says.

It's tradition. And tonight is no time to break tradition. Because tonight, the Giants—L. T., Simms, Meggett, Bavaro, and the rest—are here, at Candlestick, for "Monday Night Football." If this season, if the quest for history is going to go anywhere, then it's going to have to begin tonight. Against the only other 10-and-1 team in the NFL.

Sitting on the stool next to Harris Barton, Jesse Sapolu also is trying his best to ignore Joe Montana. Sapolu is the 49ers' center, a 6-foot-4, 260-pound rock in his eighth year out of the University of Hawaii. Less than

30 minutes before the blood feud with the Giants, Jesse Sapolu is trying to calm down. He is trying to find peace.

When Sapolu was growing up in Hawaii, his dad was a minister. Back in the islands, his dad taught Jesse not to think bad thoughts about the other players he was competing against, but to trust God and just do the best he possibly could. *Don't worry about whether your best is going to be good enough,* Jesse's dad had told him many times before he died. *If you've done everything you can do and it's still not good enough, then maybe that's the way it was supposed to be. You must learn to be at peace with yourself.*

For Jesse Sapolu, peace comes in a color. As he focuses deeper and deeper on the game ahead, everything—people, words, the weather—begins to gray, losing shape and form until all that's left in his mind is a canvas of black. *"My black magic,"* Jesse calls it. *"My black magic."*

Normally, Sapolu is fairly calm before a game—keyed up, of course—but mostly at peace with himself and the war ahead. Tonight, though, Jesse Sapolu is having trouble finding peace. He can't seem to summon his magic. Perhaps it's because he knows that in less than half an hour L. T.—Lawrence Taylor—will come shuddering toward him and his linemates. Perhaps it's the pressure of protecting the greatest quarterback in the world from one of the roughest defenses in the world. Or perhaps it's because this "Monday Night Football" game is beaming back to Hawaii and Los Angeles, where family and friends—a whole state and part of a city—are watching and *expecting* him to do them proud. But then again, maybe it's none of these reasons. Maybe tonight Jesse Sapolu is just nervous. Number 61 takes a deep breath and lets it all out. Fade to black.

A few lockers away, Roger Craig is meditating. Jazz rhythms glide through his headphones. The feet bounce on the toes. Up. Down. Up. Down. Seven days of pent-up nervous energy straining for release.

Craig's countdown began last Monday, the morning after San Francisco took its first loss of the season, to the Rams at Candlestick. For seven days, the 49er running back has visualized this game in his mind. Taking the handoff. Running up into the hole. Teammates blocking like the diagram in the playbook. Slashing up the field. Pounding his knees like jackhammers. A linebacker or a safety flailing at him as he churns by gaining yard after yard. That's the most important part. To Roger Craig, that's what mind over matter is all about. Running. Gaining yards. Those are the things that win football games.

Roger Craig's game-day ritual began about two hours ago when equipment assistant Ted Walsh drew a small triangle in red ink at the top of each of Craig's ankles. To Roger, the triangles carry spiritual strength, a power the Niner running back believes protects him from misfortune and injury. To teammate Jamie Williams, Roger Craig is Captain America, the comic book superhero who, after the army injects him with a serum, possesses superhuman endurance and is feared ever after as one of the finest hand-to-hand combatants the earth has ever known. Captain America's only weapon, according to comic book legend, is a shield that cannot be penetrated or destroyed. With his shield as protection, Captain America is virtually indestructible. Tonight, against the Giants, there will be a crack in the shield. But not before Captain America has helped save the day for the good people of the city.

Several lockers to Craig's right, Dexter Carter is waiting. Unlike some of his teammates, San Francisco's rookie running back does not hate these moments in the locker room before the game. Dexter isn't nervous. And he doesn't need to slam his head against the wall to get fired up. During the week, he's watched films, read the playbook, and run every play 60 yards down the field in practice. Dexter is ready. Because he knows he's not alone out there on the football field.

The Lord has always taken care of Dexter Carter. No matter what the problem—no matter *who* the problem— the Lord has always delivered exactly the reward Dexter deserved. Gloria Carter, Dexter's mother, taught her son that no problem was so difficult that hard work and a prayer couldn't simplify it. In high school, before the bus came to take Dexter to school, Gloria Carter would gather Dexter and his older brother in the living room, where the three of them would hold hands and say a prayer for the day ahead. *Lord, bless us and protect us from all hurt, harm, and danger. And let nothing come before us that neither the Lord nor we can't handle.* In Baxley, Georgia, praying had always worked for Dexter Carter. It had worked when he went away to college in Florida, too.

But that was then. This is Candlestick Park. Do prayers work for blood feuds with Giants? As the game draws closer, Dexter is talking silently to himself. *Bless me, Lord. And Lord, when I get in there and they give me the ball, I'll run just like you tell me to.* Amen.

At the far end of the upper level of the locker room where the 49er offense dresses, tight end Jamie Williams sits reading a comic book. To the linebackers and line-men around the league, Williams is a force to be reck-oned with—a punishing, relentless blocker who some football people say is the best-blocking tight end in the NFL. To his teammates, however, Jamie Williams is Spider. Spiderman.

Growing up in Davenport, Iowa, a hard-scrabble factory town on the banks of the Mississippi River, Jamie loved to read comics. Spiderman. The Invisible Woman. The Incredible Hulk. Batman. Whatever. For Williams, comics took the edge off a dead-end neighborhood and a father from the old school who thought pumping gas or fixing plumbing was the way to make a living. To Jamie's dad, footballs and basketballs—even A's in school—were all just a waste of time.

Years ago, after Jamie got out of Davenport and into the University of Nebraska, he'd been shocked by the cutthroat world to which he had ascended—Division I football. Fifteen tight ends competing for one position. Pressure. Drugs. And fear. So Jamie called on the comic book world to which he had retreated for support back in Davenport. Inside, Jamie cultivated a feeling that, like Spiderman, he had problems just like everybody else. But that when it came right down to it, good always triumphed over evil. And Jamie Williams definitely knew that he was good.

In the world of the superheroes, Jamie could insulate himself from the harsh realities of his life. It wasn't an escape really, but a buffer, a shield he used to keep the big, bad world away so it wouldn't—*couldn't*—trample his confidence in himself. Spiderman kept Jamie sane, kept him strong, and taught him that he could do whatever he wanted to do as long as he decided that evil would not stop him. In comics, no matter what the problem was, no matter who the villain was, Spiderman always found a way to let good triumph over evil. Spiderman always found a way to rise above problems with his girlfriend or another villain. Spiderman always found a way to save the people of the city.

Inside of 20 minutes before the blood feud with the Giants, Jamie Williams is preparing to fight. As Jamie reads at his locker, Spiderman has his hands full with a ruthless supervillain known as Hobgoblin. The city is in danger, and Spiderman is the only hope for its people. Soon Jamie Williams will be fighting his own battle with the forces of evil. He will come face mask to face mask with his own threatening villain out to destroy him and his teammates—L. T.

To Jamie Williams, however, tonight means more than triumphing over evil and saving the game for the

Niners. For Williams, the New York Giants are more than just another team on the schedule. The Giants are the team that drafted him out of Nebraska in 1983. And the Giants are the team that cut him in 1983. Jamie Williams has never forgotten what it felt like to be released—severed—from football against his will. When the Giants cut him, Jamie was hurt and frustrated and unsure of himself. *Man, I thought I could play with these guys. Can I?* Then he felt anger. As the Hobgoblin slaughters more innocent people, Jamie Williams remembers the anger. The rage builds inside him. *I hate those fucking Giants. I hate those fuckers.*

Downstairs from Jamie Williams's locker, Jim Burt paces like a caged tiger. Burt is always wired before a game. Before last year's 34–24 win over New York at Candlestick, he was so charged up that when the 49er offense ran onto the field for the start of the game, he—*a defensive lineman*—ran in with them. He hummed around the huddle, banging on shoulder pads and screaming unintelligible things before his teammates made him run back to the bench.

Jim Burt is always wired before a game. But this game has been ridiculous. He hasn't slept in three nights. Fourteen years of football—four at the University of Miami and 10 in the pros—have come down to these three hours. On this field. Against the Giants. To Burt, football is a simple game. *Either you win or you lose. There's no inbetween. And losing—losing is the worst. When you lose, there's nothing. You're empty.*

Fifteen minutes before the blood feud with the Giants, Burt paces in the center of the locker room, thrusting his hands up into the imaginary shoulder pads of his enemy. Tonight his enemy is the Giants' center, Bart Oates. For eight years, Burt and Oates played together in New York. For eight seasons as teammates, Burt and Bart practiced and played together. And after bitter playoff losses to San Francisco in 1981 and 1984, they hated the 49ers together. Now only one of them hates the 49ers. After the game, they will be friends again. But now and for the next three hours, Jim Burt is going to try his hardest to hate Bart Oates.

Ronnie Lott stares out from his stool in the corner of the locker room. Like Joe Montana, Jesse Sapolu, Jim Burt, and the rest of the Niners, San Francisco's ferocious, moody free safety has his own way of preparing for war. Once last year, his first as head coach, George Seifert walked over and said something to Lott on his stool before a game. Lott looked up at Seifert with glassy, pained eyes. With the faraway look that Lott's teammates know means *Don't Mess With Me*. George Seifert learned.

Three months ago, it was Lott who had marked tonight as a watershed moment in the quest for Three-peat. San Francisco had just lost an exhibition game to the Chargers. In the locker room after the game, someone asked Lott how long it would take before he could assess whether this year's team was going to be able to play up to the level last year's team had. Lott had said, "We won't know what kind of team we are until Week 12. Great teams don't become great teams until Week 12."

On a warm August night in San Diego, Week 12 looked and felt like a long ways away. And it was. But now it is here. It is time to see what kind of team the 49ers are this year.

For Chet Brooks, there will be no football tonight. No Meggett. No Simms. No Monday night. Brooks is on the inactive list for the war with the Giants. A month ago in Green Bay, the reckless, relentless Niner strong safety tore cartilage in his left knee against the Packers. Brooks has missed three games after having arthroscopic surgery to repair the damage.

Growing up in Oak Cliff, a middle-class neighborhood in the shadow of downtown Dallas, Chet Brooks and his buddies had a saying, a code of honor they wore on their sleeves whether they were playing Kimball for neighborhood bragging rights or taking on the white boys from Odessa for the championship of the state of Texas. *You gotta bring some ass to get some ass,* is what they said. For his coaches and his parents, Chet shortened it to, *You gotta bring it to get it.* But either way, the message was clear. You either brought some, or you didn't bother playing at all.

Ever since his injury, Chet Brooks has been fighting the fact that he hasn't been able to play. In fact, it's been tearing him up. Ever since his injury, he hasn't come to the games because it's too hard to be so close and yet so far from the hitting. It's easier to stay home with his girl and watch it on TV, because then, when the void and the hurt get to him, he can just turn it off and walk away.

But tonight, Monday night, Chet Brooks is here at Candlestick where he loves to be. In the locker room. *With my boys.* Brooks paces, but there's a smile on his face. If he can't bring it against the Giants, then at least his boys can.

One minute before 6 o'clock, George Seifert gathers the San Francisco 49ers in the center of the locker room at Candlestick Park. The 49ers' head coach is holding the notes of his pregame speech. But his players seem too tight—almost *too* tense—for yet another talk. So Seifert stuffs the notes back in his pocket. Most of his players are kneeling in a circle around him as the words rumble forth like the deep measures of a waterfall in the night.

Our father who art in Heaven, hallowed be thy name.

Thy kingdom come, thy will be done on earth as it is in Heaven.

Give us this day our daily bread and forgive us our trespasses as we forgive those who trespass against us.

Lead us not into temptation but deliver us from evil.

God is the Kingdom. GOD IS THE POWER. GOD IS THE GLORY.

They rise and file out to the field.

They are ready for some football.

Chapter 1

Camp Super Bowl

Little globs of sweat race across Hanford Dixon's bald head, plunging down his forehead and into his eyes. It's a Friday afternoon late in July 1990, the first week of training camp. Practice ended a few minutes ago. Now Dixon sits on a square wooden bench at the entrance to the locker room at Sierra College in Rocklin, California. He's cutting the tape off the outside of his cleats. It's almost 100 degrees outside, and as the sun broils the blacktop, waves of heat shimmer in the distance, distorting the view over the football fields from where the San Francisco 49ers have launched four Super Bowl quests since 1981.

The year San Francisco won its first world championship, 1981, was the same year the Cleveland Browns drafted Hanford Dixon in the first round out of Southern Mississippi University. Dixon spent nine seasons as a cornerback for the Browns. He went to the Pro Bowl four times. One year he was named the defensive back of the year in the National Football League. Another year, he was looking for a way to fire up his linemen to go after the quarterback, so he started barking at them in the huddle. When the fans and the press got hold of what he was doing, "Dawg Mania" consumed Cleveland. Bronze statues downtown were outfitted with orange helmets and giant white milkbones. Schoolchildren went to class wearing handmade paper headbands with floppy ears. The mayor paraded around town wearing an orange dog snout and brown basset-hound ears. The defense was the Dawgs. Cleveland Stadium was the Dawg Pound. And the creator of the whole thing, Hanford Dixon, wasn't just one of the best corners in the NFL, he was the Dawg. In 1984, the year Dixon walked into the huddle and started barking, the Cleveland Browns won 5 games and lost 11. The next year, Cleveland went 8 and 8. In 1986, the Browns soared to 12 and 4 and played Denver in the AFC Championship Game. That year, Hanford Dixon was named to the AFC Pro Bowl squad, the All-NFL team, and the All-AFC team. Those were the good times. The best.

For Hanford Dixon, that life and career are gone now. The Dawgs, the Browns, the Pro Bowls—they are all just memories, reminders of what he used to be. The reason for the past tense is simple. Hanford Dixon is no longer the player he was in Cleveland. After nine seasons in the NFL, he's lost much of the speed he had when he was younger and barking his way to the Pro Bowl. At 31, Hanford Dixon now relies on savvy and technique—on *thinking* himself into the right place at the right time on the football field.

After last season, Cleveland head coach Bud Carson decided that Dixon was an uncoachable prima donna— Carson even said so in the newspaper. In the NFL, however, coaches frequently tolerate uncoachable prima donnas as long as they can still make plays. Early in 1990, Bud Carson named another player to start in Dixon's place at left cornerback. And the Browns left Dixon unprotected in the Plan B limited free-agent pool, a system in which teams can retain rights to 37 of their 47 players. Those who are left unprotected are then free to jump to any team that wants them. The Browns figured nobody would have any use for an old cover man, and that would be that. Dixon would still be a Brown and they would either cut him or he would retire. The Browns were wrong. In March, soon after Cleveland sent its Plan B list to the league office, the 49ers called. The Dawg jumped at the chance to show a new owner that he still had a little play, a little bark, left in him.

After his fourth practice as a Niner, Hanford Dixon sits on the wooden bench outside the Sierra College locker room, shearing the tape off his right shoe. The Dawg is talking about how he's hoping to bring some of his bark to San Francisco to bite down on the one thing he got close to three times as a Brown but could never quite get his paws on: a Super Bowl ring.

"I feel like a rookie," Dixon says. "I'm just working as hard as I can, trying to get better each day, to see if I can help this ball club. Wherever the coaches want me to play, that's where I'll play. Corner. Free safety. Strong safety. I don't care. My biggest thing is to get one of those rings.

"This [training camp] is different than Cleveland," Dixon adds, tossing a wad of tape over his shoulder into the garbage can behind him. "This is a championship atmosphere. We don't work as long as we did in Cleveland, but we work as hard. I think that's important. Once we hit the field, it's quality time. A lot of teams use training camp to get ready for the season hoping they make the playoffs. These guys go through camp expecting to make it to the Super Bowl. Whatever they want me—"

In midsentence, Dixon cuts himself off and calls out to Jerry Attaway, San Francisco's conditioning coach, who is walking into the locker room. Attaway stops and looks at Dixon.

"I was a little weak today," Dixon says. "I don't know what it was, but I got a little weak." Attaway has a blank look.

"I don't know, Hanford," he says. "Old age, maybe?"

The Dawg grins, but goes quickly back to looking concerned.

"I felt drained. Any ideas?"

"You been eatin'?"

"Yeah."

"Drink some of the stuff on the right over here." Attaway points to a table just outside the locker room door. On the table are dozens of cups of bottled water and PowerBurst, a high-performance sports drink. "It's got a lot of carbohydrates and calories," Attaway adds. "All the things guys your age need."

Attaway grins at Dixon, then disappears into the locker room. Dixon walks over to the table and picks up two cups of PowerBurst.

"I don't know what it is," he says, taking a long gulp out of one. "I felt like my legs were in cement today. I couldn't get goin'. Maybe I am gettin' old."

Maybe.

Plan ahead. Get ahead.

This is one of John McVay's favorite sayings. McVay is San Francisco's executive vice-president of football administration. This fancy title means that he's in charge of what Bill Walsh, the architect of San Francisco's Super Bowl machine, often called the most important part of building and sustaining a sports franchise: finding, acquiring, and developing talent. In nine years with the 49ers, John McVay has put his favorite saying to use more than once.

Before this year, the classic example for McVay's motto came to fruition on the field in 1987, when the NFL players went on strike in a dispute with league owners over free agency. At the NFL meetings in Hawaii that spring, Bill Walsh, then in his ninth year as head coach of the Niners, called McVay and told him the talk was true. If the players walked, the owners were serious about playing the season anyway by hiring "scabs" to play in place of their regular players. John McVay went to work, combing the United States for former NFL players, former 49ers, former Division I college players—the best-quality free agents he could find. If the owners were serious about playing the season with replacements should a strike be called, then McVay and Walsh were determined to be prepared to field the best team possible. That summer, San Francisco invited a record 118 players to Rocklin, nearly a whole football team more than the usual number. Walsh and McVay kept the throng around most of camp, giving them plenty of practice time. Just in case they needed them back later on.

In late September 1987, the National Football League Players' Association voted to walk out, and the owners said, "Fine, we'll play the season anyway." Although some of the NFL's brightest executives were caught unprepared, McVay and Walsh put together a strike squad that featured 17 temps who had played in the NFL before. Only one other team in the league, the Indianapolis Colts, had that many strike players with NFL playing time under their belts. San Francisco's chief NFC West rivals, the Los Angeles Rams, on the other hand, had only three strike players with NFL experience. Not surprisingly, L.A. lost all three of its games during the strike. Coupled with a 0-and-2 start before that, the Rams' regulars came back to finish the season staring down the short end of a 0-and-5 record. It was a hole L.A. never escaped. The 49ers, meanwhile, went 3 and 0 during the strike, and streaked to the NFL's best regular-season record, 13 and 2, before unexpectedly losing to the Minnesota Vikings in the first round of the playoffs.

In 1987, John McVay planned ahead to get ahead. Before and since, there have been many other occasions when he has looked into the distance and acted with foresight to perpetuate the Super Bowl machine. There have been other players he has brought into the organization just in case they were needed—for a few games, for one game, for two plays. But none of these moves has been as brilliant—or more productive—as the acquisition of two players who are now running before him on the green grass in the sunshine at Sierra College.

John McVay's knobby legs are propped up on the front of a golf cart one afternoon early in Camp Super

Bowl. The cart is parked on the dirt infield of a baseball diamond next to where the 49ers are practicing. The drill is called seven on seven: Receivers and running backs run plays against defensive backs and linebackers. As McVay squints out into the sun, quarterback Steve Young barks the signals.

"THREE EIGHTY-FIVE. THREE EIGHTY-FIVE. SET . . . HUTHUT."

The receiver on McVay's side of the field is tall, with long legs and thin arms. As Steve Young drops back to throw, Mike Sherrard launches off the line into his pattern. Sherrard bounces like a rubberband up the field as he cuts inside, then quickly outside trying to lose the cornerback with his fake to the inside. The corner bites. Steve Young sees it and rifles a spiral toward Sherrard. Eighteen yards downfield, Sherrard surges toward the sideline and looks back for the ball.

Young's pass is too high and too far inside. But Sherrard knows where he is on the field. As the ball arrives, he whirls his body back toward the middle of the field and springs up into the sunshine. Sherrard snags the ball, then somehow suspends his momentum and falls, touching the tips of his toes inside the white line. Written down, the steps are separate and distinct. Drive off the ball. Fake the corner to the inside. Break the route off sharp outside. Find the sideline—*how much room?* Look back for the ball. Pick up the ball. React. Glide up an invisible elevator toward the sun. Reach up for the ball. Catch the ball. Somehow halt momentum and fall in the same place so the feet stay in bounds.

Separate steps on paper. But out on the field, Mike Sherrard blurs them all into one motion—a graceful act so precise, so athletic, so extraordinary that a chorus of whoops and yells erupts from his teammates as Sherrard picks himself up off the turf after what would have been a big play in a game.

"OOOOOOO . . ."

". . . VENUS . . ."

". . . OOOOOO."

The nickname has been Sherrard's since early in camp. He's been catching everything thrown his way like he's a butterfly net. Or a trap. A Venus Fly Trap. Camp Super Bowl was little more than a week old when George Seifert told reporters that one of the stars of camp had been Mike Sherrard. Some of the reporters decided that Sherrard's comeback saga was indeed remarkable, and so they wrote 20-inch features for their next day's papers. But no matter how accurate or poetic their stories were, words could hardly capture what Mike Sherrard had been through since splashing into the NFL as a rookie with the Dallas Cowboys in 1986. Words could hardly describe how low he had been and how far he had climbed to be at Camp Super Bowl catching everything thrown his way and earning the nickname Venus Fly Trap.

As Mike Sherrard lopes back to the huddle after making his graceful circus grab, John McVay is one man who is not surprised. All along, McVay had a hunch that what he has just seen along the sideline—the grace, the speed, the savvy, the skying, the catching, the stopping in midair, and the landing with delicate feet just inside the line—was possible from Mike Sherrard. In fact, with Sherrard, McVay had a hunch that *anything* was possible. Hunches, McVay says while sitting on the golf cart in the sunshine, are part of the way you plan ahead to get ahead. Sometimes, they are the only way.

Mike Sherrard broke his right leg the first time in 1987. Sherrard had gone out for a pass in a drill at the end of one training-camp practice. Someone kicked his heel, and his right leg hit his left. When the play was over, Sherrard had shattered both of the bones—tibia and fibula—in his right leg. To help the bones heal, doctors inserted a metal plate and six screws.

Seven months later, after both the plate and the screws had been removed, a Cowboys doctor told Sherrard that he should run on the beach to condition his leg for football. The doctor went so far as to run the course with him. A week later, Sherrard was almost at the end of a days' workout when it happened again. This time it was the tibia, the larger of the two bones. Mike Sherrard spent five more months in a cast.

He never played another down for Dallas.

After the second break, the Cowboys' doctors wanted to insert a rod in his right leg. The doctors also told Mike Sherrard that he would never play football again unless he had the rod put into his leg. Sherrard refused to let them operate. He went to four or five specialists, who all gave the young receiver the same basic message: "Your bones are not brittle. Rest and there is no reason you can't play again."

The specialists also told Sherrard that the last thing he should have been doing was stressing the bones in his leg running in sand. For Sherrard, that did it. He wanted out of Dallas. When he refused to let the doctors put the rod in his leg, the Cowboys were furious. Soon afterward, when Cowboys' general manager Tex Schramm put together his Plan B list, he left Mike Sherrard unprotected. For Sherrard, his career had reached its lowest point. It had started out so differently five years before.

At UCLA, Mike Sherrard was a football walk-on who ended up setting school records for catches in a season and a career and yards gained in a career. The Cowboys drafted him in the first round in 1986. That season, Sherrard caught more passes—41—than any Cowboy rookie since Bob Hayes in 1965. But then he kept breaking his right leg, and it looked like Mike Sherrard's career as a professional football player was through before it ever really got started.

Then, late in the summer of 1989, the 49ers called. John McVay, George Seifert, and Sherm Lewis, San Francisco's receivers coach, all agreed that, if he could get healthy and stay healthy, Mike Sherrard was a football player who still could make plays in the NFL. The 49ers were not afraid to wait and see how Sherrard was going to turn out. San Francisco had just won its third Super Bowl, a come-from-behind thriller in Miami in which John Taylor caught the winning pass with only 34 seconds left—so there was really no rush to get Sherrard on the field. Montana still could throw to Taylor and Jerry Rice and Roger Craig and Tom Rathman.

But in the NFL, a team can never have too many good receivers. With quarterbacks like Montana and Young, and an offensive line like San Francisco's, good receivers mean touchdowns. In July 1989, John McVay signed Mike Sherrard to a $200,000 contract. The Niners even threw in a $125,000 signing bonus. For most of the season, the team paid Sherrard's salary while the young receiver worked to rehabilitate his jinxed right leg. And although Sherrard was activated for the playoffs in 1989—he caught two passes in the NFC Championship Game against the Rams and one in the Super Bowl against the Broncos—1990 was the year John McVay was planning for all along when he signed Mike Sherrard.

This year.

Two weeks into Camp Super Bowl, it's clear that San Francisco's patience is paying off. Mike Sherrard is showing the 49ers what the Cowboys could not—did not—have the patience to discover. That he is through with bad luck. That he is through with broken bones. That he is, in fact, ready to make some plays in the NFL. Two and a half months from now, on a cold, windy fall afternoon at Candlestick, with the clock winding down and the Niners desperate for somebody to make a play to win them a game, Mike Sherrard will show everyone once and for all that one of those three claims is true.

After Mike Sherrard pulled down Steve Young's pass in practice, and after the whooping for Venus Fly Trap had died down, another player John McVay could say exemplified his philosophy of planning ahead to get ahead made his presence felt. Dave Waymer was kneeling on the sideline where Sherrard made his play. When the rookie corner who was covering Sherrard got turned around on the fake to the inside, Waymer exploded.

"MAKE A PLAY, GODDAMMIT! MAKE A PLAY OUT THERE!"

A few plays later, another receiver ran the same route and Dave Waymer didn't bite on the fake and he picked the ball off and ran it all the way back to the end zone. He had made a play. During the long, torturous quest for Three-peat, he would have to. Somebody would.

By the time the Niners blew out the Broncos in Super Bowl XXIV, Bill Walsh had traded coaching for the broadcast booth at NBC television. But John McVay was still planning ahead to get ahead. While the offense got much of the press in the wake of San Francisco's big win—the Niner offense *did* outgun the Vikings, Rams, and Broncos by a combined score of 126–26 in the playoffs—one of the most important reasons for the team's second-straight Super Bowl victory had been the consistent defense. Especially the play of its leader, Ronnie Lott. In the fourth quarter against the Vikings at Candlestick in early January, Lott picked off a pass and motored 58 yards for a touchdown. The next week, in the NFC Championship Game against the Rams, Lott streaked across the field to knock away a touchdown pass at the goal line. The play set the tone for San Francisco's 30–3 win that put it into the Super Bowl.

At 31, Ronnie Lott has played nine seasons in the National Football League. Relentless, brutal, and intelligent, he defines the 49ers' defense. But Lott's age, coupled with his reckless style of play, have kept the Niner safety on the sidelines and out of more and more games in recent seasons. In fact, the last time Ronnie Lott played every game in a season, he was 27 years old, and the Niners only had two Super Bowl wins.

In mid-February, less than a month after the 49ers beat the Broncos in the Super Bowl, John McVay scanned the list of players who had been left unprotected by their teams under Plan B. For some time, McVay had known that it would be wise to pick up some experienced help at safety for those times when Ronnie Lott has banged himself up so badly that he can't play. As he looked at the Plan B list, McVay saw a name that started his wheels turning. He had the urge to plan ahead to get ahead.

Dave Waymer played 10 seasons for the New Orleans Saints. In 1987, he picked off five passes and was named to the NFC Pro Bowl team. In 1989, Waymer made pick-offs in the last two games of the regular season to become the Saints' career interception leader with 37. Nevertheless, when the Saints' management made up its Plan B list at the end of the 1987 season, it decided that younger players were going to be more useful than a guy who'd been banging around the NFL for a decade. New Orleans left Waymer unprotected. Some two weeks later, the 49ers called.

At first, Waymer looked at Lott, Chet Brooks, and the rest of the secondary and didn't see quite where he fit in. But John McVay assured him that he would have a place. That he was going to be more than a backup. Back home on his ranch in North Carolina, Waymer realized the same thing Hanford Dixon had. *This is the chance of a lifetime.* Like Dixon, Waymer saw the means to reach the one end he had been working for all those years in New Orleans. A ring.

"I'm hungry, damn hungry," Waymer says after a workout at Camp Super Bowl. "For 10 years I've been on the outside looking in at this franchise. For 10 years I watched this franchise win division championships and get all those rings. Now I see why. Four Super Bowls, and all these guys talk about is winnin' another one."

Waymer talks about the play Mike Sherrard made, and how he feels when a receiver catches a pass against the defense.

"Damn right I take it personal," he says, his Southern drawl twanging in the afternoon heat. "I've always treated football as a career, not just a job. If you treat something as a job, you don't care about it as much. This is my livelihood. When we're out there, it's me against the other guy. If he catches one on me, then he's affectin' my livelihood. Fuck, man, I'm no engineer. I'm a damn football player. I hate it when some guy does somethin' better than me. A lot of these guys are the same way. They care about their football.

"You play all your life to get into that game they'll be playin' in Tampa next year. When I played on the side of my house as a kid, that's the game I pretended I was playin'. When I played in the church parkin' lot, I pretended I was playin' for the world championship. Havin' a chance to play in an organization where everybody is thinkin' about one thing—gettin' one of those rings—is, well, it's somethin' I almost can't even talk about because it makes me so emotional. This is what I've waited for my whole career, my whole life. For the next six months, it's all I'm gonna be thinkin' about."

In the early days at Camp Super Bowl, reporters canvassed almost everyone connected with the 49ers to find out what they thought about the quest the team was about to embark upon. The analogies were all over the map.

"Everybody talks about how other teams are going to be hunting us," running back Harry Sydney responded after practice one morning. "Well, why can't we go hunt them? Why can't the hunted be the hunters? I see no reason why we can't go out and attack instead of just defend."

Dr. Harry Edwards, a professor of sociology at the University of California, Berkeley, and a consultant with the Niners, looked at the season ahead in a different light.

"We're trying to do something that nobody else has ever been able to do," Edwards said one morning, his foot propped up on a red blocking dummy out on the practice field. "Franco [Harris] and [Terry] Bradshaw and Mean Joe Green and the Pittsburgh Steelers couldn't do it. [Jim] Kiick and [Larry] Csonka and Mercury Morris and the Dolphins couldn't do it. We're the third one to ever get to this door. The issue is: Can we be the first to pass?

"When I look at the schedule, I know we're going to be tested like we've never been tested before. We've got L.A. twice in a month, the Giants in the middle, there's the Steelers and Cincinnati, the Vikings in Minnesota at the end, and we can't forget about Atlanta. Every time we go down there we come out all broken up. This thing, this Three-peat, is going to test us—every one of us—like we've never been tested before. Teams are going to be coming after us. Every week is going to be another Super Bowl. It's going to get ugly."

When he's finished talking, Harry Edwards takes his foot down from the blocking dummy and stretches his arms up over his head. Already 6-foot-8, with his arms up over his head he looks as tall as a mountain. The image will remain because, for all the analogies and theories surrounding San Francisco's quest for the Super Bowl, the description used most often involved a mountain.

Last year, his first as head coach of the Niners, George Seifert talked constantly about pushing a boulder up a mountain. Before Seifert, it was Bill Walsh who spoke of the mountain. Getting to the top, Walsh would tell his players, required setting up a series of temporary base camps along the way. That's the way to get to the Super Bowl. Hike and climb and scratch and claw from one base camp to the next. Do that, and someday, if every man and every day fit together in the right way, there will be a chance to reach the summit and enjoy the view.

After morning practice one day early in camp, Dwaine Board, a former Niner defensive lineman and now an assistant coach, put the mountain, the boulder, and Three-peat into proper historical perspective.

"What some of the younger guys don't realize is that, way back in 1981, we started pushing this big boulder up a mountain. For the last 10 years, the mountain has been getting bigger and bigger, and the boulder has been getting heavier and heavier. But what some of the younger guys don't realize is that they can't say, 'Hey, I'm tired of pushing this boulder to the top, so I think I'll quit now.' You can't stop. Because if one guy stops, another guy might stop. And if we all stop, the boulder's going to fall right back down to the bottom again and we'll be right back where we started."

Even John Madden talked about mountains and boulders. Up in the CBS television booth at Candlestick the night of San Francisco's first preseason game, against the Los Angeles Raiders early in August, the former Raiders coach was explaining how George Seifert must approach the new season. "He has to remember that you don't start out where you ended up," Madden said. "Last year, they were the best team in football, and the gap between them and the next best team was a wide gap. Maybe it still is a wide gap. But, as George Seifert said, 'Last year, we were at the top of the mountain. Then [during the off-season], the boulder rolled down the mountain.' He said he told his guys that 'We have to start rolling the boulder up the mountain again. And we have to start tonight.'"

Against the Raiders, San Francisco's push up the mountain meets with an avalanche. The 49ers bury themselves under a torrent of mistakes. Roger Craig fumbles. Steve Young fumbles. Dexter Carter, the team's number-one draft pick, muffs a punt. Steve Young throws two interceptions. Steve Bono throws another interception that's almost returned for a touchdown. There are penalties and dropped passes and missed blocks. The Raiders are crisp and tenacious on defense, and L.A.'s 23–13 win is a reminder that John Madden was right. In the NFL, you don't start out the season where you ended the last one.

As the blood leaks from the cut on his nose, Joe Montana knows it's happening again. It's open season. On him. And on the Niners. Montana has been through it before. It always happens after a Super Bowl win. No matter how good the teams are, no matter what their records are, they all play the Niners as if it's *their* Super Bowl. This season, Montana knows, will be no different. Teams that have no business being anywhere close to the world champions will be right there, in the game at the end, ready to notch a W and salvage a losing season with one glittering moment against the Niners.

Tonight, at Mile High Stadium in Denver, Joe Montana knows the hunting has started again. He knew it sitting in the locker room before the game. Overhead, Mile High rumbled as more than 74,000 people stamped their feet and screamed for violent and total atonement for the humiliating Super Bowl loss they had endured to these same Niners in the Superdome nearly seven months before. The walls of the locker room reverberated with the venom and the anger. Open season was about to begin.

Out on the field, Montana was running for his life. On one play in the first quarter, Karl Mecklenburg, Denver's 6-foot-3, 230-pound linebacker, roared past Niner left tackle Bubba Paris and dragged Montana to the ground. On another, Mecklenburg barreled right through running back Tom Rathman and slung Montana down again.

Right before he came out of the game for the night, Montana took matters into his own hands. At the end of a long San Francisco drive, he took the snap and snuck over the goal line for San Francisco's first touchdown. As

Montana lay at the bottom of the pile, one of the Broncos shoved a hand inside his face mask and clawed at the side of his nose. Joe ran off the field as if it were no big deal. On the sidelines, he slipped off his helmet and put a white towel up to his face. As Montana sopped up his blood, the words of Harry Edwards came to mind.

Three-peat has already gotten ugly.

The 49ers beat Denver when two rookies, Dexter Carter and nose tackle Dennis Brown, make big plays in the fourth quarter. In San Diego the next week, San Francisco loses both the game and, at least until the regular season, Joe Montana, who bruises his throwing arm. Before the last preseason game of the year, against the Seattle Seahawks at Candlestick late in August, Jesse Sapolu and Guy McIntyre finally end their holdouts and start practicing. And now, defensive starters Kevin Fagan, Chet Brooks, and Charles Haley are all finally in camp. All the pieces are there. Now it's only a matter of fitting them together.

It doesn't happen against the Seahawks. For San Francisco, the game is a disaster. After a scoreless first quarter, Roger Craig lunges in from the 1-yard line and the Niners lead, 7–0. On the next series, a face-mask penalty on Dennis Brown gives the Seahawks a first down on the San Francisco 31. Seattle fullback John L. Williams takes the handoff and lumbers up the middle. Six 49ers miss tackles as Williams rumbles into the end zone. After Seattle kicks off, Steve Young floats a ball over the middle for Jerry Rice. It's too high and Seattle safety Eugene Robinson picks it off near midfield and runs all the way to the 49er 16. Four plays later, Seattle leads, 13–7. On the first play after Seattle kicks off, Roger Craig fumbles, and the Seahawks are in business again. In less than five minutes into the second quarter, Seattle scores three touchdowns. At halftime, the Seahawks lead 20–7 and the rout is on.

For the Niners, the final stats are not pretty. With Jesse Sapolu, Guy McIntyre, and Harris Barton playing their positions on the offensive line for the first time together this season, the Niner quarterbacks are sacked four times. Not counting the 32 yards Steve Young makes running for his life, San Francisco manages only 32 yards rushing on 14 carries when the starters are in the game. The Niners are flagged for nine penalties and 99 yards, including a personal foul call on rookie defensive back Anthony Shelton, who belts a Seattle receiver in the back of the head at the end of a running play. There is also a costly pass interference penalty and three missed field goals. And that doesn't count the dozens of missed tackles and blocks, mental errors, and Craig's fumble.

For Roger Craig, life is a time of contradictions right now. Off the field, things have never been better. During the off-season, San Francisco's star running back played an undercover cop in his first movie role. He starred in his own fitness video. And his Macy's newspaper ad—a full-page shot in which Craig wears only a pair of Calvin Klein bikini briefs—has recently made him San Francisco's newest sex symbol. During Camp Super Bowl, Craig's public-relations manager tells the *San Francisco Chronicle* that the player's endorsements stand to make him more than $1 million in 1990.

Ironically, life on the football field is a different story. Craig has had his worst preseason in years. He's not gaining yards. And, most disturbing of all, he's fumbling. In his seven seasons in San Francisco, Roger Craig has never been a fumbler. He's been a Pro Bowl player. He's been an All-Pro player. He's been an All-NFC player and a *Sports Illustrated* Player of the Year. But he's never been a fumbler. Until now.

In the last month, Roger Craig has coughed up the ball twice. He made San Francisco's first turnover of the preseason, a fumble against the Raiders. And he made the first turnover of the last game of the preseason, the fumble tonight against the Seahawks. After the game, reporters mill around Roger Craig's locker. They're waiting to ask him about the fumbles and about the problems the 49ers are having running the ball in general as the regular season approaches. But Roger doesn't want to talk to anyone tonight. He just wants the season to start. Then everything will be all right, just like it always has been.

George Seifert is beside himself. After a month of preseason games, his team is not coming around. The Niners look sloppy and out of whack. The Raiders beat them up in the first preseason game. They played sloppy but beat the Broncos in Denver. They played a little better but still lost to the Chargers. And now, in the final tune-up before the regular season, they get pushed around by the Seahawks. In four games, the Niners have fumbled eight times, thrown five interceptions, and been called for 30 penalties. For the first time in seven years—and only the second time in 11—the 49ers have more exhibition season losses than wins. And although the games don't count yet, George Seifert is disgusted.

At the podium in the interview room after the game, a reporter asks the 49ers' head coach if he's concerned that his field-goal kicker missed three out of four attempts.

"Yes, I'm concerned about the missed field goals," Seifert admits as coldly as the bitter wind blowing through the empty orange seats at Candlestick. "I'm concerned about the fumbles. I'm concerned about the pass interceptions. I'm concerned about the penalties. And I'm concerned about the blocking of the offensive line and the play of the defense. We've said this is a players' team. It's obviously about to become my team."

The season is only nine days away.

Chapter 2

Professor X

*T*he cold sore above George Seifert's lip appears about a week before training camp ends. At first it's just a small blemish. Then it gets bigger. Finally there's no hiding it. George Seifert is stressed out. Holdouts, injuries, and mistakes have turned his Super Bowl sports car into a sputtering, unpredictable clunker. And as the man in charge, he knows it's his job to get the thing running again. He feels the pressure. There is a gun pointed at his head. His finger is on the trigger.

It's all so different from last year. In 1989, nobody expected the 49ers to win anything. Bill Walsh, the imaginative architect of the 49er dynasty, was gone. The Niners, many snickered, are Bill Walsh's team, Bill Walsh's creation. Watch how they fall apart now that he's not around to take care of his baby. It didn't happen. George Seifert put on Walsh's headset, and the result was the same. San Francisco started fast, finished fast, and got the job done in the Super Bowl. Last season, San Francisco had done what everybody said was all but impossible to do in professional sports anymore: win back-to-back league titles. In a time when parity and a smorgasbord of enticing distractions intrude upon a champion team, Seifert's ability to focus his charges on the job was an accomplishment of monumental proportions; 55–10 was proof of that.

Which is the real problem as Camp Super Bowl comes to a close late in August. The same people who were saying the Niners had no chance to win the Super Bowl last year are the same people who are expecting them to win it this year. To Seifert, the message is such a burden his body is talking to him. *Win the Super Bowl. Anything else is failure.* Now, in effect, two guns are pointed at George Seifert's head. The one he is holding and the one the press and the public are holding with their expectations of greatness. As the Niners leave Rocklin, the question is, Who will fire first?

Jamie Williams spent most of 1989 on injured reserve (I.R.). After signing with San Francisco as a Plan B free agent from Houston, he broke a finger in training camp and didn't play in a game until December. Spending all that time on I.R., Williams had ample time to decide where George Seifert fit into his imaginary world of superheroes. As he watched the first-year head coach juggle holdouts and injuries, and concoct game plans aimed at foiling all of the hungry teams who wanted to block the Super Bowl champs from repeating, Williams knew exactly who George Seifert reminded him of. A comic book genius called Professor X.

"He's a mutant, a telepath," Williams explained at lunch one day early in the season. "He reads minds. He put together a group of mutants with varying weird powers. No one wanted them. No one knew what to do with them. But Professor X taught them to use their powers to save the world."

But last year, there were no guns pointed at Professor X's head.

For most of 1989, the question that dogged George Seifert was whether the 49ers were his team or still Bill Walsh's team. The point grated on Seifert, who viewed the change in coaches as a simple deal. Bill Walsh was gone, and he was the coach now. The Niners were his team. "I'm not trying to copy Bill," Seifert said at an early press conference. "I am not a clone of him."

Many people, however, looked at the 11 years he had

coached under Walsh—first at Stanford University and then with the Niners—and decided that George Seifert was indeed a clone of Bill Walsh. The many similarities the two football men shared didn't help matters. Both had spent decades in coaching, moving their families from city to city as the next opportunity to move up presented itself. Both demanded excellence of themselves and those who worked under them. Both locked keys in their cars and didn't hear their wives say things because they were always in their own little world of football. Both were focused, insulated, almost brooding men who could tune out everything but the game. Both were emotional men with a sense of humor. Both had been singularly obsessed with becoming a coach at the highest level of the game—the NFL. And, perhaps most important of all, both had helped build the San Francisco 49ers into professional football's premiere franchise.

But there were differences between Walsh and Seifert, too. Walsh was a brilliant offensive mind. Seifert's expertise was defense. Walsh was calculating, often using what players call "head games" to create the edge of tension he felt motivated the team to perform its best. Seifert was spontaneous and always figured that the players were mature enough to pressure themselves into playing their best. Walsh kept to himself, and players were often unsure of who he was and what he thought of them. Seifert was open and honest and players knew exactly where they stood. Walsh was irresistibly curious about a host of issues beyond football, and in general displayed a heightened social conscience. Seifert, however, did not concern himself with such matters. Walsh played tennis and drank wine. Seifert liked to hike and fish and have a beer on his boat. Walsh loved classical music. Seifert got fired up over Billy Idol.

They were the same. But they were opposites.

In coaching, replacing a legend is difficult. In Green Bay, Wisconsin, in 1968, a quiet, cigar-smoking little man named Phil Bengtson took over from Vince Lombardi the season after the Packers won the first two Super Bowls. For three years, the Packers lost more games than they won and Bengtson was fired. In the 1970s, a basketball coach named Gene Bartow took over from John Wooden at UCLA, and the pressure of replacing the college-hoops monarch got to Bartow and he resigned in frustration. George Seifert, however, succeeded where the others had failed. He had replaced a legend. He had done what nobody said could be done.

But now, after a sloppy, stressful August, that rich success is disintegrating. In only a few days, the Niners will set out to defend their championship. With a cold sore to prove it, George Seifert is anxious over his team's chances. There are so many questions right now and so few answers. The regular offensive linemen have had only a few days practice together. The running game is going nowhere. The quarterbacks hardly have any time to throw the ball. The defensive secondary is a banged-up mess. So is the defensive line. The defense, in fact, is the most unsettled it has been in the 12 years he has been with the team.

Seifert is not sure how the defense is going to play. He's not sure how long it's going to take the offensive line to jell. He's not sure whether defensive back Eric Wright is ever going to be healthy enough to play again. He's not sure how much football linebacker Keena Turner has left after 10 years in the league. He's not sure if nose tackle Michael Carter's foot is going to heal from last year's bone graft so he can play back to his Pro Bowl form. He's not sure how much rookies such as Dexter Carter and Dennis Brown will be able to contribute to the team in their first year in the league. He's not sure about his field-goal kicker or his punter or his running backs. He is not sure of anything anymore.

All George Seifert knows right now is that almost every unit of his football team has a problem that needs to get squared away or it could mean trouble later on. Seifert has fished in enough oceans—he's had his boat tipped over enough times—to know that great storms often announce themselves as gentle breezes. "How long do the great teams hang in there?" Seifert asks *Chronicle* columnist Lowell Cohn one afternoon before the first game of the season, against the Saints in New Orleans. "To keep [things] going, it's so damn tough. . . . There's pressure. I want to do everything just right, and you can't do that. I'm trying to make it the most perfect I can. You anguish about it, about every little thing you do."

He has always been this way.

George Gerald Seifert grew up in San Francisco's Mission District. His high school, Polytechnic, was right across the street from Kezar Stadium, where the 49ers played from 1946 to 1970. On Sundays in high school, Seifert was an usher at Kezar. He got into the games free. And he made a few bucks, too. On the football team at Poly High, Seifert was good enough to play both ways. He wanted to play fullback. But when that didn't work, his coach moved him to tight end. As a senior, he played tackle and linebacker. Seifert was good, but for almost 30 years, when he looked back on his career as a football player, the one thing he remembered was a game at Kezar on Thanksgiving Day in 1957.

In those days, Poly High made a habit of winning the San Francisco city championship. Not Seifert's senior year. In the city title game that day, the winning touchdown was scored on a pass on which he was the cover man. The ball went right over his shoulder. He could have knocked it down, batted it away, or intercepted it. He did none of those things, and the guy caught the ball and Poly High lost. Up until San Francisco's first Super Bowl win in 1982—a five-point thriller made possible when Seifert's defense kept Cincinnati out of the end zone on four consecutive plays near the Niner goal line— George Seifert thought about that play at Kezar every day of his life. Every day. For almost 30 years.

You anguish about it, every little thing you do.

At the University of Utah in the late 1950s and early 1960s, George Seifert studied zoology. He'd gotten a love for the outdoors from his father, who drove a truck for a living. Ernie Seifert had absolutely no interest in football, but he did love the outdoors. So would his son. George spent his sophomore year of high school in Humboldt, a coastal mountain county some 100 miles south of the Oregon border. Part of the time, he lived on the Hoopa Indian Reservation. The rest of the year he lived with his grandparents in a cabin heated by a potbelly stove. Later, when he married, he took his bride hiking and fishing on their honeymoon. In college, Seifert's roommate was an All-Western Athletic Conference football guard named Lynn Stiles. In college, Seifert and Stiles used to talk about how someday they were going to sail around the world in a boat.

Seifert's first coaching job was as an assistant at Utah after graduation and a six-month stint in the army. At 25, he was ready to be a head coach. But where was a 25-year-old zoology major supposed to get a job coaching a football team? For Seifert, it was tiny Westminster College in Salt Lake City. Conditions were far from perfect—the college hadn't had enough money to field a football team in several years—but it was all he could get. So with no players, no schedule, and no staff, George Seifert took the job. He scrounged equipment. He ferreted out two players still in school from Westminster's last team. And he recruited others—some of them older than he was. The team went 3 and 3 that year, and afterward Seifert felt like he was ready for a major college program.

He spent 1966 as an assistant on the staff at the University of Iowa. During the year the Seiferts spent in Iowa City, George worked on his Master's degree in physical education and helped his wife operate a lodge. Eight years later, after assistant positions at the University of Oregon and Stanford University, he was ready to become head coach at a major college program. The only problem: The major college program he picked was not ready for him.

When Cornell University hired Seifert as its head football coach in 1975, it was a case of a man being in the wrong place at the wrong time. For months, a powerful alumni faction led by Roger Weiss, a New York stock-broker—and big-time Cornell contributor—had been trying to get the Ivy League school to hire Tom Matte, a former running back for the Baltimore Colts, as its head coach. Seifert was hired instead, and things just never worked out.

Because he wasn't Tom Matte, the Cornell alums took their displeasure out on Seifert. Contributions and alumni support for the Cornell football program dried up in a hurry. In the Ivy League, where athletic scholar-ships are not allowed, this was death by asphyxiation. After two losing seasons—1 and 8, then 2 and 7—George Seifert was fired. Later Seifert would realize that he had learned invaluable lessons during his two years in upstate New York. But at the time, all he knew was that he felt burned. He had done everything he knew how to make things work, and he had failed. The more he thought about it, the more he soured on being in charge. He was not sure if he ever wanted to be a head football coach again. He was not sure at all.

You anguish about it, every little thing you do.

After Cornell, it was back to Stanford, where Bill Walsh was in his first year as head coach. Walsh had learned the game as an assistant on Al Davis's Oakland Raiders' staff in 1966, before spending eight years in Cin-cinnati under Paul Brown. At 45, after nearly two de-cades and six different jobs, Bill Walsh was finally getting his chance to take charge of a football team. At Stanford, George Seifert went to school. He was the student. Walsh was the teacher.

During the three seasons Seifert had spent at Stanford before Cornell, he had shown promise as coach of the defensive backs. In both 1972 and 1973, Stanford's secondary was the PAC 8's best. Six years later, the magic was back: Under Seifert, Stanford's pass defense was ranked second in the PAC 10. But there was something else that Seifert gleaned from his year under Bill Walsh. He began to figure out what he did wrong at Cornell.

As he watched Bill Walsh work at Stanford, Seifert noticed that Walsh's way of doing things contrasted sharply with the way he himself had done things at Cornell. Walsh's focus at Stanford, Seifert could see, was always on football. At Cornell, Seifert's focus often had been on everything but football. He supervised recruiting. He answered each and every letter by hand and then had a secretary type it over. He played politics and tried to keep the alumni factions happy. He would come home late at night in the off-season after a day spent trying to get a feel for Cornell's complicated budget process. Seifert also made a mistake coaches often make their first time in charge of a team: He drew up a system of football and tried to fit his players into it. At Cornell, where some of the offensive tackles were faster than the defensive backs, the players just weren't good enough to do the things Seifert wanted of them. He decided he would never make the same mistake again.

In 1979, Bill Walsh left Stanford to take the reins of professional football's worst franchise—the San Francisco 49ers. Seifert had always been a little hesitant about coaching in the NFL. He wasn't sure he had what it took to deal with high-priced athletes. In fact, he said later that he felt threatened by the whole idea. But at Stanford under Walsh, Seifert changed. He once told Ira Miller of the *San Francisco Chronicle,* "I got to a point where I developed an inner confidence that, hey, I could go in front of a group, I could get a guy one on one, I don't care how long he [had] played, and still make him a better player."

By the end of the 1978 season, Seifert felt he was

ready for the NFL. But when Bill Walsh left Stanford for the 49ers, he didn't take Seifert with him. The next year, when Walsh did call, he was almost too late. Bart Starr needed help in Green Bay, and Seifert saw it as the chance he had been waiting for. His chance to see if he could coach in the NFL. Seifert had already convinced his two children that they would get used to playing in the snow. When Bill Walsh called and offered their father a job, Eve and Jason Seifert cried. They were staying home.

With the 49ers, George Seifert did not wait long to prove he belonged in the National Football League. In 1981, San Francisco drafted three rookie defensive backs: cornerback Ronnie Lott from USC, cornerback Eric Wright from Missouri, and safety Carlton Williamson from Pittsburgh. Seifert was in his second year in the league, and he had three rookies in his secondary. But he made it work. That year, the 49ers gave up the lowest number of points in the NFL. And after Dwight Clark's touchdown catch in the back of the end zone at Candlestick beat the Cowboys in the NFC Championship Game, San Francisco was on its way to its first Super Bowl title of the 1980s.

Two years later, Walsh promoted Seifert to defensive coordinator. In 1984, San Francisco won its second Super Bowl over the Miami Dolphins. Shortly after the Niners' 38–16 win, Jim Irsay, general manager of the Indianapolis Colts, asked Seifert to become his head coach. But when Irsay wouldn't consent to give him as much say in the draft and on trades as he felt he should have as head coach, Seifert turned Irsay down. Afterwards he wondered if he had done the right thing.

"It gave me confidence that somebody thought I was good enough to do the job," Seifert told Glenn Dickey of the *Chronicle*. "But I wondered if I'd ever get another chance."

You anguish about it, every little thing you do.

In 1988, Green Bay was looking for a replacement for Forrest Gregg, who had resigned to become the head man at Southern Methodist University in Texas. During the 1987 season, despite injuries on the defensive line, Seifert's unit had allowed the fewest yards in the NFL. San Francisco was also ranked number one in pass defense. After Forrest Gregg resigned, Bill Walsh called Tom Braatz, Green Bay's executive vice-president of football operations, and gave the Packers permission to interview Seifert. The Packers did, and they liked him. But the job eventually went to Lindy Infante, who, like Walsh, had built a reputation as an offensive wizard as coordinator for the Cleveland Browns. George Seifert was still waiting for his chance.

On a winter day late in January 1989, George Seifert was on a plane headed for Cleveland. Browns' owner Art Modell had recently fired head coach Marty Schottenheimer, even though Cleveland had put together the fifth-best record in the NFL in Schottenheimer's five seasons with the club. Three days before, the 49ers had won their third Super Bowl in Miami. In the two weeks before the game, the media had cranked the rumor mill into overdrive. If San Francisco won, would it be Bill Walsh's last game as coach? The consensus in the press was *yes*.

At the coaches' first meeting back in Santa Clara after the Super Bowl, however, Walsh was business as usual. He talked about the upcoming scouting combine that the coaches would attend. He talked of next year's team. Later Seifert would learn that Walsh was meeting with owner Eddie DeBartolo Jr. and Carmen Policy, DeBartolo's number-two man in the front office. Walsh already knew he wanted to leave coaching. But he wanted to make sure the right man was handed the responsibility of carrying on the dynasty he had built. In his meetings with DeBartolo and Policy, Walsh was lobbying for the one man he felt could handle the job. George Seifert.

Although he had heard the rumor that he was the leading candidate to replace Walsh, no one from the club had made a move in Seifert's direction. So, during the last week in January, three days after his defense helped the Niners win another Super Bowl, George Seifert was on his way to Cleveland to see Art Modell. He wanted to be a head coach in the National Football League. That was the goal, and he wanted to reach it so badly that he was prepared to do anything to reach it. Even leave home for a place like Cleveland.

There was bad weather in Cleveland that day, and because his plane had to stop in Dallas, Seifert knew he wouldn't have time to call his wife, Linda, before his connecting flight took off for Cleveland. So he stuck a credit card into the airphone. Linda Seifert told her husband that Carmen Policy had called. Policy, Linda told George, wanted to talk to him about becoming the head coach of the 49ers.

In the air on the way to Dallas, George Seifert made his choice. San Francisco was home. The 49ers were home. That was the job he had wanted all along, not Cleveland. On the plane into Dallas, Seifert mapped out his game plan. He decided what he would say in the interview with Eddie and Carmen. At Dallas–Ft. Worth International Airport, Seifert bought a ticket back to San Francisco. On the flight back home, he thought and planned and rehearsed some more. He was excited. And as always when it came to football, he was anxious. On the plane, he didn't talk to anyone. He drank a glass of white wine. The next day, he was finally a head coach in the National Football League.

Back when he was an assistant, some of his players hated George Seifert. He was like a Marine drill sergeant. He was demanding, and he expected perfection. Then there were his meetings: too long and too many. When practice was over, most of the other players would be getting ready to go home. Not the defensive backs. They were getting ready to watch another hour of films. In those early days, Seifert was tough on his players. He knew the bunch was young and that they needed all the preparation they could get. So Seifert drove them and bullied them and got them to play above their heads.

Although Seifert rode everyone in those days, the player he rode the hardest was Eric Wright. A thin, cat-quick cover man, Eric Wright could play. He knew it, and George Seifert knew it. But Wright liked to talk. He wasn't like Ronnie Lott, who usually kept his mouth shut and let his play on the field do his talking. Eric Wright wasn't as polished as Ronnie Lott was, either. Seifert rode Wright mercilessly, trying to keep his young corner focused on embellishing his obvious physical talents for playing football. The 49er defensive backs used to joke about thinking up a plot to "get" Seifert for riding Wright so hard. A group of teammates once approached Lott. As their leader, they wanted Lott to tell Seifert that they'd had enough, that they needed a rest from his meetings and his demands. Lott never did. Like most everyone else, he didn't have the guts to say something like that to Seifert.

In 1990, almost a decade later, Eric Wright and Ronnie Lott are still playing defensive back for the 49ers. But much has changed in 10 years. Eric Wright played three brilliant seasons for the 49ers. Between 1983 and 1985, no defensive back in the NFL could cover a receiver like Eric Wright could. Wright made the All-NFC team three seasons in a row. He was named All-NFL twice. Then, on November 3, 1985, in a game against the Philadelphia Eagles, Eric Wright pulled a muscle in his groin. He hasn't been the same since.

The seasons have been more fulfilling for Ronnie Lott. He has played in the Pro Bowl seven times. He has been named All-Pro four times. Lott is 31 years old now, and every year it seems he gets a little more banged up than the year before. But 10 seasons after being shoved into the starting lineup, Lott is still there, watching film, going to meetings, and playing football for George Seifert.

So are other veterans like Keena Turner. A tall, quiet leader, Turner came to San Francisco in 1980, the same year Seifert did. Since then, the linebacker has played in the Pro Bowl and four Super Bowls. For Ronnie Lott, Eric Wright, Keena Turner, and George Seifert, things are just like they have always been. Football season is starting, and they are getting ready to go to war together. Everything is as it has been for 10 years. With two differences. Lott, Wright, and Turner are not young anymore. And George Seifert isn't just their position coach now, he's their boss.

Two days before San Francisco's final exhibition game, the blowout loss to the Seattle Seahawks, the 49ers break camp in Rocklin and set up for the season at their practice facility in Santa Clara, 40 miles south of Candlestick. The letters on the sign at 4949 Centennial Boulevard read:

THE MARIE P. DEBARTOLO SPORTS CENTRE
HOME OF THE
SAN FRANCISCO
FORTY NINERS

Eddie DeBartolo Jr., the 49er owner, dedicated the facility in honor of his mother, who died of lung cancer in 1987. To the 49er players and coaches, the place is known as the Taj. And, with three football fields, a cavernous locker room, and comforts that include everything from a whirlpool and hydrotherapy pool to a private lunchroom and racquetball courts, it's clear that this is indeed the Taj Mahal of NFL training facilities. The Niners have barely settled in at the Taj when George

Seifert sits down to make the hard decisions that a position coach never has to make.

On September 3, the 49ers announce 13 cuts from their active roster as the team trims down to the 47-player limit required by the National Football League. Keena Turner is one of the players cut. A day later, when no team picks him off the waiver wire, the 49ers reclaim Turner's contract and he's brought back onto the roster. As the season starts, he's penciled in as the backup at right outside linebacker behind Bill Romanowski, an exuberant third-year player San Francisco has been grooming to replace Turner.

Eric Wright is not cut. But he's still hurting with the latest in a series of groin injuries. A day before the cut-down deadline, the 49ers offered Wright an injury settlement to retire. But because accepting the team's offer would have meant losing the benefits he had earned during nine years in the NFL, Wright declined and said he wanted to get healthy so he could play again. As the opener in New Orleans draws closer, it looks like it will be a miracle if Eric Wright can just finish the season.

Ronnie Lott has had what several teammates call his most intense training camp ever. Some say it's because Lott is feeling the heat from Dave Waymer, who Seifert freely acknowledges as one of the stars of Camp Super Bowl. Others say it's because Lott wants to renegotiate his contract and is trying to show management that he can still play like he once did. Still others say it's simply because the proud warrior absolutely hates it when reporters write that he's too old and too slow, that he's through and can't get the job done anymore. For his part, Lott says he doesn't want to talk. All he wants to do is play football.

Play football. That's all that Hanford Dixon wanted to do. But after tearing a muscle in his thigh halfway through training camp, Dixon accepts an injury settlement and retires from football one afternoon late in August. The Dawg isn't going to get one of those rings. But there's nothing he can do about it now. "There's no sense in [kidding] each other," Dixon says as he leaves the Taj before flying home to Cleveland. "It never got any better and I still can't run on it. So I'll retire. I've had a good career. And I hope they win the Super Bowl—it's a class organization."

The week of the 1989 Super Bowl, George Seifert talked with Lowell Cohn of the *Chronicle* about the pressure that would build on the 49er franchise if the team beat the Broncos and set up the possibility of a Three-peat.

"There's maybe even more pressure if we win," he said. "And you know what? I'll think, Here we are. We go out to practice every day. We've got to play these games. Let's try to do it again. What the hell else is there?"

Indeed. In early September, now that the first weekend of the NFL season has arrived, there is nothing left to do but go out and play the games. It's time for the Niners to defend their title. Time to seek a new one. They are hungry to do it again.

Three thousand miles away, two professional football players have ended their training-camp holdouts and are ready to go to work. One is named Lawrence Taylor. The other is named Leonard Marshall. Both play defense. The team they play defense for is the New York Giants. The Giants are starving for what the 49ers have.

Chapter 3

"Scared Shitless"

*I*t's late, around 11 on the Tuesday night before the Atlanta Falcons come to Candlestick in September. All of the 49er coaches have gone home for the night, except George Seifert, who sits watching a video screen in the workroom across the hall from his office upstairs at the Taj. Seifert has spent the better part of the past two days watching films of the Falcons' defense from their first game of the NFL season against the Houston Oilers.

By now, Seifert has memorized the images so clearly that they frighten him. Atlanta linebacker Aundray Bruce, exploding huge, fast, and mean through Houston's offensive backfield to separate Warren Moon from the football. Fumble. Touchdown Falcons. Cue further. Linebacker Jessie Tuggle rocketing past the blockers on the outside and slamming Warren Moon to the turf. Fumble. Touchdown Falcons. Cue further. In one five-play sequence, Bruce, 6-foot-5, 250 pounds and a chip on his shoulder, tomahawks Warren Moon to the ground four times. No matter what Houston's blockers do, the videotape shows Seifert, the Oilers cannot keep the Atlanta Falcons away from Warren Moon, Houston's quarterback.

Quarterback.

George Seifert's mind flashes ahead. The thought of Aundray Bruce or Jessie Tuggle exploding huge, fast, and mean toward *his* quarterback makes him shudder. It's the kind of queasy, hollow feeling that makes head coaches turn white like Seifert did yesterday at his weekly press luncheon when the subject of Joe Montana and the Falcons defense came up. Seifert has good reason to be worried. Two weeks ago, in the last-minute win at New Orleans, the 49er offensive line had played like it had two guys learning new positions, two training-camp hold-outs, and only a few days of practice together. There were six sacks. And nearly twice that many passes got knocked down or were thrown before they should have been because the line couldn't keep the Saints from chasing Joe Montana all over the Superdome. San Francisco's blocking had been much better last week in the win over the Washington Redskins. But Aundray Bruce, Jessie Tuggle, and Scott Case, Atlanta's kamikaze cornerback, do not play for the Redskins. They play for the Falcons, who, on this Tuesday night at the Taj, are destroying Warren Moon, a quarterback, before George Seifert's very eyes. The Falcons who in five days will be foaming at the mouth to do the same thing to Joe Montana.

It was easy enough to dissect Atlanta's 47–27 win over the Oilers. The first quarter said it all. Sixteen plays from scrimmage for Houston. Sixteen Atlanta blitzes. The assault produced five fumbles, five fights, three personal-foul penalties, and, most important, 21 Atlanta points in less than two minutes. By halftime, the Falcons led 27–7 and, with help from George Thorogood music blasting through the stadium speakers, Atlanta was "Bad to the Bone" for the first time in years. Against Houston, Aundray Bruce, Atlanta's number-one draft pick of three seasons ago, was unstoppable. Five tackles. A sack. The forced fumble on Moon. And three passes batted away.

Shortly after 11, George Seifert stops the film and heads for the back stairs at the Taj. As he walks silently across the carpet and down the stairs, an image leaps about in the fluorescent light. Joe Montana dropping back to pass . . . the blocking is breaking down . . . and Aundray Bruce is . . . coming . . . coming . . . coming. Sei-

fert approaches the back door. Here, away from his players, away from his coaches, away from reporters, and
away from Eddie and Carmen and McVay, Seifert wres-
tles with the fear ricocheting around in his stomach. A
fear that got worse and worse every time he watched
Aundray Bruce and Jessie Tuggle hit Warren Moon. Seifert's mind races.

If they play like that, there's no way we can win.

San Francisco's week of practice is tense. On the field,
George Seifert paces like an angry bird of prey. As play
after play is rehearsed before him, Seifert stands rigid,
his feet bolted to the grass, his arms folded like the steel
spokes in a wheel. Seifert's instructions—to players and
coaches—are short and clipped, like the thump of a gun
at a carnival. Once, when a pass rush clogs up the quarterback's throwing lane, Seifert jackhammers out of his
silence and stalks to the center of the offensive huddle.

"If they're blocking off on the weak side, just blast
them the fuck out of there!" Seifert blurts angrily, slamming his fists together.

Eleven pairs of eyes stare down at the grass. For a few
awkward moments, Seifert stares into the face masks,
venting his fear and his anxiety. Then he walks away,
muttering, "Goddamn . . . for Chrissakes. . . ."

By Wednesday, Seifert looks completely exhausted.
There are deep circles under his eyes. His face is pale and
drawn. The wrinkles at the corner of each eye seem
deeper. But at least the cold sore is gone. After practice, a
reporter trys a joke. Seifert smiles weakly. He cannot
even laugh. He is too tired. Too tense. Or both.

Saturday night, around 8:30, the Newport Beach
Room, the Airport Marriott, Millbrae. A warm rain driz-
zles against the windows of the hotel. Inside, members of
the 49ers' offensive unit are watching films of last week's

26–13 win over Washington, the Niners' second-straight victory of the young season. On Saturday night, the Niners always watch films of last week's game—if that game was a win. Half an hour or so before the team's usual night-before-the-game snack—hamburgers and french fries—the screen lights up with the Redskins. Wide receiver John Taylor had been San Francisco's big weapon, catching eight passes for 160 yards—including a 49-yard catch-and-run in the second quarter that gave the Niners a 17–3 lead. But it's not what Taylor did against the Redskins that fascinates Brent Jones. It's *how* Taylor makes many of his yards that the 49er tight end notices.

The stiff arm is a technique football coaches teach starting in pee wee league. A guy is closing in to make a tackle. No problem. Stick out an arm, shove a hand in his face. The guy goes down. You keep running. Against the Redskins, John Taylor puts on a stiff-arm clinic. The best one comes with a little more than two minutes left in the third quarter. The play is simple. Taylor lines up on the right side of the formation. At the snap of the ball, he takes three steps forward and looks back for the ball. He catches Montana's flip, and tries to juke Redskin cornerback Martin Mayhew to the inside. Mayhew doesn't bite on the fake, so Taylor heads for the sideline. Just before Taylor heads out of bounds, Mayhew latches onto his left shoulder. That's all Mayhew gets, though, as Taylor brusquely shoves his left hand up under Mayhew's face mask and pushes the beaten Redskin cornerback to the ground. The play only gains seven yards.

But on this rainy night a week later, Brent Jones sees more than a simple seven-yard play. He sees *possibilities. Man,* Jones thinks to himself as the film rolls, *if I ever get a chance to use that, I'm gonna try it and see how it works.* The chance comes tomorrow at Candlestick. Prime Time.

On Falcon Sunday, George Seifert walks out of the hotel into the sunshine. He finds his navy blue Volvo 740

in the parking lot, settles in, and heads out to the freeway
and Candlestick. Some of his players are already at the
stadium getting ready for the game. Surging north on
Highway 101, George Seifert pops the tape into the cas-
sette deck.

The first sound he hears is the organ. Then it's the
pitter-patter of drums, then the bass guitar, then the
voice, deep and full, then soft, like tiptoes. There are
words, then more keyboards, bass, and drums. Then
everything speeds up. The drums tumble, the voice trips
on. The words are soft, but they sing of guns and domi-
nation and whiplash smiles. Seifert is waiting. He knows
what's coming. The part he's waiting for is almost here,
almost here. It's all getting louder now. Louder. Here it
comes . . . there it is, the screeching voice, the pounding
drums, then yes, oh God, yes, those squealing guitars
exploding raw, loud, and angry like 10 tomcats hissing
because somebody is holding them upside down by their
tails.

Screaming toward Candlestick, George Seifert loses
himself in the noise. Later he will describe why he likes
this raw, loud, angry music, which he pops into the cas-
sette player on his way to Candlestick before every home
game early this season.

"I'm not what you'd call a cult fan," is the way he put it.
"It's just like—oh, God—I like those squealing guitars."

The song is finished by the time Seifert pulls off the
freeway and parks in the lot reserved for players and
coaches at Candlestick. He walks past the security guards
and down the tunnel to the locker room. It's game day,
and he is anxious. But he feels good.

Thank God for Billy Idol.

Half an hour before kickoff, Jerry Glanville scuffs the
turf at Candlestick with a pointy black cowboy boot.
"Let's git this dance started," Glanville drawls aloud to
himself. George Seifert is not the only anxious NFL head

coach in San Francisco this week. The Atlanta Falcons have tried just about everything in the last decade. Now it's a loudmouth in black.

Jerry Glanville clamored in from Houston with a promise when the Atlanta Falcons needed one. Six-straight horrible losing seasons had drained all life from the franchise. Last season was the worst. Two players had died in automobile accidents within a month of each other. There was the rash of paternity suits that had included even Rankin Smith Jr., son of the Falcons' owner, Rankin Smith. Then there was Christmas Eve in Atlanta when only 7,792 people showed up in 12-degree weather—minus 20 with the wind-chill—to see the Falcons end another nightmare season with a 31–24 loss to the Lions. The Atlanta Falcons had hit bottom. Again.

When the Smith family hired Jerry Glanville, it knew exactly what it was getting. A coach with a huge ego, a personality like an active volcano, and a reputation as one of the biggest jerks in the National Football League. "We knew the way he was," Rankin Smith Jr., told the *New Orleans Times Picayune*. "We wanted the whole package."

From the time in early spring when Glanville launched Operation Headstart—a six-week training camp designed to introduce the Falcons players to his Red Gun offense and Hit Anything That Moves style of defense—Atlanta has been on fire. For the first time in the team's 25-year history, the Falcons win every pre-season game. It's only preseason, but the 4-and-0 start still ignites a city that has seen its professional football team post just five winning seasons since joining the NFL in 1966. A whole city is hoping that Glanville will be known in Atlanta for winning football games instead of for his mouth or for his all-black getups or for leaving tickets at will-call for dead heroes like Elvis and James Dean. In the newspapers, on radio, and on television, Atlanta has lined up to hail its new conquering hero. And,

as usual, one of Jerry Glanville's biggest and loudest sup-
porters is Jerry Glanville. "I can promise you one thing,"
he tells the *Atlanta Journal and Constitution* during training
camp, "the fans are going to see us spill our guts out. . . .
We're going to have players here who will kill their
mothers to get to the football."

George Seifert knows. He's seen the films.

The game starts slowly. It's 3–0 Atlanta after one
quarter, 5–3 San Francisco at halftime. Although the Falcons are shutting down the run—Roger Craig and Tom
Rathman have gained just 23 yards on the ground after
two quarters—the 49ers are moving the ball through the
air. At halftime, Montana has 187 yards passing. But
Roger Craig fumbles deep in Atlanta territory on one
drive; and right at the end of the half, another possession
ends when the Falcons block Mike Cofer's field-goal try.

Curiously, Atlanta is not blitzing as much as they did
against the Oilers. And with the exception of two sacks
for 19 yards, the San Francisco offensive line is keeping
Aundray Bruce, Jessie Tuggle, and the rest of the Falcons' defense away from Montana. The running game is
going nowhere, but Joe has had enough time to throw.
And, as one Falcon will say after the game, when Joe
Montana has time to throw, it's only a matter of time before he beats you.

Early in the third quarter, Joe Montana starts to beat
the Atlanta Falcons. On second and nine from the Atlanta 35, Montana drops back to pass. On his blind side,
left tackle Bubba Paris walls out Falcon end Tim Green.
To Montana's right, Harris Barton deals with nose tackle
Tory Epps, and Steve Wallace stuffs Mike Gann, Atlanta's 6-foot-5, 270-pound end. Montana scans the field
from the pocket. He's sent Mike Sherrard deep on a
crossing pattern from the left. Sherrard's route draws
both Atlanta safeties to the middle of the field, leaving

Jerry Rice wide open crossing underneath from the right. Rice makes the catch at the Atlanta 14. No Falcon is within 10 yards of him. Touchdown, 12–3 Niners.

After the Falcons score to make it 12–10, Brent Jones gets his chance to use John Taylor's stiff-arm tactic. On second down from the 49er 33, Jones catches a Montana flip over the middle and takes off for the end zone. Atlanta cornerback Deion Sanders is the closest Falcon. As Jones crosses midfield, the footrace is on. Sanders runs the 40-yard dash in 4.27 seconds. Brent Jones does not. On paper, it's a mismatch. But football is not played on paper. Jones is still in the lead as he reaches the Atlanta 15. But Sanders, a flamboyant talker who wears a ton of gold jewelry and boasts the nickname Prime Time—a registered trademark with the federal government— puts on a burst and catches him.

As Prime Time grabs for him, Jones remembers what John Taylor did to Martin Mayhew. Still chugging toward the Falcon goal line, Jones unfolds his left arm into Prime Time in an effort to keep Sanders away from his legs. Sanders stays on his feet, clawing at Jones, but he can't get close enough to push Jones out of bounds. With Sanders scratching at his heels, Jones flails into the end zone to give San Francisco a 19–10 lead. Deion will get one more chance today to make a Prime Time play.

The game clock shows 1:12 left. The Falcons have just kicked a field goal to close San Francisco's lead to 19–13. On third and three from the San Francisco 41, the Niners are just trying to get a first down. Make a first down, and Atlanta won't even get the ball back and have a chance to win the game. As Montana calls the signals, Jerry Rice goes in motion behind the line of scrimmage. Montana takes the snap, and Rice shoots out into the right flat. Montana throws. Deion Sanders knifes over from the middle of the field to cover Rice. All Prime Time sees is green. If he steps in front of Rice and makes the catch, Deion knows that no Niner is going to catch him before he scores the winning touchdown. Prime Time breaks for the ball. He gets a hand on it. No touchdown. But Atlanta still isn't dead. Not yet. The Niners punt. Atlanta takes over on its own 29.

With seven seconds left, the Falcons have reached the 49er 29. With the clock ticking down, Atlanta quarterback Chris Miller takes the snap, juggles the ball, and pushes it to the ground. It's supposed to be a pass—an incomplete pass that stops the clock without wasting the time it takes to drop back and whip the ball out of bounds. That is what Chris Miller was trying to do. With four seconds left, however, referee Jerry Seeman rules that Miller never had possession of the snap from center, and so he couldn't have thrown any pass at all. Therefore, Seeman says, the play is a fumble, recovered by San Francisco. The Falcons are dead. Finally.

The Niners have dodged a bullet. On defense, the Falcons did not play the way they did against the Oilers. Strong safety Brian Jordan leads Atlanta in tackles with 11. Jessie Tuggle has nine tackles, and he recovers Roger Craig's fumble at the end of the first half. But Tuggle does not get to Joe Montana, who completes 24 of 36 throws for 398 yards and two touchdowns. Aundray Bruce doesn't even show up on the stat sheet. No tackles. No sacks. It's like he wasn't even there on the field at all. Atlanta didn't play the way it did against the Oilers, and the Niners get another win, their third straight of the season. As he disappears into the coaches' dressing room after speaking with reporters, there is no one in San Francisco who is more relieved about this than George Seifert.

In the tunnel that runs from the locker room to the field, offensive coordinator Mike Holmgren leans against a concrete wall, talking to a handful of reporters. Holmgren has just showered, and his hair is still wet.

There are deep circles under his bloodshot eyes. He sips a bottle of Michelob Dry. When he speaks, his words come slowly, as if each one is a great effort.

"This is a big win for us," Holmgren says. "The Rams lost, so we're two up after three. That's nice, but it's way too early. . . ." Holmgren's voice trails off before he finishes. His point, however, is well taken. A win is a win, and in the NFL every win counts. But there is a whole season left to play.

A reporter asks Holmgren about how anxious George Seifert had been during the week over Atlanta's swarming defense. Holmgren takes another sip of his beer. This one is longer than the first.

"After watching the films of their game with Houston, I was more than concerned," he finally says. "I was scared shitless. I think we all were." Then Mike Holmgren finishes his beer and walks up the tunnel and out into the wind.

Later, Candlestick is empty. The wind has died down, and the streets outside the stadium, swollen only an hour ago with traffic snaking its way toward Highway 101, are dark and silent. Out over the bay, the lights of the planes blink as they land at San Francisco International Airport. One by one, they settle down, their red beacons falling out of the night lower and lower until they're gone, each replaced by another copying its path to the ground.

Soon, the Niners will be on one of those planes bound for Houston. Where Jamie Williams's dream finally came true.

Chapter 4

Jamie

*T*here's a little bit of everything in this crowd. White skin with freckles. Black skin with armbands. Blond hair with curls. Brown hair in ponytails. Two hundred eighth graders sit in a tiny auditorium, listening to a guest speaker. It's "Red Ribbon Week" at Ralston Middle School, high in the hills of Belmont, California. The message this early fall day is, "My choice: drug free." The speaker is tight end Jamie Williams of the San Francisco 49ers.

Twenty minutes ago, at the 9:25 A.M. bell, the deserted hallways at Ralston had filled suddenly with hundreds of teenagers. They wore baggy M. C. Hammer pants and braces, Bermuda shorts, and high-top sneakers. Lockers banged. Shoves followed pushes. One girl, who couldn't have been more than 14, looked 20 in a skin-tight black leotard, a neon yellow tank top, and spiked, black leather boots.

But as Jamie Williams walks to the front of the little auditorium at Ralston to start his talk, it's another girl who stands out above the rest. She sits in the ninth row, about three-quarters of the way back in the room. A big, tough-looking Hispanic girl, she has scraggly black hair tied up in a white bow. She has a tattoo. Everything about this girl—the way she sits there, her head cocked back, her mouth pursed down, her arms folded tightly across her stomach—reads defiance in big, capital letters like the ones that spell out RALSTON RAMS on the wall of the gym. She knows why this big, black big shot with the

53

goofy dreadlocked hair has come to her school: To swag-
ger around with his Super Bowl ring and fill himself up
with the foolish worship of a school full of stupid people
who don't know any better. But Little Miss Defiance isn't
fooled. *Show me, big man,* she seems to be saying to Jamie
Williams. *Show me—if you can.*

Jamie started going to schools to talk to kids about
drugs when he was playing for the Oilers. In five years in
Houston, he gave dozens of talks like this one. In Houston, the kids usually were out of control, hooting and hollering so loud Jamie had to practically yell to be heard
over the din. But here at Ralston, the kids are silent, mes-
merized. So Jamie begins.

"I'm going to tell you a story about a guy," he says. "It's
kind of a sad story, but it's one that I think might hit home
to you guys. Now, a lot of us, we know about drugs. We
know what that stuff can do to you. And we know what's
destined for you if you go out and start hanging around
with gangs. But let me tell you about a guy who just didn't
feel like going to class.

"In high school, this friend of mine and I, we were the
stars of the football team. He was a receiver, and so was I.
When we were in high school, they came out with a report
on the top 10 receivers in the country. My friend and I
were both on that list. The day [it] came out, we were giving high fives to each other. We were both getting ready
to go to college. At least we thought we were.

"All of a sudden, here comes Notre Dame to talk to
Jamie Williams and his friend, Alexander. And here
comes Nebraska to talk to Jamie and Alex. The University of Illinois, Missouri, Cal Berkeley—all of these
schools are coming in to talk to us when we were in high
school. And you've got to understand, Alex was one of
the most talented football players I've ever seen. As a
matter of fact, this guy was so good that, for awhile,
Roger Craig was his backup. You know Roger Craig.

Super Bowl man. Touchdown man. He had to play back-up—*backup*—to this guy.

"But you've never heard of this guy. Why? Because when it came time for the colleges to sit down and offer us a scholarship, they said, 'We're sorry Alex, we can't offer you anything because your grades aren't good enough.' On a scale of one to four, this guy probably had something like a point O nine. That's like F or D minus minus. All that talent and he couldn't even get into college. Me? I studied. I went to class. I got A's. I got an education. Now I've got a Super Bowl ring."

Unfortunately, Jamie tells the kids at Ralston, his friend's situation got more complicated—and it got worse. "Alex," he says to the teenagers, "hadn't even graduated from high school yet, and he had three kids. That didn't have anything to do with drugs. But it had everything to do with education, and I'm going to tell you how in a minute.

"But first, I want to tell you about something that happened last year right before the Super Bowl. I'm getting ready to pack up and fly to New Orleans, when I get a call from Alex. He wants some Super Bowl tickets. I asked him how he was doing. He said he had six or seven kids now, and that he works hard labor in a factory. The guy had the talent to do whatever he wanted to with his life, and here he is working hard labor in a factory. I don't know how much you guys know about factories. But I grew up in Davenport, Iowa, where about all we had was factories. So I know a thing or two about what factories are like. They have a line of guys, and every guy does the same thing—the *same thing*—for eight hours. You think English is boring? You think history is boring? Try taking a bolt and putting it on a screw, taking a lunch break, then coming back and doing it some more, eight hours a day. Then go home and take care of six or seven kids.

"You know what Alex told me when I talked to him?" Jamie asked the eighth graders. "'Jamie,' he said, 'I should have listened to you. I should have listened to you when you told me to study. I should have listened.' But he didn't. Now it's too late. He's got all these kids. And kids—kids are forever."

As Jamie's words echo in the little auditorium, all eyes drop to the floor. There's silence, except for the sound of 200 teenagers shifting awkwardly on brown metal chairs. Jamie Williams looks out over the hushed room. He knows he has hit home. He knows he has struck a nerve. Now, when they are a little scared and more than a little vulnerable, it's time to drive home a point.

"When I was growing up in the neighborhood," Jamie says, "all I knew about was going to the park to shoot some hoop. 'Who's got the best jump shot today, boys?' All I knew about when the weekend was over was that I had to go back to English class, back to math class. But I went back to class, and you know what it got me? I'll tell you. It taught me how to *think*. Why is knowing how to think important? You don't have to be very smart to get hooked on drugs. You don't have to be very smart to start hanging out with a gang. And you don't have to be very smart to have three or four kids before you even graduate from high school.

"But it's the people who know how to think who don't get into situations like that. Because they think about what they're doing. When you go to class, when you study English and math and history, you teach yourself to go, 'Well, I really like this girl, but I'm not ready to be a daddy.' When you go to class and study, you learn something about yourself that you'd never know unless you know how to think. Here it is.

"You can never be anything if you don't want to be anything. And to be anything, you've got to know how to think. *That's* why education is important. There's a million stories like Alex's, stories of people who've blown away their education. You guys have to think about it."

Jamie talks for another half hour. He talks about how

drugs are dangerous because they "make you someone you're not." He talks about the time, as a freshman— "freshmeat"— at Nebraska, when some football players tried to get him to smoke dope—and how, when he refused, the guys had called him things like "wimp" and "punk" and it took guts to tell them where to stick their dope but he did it. And he talks about how some of his own brothers and sisters sat back and never studied and figured "somebody was going to hand them something in life." The words come from his heart. And that's where most of what he says hits the kids at Ralston.

When Jamie finishes, he sets down the microphone and waits for the ambush. Dozens of teenagers rush the stage, pushing and shoving to get close to him. For several minutes, they press in close. Then, one of the teachers orders the kids back to class. As most of the students head grudgingly for the door, one girl stays, hovering nervously about 10 feet in front of Jamie. It's Little Miss Defiance. She stands, shyly scuffing the bottom of her right shoe on the top of her left one. She looks at Jamie. She smiles, a small, timid one at first, then a wide, ear-to-ear grin that pushes her chubby brown cheeks up to her eyes.

"Hi Jamie," she says, finally. Then she giggles and squeals out toward the door.

As Jamie watches her disappear, he turns to the group of teachers clustered around him at the front of the auditorium.

"There's going to be a lot of kids coming out of here with something in their heads for the future," he says.

It's noon before Jamie Williams reaches the parking lot and unlocks the door of his white Mercedes. He's stayed longer than he'd planned to today. Much longer. After inspiring a whole auditorium, he spent almost two hours dropping in and out of a half dozen other classes. One by one, the teachers had pleaded with him. "*Can't you spend just a few minutes with my kids?"* And Jamie looked down at the kids, standing in the doorway around their teacher, staring up at him with their big, searching eyes. And, almost every time, he had smiled and said, *"How can I say no?"*

The next day, back in the locker room at the Taj, Jamie Williams explained why he can never say no when it comes to kids and drugs. His father had died the day before Jamie spoke at Ralston. He was murdered, Jamie said, adding that it was not the first time that a member of the Williams family had fallen in with the wrong kind of people. Jamie never forgot what had happened the first time. To his older brother.

Jamie was 13 when Dennis Williams almost died. He can still remember walking home from school and seeing his neighbors milling around in the front yard. One said the ambulance had been there. That Dennis Williams had been taking drugs, and that *they don't know if he made it yet.*

Dennis Williams made it. The heroin didn't kill him. But Jamie Wlliams's older brother has never been what he could have been. "Drugs cut Dennis in half," Jamie said that day at the Taj. "That's the pain I play with to this day. He could have been out there doing what I'm doing. My older brother should just be getting out of the NFL about now. My brother should have *played.* He should have done so many things. But drugs took all that away. Drugs took my brother."

Back in Davenport, Dennis Williams was a legend. All the kids looked up to him. He stood a stocky 6-feet-3-inches tall. And he was everything every kid in the neighborhood wanted to grow up to be. Tough. Strong. And independent. Dennis Williams didn't take trouble from anybody. "Dennis," Jamie remembers, "was the type of kid who, if he got in a fight and lost, he went back the next day and fought again until he won. But Dennis didn't have to go back very often. He kicked everybody's ass. He was extremely hard." Part of the reason Dennis Williams was extremely hard was his father.

Claude Williams had been born in Florida, and like many blacks from that part of the country around the time of World War II, he had been taught that life meant learning a trade to make a living. Claude Williams became a welder.

By the time Jamie was 9, Claude Williams was already an angry man. There wasn't much work in Florida for a black man who made his living welding pieces of metal together. And because he had mouths to feed—there would be seven children in all—Claude was under the gun. Already he was angry and frustrated at a society that treated blacks the way it did, but even more so at the advancing conflict he was feeling between what *he* thought was important in life—learning a trade and making a living—and the things that his three oldest sons thought were *their* tickets to a better life—football, basketball, and school books.

In the summer of 1969, Claude and Bernice Williams moved their family to Davenport, Iowa. Claude was still angry, but at least there was work. In Davenport, about all a guy needed to find a steady paycheck was a Social Security card and an alarm clock. If you could show up on time and weren't always drunk, there was usually a job at John Deere, Ralston Purina, Caterpillar, or any one of the other plants that defined life in the factory town on a curve of the Mississippi River.

Jamie says the tension growing up with his two oldest brothers, Claude Jr. and Dennis, and his father, shaped his family's life in Davenport. There was always a lot of yelling and screaming, he remembers—screaming that came from people fighting to live in different worlds. *"You wastin' yo time playin' ball!"* Claude Williams would scream at the top of his lungs to his sons in the tiny white house on the hill at Ninth and Gaines. *"You don't know nothin' about tools and mechanics. You gonna be sorry. You gonna grow up and be sorry and good for nothin' in life 'cus you don't know tools and you don't know a trade. You don't know nothin'."*

"At that point," Jamie remembers, "my dad was like a lot of my friends' fathers. He just didn't have it in his mind that kids could go on to college and be great athletes and that that could lead to a career. He thought we should be learning a trade, and that when we got out of high school we'd get a job down at the gas station. Instead, we were out there playing ball and going to bonfires and being rah-rah with the high school. He thought we had our priorities screwed up. My dad never finished high school, and so he didn't understand that getting good grades and being a good athlete opens up doors and makes opportunities for you."

With a father he couldn't get close to, Jamie looked around for someone—another father—to help him figure out who he was so that he could someday get out of Davenport and be somebody. He didn't have to look any farther than his extremely hard older brother, Dennis. "Growing up, he was more of a father to me than my father was," Jamie said one day during the season, adding that one of the first skills his older brother taught him was how to be tough. "When I was a kid, he used to take me to his friends' houses and make me race their brothers and cousins. Sometimes, he'd make me wrestle them. And sometimes, he'd make me fight them. To some people, that might sound a little hard, but to me it was an honor. This was my older brother, man, and he was just trying to teach me to look out for myself."

But Dennis Williams did more for Jamie than teach him how to fight. He taught him how to think, too. "He was somebody who showed me that it was really good to get A's," Jamie says, remembering how, whenever he would bring home a report card with an A on it, Dennis would do something nice for Jamie. Take him up to the store for a soda and a bag of chips. Or let Jamie ride his bike down the hill to the park. For Jamie, his older brother's teaching was just what he needed. Jamie got bunches of A's.

But if there was one piece of the puzzle of Jamie's life that Dennis Williams did more to help his younger brother put together than any other, it was that little piece with no edges called *direction.* Robin Ewing, Jamie's best friend in Davenport, remembers spending the night at the Williams' house. He remembers how at times all the banter about comic books and superheroes and playing basketball in the alley behind Jamie's house would end and, suddenly, Dennis Williams would be serious. Deadly serious. "What I remember most is how we'd be up late talking, Dennis beating up on Jamie—slap fighting—and how, all of a sudden, Dennis would get all serious," says Ewing, now a basketball and track coach in Davenport. "And then he would look at us real hard, and he would tell us, 'If you guys want something beyond all the crap you're seeing here in this neighborhood, you're going to have to go out and take it. You're going to have to work for it, and you're going to have to do it by yourself. Nobody's going to do it for you." Then, Ewing remembers, Dennis Williams would issue a challenge. *"If you don't do it, who will?"*

Dennis Williams, Ewing says, "helped Jamie learn that there's a right way and a wrong way to do things. And that sometimes the right way is the hard way. Because of Dennis, Jamie accepted the fact that he was going to have to go through some hard times to get where he wanted to be."

By the time Jamie was getting ready to go into high school, the war between Claude and Dennis Williams was raging. As the impatient, aggressive father clamped down harder and harder on a son who flaunted his distaste for his father's attitudes and discipline, the strong-willed son with his own ideas rebelled more and more. It was a vicious cycle. It was a cycle that led to drugs. With the athletic scholarship offers piling up, Dennis Williams joined a traveling rock band. He wanted to be like Jimi Hendrix. He even played the guitar left-handed, just like Hendrix. At 18, Dennis Williams was just like Jimi Hendrix in one other way: He overdosed on drugs.

One day shortly after he got out of the hospital, Dennis Williams told Jamie he wanted to talk to him. He had that look on his face. He was deadly serious. "Hey, man," Dennis Williams said to his younger brother, "don't do what I did. Don't mess with the drugs. My dreams got cut short because of that shit. Don't you make the same mistake. I didn't make it out of here the way I wanted to. You can. And if you don't do it, who will?"

Today, Dennis Williams lives in Vero Beach, Florida, where Claude and Bernice Williams started their family more than three decades ago. Jamie says he works in a club. He hardly ever sees his younger brother, who plays pro ball on another coast. Both are horrible at writing or dialing the phone. For Jamie, it's half a country away from where he now lives, and more than half a lifetime since the day he walked home from school in Davenport and found out that the ambulance had been to his house, that Dennis *had been takin' drugs,* and they *don't know if he made it or not.* But sometimes, like those 50 minutes in front of the eighth graders at Ralston, it's like it all happened yesterday.

"Drugs took my brother," Jamie said a few days after his talk. "And because of that, I had somebody to help me avoid making the mistakes Dennis made. Do they have that somebody? That's why I talk to the kids. They have to know that they can make their own futures. They have to know that they can make their own opportunities. They have to know that if they want to be somebody, they have to want to work to be somebody. Because if they don't do it, who will?

"A lot of people think, 'Your brother overdosed on drugs, he didn't make it, so you must think you're better than him.' That's the part that hurts. Hurts not just because it's not true, but because of how far from true it is. Dennis helped me more than anyone will ever know. If it wasn't for him, I might not be where I am today."

Indeed. But in Davenport, his older brother wasn't the only one who helped Jamie Williams grow up. There was one other person. Some might call her a second mother. Others would say she's just a teacher.

It's the day after Halloween in Davenport, Iowa. Pumpkins sit on stairwells. Paper ghosts hang from porch ceilings. And leaves of every fall color—bright oranges, yellows, and reds—tumble across sidewalks in the advancing winter wind. A few minutes after 2:30 in the afternoon, Barbara Hess is alone in Room 530 at Davenport Central High School. Alone, that is, except for one student, a bright but undirected sophomore, a boy who now lingers before her, scuffing his Air Jordans on the dirty schoolroom floor. The young man is about to catch hell, because he has committed the one transgression that Barb Hess has never pardoned in her almost 30 years of teaching at Central: He has piddled away an hour he could have spent learning. And so a scolding is in order. "What did you do today?" asks Hess, a short, round woman in her early fifties. Hess, of course, knows the answer. "You were all over the room today," she says, "and your mouth never stopped moving."

The boy fidgets. The Air Jordans paw the floor some more. Tomorrow, Friday, there will be a substitute in her class, and Hess hopes her little lecture today will forestall a disaster tomorrow. "If you want to sit here tomorrow and pout, that's fine with me," Hess says to the boy. "At least when you pout, you're quiet." As the student leaves, Barb Hess walks over to her desk, a huge, rectangular thing covered by several inches of homework and other papers. She pulls four Kleenexes from a box. She will use them all.

Barb met Jamie Williams before a junior varsity basketball game one Saturday in the fall of 1975. Jamie was a sophomore. Barb was the statistician for the basketball team. She was also the unofficial team "den mother." On this day, Hess was sitting off to one side of the court when the sophomore basketball coach brought Jamie over and introduced him to her. "Jamie sat down and just kind of leaned into me," Hess remembers in Room 530 as the bump and throb of rap music sifts in through the open window from the parking lot below. "I had no idea what had just happened in his life, but it was clear from the minute we met that he needed me." Before long, that need would work its way right back. Because if Jamie Williams needed someone to love him, Barb Hess wanted someone to love.

To look at them, Jamie and Barb were an odd couple. One was a huge, muscled black kid, with long legs that he stretched out under his desk. At six-foot-four, Jamie had massive, broad shoulders, a thick chest, and these serious pipes—biceps—that he had forged through countless hours in the weight room. But, Barb could also see, Jamie was quiet, and he was gentle. And he loved to touch and to hug. Barb was just the opposite. She was a small, no-nonsense white woman who had always lived alone and, although she had never considered herself particularly cold before then, had never really gone in for touching and hugging and a lot of outward affection. That changed when she met Jamie and Robin.

Robin Ewing was Jamie's best friend in Davenport. Jamie called Robin "Bird." Bird was tall—six-three—and rail thin. Like Jamie, he loved comic books—Flash, Batman, the Incredible Hulk, all of them. Bird was also renowned as the clown of Davenport Central. Bird would do anything. Hang himself from a movie screen at the front of the room. Crawl on his hands and knees through the hallways all the way to gym class. Act out the scene in the *Wizard of Oz* in which the Cowardly Lion, dressed up in soldiers' garb to rescue Dorothy from the castle of the Wicked Witch of the North, frantically flails behind him to hide his flying tail, while belting out, in his deep baritone, the soldiers' ominous refrain, "O-EEEE-O, EE-O-O."

Together, the two towering sophomores gave Hess all she could handle. They were toughest when they teamed up on her. Like the day in March 1976. The principal had shown up at Hess's room and requested her company in the hallway on a school matter. Hess was teaching a class that included Jamie, Bird, and several other members of the sophomore basketball team. When the principal asked Hess to close the door while they talked, Hess told him that she didn't dare turn her back on *this* group. So when she went out into the hallway with the principal, Hess kept her hand on the doorknob. Her arm, up to the elbow, was still inside the classroom. While she stood in the hallway talking to the principal, Hess felt something itchy crawling up the back of her arm.

That damn Robin, she thought. *He's kissing me.*

When she could stand it no longer, Hess flung open the door and bellowed.

"ROBIN!"

But it wasn't Robin. It was Jamie, who stood in the doorway, smiling down at her.

"I knew you'd blame Robin," he said.

From the time Barb had the two basketball players in her class, it was obvious that both Jamie and Robin needed something—someone. At home, both had lives filled with tension and trauma. During high school, Robin's parents would consider—but reject—a divorce. And with both of Jamie's older brothers gone from home—both had run away—Claude Williams was riding Jamie hard like there was no tomorrow. *"You wastin' yo time playin' ball,"* he would rant. *"You don't know nothin' about tools and mechanics. You gonna be sorry. You gonna grow up and be sorry and good for nothin' in life 'cus you don't know tools and you don't know a trade. You don't know nothin'."*

"What Jamie and Robin needed," Barb Hess said, "was somebody soft, somebody who didn't feel that their primary value was the number of points they scored or the number of passes they caught. Jamie and Robin needed somebody who accepted and cared for them as they were."

Bird says Barb was right about what they needed from her. "Barb was always there, for me and for Jamie," he remembers. "She was our second mother. Without her, I don't think either of us would be where we are now. She gave us the one thing both Jamie and I needed more than anything in the world. She gave us her love."

From the beginning, Barb knew her relationship with Jamie was finite. There was a set deadline—graduation—and from the moment Jamie leaned into her on the side of the basketball court that day before the junior varsity game, the clock was ticking. "I've lived in Davenport almost my whole life," she recalled in her classroom that first day of November. "And it's a good, middle-class place to live. But for Jamie, it would have been a dead end. Where would he have gone with his talent here? He had to get out—up and out. And he was comfortable with that. He was comfortable with who he was, and with where he was going. It meant that the attachments he had here were often times not as deep as they were with some of the other kids like Roger [Craig, Jamie's 49er teammate, whose family also lived in Davenport]. Jamie knew it had to be that way. He knew he didn't have time to get immersed in the place or people, because he wasn't staying. This was just the first stop on his journey upward."

For Jamie and Barb, the journey began on the basketball court. One of the first things she taught Jamie was the same thing Dennis Williams was trying to get across to his younger brother: Survival. Hess went about it in a different way than Dennis Williams did, but the goal of the tutoring was the same. Jamie needed to be able to take care of himself. "Every Monday during the basketball season," Hess remembered, "the sophomores got a chance to practice against the seniors. Those seniors used to beat Jamie bloody. They were doing all the cheap shots—elbows, hips, knees—and we had two of them who were pretty good at it. After one scrimmage, Jamie was telling me, 'Man, I'm all black and blue.' And I remember asking him, 'Well, what did you do to them?'

" 'I tried to get out of the way,' Jamie answered.

" 'You didn't throw an elbow back?'

" 'Oh no, man, these are *seniors*.'

" 'Jamie, the idea of playing basketball is for you to learn something you can use in your life later on. This is where you learn to throw elbows in life.' "

Hess remembers the time when she knew Jamie had learned his lesson. It was after a scrimmage, and she was back at home when the phone rang. It was one of the seniors.

"Did you tell him to use his elbows?" the senior asked.

"Yeah, I did," she answered. "And his knees, too."

Before long, it was the spring of 1977. Jamie was a junior, and basketball season was over. Jamie had nothing to do. The only sport available was track. And that, Barb remembered, posed a problem. "Running was not Jamie's thing," she said. "He was pretty fast, but he was so big, and his legs were so long that about all he could do was lumber along. And jumping wasn't much better." Finally, Jamie settled on an event where he didn't have to run or jump, where he could use his height and years of pumping weights to his advantage. He chose the discus.

After Barb went down to the sporting goods store and

bought Jamie a discus—the high school didn't have enough to go around—the two of them trudged out to Brady Street Stadium off Highway 61. There, every Saturday morning, while the track team was off at a meet in Clinton or Cedar Rapids, Jamie Williams learned to throw the discus. And Barb Hess learned how to fetch it. Three months after they started, Jamie finished fourth in the Iowa state track meet with a throw of 156 feet.

Under Barb's care, Jamie was growing up. But the most important collaboration between student and second mother did not take place in a sport. It involved school. Jamie had always loved to read—even if it was about Spiderman, Flash, Captain America, and the other superheroes in the jillion comics he had stashed all over the place in his room at home. Jamie was a good listener. And he was the most inquisitive student Barb had ever met. But, Barb knew, if Jamie was ever going to make it out of Davenport, it was going to take more than good grades, sharp listening skills, and curiosity. It was going to involve a choice.

"Academically, I knew Jamie would have no trouble getting through any of the schools he wanted to go to," Barb said. "But before he'd get the chance to go to college, he had to decide he was going to make something of himself no matter what it took. And he did. Jamie could have chosen to wallow in misery like some of the other kids he went to school with. He could have chosen to get mediocre grades and go to a mediocre college. But he chose to dream higher. And he chose to give up things— like a social life and friendships—to make his dream come true. He chose to do the running and the weight lifting that were necessary to make him a better athlete. And he chose to study while a lot of kids his age were out doing their dippy stuff. These were hard choices for Jamie—for any kid. But there was no way he was going to get trapped over there [Ninth and Gaines]. He would have died over there."

By the fall of 1977 and the start of Jamie's senior year at Davenport Central, his dream of landing an athletic scholarship and a ticket out of Davenport was in sight. The letters from the universities were piling up. Barb kept them all in her desk drawer at school. Penn State, Notre Dame, Tennessee, Iowa, Iowa State, Illinois, and Missouri were among the schools beating a path to his door. Barb wanted Jamie to pick Tennessee. She had been impressed by a letter the Volunteers' football coach, Johnny Majors, had written pointing out his commitment to guaranteeing athletes their degrees. Barb liked Tennessee, but she knew there wasn't much chance that Jamie would end up there. To Jamie, there was basically only one school on his list. If it checked out, his choice was made. The school was Nebraska. That was where Curtis Craig, Roger's older brother, had gone several years before. In many ways, Curtis and Jamie were alike. Both were quiet. Both had been prodigiously talented athletes at Central High. And both had, at young ages, realized that school and sports were going to be their ticket out of Davenport to the world beckoning from beyond.

Barb took Jamie to the airport one day in the spring of 1978. She had never seen him so nervous. His hands were twitching, and he was making nervous cracks about how safe the airplane was going to be. It was Jamie's first trip anywhere. Now, he was going to *Nebraska*. And he was terrified. Barb tried to soothe him.

"Jamie," she said before he got on the plane, "the only trouble you're going to have is fitting into the seat. After that, everything will be fine."

Barb was right. When she picked Jamie up a few days later at the airport in Moline, Illinois, across the Mississippi from Davenport, she knew that Nebraska had indeed checked out. She knew it the minute she saw the look on Jamie's face.

"He looked like someone had just handed him his dream," Barb said, "and all he had to do was close his fingers and it was his."

At the Astrodome on October 7, Jamie Williams's return to Houston, where he spent his first five seasons in the NFL, is hardly monumental. He catches two passes for 14 yards. Fortunately for the 49ers, however, John Taylor does have a big day. Taylor pulls in two touchdown passes—the second one a 46-yard catch-and-run late in the fourth quarter—as San Francisco wins its fourth straight game of the season, 24–21.

But for the second week in a row, the Niner defense barely survives against the run-and-shoot, a passing offense in which four wide receivers run routes and react to the defense on the field instead of having specific patterns laid out before the snap. In the first half, Houston quarterback Warren Moon rips the 49er secondary for 120 yards passing on 11 completions. Moon runs for one touchdown and throws for another. At halftime, the Oilers are up 14–7, and the Niner defense doesn't look like it has a clue how to stop the run-and-shoot. But the Oilers only find the end zone once in the second half. And Joe Montana twice hits Taylor on long passes, and the Niners pull another one out at the end.

In the visitors' locker room after the game, Eddie De-Bartolo Jr. stands in the hallway between the trainers' room and the showers. The 49ers' owner has come down into the locker room to congratulate his players and coaches on a job well done. Guard Guy McIntyre walks by. DeBartolo likes hugs, but McIntyre is wet from a shower, so a handshake suffices. Handshakes follow with special teams and tight end coach Lynn Stiles, cornerback Darryl Pollard, and safety Dave Waymer.

Then it's Bill McPherson's turn. The 49er defensive

coordinator is tall and lanky, with knobby, bean-pole legs that make his movement a shuffle as much a walk. As usual, McPherson has a wad of Red Man stuffed in his cheek. Without his 49er hat, McPherson's hair strays in several directions. His red 49er golf shirt spills out over his belly. His face is flushed a bright shade of red; it's humid as hell in here. McPherson shuffles up to De-Bartolo.

"Congratulations," DeBartolo says, offering his hand to McPherson. And then it's like he has pulled the back off a dump truck with a full load of sand. McPherson spills out everywhere.

"I HATE THAT FUCKING OFFENSE!" McPherson booms, pumping DeBartolo's hand. "I HATE THAT THING. I DON'T KNOW HOW TO DEFENSE IT. ALL THOSE WIDEOUTS RUNNIN' EVERY WHICH WAY."

Bill McPherson shakes his head at DeBartolo, who just looks up at the coach who's at least a foot taller than he is. McPherson isn't finished. But at least he's stopped yelling.

"I hate that offense," he says again.

McPherson and DeBartolo stop shaking hands and McPherson leaves. As he shuffles down the hallway to the coaches' dressing room, Bill McPherson can be heard muttering, to himself, about how much he hates Houston's run-and-shoot offense.

The Niners had pulled out another one at the end. Just like New Orleans. Just like Atlanta. But this win had come with a price. In the second quarter, one play after he'd broken Walter Payton's NFL record for the most pass receptions by a running back, Roger Craig hurt his right knee. Tomorrow reporters will learn that Craig has suffered a partial tear of the posterior cruciate ligament, one of two ligaments that cross at the center of the knee and prevent the tibia, or shin bone, from moving backward. The 49ers do not release a schedule for Craig's re-

turn or allow reporters to interview team physician
Michael Dillingham about the injury. John McVay, however, tells a reporter privately that Roger Craig could
miss as many as six games.

Which means that there is now a hole at running back.
And an opening for the San Francisco press. The National Football League trading deadline is only nine days
away. And with only rookie Dexter Carter as a backup,
will the Niners make a deal for some big-name back to fill
Roger Craig's shoes? The prisoners from Stalag 49
thought they knew.

Chapter 5

Stalag 49

*T*uesday morning, October 16, the O'Hare Hilton, Chicago O'Hare International Airport. John McVay is drinking coffee. So is Al Davis, who is standing next to McVay. McVay and Davis, owner of the Los Angeles Raiders, are in Chicago for the NFL's annual fall meeting. According to the nation's sporting press, the two men are plotting the biggest trade of the year in professional football—an all-star running back for a first-round draft pick. For weeks, the press has been reporting that McVay and Davis have been exchanging phone calls. Now they have come to Chicago to hammer out a deal. What the negotiations amount to is this:

"If you could trade for a great running back," the Black Knight says to McVay, taking a sip of his coffee, "you'd win the Super Bowl."

"Al," McVay answers, "if you could guarantee that, you could have all 12 picks."

That was the end. The beginning seemed like a long time ago. It was only seven days.

Ten in the morning, and already John McVay knows things are out of control. It's Wednesday, October 10, three days after San Francisco's win at the Astrodome, and about all Hilary Heuermann, McVay's administrative assistant, has been doing this morning is fielding phone calls. One after another. From reporters, who are all asking to speak with John McVay about the same thing. Marcus Allen.

In this morning's edition of *The National,* unnamed "sources" have revealed that the "49ers are considering a trade" for Allen, the Raiders' all-time leading rusher who is presently in Al Davis's doghouse—again—after asking to be traded during training camp. The 49ers, according to *The National,* "are willing to surrender a first-round draft choice" to get the 30-year-old running back, who was the Most Valuable Player in the Raiders' 38–9 Super Bowl win over the Redskins in 1984.

With Roger Craig out indefinitely, and with the NFL trading deadline only a week away, John McVay knew the rumors were going to fly. They always do at this time of the season. But this Marcus Allen rumor, McVay realizes on the morning of October 10, is going to be a bigger pain than usual. So, escorted by Rodney Knox of the 49ers' public-relations staff, McVay arrives downstairs in the press room at the Taj around 11 A.M. He tries his best to throw cold water on the flames that the media are quickly trying to stoke into a bonfire.

"Everybody knows we're a week away from the trading deadline," McVay says, "so this activity now gets a new impetus. . . . [But] as has happened with most trades here, there has been a whole lot more conversation than activity. . . . We talk to lots and lots of people. We call around; we talk to people constantly. People call us. There is a constant flow of information back and forth, [with] us talking to other teams and them talking to us. . . ."

"Have you made the Raiders an offer?" Ira Miller of the *Chronicle* asks McVay.

"No," McVay answers without hesitation. "I'm not going to deny that [I've] had conversations with Al. But we've had [such] preliminary [types of] conversations that I could hardly say we're talking about a trade. . . . This thing is way out of proportion with the Raiders. The Raiders aren't very happy about it, and we're not very happy about it. It's way, way, way, *way* exaggerated."

The reporters hear McVay's words. They write them down. Later they will play them back on their tape recorders. But many don't believe what they hear, because many of the reporters who cover the 49ers assume that there are always two ways to interpret anything a team member says to the media—especially when it comes to trades and injuries. First, the thinking goes, there is what is said. Then there is the truth. On the morning of October 10, some Bay Area reporters decide that this axiom is working perfectly in the case of Marcus Allen. John McVay, they are sure, is telling them a story.

The early reports have the Raiders offering Allen to San Francisco for a player—either Pro Bowl defensive lineman Charles Haley or third-year defensive lineman Pierce Holt, who was named to the NFL's All-Rookie Team in 1988—and was the team's first-round pick in the 1991 college draft. As for Haley and Holt, one Niner source tells the *San Mateo Times* that the team isn't about to give up either of its young stars "for a 30-year-old running back." As for the draft pick, John McVay is covetously protecting San Francisco's top three picks, one first- and two second-round selections. This is mainly because the undefeated Niners are headed again to the NFL playoffs, which means they'll be picking at or near the bottom of the 28-team drafting order. By drafting so low, McVay knows, San Francisco's first-round selection is essentially another second. And, McVay also knows, the farther down a club picks in the draft, the worse the chances are of getting a player who can fill a real need on the roster of the two-time defending world champions.

During the week of San Francisco's 45–35 win over the Falcons in Atlanta, the Niners' trouble at running back is the talk of professional football. "49ERS WANT MARCUS ALLEN FROM RAIDERS," trumpets the headline in *The National*. "WHY NINERS SHOULDN'T

PASS ON CHANCE TO ACQUIRE ALLEN," says the *San Francisco Examiner*. Frequent accounts of the "trade" also appear in the *San Francisco Chronicle, San Jose Mercury News, Sacramento Bee, Peninsula Times Tribune,* and almost every Northern California newspaper that covers the 49ers. The circus is just beginning.

Over the next week, the press churns out hundreds of inches of copy on the rumors surrounding Marcus Allen and the 49ers. Every reporter in the Bay Area—and many from around the country—is trying to dig up something nobody else knows about the deal. The result is like repeatedly tilling a field: After awhile, it's hard to tell the old dirt from the new dirt. And when it gets too hard to tell the difference anymore, some reporters fire up their own rototiller.

"I think I'll start a rumor," one reporter says in the press room at the Taj one afternoon a few days before the trading deadline. Who knows if he's joking.

In all the talk and rumor, there are conflicting truths. The deal for Allen, some reports say, will never happen—just pick a reason. First, the 49ers' medical reports on Roger Craig are encouraging. Craig, it's now thought, will only miss another game or two, making the addition of a running back less urgent than if Craig were to be out for a month or longer. Another red flag is the high price—that first-round draft pick—that Al Davis is demanding for Allen, who is in his ninth year in the NFL.

In Los Angeles, too, most of the reports indicate that Marcus Allen probably won't be moving to San Francisco. For days, Raiders' coach Art Shell has been insisting that, just because Bo Jackson's rocket will soon land in El Segundo for the football season, it doesn't mean that he wants to unload Marcus Allen—even if Al Davis does. "Marcus Allen right now is a member of the Los Angeles Raiders," Shell tersely tells the *Los Angeles Times* on October 15. "[And] I expect him to be a member of the Los Angeles Raiders tomorrow at this time."

Another snag on the L.A. end is that Davis is still fuming over what happened last year with Matt Millen, a Raider linebacker for nine seasons. In training camp in 1989, the Raiders decided Millen was through, so they cut him. Several weeks later, Millen showed up in San Francisco, where he started the final 12 games on the Niners' march to New Orleans. Al Davis does not want to make the same mistake twice.

Other reporters, however, have sources who tell them exactly the opposite. The deal for Marcus Allen *is* alive, says the *San Mateo Times* on October 15: "[L]ook for [the] Los Angeles Raiders' running back . . . to be in a Forty Niners uniform before Tuesday's 1 P.M. trading deadline." Garry Niver's story in the *Times* also mentions a meeting between John McVay and Al Davis that will take place tonight when the league executives gather in Chicago. The high-level meeting that is the culmination of weeks of phone calls and negotiations. The high-level meeting that will result in the blockbuster trade of the year in professional football. The meeting that lasts less time than it takes to drink a cup of coffee.

Nine in the morning, Friday, October 19, John McVay's second-story office in the Taj. The NFL trading deadine is three days past. John McVay sits behind his desk. Sun filters in through the windows behind him. McVay wears a white oxford shirt, a green tie, and gray slacks. He is talking about the media and Marcus Allen. About how the media suddenly decided that Three-peat was old news and so they decided to make some news where there was none.

"I told everybody that it was all just a lot of conversation," McVay says of the trade rumors. He walks around his desk to pour himself a cup of coffee. "But nobody was listening. Some guys got it in their heads that it was big news. It really wasn't. I don't think Al ever really wanted to do anything. We were just talking."

McVay walks back behind his desk. He sets his coffee down and stands looking out the window. He reaches down and hitches his slacks up with his fingers. For several moments, he gazes out across the three practice fields toward the mountains in the distance. Then John McVay shakes his head and says, "Some wild things get printed just because some guys get it in their heads that something is news."

It's happening again. Richard Weiner figured it would. It was inevitable. But, Weiner figures, the guy will get his. *Sooner or later, he'll get his.*

It started back in training camp. The problem was simple. Almost every time Weiner would make a call in the press room at Sierra College—a series of tables crammed side-by-side in what is normally a staff and faculty dining room—the keyboard of a certain laptop computer near him would fall silent. That reporter, like at least half a dozen others in the room, was listening to what Weiner was saying on the phone—for a quote, a salary figure, the name of an agent, something, *anything* that he had missed. On the 49er beat, there is but one thing worse than death.

Getting scooped.

Richard Weiner covers the 49ers for the *Peninsula Times Tribune,* an afternoon daily in Palo Alto. Weiner isn't a big name in pro football coverage, but he's one of the best reporters on the Niners beat for several reasons. He has a nose for news. He's discreet and knows how to listen. And he's relentless in a low-key sort of way. Weiner isn't the toughest of the beat reporters. And he's not the most aggressive. But he doesn't need to be.

Unlike many reporters, Weiner doesn't treat the 49er players, coaches, and administrators like high-priced quote machines. Weiner's rapport with the team—especially the players—is relaxed and professional, cultivated and perpetuated by a sense that, hey, you may be a player and I may be a reporter, but we're both people so let's be honest and responsible and do our jobs. For Weiner, the approach works. Big time. He has more players' home phone numbers than most of the reporters in the press room, which means that he comes up with stories and pieces of information that many of the other reporters don't—or can't. That's why some listen to his phone calls.

Five days before the National Football League trading deadline, it was happening again. Richard Weiner figured it would. Competition is competition. But this time, Weiner decided, it was time to get even. It was time for someone to get what he had coming to him.

On Tuesday October 9, the 49ers bring several former NFL running backs in for workouts at the Taj. The most conspicuous is Joe Morris. In seven seasons with the New York Giants, the 5-foot-8 Morris rushed for more than 1,000 yards three times. But in 1989, he broke his foot and missed the whole season. Two months ago, at the final cut in training camp, the Giants let him go. Morris, John McVay tells reporters, "looks like he can still play." But are the Niners going to be the team that signs him? John McVay does not say. On Thursday night, with the trade deadline only five days away, there is only one way for reporters to find out just how serious the Niners are about Joe Morris. The Niner writer's scramble drill is simple. Call the Santa Clara Marriott. Run down the list of players to see if any of them are registered. *No?* Call the Doubletree Hotel up the road. Do the same thing.

Around 8 P.M., Richard Weiner is on the phone, doing the Niner writer's scramble drill. First, he calls the Marriott. No Joe Morris. Next, the Doubletree—and it happens again. When he runs down the list of the players with the voice at the front desk, Weiner notices the same thing he did back in the press room at Sierra College.

That same reporter who was listening to his phone calls in Rocklin is listening to his phone calls now in the press room at the Taj.

On the 49er beat, few reporters are as persistent as the one who has stopped typing to listen to what Weiner is saying. Few reporters hustle for stories and quotes as hard as this one does. And few reporters are, as one 49er player says, as "bloodthirsty" for a story or a quote as this one. Less than two weeks from now, this same reporter will anger several players—and as many beat writers—by barging into an injured 49er's hospital room in pursuit of news. The players will be livid because the reporter has brusquely violated the privacy of one of their comrades at a time when he's most vulnerable. The beat writers will be angry because, in the eyes of the players, the reporter has made them all look like heartless ambulance chasers who will do anything for a story.

Anything for a story. When the Niner writer's scramble drill fails to turn up Joe Morris, and with *that* reporter listening to his phone calls again, Richard Weiner snaps. Competition is one thing. Nosiness is another. Weiner gets an idea.

"J. B.," Weiner whispers quietly to Jarrett Bell, the beat reporter for the *Marin Independent Journal,* who sits to his right. Bell looks at Weiner. Weiner winks. Then in a voice loud enough that the other reporter can hear, Weiner launches his prank.

"Oh, yeah, there's another hotel," he says. Weiner dials his phone. He wants the other reporter to think he's talking to the front desk at the third hotel. In fact, there is no such hotel. Weiner waits, then begins to run down the list of players, beginning with Joe Morris. On the other end of the line, Weiner hears, *At the tone, Pacific Standard Time will be eight o'clock and thirty seconds.* When the Time Lady informs Weiner that a Joe Morris *is* registered, he asks to be connected. For several minutes, Richard Weiner "interviews" Joe Morris. After each question, he types for a few seconds to make it sound real. *This is the stupidest shit I've ever written. This is the stupidest shit I've ever written.* Toward the end of his "interview," Weiner isn't sure he's hooked the other reporter yet. So, before wrapping things up, he devises a key test.

"How long are they putting you up?" Weiner asks Joe Morris a.k.a. the Time Lady. "Until Friday. Well, all right, sir, just thought I'd check in. Maybe we'll see you then. Take care."

After he hangs up, Weiner does some eavesdropping of his own. The other reporter is back on the phone, re-doing the Niner writer's scramble drill. He is under the impression that Richard Weiner has just talked to Joe Morris—he is under the impression that somehow he has *missed Joe Morris.* That isn't going to go over well back at the desk. That won't go over very well at all. Weiner listens to the reporter for a couple of minutes. Then he ups the ante again.

"J. B.," Weiner calls out to Bell in one of those hoarse whispers used by people trying to make it look like they want to be quiet when they're really trying to be loud enough to be overheard easily. "Is there anybody else here?"

Bell plays along. "I don't know. What's up?"

Weiner and Bell walk out of the press room into the lobby at the Taj. There the two reporters talk about Weiner's joke—they even tell Aaron Guglielmelli, the security guard, about the mystery hotel. After a couple of minutes, the two reporters return to the press room. Each pretends to call his desk, talking in exaggerated whispers so, on the other side of the press room, the other reporter will think they are trying to keep the big scoop to themselves.

By Richard Weiner's count, the reporter works for another 90 minutes trying to find Joe Morris. At one point, the reporter walks out to the lobby and interrogates Aaron Guglielmelli about the mystery hotel Weiner was talking about on the phone. Guglielmelli says he doesn't know anything about any of the hotels. Finally, when Weiner and the reporter are the only beat writers left at the Taj, the reporter walks around the wall that separates the two sides of the press room.

"Are you scooping me?" he asks Weiner. "Or are the 49ers lying?"

Weiner turns and looks quizzically at him. "What are you talking about?"

"Are you scooping me?" the reporter asks again. "Or are the 49ers lying?"

"No on the first," Weiner answers. "Yes on the second."

The reporter is confused. "What about Joe Morris?"

Weiner keeps typing. "I didn't say anything about Joe Morris," he says.

The reporter, Weiner remembers later, returns to his cubicle and makes more phone calls. Half an hour later he's watching the TV in the press room when he turns to Weiner.

"I can't stand it," he says. "What have you got on Joe Morris?"

Weiner continues typing. "What're you talking about?"

Shortly after this, Weiner remembers later, the reporter gathers up his things and rushes out the door. Has he been scooped? Or has he been had?

No on the first. Yes on the second.

Tomorrow, two other reporters, Mike Silver of the *Santa Rosa Press Democrat* and Tim Keown of the *Sacramento Bee,* will perpetuate Weiner's prank in their own interview with Joe Morris a.k.a. the Time Lady. It will be days before the other reporter speaks to Richard Weiner again.

After the other reporter storms out of the Taj late on this Thursday evening in October, Richard Weiner smiles to himself as he thinks back at how perfectly his prank had worked.

He finally got his, Weiner thinks to himself. *He finally got his.* It was inevitable. He smiles again and finishes his story for Saturday.

To some of the writers and columnists who cover the 49ers, the Taj is not known only by that name. Every year, one beat writer has T-shirts designed and printed that depict the struggle of the prisoners in the battle against the oppressive keepers of the jail at "Stalag 49."

The nearly two dozen reporters who toil in Stalag 49 are there for a host of different reasons. Some write about football because they like football. Others write about football because they like news reporting. Others write about football because they have been doing it so long they don't know anything else. Only a few reporters do their jobs because they actually like them. Most of them are men. Some are in their forties, veterans who have covered the Niners or pro football for decades. Others are still in their twenties and just getting started. Some of them are wonderful writers. Some are not. Some are fantastic reporters with contacts all over the country. Others aren't. Some have a fine eye for detail, and are able to offer insights into the game that their readers see only from a distance. Others just get quotes. Some of them are pushy and obnoxious, while others are polite and professional. Some are arrogant and irritatingly self-absorbed, while others are humble. Some have a remark-able sensitivity for people. Others have no such sense at all.

Whatever their differences, all of the prisoners in Stalag 49 have one thing in common. They are partners with the 49ers. In a fixed arrangement in which each side uses the other to get what it wants. In which each side tol-erates the other because the NFL says they must.

Chapter 6

Strained Relations

Jesse Sapolu pads across the charcoal-colored carpet toward his locker at the Taj. It's a Saturday afternoon in September. Last night, after San Francisco's sloppy loss to Seattle in the last preseason game of the year, George Seifert stood at the podium and told reporters, "We've said this is a players' team. It's obviously about to become my team." Then Seifert left the room, leaving reporters to wonder whether he was just frustrated over the Seahawk debacle or whether he was about to crack the whip on his world champions.

The next day, Jesse Sapolu is sitting in his undershorts on the bench in front of his locker when Bill Soliday, a reporter for the *Hayward Review*, walks up, turns on his tape recorder, and goes to work.

"George said something after the game," Soliday says. " 'This used to be a players' team, now it's my team.' What does that mean to you?"

Sapolu stares out across the almost empty locker room. Soliday is just doing his job. But so is Sapolu. Soliday waits for an answer to his question. Silence. Finally, after a full minute, the reporter clicks off his recorder.

"Okay, Jesse," Soliday says, sarcastically. "Thank you."

Sapolu ignores him and continues to sit, with his elbows resting on his knees, on the bench in front of his locker. Soliday is gone but 30 seconds when Ric Bucher, the *San Jose Mercury News* beat reporter, stops by. Bucher swings his leg over the bench, and sits facing Sapolu. Bucher cuts to the chase.

"George says this used to be a players' team, now it's his team. Do you buy that?" For half a minute, Sapolu says nothing. Then in a half-grunt, half-whisper, "We'll find out."

Bucher stares at the center of the 49ers, waiting for an elaboration. One is not offered. Finally, Bucher gives up.

"Doesn't seem like a Saturday, does it?" the reporter says.

Jesse Sapolu looks out across the locker room. A little smile comes into his face. He has done his job. Two reporters have tried to stir the peace. And he has been solid. He has protected the peace. Twice.

"No," Sapolu says. "It doesn't."

Then he stands and walks slowly off into the lunchroom.

Dr. Harry Edwards knows exactly what has happened. Edwards has been "inside" the 49er locker room ever since Bill Walsh brought him in before the 1986 season. Edwards is not listed anywhere in the team's media guide. He doesn't have any power to make decisions—after all, he's just a "consultant." Technically, Bronco Hinek, the equipment manager, is in charge of the Niner locker room. But so is Harry Edwards.

Edwards isn't in charge of what people think or say or do. But he most certainly is in charge of making sure the Niners are all thinking and talking about going in the same direction. Is Ronnie Lott getting along with Chet Brooks? Has Charles Haley patched up his thing with Jim Burt or Matt Millen? If Chet Brooks is unhappy because he isn't playing every down, how is he handling it? How is Brooks's frustration affecting his teammates in the secondary? How is Steve Wallace feeling now that his parents are suing him over a house he bought them in Georgia four years ago? Is Jim Burt's baby girl still sick?

Harry Edwards is a sociologist. He is a rebel and a boat rocker. But in the Niner locker room, Edwards is also a savvy chemist, a savvy scientist who deftly monitors the volatile mix of personalities to make sure that each meshes with the others so that the experiment on Sundays will be a success.

Harry Edwards does his job with a comment here, a little advice there. He does a lot of listening. He does even more talking. Once, when he was getting ready to sit down with Eddie DeBartolo to talk about his contract, Harry Edwards came up with a list of 19 things that he does for the Niners. None of those functions is more important than helping the players survive their relationships with the media.

"The locker room is where the guys live," Harry Edwards is saying. "It's their office, their home. It's the place where they come to grieve when they lose. The place where they are attended to when they are injured. The place where they come to celebrate when they are happy. It's the place where the respect that is generated out on the field is communicated among the guys. This is as private as these guys get. They are exposed. Completely vulnerable. The press can literally come into the locker room and see if a guy's underwear is clean—or if he even wears underwear. It's very private, almost sacred, ground, and I think the media often fails utterly to appreciate that. There is a very fine line between the media doing its job and the media using a proctoscope to invade the privacy of the guys. I know people in the media who have a very fine sense of where that line is. I know others who don't even know there's a line."

The line. On one side are the reporters who want to stir the peace and get their stories. On the other side are the players and the coaches who want to protect the peace and win football games. What happens when the line is crossed?

"That's my shop," Harry Edwards says. "Bullshit."

"There is a linkage, an interdependence, between the sports institution and the institution of the media that is both necessary and symbiotic," Edwards says. "Sports help the media sell advertising. Sports help the media gain adherents and subscribers. Sports help the media keep their jobs. At the same time, the media help sports generate fans. The media help sports create and sustain tradition. The media are literally the scribes of the secular religion of sport.

"Within the context of that relationship, however, there is a tension, a contentiousness that is borne of the fact that both in the press and in sports organizations you zation are conflicting and actually contradictory. On one hand, the press is pushing to get as much of the "story" as possible in all its dimensions—institutional, organizational, tactical, human—within and beyond the boundaries of the sports endeavor itself. The media comes in and picks the bones down to the last morsel of flesh to get their story. And then, just about the time you think you're out of it, you get to the middle of the week and somebody comes in and cracks the bones for the marrow. With all of this going on, the sports organization has a tremendous interest in keeping the internal operations and conduct of the organization and the relationships in the organization as private as possible. No organization likes to have its backstage operations and relationships exposed to public scrutiny. All an organization wants is to take care of its business.

"When you add all of this to the human factor—the fact that both in the press and in sports organizations you are going to have your proportionate and representative share of assholes—contentiousness can actually turn into embattlement. This is where you begin to get boycotts of the media by certain players or entire teams. You begin to get certain members of the media dogging certain players or entire teams because of an injury felt or imagined. The alliance between the sports organization and the media is a necessary relationship. But it's not always, let's just say, appreciated. And I'm quite certain that the media feel the same way about the football players. The feeling of cooperation in an atmosphere of skepticism and distrust is mutual. There is a contentiousness there which is inevitable and unavoidable."

Stir the peace. Protect the peace. Reporters and editors. Football players and football coaches. The Niners. The press. Enemies. And partners. In a strained relationship that was formed in San Francisco way back in the magical year of 1981.

Three years after taking over the worst team in professional football, Bill Walsh won a Super Bowl with a club that had no running game, three rookie defensive backs in the starting lineup, and hardly any depth. To Bay Area reporters, who had been used to nearly a decade of losing, Walsh's achievement was a miracle. In print and on the air, it was a time to coronate the man responsible. The Genius was born.

Bill Walsh never liked the label. Years later, Walsh would say that being called a genius didn't make sense for someone who was as insecure as he was. In 1981, Walsh was still busy establishing himself. He did not consider himself a genius. Not at all. Three seasons in the NFL—the Super Bowl year his first winning one—had not instilled in him enough confidence to make up for the nearly 20 years of uncertainty he had spent wondering if he would ever get a chance to be a head coach.

But if Walsh was uncomfortable being called a genius, for the press the tag was perfect. Because to reporters Bill Walsh was something of a mystery, a wizard who kept himself cloaked in a robe with bright moons and stars. The reflection from Walsh's robe always seemed to send out too many splinters of light for the press to make sense of them all. When he answered their questions, reporters often asked themselves, *Okay, but what does he* really *mean by that?*

To members of the press, Walsh's behavior was often erratic. They could never predict how he would act or what he would say. He could be angry and austere one minute and then make dry jokes or kibitz about boxing the next. He could be modest and placating one minute and haughty and dictatorial the next. He could be enchantingly impertinent one moment and obstinate and manipulative the next. After a big win in, say, Atlanta, Walsh could be icy and emotional, as if the flea-bitten Falcons had blown his team away and sent Joe Montana to the hospital. After a loss, on the other hand, Walsh could be witty and completely accommodating. He would have a story for everyone. And so the press was confused. Just who was Bill Walsh?

Then the 49ers won the Super Bowl and someone came up with the Genius tag, and reporters' problems were solved. They no longer had to worry about what they were supposed to think about San Francisco's head coach. They now had a box into which they could dump everything. The Genius said it all. Except that Bill Walsh did not like being put in the box. Especially in 1982.

The season after their first Super Bowl, the Niners stumbled, missing the playoffs altogether in a season shortened by a players' strike. To the press, the Genius tag took on a whole new meaning. Instead of being a genuine term of recognition—even wonderment—that described the visionary who had performed magic right before their very eyes, the label of Genius was now a snide dig at the mad scientist who had lost his notes and couldn't remember how to put his fantastic football machine back together again. Reporters began to write stories wondering what had happened to the Genius and his magic formulas. They began to write stories that second-guessed his play calling and his penchant for tinkering with things that seemed to be working just fine. They began to write that his offense was outdated, that the rest of the league had caught up with his offensive wizardry. Perhaps most condescending were the caustic remarks Walsh began to hear from certain executives with other clubs around the NFL, who were using the term to embarrass the proud coach and highlight the sudden demise of the Genius's dream team.

To Walsh, the needling cut deep. He had spent nearly two decades working for his chance to be a head coach in the NFL. He had won a Super Bowl in just his third season. And then, his reputation—and his ability and even his character—was going to hell all in one wrenching season. Walsh began putting up barriers to protect himself from media mortar fire. "He's very difficult to penetrate," Lowell Cohn, a columnist for the *San Francisco Chronicle,* said in an interview in the early 1980s. "It's not just a matter of getting close but getting near. He always strikes me as a guy who is more self-protective than he needs to be."

In the years that followed, Bill Walsh would progress from being cautious to being annoyed with the press. After that, he was impatient and suspicious. Finally, he would retreat completely. It was the drug rumors that drove everything off the cliff.

During the 1982 season, as the Niners plummeted from their Super Bowl success of the year before, Joe Montana stopped using public restrooms because he knew that people were watching him and thinking, *He's in there snorting a line of coke or something.* So Joe sat with his legs crossed and hoped he could wait until he got home. In 1982, one season after everything the 49ers did went right, nothing they did went right. Rumors of drug use on the team began to circulate in San Francisco. Some of them made the newspaper, others just traveled through the grapevine. And, although the rumors about Joe Montana taking drugs were not true, the rumors about other 49ers taking drugs were.

"After our first Super Bowl year in 1981, I heard that several of our players had been using cocaine during the season," Bill Walsh wrote in his book, *Building a Champion*. "I later learned that one substitute, who did not play in the game, was snorting cocaine in the john at halftime of the Super Bowl." Drug use, Walsh added, "may have curtailed the careers of as many as eleven players on that team." In 1982, however, not much was written about such troubles. Then the team was able to keep such personal struggles out of the newspapers. But three years later, after another Super Bowl win and another fall from grace, the drug rumors returned, and Bill Walsh's attitude toward the media changed from annoyance to disgust and then to suspicion. Media relations would be strained, never to be mended.

In 1985, the Niners gasped out of the blocks much like they did in 1982. A year after winning 18 out of 19 games and blasting Miami in the Super Bowl, San Francisco was 5 and 5 at midseason and going nowhere. And the press, now expecting every season to be a Super Bowl miracle, wanted some answers. In 1984, San Francisco led the league in rushing. Where, reporters wondered, was the running game now? In 1984, Joe Montana threw a team record 31 touchdown passes and won his first NFL passing title.

What's wrong with Joe now? In 1984, in the aftermath of the demolition of the Dolphins, there was talk that San Francisco was professional football's newest dynasty. Now where were those Niners? Just another .500 team.

In 1985, following a 17–16 loss to the Broncos on "Monday Night Football," the Niners had lost three of their last five games. In the snow in Denver, Joe Montana had one of the worst games of his career, completing only 17 of 40 passes, and many of the incompletions weren't even close. A month earlier, Montana had played poorly in a 23–21 loss to the Lions in Detroit—a game he couldn't finish because he had a bad case of the flu—so now the press put two and two together and got six. If Joe Montana is playing lousy and he's ill, then he must be doing drugs. As the 1985 NFL season reached November, the press wanted some answers and was willing to look anywhere to get them.

The first rumors had Joe Montana being arrested for speeding in his red Ferrari in Rocklin: the same rumor that had made the rounds three years before. Another story had the Niner quarterback being stopped in Monterey for driving 100 miles an hour in the same car. In Monterey, the story went, police officers found cocaine stashed somewhere in Joe's car. Later in the season, a report from Atlanta had Montana drunk and carrying more drugs. In that version, Willie Brown, speaker of the assembly of the California legislature, called the mayor of Atlanta and got Joe out of jail.

One time, a reporter got a phone tip that Montana had been arrested at nine o'clock in the morning, four hours before a game at Candlestick against the New Orleans Saints. Other versions had Montana being arrested just four hours before a home game against the Chicago Bears. Still another rumor had Montana being arrested for drug possession in his hotel room the night before the Chicago game. Some rumors involved Montana's red Ferrari. Others had him being arrested in a limousine.

Another rumored event took place before San Francisco's loss in Detroit, where Walsh supposedly took Montana up to his hotel room right before the game. There a doctor revived the quarterback who presumably had passed out on drugs. Still another bit of gossip—one that got some play in the newspapers—had the doctor at a Bay Area hospital telling a nurse, "Get ready to have Joe Montana admitted. He'll be under my private, confidential care."

Reporters began to confront Montana, Walsh, and other members of the team with the rumors. One reporter questioned a neighbor of 49er linebacker Riki Ellison to see if he knew anything about the Joe Montana rumors. And in his autobiography, *Audibles*, Montana wrote that another reporter put Randy Cross, San Francisco's left guard, on the spot one day.

"Where was Joe between nine and nine-thirty the night before the Chicago game?" the reporter asked Cross.

"He was in a meeting," Cross replied.

"Yeah, but are you sure?"

"Hell, yes, I'm sure he was there, because I was there."

The rumors were flying east as well. There was, for instance, the story that ran in a gambling tip sheet in the Boston area; its headline read, "IS MONTANA ON COCAINE?" Montana said later that he knew things were getting out of hand when Paul Zimmerman, *Sports Illustrated*'s pro football writer, approached Frank Cooney of the *San Francisco Examiner* to see what Cooney knew about the rumors.

Finally, in late November 1985, Bill Walsh and Joe Montana decided that enough was enough. The coach, the quarterback, and the rest of the team had endured the rumors for weeks. Walsh, in fact, had been calling Montana's agent, Larry Muno, since the second or third week of the season to see if Muno had been hearing the same rumors he was hearing and if he knew whether any of them were true. Every time Walsh called, Muno said the same thing. The rumors about Joe Montana using drugs and being stopped in his red Ferrari were not true. Inside, Walsh knew the rumors weren't true. Joe had told him that he wasn't using drugs, and he believed him. But then Walsh would hear a rumor worse than the last one and he would start to wonder again.

Walsh was concerned for Montana. But the fact that his quarterback's life was in chaos wasn't the worst part of the whole thing. When it came right down to it, the worst part about the rumors was that, with the team stumbling on the field, it was quite possible that all the talk might be distracting his players from the job of playing football. To Walsh, the rumors were extremely annoying. That professional journalists would resort to such snooping and gossip was unfair, unfortunate, and unnecessary. And when Walsh realized that the press might be affecting what was happening on the football field, that was totally unacceptable. Whether it was just the rumors or a combination of the rumors and the reporters, anything that interfered with the 49ers' football had to be dealt with. There was no other choice. On Friday afternoon before the Broncos game in early November, Walsh called Larry Muno and told him that things were getting out of hand, and that perhaps the best way to calm the storm would be for him to issue a public denial of the rumors that linked Montana to drugs. It was time to use the users.

The next Tuesday, at his weekly press conference the morning after the Niners' loss in Denver, Bill Walsh cleared the air with the team's first public comments on the rumors involving drugs and Joe Montana.

"These are absurd, ridiculous, factless strings of gossip about a player, and it has affected Joe," Walsh told reporters. "But nothing has happened, and I know it's going to wreck some of the people who have been so joyously going to others with these kind of absurd stories. None of them has any basis at all. . . . I think it has been a very unfair thing. The team has not done well, Joe has not had a great season, and people are looking for explanations. And the juiciest would be that the great player is now at the mercy of a drug substance. . . . At some point we have to go public because some of these stories are compounding each other to the point where people almost assume they're fact.

"We have had at least five stories . . . of him being stopped in his red Ferrari with cocaine in the car . . . all the way from the East Coast to the West Coast. . . . I bought him off in one. Eddie bought him off in the other. Top politicians have saved him. . . . We've had stories of Joe being admitted to hospitals. We've had stories of him in back of a famous restaurant using drugs. I can categorically say that none of these instances ever occurred. Joe Montana has never ever been pulled over on the highway. Drugs have never been found on Joe Montana. He has not used drugs in public. . . . He categorically denies the use of drugs. He has in the past, whenever asked to, taken a drug urine sample for us, never showing any drugs. And so all the stories—and I hate to disappoint people—are absurd."

The next day, Joe Montana's supposed affair with drugs made front-page news in almost every paper in Northern California. The *Chronicle* headine read: "WALSH ATTACKS RUMORS LINKING MONTANA TO DRUGS." The other big news story of the day was about Rock Hudson's lover, who was suing Hudson's estate because Rock had lied to him about having AIDS. On the swag board in Redwood City—where players lampoon one another—one of Montana's teammates cut out the story and put Joe's picture in place of the guy who had lived with Rock Hudson. Even Joe laughed when he saw it.

Later that day, Montana held his own press conference. He talked about the rumors. About how ridiculous it was that he supposedly had been stopped in his Ferrari because the Ferrari had been in the garage of his house in Los Angeles since the previous year. About how, when he was rumored to have been drunk and rescued from jail by Willie Brown in Atlanta, all he did was take a cab out for dinner with some of his linemen. About how the only time he left his hotel room in Detroit was to eat dinner in the hotel restaurant. Alone. About how difficult the two months of rumors had made life for him and his family. Then he talked about the lasting damage the whole mess had done to him.

"It's like when the girl screams rape and they prove

the guy innocent and no matter what happens that doubt is still left."

In San Francisco, the reaction to Montana's outpouring was incredible: The rumors increased.

In the relationship between the 49ers and the media, the roles of hero and villain had now been cast. To the 49ers, reporters could no longer be trusted to go about their jobs with respect for the lives and feelings of the people they covered. The team did not expect the media to care about how their coverage affected the team. That was not the job of the press. But there was something personal in the attacks on Joe Montana that to Bill Walsh, the man in charge of the daily operations of the team, crossed the line between journalism and maliciousness. To Walsh, poking and probing into someone's personal life as the press had done with Joe Montana was completely unnecessary. But even more inexcusable was that reporters had affected how his 49ers played on the football field. That was an offense for which there was no excuse. But one for which there was one remedy. Distance.

In Redwood City, before the Taj, the Niners trained at a facility that resembled a college dormitory—two floors, with rows of rooms on each side connected by a central hallway. There were no press facilities, but reporters loved the cramped old building anyway, because players and coaches had to walk through the hallway to get almost anywhere else. All reporters had to do was loiter in the hallway and, sooner or later, they could get just about anybody they needed to. Coaches. Players. Even Joe Montana. They could walk down the hall into the locker room and talk to anybody there. Even Lindsy McLean, the trainer, would stop and chat. Reporters would often interview players outside on the steps. Across the street was a senior citizens' center. Sometimes, reporters and players would hold their interviews to the sound of singing.

Then in August 1988, the Niners moved into the Taj

in Santa Clara. The team's new $8 million facility mir-rored Bill Walsh's deteriorating opinion of the press. Al-most as soon as the team moved in, the inmates at Stalag 49 began to groan about their new prison.

Lowell Cohn of the *Chronicle* outlined his thoughts in a column headlined "PRESS HELD CAPTIVE INSIDE FORT WALSH."

"The strange configuration of the fort," Cohn wrote, "leads you to believe that 49er management is paranoid about the press and wants to control the flow of informa-tion. Reporters are assigned to a room that faces away from the field.

"The press room is as far from the field as you can get without leaving the premises. Then there is the issue of the key card the team issues each writer. When you stick it into the press room door, your name lights up on a cen-tral computer. . . . George Orwell would have loved it."

Cohn also satirized the security at "Fort Walsh." Guards sat at a security desk with television monitors be-tween the press room and the door that leads to the locker room and the stairs that lead to the management and administrative offices. At the end of his column, Cohn recounted a conversation between "an executive for another team," who "recently asked a Bay Area re-porter what gives with the press room at the 49er facility? Never having been there, the reporter said he didn't know. The executive smiled. He said Bill Walsh was tell-ing people around the league how he'd stuck the press in Siberia."

Distance. It was about the only way the 49ers were ever going to escape the prisoners from Stalag 49. There were just too many of them now.

The National Football League's 1990 telephone direc-tory—known to most reporters as the Black Book—lists members of the print media who regularly cover the San Francisco 49ers. The *San Francisco Chronicle,* for instance, has one beat reporter, two feature writers, and four columnists. The *San Francisco Examiner* has a beat reporter, an NFL writer, two reporters, two columnists, and two radio and television reporters. At the *Mercury News* in San Jose, the reporting staff includes a sports editor/columnist, a beat reporter, a feature writer, and two columnists. The *Bee* in Sacramento has a beat reporter, two columnists, and a feature writer.

The Black Book roster also lists beat reporters for the *Oakland Tribune, Sacramento Union, Peninsula Times Tribune, San Mateo Times, Hayward Review, Contra Costa Times, Marin Independent Journal,* and *Santa Rosa Press Democrat.* In addition, journalists also represent such news organizations as *49ers Report,* Skinner Syndicated News Service, the *S.E. Sun Reporter, Santa Cruz Sentinel, Associated Press,* and *United Press International.* In all, the Black Book lists 22 print journalists who cover the 49ers on a regular basis, more than cover any other team in the National Football League, whether they be the New York Giants, the Chicago Bears, or the Los Angeles Raiders. And more reporters than the Washington Redskins, Denver Broncos, and Atlanta Falcons *combined.*

It hasn't always been this way.

In Bill Walsh's early years with the 49ers, there was no media horde to deal with or even worry about. In fact, sometimes before his weekly press conference, the public-relations staff made it a point to call reporters so they could be sure Walsh would have someone to talk to. But the Super Bowls changed everything. As San Francisco won the big prize once, and then twice, in the early 1980s, an ever-thickening torrent of media recorded every move the storybook team made. *Sports Illustrated, Inside Sports,* ESPN and NFL Films began to show up on a regular basis. So did CBS and the other television and radio networks. Locally, a smattering of smaller papers between Santa Cruz on California's central coast and Sacramento, the California capital, began to offer or to expand their daily coverage of the team.

To the newspapers of the Bay Area—especially the smaller ones—the 49ers were an important drawing card. The Niners once were a bad joke that nobody wanted to hear about, but that was no longer the case. The 49ers were now a sports dynasty and everybody wanted to read about the people who were doing things of which they could only dream. And so the reporters came. Day after day. Week after week. Season after season. The procession never stopped. To the players, the threat of what had happened to Joe Montana was always there. Always. So they kept their distance.

One day early in the 1990 season, a reporter who began covering the 49ers several years ago when Bill Walsh was head coach explained the difference between the way covering the 49ers used to be and how it is now.

The reporter used the analogy of a small town that mushrooms into a big city. He described how it's natural for people to long for the days when anyone could ride a bicycle to the store and get ice cream for a quarter. But they can't do that anymore: Now ice cream is a dollar and there's too much traffic on the way to the store to ride a bike. And there are more people in line to buy ice cream. The storekeeper is an honest man. But not everyone is as honest as they used to be. The city is full of criminals now. And because the storekeeper never knows when someone will try to rob him, he keeps a close eye on those who come into his store. He also keeps a gun under the counter. It's the only way he can protect what's his. The only way he can keep his distance from those who can hurt him.

Dr. Harry Edwards has his own analogy about the change that came over the 49ers after the Super Bowls brought the media. "It's like the old saying, 'Once bitten by a snake, you come to be frightened of ropes.' Even if it's a rope somebody throws to pull you up a little bit, you're gonna look before you pick it up. Nothing is exactly what it seems. And anybody who's not suspicious of other people's motives has either got to be a mind reader or a fool."

A few days after the scene between Jesse Sapolu and the two reporters in the locker room at the Taj, Guy McIntyre, San Francisco's Pro Bowl guard, talked about how he and his teammates feel about sharing themselves with the media. "One of the problems some of the guys have is that they just don't have any control when it comes to reporters," McIntyre said as he dressed for practice. "The reporter always has his own agenda. The reporter asks all the questions. And then, once you've answered all the questions, he's going to write what he wants to anyway. Some of the guys have been burned by the media. So they just feel, 'Why should I bother talking at all?' "

Before McIntyre went out to practice, he offered another important reason for the strained relationship between the 49ers and the media. It involved the place reporters conduct most of their interviews. A place that Guy McIntyre said the Niners consider as private as their bedrooms.

Chapter 7

Bedroom Eyes

More than a few players have said that if they had their choice, reporters wouldn't be allowed in the locker room. Period. "It's like having somebody you didn't invite come walking right into your house, into your bedroom," Jamie Williams said one day. "Wouldn't you at least like the chance to tell the guy, 'I don't want you coming over?'"

Of course.

But it's a good thing the players don't make the decision on whether reporters are allowed in the locker room. Because the locker room is where it's possible to see and hear things that could never be repeated, much less duplicated, in mass interview sessions. The locker room is where the spontaneity, the jokes, the anger, the frustration, the friendships, the respect, the animosities, and the crudeness of professional football takes place. All of that would be lost if writers weren't there to see, hear, and ask questions.

By being so close, it's the little things that become obvious. Blood on an elbow. A bag of ice wrapped to a knee or a shoulder. The welts on an arm that were pink in September but by Thanksgiving have become a greenish purple. The look in Joe Montana's eyes as he runs, still in his cleats and helmet, through the locker room to avoid reporters. The puckish grin on Montana's face, and the little squeal—"*Ooooooooooooo*"—that slips from his mouth, as he runs knock-kneed like a six-year-old toward the bathroom.

Those are the scenes that bring the people who play the game to life. Those are the scenes that no photograph or any number of words in an interview could ever record. Scenes like the one that unfolded the day Jim Burt planted a heat bomb—a glob of Ben-Gay—in Kevin Fagan's underwear.

Actually, it had all started the week before on United charter flight 5073 to Houston. At 40,000 feet, Kevin Fagan's watch had disappeared. Jim Burt was at the bottom of the whole thing. Today, the games continued on the practice field at the Taj.

While the defensive linemen were waiting around to join a drill, Burt and Fagan were spitting at each other like two boxers waiting for an opening. Burt would cock his head left, then right, waiting for just the right moment. Then he would let fly and get Fagan. Fagan would wipe off the spit, cock his head left, then right, waiting for just the right moment. Then he would launch and hit Burt. Burt would lie down on the grass and wipe off, and the whole thing would start again. Burt got Fagan about as often as Fagan got Burt. They were even. Until they got to the locker room.

At the lockers used by the defensive linemen, Kevin Fagan has put on a clean pair of shorts, but he is still pissed off. Jim Burt has gone too far. Again. As Fagan pulls on his jeans, Burt walks out of the trainers' room and turns in front of Fred Smerlas's locker. Smerlas, who signed with the Niners in the off-season after playing 11 years in Buffalo, is sitting nonchalantly on the bench in front of his locker clipping his fingernails. Smerlas looks up as Burt walks by.

"Fags is upset with us," he says.

"He iiis?" Burt says, mocking Fagan.

"No," Smerlas says, looking right into Burt's eyes, "he's *really* upset."

"Whaddya tawkin' abowt," Burt fires out in his New

York squall, stalking three lockers over and getting right in Fagan's face.

"Is Fags upset?" Burt tries to pat Fagan's shoulder.

"Don't fuck with my underwear," Fagan grunts brusquely, pushing Burt's hand away.

"Stop," Burt answers, realizing that Fags is indeed truly upset. "Stop whining. Stop fucking whining. You're whining. You're a whiner."

Fagan starts to explain, but Burt tunes him out.

"I'm gonna do it to your underwear tomorrow, too," Burt announces, standing within an arm's length of Fagan. "Whaddya gonna do about that?"

"I'm gonna punch you in the mouth."

"Okay. Then what?"

"I'm just tellin' all you guys, anyone who fucks with my underwear again, they're gonna get punched in the mouth."

"WHHOOAAAAAA!" Burt hollers, throwing his hands up, bugging out his eyes, and recoiling in mock fear. "I won't sleep tonight, Fags. WHHOOOAAAAA! Tiptoe around Fags."

Then Burt, who at a stocky six-foot-one and 270 pounds reminds some of his teammates of the Oompa Loompas, the short and squat little helpers at Willy Wonka's famous candy plant in *Charlie and the Chocolate Factory*, starts prancing up on his tiptoes in a circle in front of Kevin Fagan.

"Fags," Burt says when he's finished tiptoeing around, "you're a fucking pussy. You know that?"

"Tell him why you're upset, Fags," says Fred Smerlas, now clipping his toenails.

Fagan glares at Burt like he's an older brother who was supposed to keep his mouth shut in front of mom but now dad has found out what he did and, boy, is he angry.

"First," Fagan says to Burt, "you were spitting on me on the field in front of the coaches. Then, we're standing in here, and you throw this huge glob of shampoo all over me. *Right in front of the coaches.* Jesus, man, Seifert was standing right there, watching us fuck around like idiots. You always go too far. Too fucking far. It's your trademark."

"Whaddya mean, I go too far?!" Burt shrieks, looking around at Smerlas, Pierce Holt, and then finally back at Fagan.

Fagan repeats his punch in the mouth threat, which elicits a sarcastic chorus of "WHOOOAAAAA!" from Burt and Holt.

It's now time for the Oompa Loompa to leave. And Jim Burt knows only one way to end a practical joke. With the last word. Burt clears his throat, and announces to an almost empty locker room, "FAGS SAYS DON'T FUCK WITH HIS UNDERWEAR."

Before Burt finishes, Kevin Fagan is stomping off toward the showers to brush his teeth. As he disappears from view, Fagan mutters a name at Jim Burt, under his breath.

"Sawed-off bastard," he says.

At other times, the scenes in the Niner locker room are more bizarre.

One Friday afternoon before he hurt his knee and went on injured reserve, Eric Wright is getting ready to take a shower after practice. As he grabs a towel and his toothbrush, he realizes he doesn't have any toothpaste. So Wright walks around to different lockers—Ronnie Lott's, Keena Turner's, Roger Craig's—looking for toothpaste. When Wright's back is turned, in front of Roger Craig's locker, Keena Turner slinks out from the showers and slings a rolled-up ball of tape at his teammate. Turner and Wright have been teammates on all four of San Francisco's Super Bowl teams. But clearly that means nothing now, when the other guy has hit you—*SSSSSNAPPPP!!!*—on the butt with a tape ball.

"Bitch!" Wright hisses, wiping the sting away and

turning around to see who has gotten him. It isn't hard to figure out. Keena Turner is standing in front of his locker, zipping up his jeans, grinning guiltily. Wright, wearing only the silver chain around his neck and the toothbrush in his mouth, prances over to the nearest ball of tape. There are dozens of the golf ball–sized weapons lying on the floor. Wright picks one up and then leers at Turner, who frantically finds a towel and holds it out in front of him like a shield.

The wheels are turning in Eric Wright's head. It's Friday. Practice is over. A week's energy is all built up for one last night of fun before they hole up at the Marriott tomorrow night for Sunday's game—the weekly war—at Candlestick. Wright loses it. He whips the tape ball at Turner. As soon as he does, someone else fires another shot at Wright.

"Bitch!" he hisses again.

For the next several minutes, the whole locker room goes wild, balls of tape whipping in every direction. Rodney Knox, Dave Rahn, and Al Barba from the 49er public-relations staff are in on it. So is Vance Bigham, a security guard at the Taj. And so is Mike Silver, a reporter for the *Santa Rosa Press Democrat.* They are all piping tape balls at Eric Wright. Some hit, some miss. No one is safe. But Eric Wright doesn't care. He's out in the center of the locker room. Like a robot, his motion is the same every time. He takes two steps to his left, bends down like a shortstop, announces his "Scoop!" in a clipped yell, and zings a ball of tape across the room. After a series of throws, someone shouts:

"NAKED AND VICIOUS! NAKED AND VI-CIOUS!"

For the rest of the season—even after he wrenches his knee in November against the Rams, ending a once-brilliant career of nearly eight years—that's the memory of Eric Wright that stands out.

Naked and vicious.

On two other occasions, the goings on in the locker room at the Taj are more serious. One involves friendship and an obnoxious reporter. The other involves a football player and a woman reporter. Both involve Charles Haley.

Ira Miller is in midsentence with Jamie Williams when the clot of people moves in. Miller has been covering the 49ers and the NFL for the *San Francisco Chronicle* since the 1970s. He has a reputation among both players and reporters for being opinionated, overbearing, and pushy. Last night, Miller went on his weekly radio call-in spot and called Charles Haley a jerk. And to one of Charles Haley's teammates, Ira Miller has crossed the line between a reporter writing or saying something critical about a player or the team—which is one thing—and attacking a player's character, his personal life—which is completely unacceptable. Charles Haley's teammate is Ronnie Lott.

Lott is one of the few 49ers who will stand and argue with a reporter over a question he doesn't like. On this afternoon, Ronnie Lott intends to argue with Ira Miller. As Lott walks toward Miller, a handful of players and reporters follow. In the NFL, a confrontation always draws a crowd. As Lott approaches, Miller turns around. Lott speaks first.

"You shouldn't have called Charles a jerk on the radio," he says, accusingly. "Why'd you have to go and call him a jerk?"

"Maybe I should have used another word," Miller answers. "But whatever you call him, he still acts like a jerk."

Lott is glaring back at Miller. He's angry, but he's also confused. He can't quite fathom how somebody could call someone he hasn't even taken the time to understand a jerk on the radio and have no sense of why that is wrong.

"Man," Lott says, still glaring at Miller, "you have no

idea how that feels to a guy. How would you like it if somebody called you a jerk on the radio?"

"That's one of the nicer things people call me," Miller says.

By this time, Charles Haley has drifted close to the argument. With Lott standing in between Haley and Miller, Haley breaks in on his own behalf.

"That's why I don't talk to you guys," Haley tells Miller. "Because no matter what I say, it's going to be misrepresented. Besides, man, I apologized to her."

Her?

If Ira Miller has crossed the line and said something that is uncalled for, it isn't the first time it has happened this season.

Ann Killion could tell anyone that.

It begins innocently enough. Wearing only a white towel around his waist, Charles Haley walks in a circle at one end of the locker room. He's holding a red-and-white football. Every week, the balls—nine of them—sit in a holder on a table outside the equipment room. When every member of the team has signed his name, the balls are packed in plastic bags and sent to friends and families of players and coaches, radio and TV advertisers, and a host of charities. This afternoon, Charles Haley is trying to get his teammates to sign the footballs.

"SIGN MY BALLS!" Haley bellows, holding the red-and-white football. "C'MON, BOYS. SIGN MY BALLS!"

Haley is walking toward the table at the front of the equipment room when he whirls around suddenly.

At times, even some of Charles Haley's teammates wish their 6-foot-5, 230-pound teammate from tiny James Madison University in Virginia would just shut up and leave them alone. In the locker room and on the field, Charles Haley can be so obnoxious that he's irritating. But he also can be so outgoing and outrageous that he makes everyone around him laugh and forget all the tension. Charles Haley can be a moody, contentious bully who rides teammates so hard with his jokes that sometimes they won't get on the same bus with him. Charles Haley also can be so thoughtful and caring it's as if he's a different person. He can be generous enough to donate thousands of dollars to help schools in poor Bay Area communities buy books and computers for their kids. Charles Haley also can be thoughtless enough to chuck a football straight at a teammate who is timidly stretching an injured leg and then stand there grinning without the slightest idea in the world why everyone is glaring at him.

Charles Haley's teammates say they respect him because he doesn't try to imitate other people. He acts like Charles. In the locker room that day at the Taj, walking around in his towel, holding the red-and-white football, and hollering for the boys to sign his balls, that was precisely the problem. That has always been precisely the problem.

Charles Haley grew up in Gladys, a tiny, backwoods Virginia town with almost as many chickens and cows as people. Growing up, Charles Haley always told his mother that he was going to play football and be on TV when he was older. When Charles said that, Virginia Haley told her son to hush up, because she knew he was way too young to be talking foolish like that. But inside, Virginia Haley hoped her son was right. Because she knew what lay ahead if he didn't make it in football. He would work in a factory like his parents. Or he would join the Marines like his older brother. And if he did neither of those two things, he would end up coaching at Campbell High School. That wasn't the kind of future Virginia Haley wanted for her boy. She wanted something better.

By the time Charles was in high school, it looked like Virginia Haley was going to be right. If Charles showed up for football practice, he didn't exactly play very hard.

Most of the time, in fact, he stood around and goofed off. When the coach benched him, Charles told his mother he wanted to quit. She told him that if he was thinking of quitting football, he shouldn't even bother coming home. Virginia Haley was no football expert, but she knew her boy could play. If only he would straighten up.

After practice one day, Virginia Haley forced her son's hand. She talked to the coach. She told the coach that Charles was good enough to play, and that she was sure he was going to straighten up and fly right soon. A week later, Charles was back in the starting lineup. Later, when he was a 49er, Charles Haley would say the reason for his turnaround was that he had to change his attitude and straighten up after what his mother had told the coach. He didn't want to let her down. As a senior, Charles Haley was Campbell County's defensive player of the year. Charles was right. He was going to play football and be on TV. But Virginia Haley was right, too. Charles had straightened up. It would be some time yet, however, before he would grow up.

To Harry Edwards, the differences between the two Charles Haleys are easy to explain. "Everybody in the locker room knows that Charles Haley has some problems," Edwards explained one day. "But everyone in the locker room also knows that Charles Haley is not a jerk. Anyone who says that Charles is a jerk has not taken the time to understand him. And it takes pains to understand Charles. He is probably the most sensitive guy on the team, in addition to being very bright. And because he is so sensitive, he has these defenses he uses to keep people away until he has time to figure out how he's going to handle the relationship. He is very quick to try to get the upper hand in interpersonal relationships because he is so sensitive. Rather than let somebody come in and get the upper hand on him, he tries to get the upper hand on them.

"Charles messes with everybody in the locker room," Edwards says. "And everybody knows that. It's constant, because that's just Charles. He'll find somebody's Achilles' heel and he'll go after it. At some point, almost every guy in the locker room has gotten into it with Charles. Jim Burt got into it with Charles. Matt Millen got into it with Charles. Dave Waymer got into it with him. H[arris] B[arton] got into it with him. I've had to get up in Charles's face a couple of times to let him know, 'Hey, Charlie, you're out of line on this one and it's time to rein it back in.' Half of the media has had some kind of words with Charles. The fact that this lady comes in there and has difficulty with Charles and then takes it to heart, that's another twist to the situation."

Ann Killion is a reporter for the *San Jose Mercury News*. Before this afternoon in the locker room at the Taj, Killion has been full-time on the 49ers beat for about two months. Killion covered the 49ers a little last year, but it was mainly backup, a feature here, a sidebar there. A petite woman with brown hair and a big laugh, Killion has been a reporter at the *Mercury News* for two years. She has a Master's degree in journalism from Columbia University. She has a double major—history and communications—from UCLA. She is bright and committed to her work. She asks tough questions and is not intimidated easily. But none of these things were going to help when Charles Haley messed with her in the locker room at the Taj.

As Charles Haley stops his whirl, he looks down and starts messing with Ann Killion.
"DO YOU LOOK?" Haley bellows, grinning down at the reporter. "C'MON, YOU CAN TELL ME. DO YOU LOOK?"
Killion knows what is happening. She's had friends

who have had things like this happen to them. Last year, Haley did something like this to Pat Sullivan, a male reporter for the *Chronicle*. Ann Killion knows exactly what Charles Haley is doing.

He is calling her a "dick watcher."

And she is trapped. But Charles Haley is only warming up. Standing in front of Ann Killion, Haley pulls his white towel away from his waist. Ann Killion tries to look everywhere but where the towel used to be.

Over the next few minutes, Killion tried to get away from Charles Haley as fast as she could, moving around the locker room, trying to get other interviews. It wasn't easy. According to Mike Silver of the *Santa Rosa Press Democrat,* Haley dogged her, saying things such as, "Watch out, it's gonna hit you in the head."

Haley's teammates were laughing—not so much laughs of ridicule, cruelty, or chauvinism, but laughs of discomfort, the sort of laugh people have when they're not quite sure what to do or say. So they laugh a little and do and say nothing. Not one of Charles Haley's teammates stepped in to tell him he was out of line. Not one of his teammates stepped in to tell him that his joke wasn't funny this time. Not one of them interrupted him to say, "Hey, Charlie, lay off, man." Not one of Charles Haley's teammates stepped in and said anything like that. But neither did any of the reporters who were there.

Back in the press room a few minutes later, Ann Killion tried to collect herself. She sat down at her laptop and started to type. But her mind and her feelings were somewhere else. She was trying to understand how in the world Charles Haley could think she was trying to get her jollies by looking at him in a locker room when she was trying to work. That's why she had gone into the locker room at the Taj. To work. To interview football players and then write a story. She had gone into the locker room with the same attitude she always had. Do a job and get out. But there was no way she could do that after Charles Haley called her a dick watcher. No way.

Later, when the whole thing had calmed down, Ann Killion would be able to go back into the locker room at the Taj and think about doing her job. But as she sat at her cubicle in the press room after Charles Haley called her a dick watcher, all she knew was that she didn't feel like writing. She just wanted to cry. A few minutes later, on the phone to her editor or her husband or a friend, she did. Then she hung up and sniffled quietly for a minute or two. Then she started to write. Just like Lisa Olson did.

Less than three weeks later, in another NFL team's locker room, this one 3,000 miles east of the Taj, another woman reporter is trying to do her job. It's September 17, a Monday. Yesterday, the New England Patriots beat the Colts 16–14 at the Hoosier Dome in Indianapolis. In the NFL, the Monday after a game is generally the slowest and least organized day of the week. All that really happens—at least as far as the players are concerned—is a film review of the previous day's game and a light workout consisting of some stretching and running to prevent stiff muscles. This afternoon, Lisa Olson, a reporter for the *Boston Herald,* has come to Foxboro Stadium to interview Patriots cornerback Maurice Hurst, who picked off two passes in New England's win over the Colts.

According to a report later prepared for the NFL by Harvard law professor Philip Heymann, Olson was sitting on a bench near the entrance to the showers interviewing Maurice Hurst when Zeke Mowatt, a tight end on injured reserve, walked naked across the locker room toward her. Olson looked up and saw Mowatt "with what she interpreted as a purposeful look in his eyes." Afraid of a confrontation, Olson turned away from him and faced Hurst more directly. A few seconds later, Olson felt someone standing "at arm's length from her at her side." "Here's what you want," Mowatt said. "Do you want to take a bite out of this?"

According to the Heymann report, Mowatt's comments brought laughs and shouts from all around the Patriot locker room. Olson would say later that she tried not to look at any of the faces standing around her. But she heard their voices.

"Make her look," one Patriot shouted. "Make her look."

"Is she looking?"

At this point, Olson looked up and saw Mowatt on a scale near the entrance to the showers.

"You're not writing, you're looking," Mowatt said. Then, according to the Heymann report, Mowatt "smiled and purposely displayed himself to her in a suggestive way."

More laughter and shouts erupted from the locker room.

"Is she looking?"

"Is she looking at it?"

After this, a parade of naked Patriots walked past Lisa Olson on their way to the showers. Two or three players paused and "modeled" themselves in front of the reporter. The parade brought more laughing and more shouting.

"Did she look? Did she look?"

"Get her to look. That's what she wants."

"Is she looking?"

One of the players, later identified as running back Robert Perryman, stood where Olson could not see him and, according to one player, "adjusted" his genitals. According to another player, Perryman also shook his hips at her "in an exaggerated fashion."

Finally, Lisa Olson realized her interview with Maurice Hurst was hopeless, and she "abruptly ended her meeting" with the Patriot cornerback. According to the Heymann report, when Olson was gone from the locker room, Robert Perryman had the last word. "If the kitchen is too hot, get out."

For Lisa Olson, the kitchen was indeed hot. But for her and others, it was only warming up.

A week later, Olson was back in the Patriots' locker room conducting postgame interviews after New England's 41–7 loss to the Bengals in Cincinnati when she saw Victor Kiam, the owner of the Patriots, looking at her.

"Do you want to watch me or follow me around?" she asked Kiam, according to press accounts of the incident. As Olson walked away, according to the accounts, Kiam turned to several people standing near him.

"What a classic bitch," he said.

When word of what Kiam called Lisa Olson is reported in the days that follow, all hell breaks loose. The National Organization for Women calls for a U.S. boycott of Lady Remingtons, the women's electric shaver that Kiam's company produces. Kiam himself spends $100,000 on ads in the *Boston Globe, Boston Herald,* and *New York Times* to claim that he never called Lisa Olson a bitch. Originally, Olson asks her editor at the *Herald* to handle the whole thing quietly. Her editor calls the Patriots and asks for an apology. While the *Herald* is waiting for an apology, the *Boston Globe* runs the first story on the incident. The *Herald* interprets the story as a snipe at its professionalism, and shoots back with an editorial. Soon, columnists for the *Globe* and *Herald* are warring, and the quiet apology Lisa Olson hoped for has now become quite impossible.

For weeks, Lisa Olson sits in the eye of a storm. She is a lightning rod for all of the American questions about reporters in the locker room. In 1978, federal courts upheld the rights of women journalists to have the same access to locker rooms as male journalists, but now people aren't so sure that it's such a good idea. Everything, it seems, is open for discussion again. Should women reporters be allowed in locker rooms where men are naked? Should male reporters be allowed in locker rooms where women are naked? Should reporters of any sex be allowed in any locker room where anyone is naked? Should athletes wear bathrobes or towels? Should curtains or partitions be put up to give players some measure of privacy? Or should the NFL require writers to slip out of their clothes so everybody would be even? For much of October and November, the topics of Lisa Olson, Zeke Mowatt, Victor Kiam, and reporters in the locker room consume the NFL season. It's all anyone wants to talk about.

Lisa Olson appears on *Nightline*, *CBS This Morning*, *Donahue*, and *Oprah*. She meets with NFL commissioner Paul Tagliabue and Victor Kiam. She suffers the vulgar taunts of Patriot fans who think the whole thing is her fault for being somewhere she had no business being in the first place. She has beer dumped on her at a Boston Celtics exhibition game. Anonymous callers threaten her life and send her copies of *Playgirl*. She tries to resume her job covering the Patriots, receives death threats, and takes a vacation in the Caribbean. She is on the beach one day when someone recognizes her. Finally, Olson leaves the Patriots beat and is assigned to cover the Celtics and the Boston Bruins hockey team.

On November 28, the day special counsel Philip Heymann's 60-page report is made public by the National Football League, Lisa Olson goes out to buy a newspaper in Boston. According to Mike Lupica in *The National*, some kids start yelling her name on the street. When Olson comes home, there is "another obscene message from someone named Frank, promising to come over with a screwdriver."

But, she tells Lupica, "At least the Bruins' locker room was uneventful. It turns out that the part of my day that is the most normal is the one that involves work. Funny, isn't it?"

America does not know about Ann Killion the way it knows about Lisa Olson. This is because Ann Killion asked for and got an apology. It was all done quietly. Then, aside from some awkwardness in the days and weeks that followed, Killion went back to work covering the 49ers for the *San Jose Mercury News*. A few weeks later, in fact, she even wrote a lengthy profile of Charles Haley. In the story, Haley told Killion why he is difficult and moody, why his jokes with reporters often carry a mean edge.

"When you're not nice to people, they don't want to have anything to do with you," Haley said. "So I figure that's one less person I have to deal with. I don't like being paraded around, because then you don't have a private life. I enjoy my private life. That's what's fun about being a person."

Like Ann Killion, Charles Haley went back to work. Back to being sensitive, loud, and moody in the locker room with his teammates. Back to being so contentious he sometimes irritated them. Back to being so outrageous he made them all laugh and forget just for a while about the pressure of being professional football players. And he went back to being one of the most dominating defensive players in the league.

As the NFL season reached late October, the feeling among some reporters around the country was that Ann Killion had let Charles Haley—and by extension the 49ers—off the hook. "Had she chosen to make an issue of the incident," columnist C. W. Nevius wrote in the *Chronicle,* "the 49ers might be fielding calls from *Nightline* right now."

A sideshow had been sidestepped, and it was time to get back to football. To see what a rookie could do.

Chapter 8

Rook

*I*t's a hot and cloudless Wednesday evening late in July. Dexter Carter is standing outside the cafeteria at Sierra College talking to half a dozen reporters, his words draining out in a thick Georgia drawl. Two of his favorites are "shoot" and "dang." He wears green Bermuda shorts and a green, short-sleeved designer shirt. A pendant of a Seminole Indian—the mascot at Florida State University, where Carter went to college—hangs from his neck. In his right hand, Carter cradles a red playbook with "DEXTER CARTER 1990 SEASON" taped to the front.

Earlier this morning, Carter signed his first contract as a professional football player. As their number-one pick in the 1990 NFL draft, the San Francisco 49ers have agreed to pay Carter more than $2 million over the next four years. For signing and reporting to training camp on time, the 49ers tacked on about $800,000 more.

Outside the cafeteria after the first dinner of training camp, Carter covers a host of topics with the newspaper reporters who stand in a semicircle around him. He talks about how two typographical errors delayed his contract signing. He talks about his June surgery to remove a cyst from his right knee. He talks about how he can't wait to get out on the football field and make some of his awesome cuts. He talks about how he doesn't think his new-found wealth will make him a different person. He talks about how the 49ers are going to win whether they have Dexter Carter or not, and that his job is to fit in and help

119

where he can. Then, just before he scoots off to his first meeting as a 49er, Dexter Carter talks about Superman.

"How fast are you?" Frank Cooney, a reporter for the *San Francisco Examiner,* asks Carter.

"You'll learn," Dexter answers. "If you see me out there tomorrow and you think I'm Superman, it only gets better."

The next day, when he sees the quote in the *Examiner,* Carter is furious. "He misquoted me," he says of Cooney, one of several reporters who ran the quote in the stories they filed from Rocklin on the opening day of training camp. "If it happens again, I won't talk to him—or anybody else who does that. He asked me if I'd had any problems with my knee, and I said, 'If you wanna come out and watch me run, you'll see that my knee is okay, that the surgery was no big deal.' I never mentioned the name Superman. It came up, but I didn't say I was Superman."

As Carter walks from the cafeteria back to the dorms on the other side of the Sierra College campus, he explains that what he meant to say to Cooney and the other reporters was that he gets stronger the more practice time he gets and the longer the season goes on.

Whoever was right—the reporters or the football player—it didn't really matter. It was one of those silly little things that happens early in training camp and is forgotten long before the season starts. Even the ribbing Dexter takes from a few of his teammates over his Superman comment lasts only a day or two. It was just as if Dexter said *No big deal.* But Carter's threat to stop talking to the media *did* portend things to come. Because, as far as Dexter Carter and the media were concerned, things were going to get a lot worse before they got better.

The morning his Superman quote comes out in the papers, Dexter Carter's first practice as a 49er is far from stellar. He drops a couple of passes, breaks off another pass route too soon, and has his helmet ripped off of his head by free-agent linebacker Sam Kennedy. But the Superman stuff and his mistakes on the field aren't the only reason Dexter Carter's first day as a 49er is memorable. On a running play in the afternoon practice, he gets his first nickname.

Dexter takes the handoff and slides off tackle. Then, instead of cutting up inside the blocks of the linemen, he bobs and jukes around in the backfield. By the time Carter spurts, half-speed, through the line, safety Dave Waymer is up in his face. When Waymer lowers his head and coils his arms to simulate a tackle, Dexter lets up— just a little. But for Waymer, it's more than enough.

"RUN IT OUT, ROOK!" Waymer snaps. "Run the damn ball."

Dang. Three weeks as a professional football player, and already Dexter Carter has hit rock bottom. Dexter is as low as he has ever been in his life. The press is on him. He's on himself. And whenever he gets in the game, it seems like he screws up. It's a vicious cycle. Will it ever end? It's only August.

The trouble continues on a windy summer night at Candlestick against the Raiders. It's the first preseason game of the year. It's Dexter Carter's first game in the pros. It's not a good one. The punts are the worst part. The last time Dexter Carter returned punts in a football game was in his senior year at Appling County High School in Baxley, Georgia. Five years ago. Before to-night, he's had less than two weeks of practice catching punts—and those have been in the hot, still air of Rocklin. This is Candlestick, where the wind makes baseball players demand trades and even football players reach for their parkas. This night, with the wind yanking the ball around, Dexter Carter is settling under punts like a man under a piano falling out of a sixth-floor window.

Against the Raiders, Dexter fumbles the first punt he tries to catch. On the last play of the first quarter, Carter and John Taylor are deep waiting for the ball. Standing at the San Francisco 12, Taylor calls for Carter to make the catch. But because of the wind, Dexter doesn't hear Taylor. As the ball tumbles down toward him, Carter doesn't know what to do. He looks to Taylor for help. By the time Dexter looks up again for the ball, the wind has pushed it 10 feet to his right. He can feel the Raiders breathing down on him. At the last second, Carter signals for a fair catch and dives for the ball. He doesn't come close to catching it. The Raiders recover and kick a field goal.

In the locker room after the game, the reporters all want to talk about the balls Dexter drops. The punt. The two kickoffs. Hardly any of them want to talk about the kickoff Dexter returned for 73 yards right before half-time. Maybe it's because he didn't score. Or maybe it's that big contract. Whatever the reason, a pattern is set. For weeks, at almost every press conference he gives, George Seifert is asked why Dexter Carter can't catch punts. Seifert says that Carter "just has to focus and get that part of it done more." Lynn Stiles, San Francisco's special-teams coach, is grilled about why Dexter Carter can't catch punts. "I told him he has three things to do every day," Stiles says. "Get up in the morning. Catch the ball. And go to bed." For most of the preseason, the questions persist, because Dexter drops a lot of punts.

By the time the regular season opens, however, Dexter Carter is no longer dropping punts: mostly because he's no longer getting the chance to drop them. In San Francisco's four preseason games, Carter did have his moments. The finest came in Denver, when his 26-yard return late in the fourth quarter set up the Niners' tying touchdown in a last-minute win over the Broncos. But now that the games count, George Seifert has decided that his high-priced rookie has enough to worry about in learning the complicated San Francisco offense. So Seifert gives the job of punt return back to wide receiver

John Taylor, who had gone to the Pro Bowl as a punt returner two seasons earlier. Taylor was hoping to get a
break from returning punts when Carter signed with the
team. But clearly that's not going to happen. At least not
this year. John Taylor isn't thrilled. Neither is George
Seifert. "He does not have enough experience to just do
it," an impatient Seifert tells reporters one day. "There'll
be a time in Dexter's career when he'll be doing it, but this
isn't that time. We might have thought he was going to return punts, but it's going to take him a little more work."

By the end of September and the first month of the
regular season, the San Francisco press is slamming Dexter Carter hard. And, according to most reporters, the
punishment fits the crime perfectly. Not only has Carter
been scrapped as the new punt return man, but also, the
press reports, he is not producing on kickoffs or out of
the backfield. Three games into the 1990 season, most of
the Bay Area press has pronounced San Francisco's high-
priced first-round draft pick a disappointment and a
huge waste of money. "Carter's contributions have been
as minimal as his 5-foot-8 [sic], 168-pound body,"
Examiner reporter John Crumpacker writes on September 30. "He has not touched the ball on a scrimmage
play. Projected as the eventual punt returner, he has yet
to field a punt and does not figure to return one any time
soon. . . . When John Taylor injured his back against the
Redskins, it was Don Griffin, not Carter, who took over as
punt returner against the Falcons. That would appear to
be a slap in Carter's cherubic face, because Seifert admitted he did not have confidence in the rookie."

The newspapers, however, aren't the only place reporters are ripping into Dexter Carter. On September
18, two days after San Francisco goes 2 and 0 with a win
over the Redskins at Candlestick, *Chronicle* reporter Ira
Miller tells his Bay Area radio sports-talk audience that
Carter isn't working out. "You draft a running back in
the first round," Miller says, "and he can't help you at all

as a rookie, you've really got to wonder. Because it's not like learning to play offensive line, where you have to mesh with other guys. It's not like corner, or someplace where you've got to learn all this technique. Running back is skill, pure talent. Every year, you see rookie running backs come into the league and return kicks, catch the ball—do *something* useful. This guy hasn't done anything. He hasn't helped them at all. He got an $820,000 signing bonus. He ought to be doing more than he is."

To Carter, the words sting. Ever since the Raider game, it's been a vicious cycle. He drops a ball. The press slams him. He reads the papers. He becomes angry and hurt about being called a fumbler and a head case who can't get his act together. Which causes more dropped balls, like the kickoff he muffed against the Redskins. And kickoffs, he knows full well, are his only shot to make something happen these days. With Roger Craig playing ahead of him, Dexter has no idea when he'll get any playing time—Craig hasn't missed a game since his rookie year. Later in the season, Dexter Carter will say that during his first month as a professional football player he felt as rotten as if he'd been fired. Later he will say it felt like he had been at his own execution.

The deepest cut is an anonymous comment from an NFL executive in a story in the *Chronicle* early in October. "We really had questions about this guy," the unnamed executive says. "It kind of befuddled you that he had as much production as he did in college. You look at him physically, and he's not built like a running back. He doesn't really have pure hands. We didn't think this guy was a true, third-down back catching the ball. Our feeling was that if you took him, you were getting a return specialist. . . . We gave him third-round (draft) grades. He's a good, darter-type runner, but we didn't see greatness."

We didn't see greatness. Dexter read the words in the paper. Then he put them together with the comments on the radio. And he understood. *They're not just saying I'm too small or that I can't catch punts. They're saying I'm never going to be a prime-time player. They're saying I can't play. They're saying I can't play.* When the message dawned on him, it was as if somebody had slugged Dexter in the stomach when he wasn't looking. Most of his life, people had been saying that he was too small or not tough enough to take the pounding that little running backs take in football. But no reporter—nobody period—had ever looked at his size and a few dropped balls and decided *we didn't see greatness.* That had never happened before.

Growing up in Baxley, Georgia, Dexter Carter was always the best athlete. He was small, but he had jets in his legs and he could accelerate like an F-16 going vertical. In Baxley, he was the kind of athlete who, when it came time to choose sides for football or baseball or basketball, everybody wanted on his team because he was the best. And because he was the best, his team usually won. Everybody knew it. Dexter didn't brag about it. He didn't have to. The whole town knew it.

Baxley also knew that Carter usually got what he wanted. As a boy, Dexter had what his mother, Gloria, calls "push." "I always used to tell him, 'To get what you want, there's going to be a certain amount of pain and sacrifice involved,'" Gloria Carter said one day during the season. "And even though a lot of times he got criticism about how little he was, Dexter didn't care about what people said. He gave his all and went for what he wanted. Ever since he started playing football, he's had people telling him he's too short, that he's too little. But no matter what it took to play better, Dexter was willing to do it. He decides what he wants and he doesn't stop until he gets it."

It was like that at Florida State. When Clemson, Alabama, South Carolina, and Georgia wanted Dexter to come to their schools on a football scholarship after high school, he turned them all down. Every one of those schools wanted him to play wide receiver. Dexter was a running back. FSU was the only school that offered him a scholarship and a chance to run the ball. Dexter took it. It was what he wanted. Sure, he played behind Sammie Smith for two seasons. And sure, there was the rule that Seminole head coach Bobby Bowden put in that didn't allow the defense to tackle Dexter in practice. But that wasn't so much a knock on Dexter's ability to play the game as it was a precaution against banging up a five-nine runner before he even got into the game.

Besides, Bobby Bowden knew what Gloria Carter knew. Dexter had guts. Bowden saw that in a game against Georgia Southern in Carter's junior year. Dexter was on the sidelines in street clothes. He'd twisted his ankle against Tulane the week before. Just before half-time, tailback Sammie Smith, the Seminoles' Heisman Trophy hopeful, took a hit and came out of the game with a sore shoulder. In the locker room, while the rest of his teammates were talking about what they were going to do without Sammie Smith in the lineup, Dexter Carter slipped into his uniform. Bobby Bowden didn't use Carter in the second half, but when a reporter asked the Florida State coach what he thought of Dexter's quick-change act, Bowden said, "You can't judge a player like Dexter by his size. [Because] he has a heart as big as this room." The game against Georgia Southern was the only game Carter missed in four years at Florida State. And after leading the Seminoles in rushing as a senior, the little guy had proved his point. He could play. He was a prime-time player.

By the end of the second month of his rookie season in the NFL, Dexter Carter is thinking a great deal about the two years he played behind Sammie Smith at Florida State. *Dang, it seems like I'm back in college with Sammie again.* He also finds himself thinking about how frustrating it was to spend two years working his butt off in practice and keeping his concentration up so that when the time came for him to go in for Sammie, he would be ready to

show everyone that he could play. At FSU, Dexter remembers, the only thing that stood between him and a
chance to play was a star running back. Now, more than
two years later, he realizes that only the name of the star
running back has changed. Sammie Smith has become
Roger Craig. Dexter is stuck and frustrated again.

While he struggles with a new face on an old demon,
Carter also realizes one glaring difference between playing at Florida State and playing in the pros for the 49ers.
In college, he went to practice and worked his butt off
and the Seminoles won and went to bowl games and that
was pretty much that. Most of the time, the reporters
wrote about Bobby Bowden and Sammie Smith and Ron
Lewis and Peter Tom Willis. Dexter's private battle to remain positive so he could make the most of his chance
when it came was not a topic he would typically read
about in the newspaper or hear about on the radio. It was
a war he could fight by himself in private, in his mind and
in his heart.

But Dexter Carter is a 49er now. And by end of his
second month as a professional football player, he knows
that fighting his battles in private is a luxury that he is no
longer afforded.

With words as weapons flying all around him, Dexter
Carter goes on defense against the press. Most of the
time, when a reporter approaches him for an interview,
he politely answers a question or two. But they usually are
barebones answers that he clearly doesn't enjoy giving
and reporters aren't exactly thrilled to be taking down.
Other times, he is uncharacteristically evasive. He has a
meeting to go to, he says. Or he has an errand to do. Or
he's tired. Or he has to go the trainers' room to get taped.
Dexter Carter just wants to be left alone. Whatever he
says he has to do is better than standing around talking to
a bunch of executioners who put on a smile, take up his
time, and then load their guns and kill him all over again

in the paper the next day. Still, the silent treatment is as hard on Carter as it is on the reporters.

"Talking to the media is a part of football that I've always enjoyed," Dexter said one day at the Taj. "I like people. I'm a friendly, out-front person. I've always been that way. And, to be honest, I love attention. But I don't like talking anymore. Football is my job now. I have to be able to concentrate so I can go out there and get better. I have a job to do, and that's all that matters. Besides, what's the media going to do for me? I don't mean to be rude. That's just the way it has to be. Football comes first. That's just me now. I want to do the best I can. I'm still learning. It's tough enough playing behind Roger [and] not getting a chance to run the ball. The media can say what they want about me. I don't care anymore."

When Dexter is finished talking, he takes off his jockstrap and bends down to pick up the towel in his locker. Then he walks slowly across the room toward the showers. He walks like a man who is sagging under a great burden. The clues are simple to spot. The drawl that danced and twanged like runaway violins two months ago is long gone now, numbed and crushed by pressure and punts. Out on the field and in the locker room, he looks and acts tired. He used to smile. It has been weeks since he's done that. Back in training camp, he would often shake hands with a reporter at the end of an interview. He may never do that again. Two months ago, Dexter Carter was a young man with his whole life ahead of him. Watching Dexter walk across the locker room, it's hard to tell if he has any life left in him at all.

When he still was coaching the 49ers, Bill Walsh used to tell a story about an animal called a wildebeest. The wildebeest is an antelope with a head like an ox, a thick mane of hair around its neck; short, down-turned horns; and a long tail. The wildebeest lives in Africa, where its predators include lions. In the grasslands, a lion usually searches out a young, very old, injured, or sick wildebeest that isn't nearly as fast as the lion. The chase is often very short. But the key to Walsh's story is what the wildebeest does when a lion has closed in and things are hopeless: The wildebeest stops running and drops its head. Its eyes glaze over. Then the wildebeest just stands and waits for the inevitable. Walsh often compared the reaction of the cornered wildebeest to a football game. The goal of the game, Walsh would say, is to wear down the players on the other team to the point where they realize—and accept—that there is no hope for them. Then, like the wildebeest, they will give up fighting and wait for the inevitable. When that happens, the 49ers will have that team right where they want it.

As Dexter Carter walked to the showers at the Taj, Bill Walsh's wildebeest came to mind. And while the African animal in the story and a rookie running back in the NFL clearly are different, by the end of the first month of the season, Carter clearly has one thing in common with the animal: He is cornered. Now that Dexter Carter had been chased and cornered by the members of the media, would he stop running? Or would he fight back and somehow find a way to escape?

In Hinesville, Georgia, Gloria Carter knows something is wrong, terribly wrong, in her son's life. She can hear it in his voice on the telephone. Gloria Carter's calls with her son haven't been as frequent as they were when Dexter was playing at Florida State. Then Dexter called before and after every game. Either that or she would call him. But now Dexter is in the pros. His life now, Gloria Carter knows, is hectic and full of pressure. And he's in California, where there are more distractions than there were in little towns like Baxley, where she raised Dexter and his three brothers and one sister. But even if they aren't talking as much as they used to, Gloria Carter still can tell Dexter is fighting something.

"How are things going, baby?" she asks Dexter one night early in September.

"I'm just trying to do my job," Dexter says. "This is a job, and if I don't do the job they'll get somebody else— even though I'm a first-round pick. I'm just trying to keep my mind on what I'm supposed to be doing. I'm working as hard as I can. I'm just trying to do my job."

Gloria Carter knows what the objective tone really means. She knows about the punts. She's heard some of the things the reporters are writing about her son. Her friends up in Savannah and down in Jesup and Alma and Lumber City have been telling her bits and pieces about Dexter's football. But in the few minutes they have to-gether on the phone every couple of weeks, Gloria Carter isn't about to press her son to talk about any of those things. Because she doesn't want Dexter to know that she knows about any of it. "If he knows I know, he'll only worry," she says.

That's always the way it's been between the two of them. They aren't so much mother and son, Gloria Car-ter says, as they are best friends. Friends who know each other so well that they can feel things the other is feeling. When Dexter was having a problem with something, Gloria usually knew it without even talking to Dexter about it. And when his mother was having a problem, Dexter knew it almost as soon as she did. Once, when Dexter was nine, Gloria Carter went to the hospital for a routine gall bladder operation. When his mother left for the hospital, Dexter had a bad feeling, a feeling that his mom might not come back. She almost didn't.

During the normally routine operation, Gloria Car-ter's liver was damaged and she spent almost two months in the hospital. One day, Dexter's dad brought home all of the flowers from her room in the hospital. When-ever he would ask his dad when his mom was coming home, Dexter's dad wouldn't answer. Later, Dexter found out it was because the doctors didn't expect Gloria Carter to live much longer and so they were saving the family the pain of having to come back for the flowers after she died. But even though she survived, Gloria Carter knew her illness had been traumatic for Dexter. So when she was well enough to come home from the hospital, in the summer of 1977, she vowed that from then on she would keep her son from worrying about her whenever she could.

Thirteen years later, Gloria Carter is still trying to keep her son from worrying about her. If Dexter knows she's heard the things that are being written about his football, he'll feel worse than he already does. She doesn't want that. Lord knows he has enough to worry about already. So before she says goodbye on that September night, Gloria Carter tells her son that she loves him and is praying for him. When she hangs up the phone, Gloria Carter goes into the living room and does what she used to do before the bus came to pick Dexter and his brother up for school—what she did whenever anyone in her family had a problem they needed help with. She opens her Bible to the third chapter of Proverbs. She used to read it to Dexter all the time. He always seemed to like it. And if there was ever a time when he needed the help of this prayer, Gloria Carter thinks to herself, it's now.

They that wait upon the Lord shall renew their strength;
they shall mount up with wings as eagles;
they shall run, and not be weary;
and they shall walk, and not faint.

When she is finished, Gloria Carter closes her Bible and looks around her living room. It's not the living room Dexter knew in the three-bedroom house in Baxley on the street with all of the trailers. She's only been renting this house in Hinesville, an hour or so closer to Savannah, since August. She still has liver disease, so she can't go to work these days. But even with Dexter's new contract with the 49ers, she's paying for it herself. She's too independent to do anything else.

Tonight, though, she feels dependent. She needs help. Dexter needs help. She gets a funny feeling. A feeling that tonight the wings of eagles in Proverbs are not enough. She knows one more passage that might be. Gloria Carter reads from the twenty-third Psalm.

The Lord is my shepherd;
 I shall not want.
 He maketh me to lie down in green pastures;
He leadeth me beside still waters.
 He restoreth my soul;
 He leadeth me in the paths
of righteousness for his name's sake.
 Yea, though I walk through the valley
of the shadow of death, I will fear no evil;
 For thou art with me;
thy rod and thy staff they comfort me.
 Thou preparest a table before me in the presence
of mine enemies;
 Thou anointest my head with oil;
my cup runneth over.
 Surely goodness and mercy
shall follow me all the days of my life;
 And I will dwell in the house of the Lord forever.

Gloria Carter closes her Bible. She has done all she can do. She is not sure it will be enough.

Sheryl Ridgeway is fixing dinner. It's a Wednesday evening early in October. Shortly after her fiance, Dexter Carter, gets home from practice, they are in the kitchen talking about the day when Dexter launches into a familiar topic.

"It pisses me off," he tells Sheryl. "They're not giving me a chance. They're pounding me into the ground and

I can't do a thing about it. I haven't even had the opportunity to contribute like I want to. It's hard enough playing
behind Roger without them being on me like they are.
How can they look at how much money I make and a few
mistakes on special teams and decide I'll never be a
prime-time player?"

Dexter stops talking. Sheryl keeps working on dinner.

"Anyway," Dexter starts in again, "it doesn't matter.
Because I'm not talking to them anymore. The last two,
three weeks, when somebody's come to my locker to ask
me questions, I've answered them if I can like I always do.
But then I pick up the paper and read all this negative
stuff about me. That pisses me off. If the media is going
to write bad things about me when I talk to them, then
they can write bad things about me if I don't talk to them.
No interviews from now on. The media can say what they
want about me. I don't care."

Sheryl has heard it all before. This was the third time
in the past couple of weeks, in fact, that Dexter has
started in on how unfair his heaping of bad press is.
Sheryl and Dexter had met at Florida State. Dexter was a
sophomore. Sheryl was dating someone else. After
awhile, though, Sheryl stopped seeing the other guy and
Dexter asked her out for pizza. They've been together
ever since. Five months from now, after his first season in
the NFL is history, they will get married. In the time
they've been together, Sheryl has learned to accept what
reporters write about Dexter. In the last few weeks, she
has gotten used to letting Dexter talk things out. She's
been trying to listen, trying to get him to see that while the
media are criticizing him, it is part of their job to criticize.
Sheryl knows that Dexter is too close to the situation to
see that. Still, she tries her own little speech out one more
time.

"I know it's hard to hear some of the things they've
been saying," she tells Dexter as they get dinner on the
table. "But you have to realize that those reporters have a

job to do. They aren't out to get you. It's nothing personal. And no matter what they say about you, you have
to go out there and play. You can't let what they say decide how you play."

Then Dexter and Sheryl eat their dinner. Dexter still
doesn't get it.

In August, Paul Tagliabue, the new NFL commissioner, mailed a videotape to the head coaches of all 28
teams. The videotape is narrated by Ahmad Rashad, who
caught passes for seven seasons for the Minnesota Vikings before landing an announcing job with NBC after he
retired in 1982. In the tape, Rashad explains the various
functions of the media. No matter how nasty the media
get, he says, reporters usually don't mean anything personal in their criticisms. When reporters come down on a
player or a coach, it's not necessarily because they have
something against them. They're just doing their jobs.
And part of their jobs is dogging professional football
players.

According to the letter that Paul Tagliabue sent with
the tape, George Seifert was supposed to show it to his
players in training camp. But it's not until early October,
a few days before the Niners fly to Houston to play the
Oilers, that the team assembles in one of the large meeting rooms at the Taj. As he listens to Rashad, Dexter Carter realizes he's heard this message before. *Dang,* he
thinks to himself, *that's the same thing she's been telling me. It
may look like they're trying to cut me up and make me look bad on
purpose, but they're just doing their job.*

When the things Sheryl has been telling him mesh
with what Ahmad Rashad is saying about the media,
Dexter realizes that his focus on what's being written
about him in the newspapers or said about him on the
radio has nothing to do with how he plays or who he is.
Not talking to the media isn't going to solve my problems, he
realizes. *I'm still going to be playing behind Roger. And I still*

have to work harder not to make mistakes. So it doesn't really even matter what the media says about me. They can't decide how I play out on that field. I'm the only one who can do that. And if I think I can do something, I can.

On the way home from practice, Dexter decides the same thing he had decided when he was playing behind Sammie Smith at FSU. *I'm going to work as hard as I can in practice so that when the time comes for me to play, I'll be ready to show what I can do.* When he gets home, Dexter tells Sheryl she was right about the reporters. He sees that now. She was right all along.

At practice the next day, Dexter Carter is a different football player. On the outside, the change isn't obvious. But the attitude—*I'm the only one who decides how well I play*—is. One particular play from that Friday's practice showed the difference.

The 49ers are working seven on seven. On one play, Dexter flares out of the backfield and cuts up into the middle of the field. Before he can finish his route and turn back to look for the ball, he is knocked completely out of his pattern by linebacker Greg Cox. Set free by the added confidence his new realization has given him, Dexter gets feisty.

"Ass," he snipes at Cox, pushing the linebacker in the chest.

Greg Cox rides a Harley, wears his hair in a ponytail, and has a tattoo of a panther on his right calf. Cox got the tattoo in college when he and some buddies were bored one night and decided that getting tattoos was just the spice they needed. Cox is reckless. Later in the season, when Harry Sydney begins calling the foot soldiers on the 49er special teams "Dogs of War," Greg Cox's nickname will be "Pit Bull." Cox is rough, and he doesn't back down from anybody. Especially a five-nine running back named Dexter. Cox pushes Carter back. *"You're the ass,"* he sneers.

Cox and Carter square off within an arm's length of each other, glowering fiercely, when George Seifert halts the grudge match before somebody gets hurt.

"C'mon, Dex," Seifert orders in an insistent, controlled voice.

Carter starts back toward the huddle, still glaring back at Greg Cox. Cox is grinning at him. Seifert walks out and stands between the offensive and defensive huddles. He glances over at Greg Cox. Then over at Dexter Carter. He says nothing.

A couple of plays later, Dexter runs a pass pattern in Chet Brooks's zone. The ball is thrown to the other side of the field. As Carter jogs past Brooks on his way back to the huddle, Brooks slaps Dexter on the butt and says: "Way to keep fightin', babe." Chet Brooks has no way of knowing it, but he has just hit the nail right on the head. Dexter Carter is no longer feeling sorry for himself about getting ripped in the press. He's no longer a helpless victim before the firing squad. He's no longer a young man carrying a great and heavy burden. Now he's ready to fight. The chance he's been waiting for is almost here.

It's the seventh week of the NFL season when the Pittsburgh Steelers come to Candlestick. The 49ers are 5 and 0 (earlier they had one week off with a bye) and, along with the Giants, are still one of two unbeaten teams left in the league. Last week in Atlanta, San Francisco's offensive explosion was the talk of the league. In San Francisco's big win against the Falcons, Joe Montana threw for 476 yards—the eleventh highest single-game passing total in NFL history—and six touchdowns. Five of the scoring touchdown passes were to Jerry Rice, tying an NFL record. The fireworks put the Niners three games up on the Rams in the NFC West.

For the Steelers, however, the 1990 highlight film shows a much bleaker picture. Pittsburgh is 3 and 3 and no one is sure where things are headed. Although it's mid-October, however, those who follow the team are still talking about a play the Steelers ran in September in Los Angeles against the Raiders. With third down near the Raider goal line, Steeler quarterback Bubby Brister walked to the line of scrimmage, the first thing wrong with the play. Brister was supposed to be waiting for the snap six yards deep in the shotgun. Then, after taking the snap, Brister turned the wrong way and tried to hand the ball off to a running back—who was getting ready to block for a pass.

For the Steelers, the play symbolizes a month of frustration as Pittsburgh fails to learn a new way of moving the ball under offensive coordinator Joe Walton. Walton is in his first year with the Steelers after being fired as the New York Jets' head coach after the 1989 season. In Pittsburgh, Walton has installed a ball-control passing offense that, much like the 49ers', depends on short, high-percentage passes. Move the chains. That's what Joe Walton's passing game is designed to do. Move the chains, make first downs, and keep the defense off the field. For the Steelers, a team that has always relied on running and long passes, Walton's world is a whole new ball game.

And, for the first month of the season, it looks like the Steelers are never even going to get into *any* ball game. On October 7, after Bubby Brister throws two touchdown passes and the Steelers beat the Chargers 36–14 in San Diego, a reporter asks Brister why the Steelers had so much trouble learning Joe Walton's plays. The Pittsburgh quarterback answers by offering one of the plays Walton has been sending into the Steeler huddle.

Deuce, split right tight, Z short motion, short sprint left, Z hide, X go, on two.

"Can you repeat that?" Brister asks the reporter. "I ain't a brain surgeon either."

In English, Brister says, the football code means that he rolls out to his left, stops, and throws back to a receiver on his right. The play has worked well for Pittsburgh in the past, he says. But this year, under Joe Walton, the names and types of plays are all different. Adding even more to the chaos, Brister says, is the fact that even the way the plays are sent into the huddle is new. Last year, when Pittsburgh almost beat the Broncos to make it to the AFC Championship Game, plays were sent in from the sideline by the "wig-wag" system, which is similar to the way baseball coaches relay their signals. Brister likes the wig-wag system. But Joe Walton doesn't. Walton prefers to send in his plays by messenger: He gives the name of a play to a player who runs into the huddle and gives the play to Brister, who repeats the play to the entire offense.

In September, the Steelers choke on Joe Walton's offense. One of the biggest problems is time. By the time a play is given to the messenger, by the time the messenger runs onto the field and relays the play to Brister, and by the time Brister calls the play for the rest of the offense and the offense gets to the line of scrimmage, there is hardly any time left for Brister to read the defense and change the play if he needs to before the play clock expires—*if* the diction of a play hasn't already gotten garbled somewhere along the line. Like it did in a Steelers' game earlier in the season when Brister called two straight time-outs without snapping the ball because nobody knew what play was supposed to be run.

While Pittsburgh's offense has played better in recent weeks—scoring more points in the last two games than any other team in the NFL—it's the Steeler defense that's clearly the heart of this team. After six games, the Steelers boast the top-rated defense in the American Football Conference and the second-rated unit in the entire NFL. On the other side of the ball, however, the 49er offense ranks first in both the National Football Conference and the NFL. On Sunday at Candlestick, it's going to be the best against the best.

On Friday afternoon, Bill Walsh and Dick Enberg attend the 49er practice at the Taj. NBC television will broadcast Sunday's game, and Enberg and Walsh have come to get their first glimpse of San Francisco's quest for Three-peat. After practice is over, reporters converge around Walsh. One reporter asks him to assess Pittsburgh's chances of beating the mighty 49ers. Walsh knows that San Francisco is banged up. He knows that the 49ers will be without four starters. Ronnie Lott strained a hamstring a week earlier in Atlanta and can't play. Dexter Carter is starting for Roger Craig, who is out for the second week in a row with the torn knee ligaments he suffered in Houston. Linebacker Michael Walter, the 49ers' leading tackler for the last three seasons, is still out with a finger he broke in the opener in New Orleans. With all of the injuries, Walsh says, the 49ers need someone to step up and have a dominating performance. "This can be as tough a game as the 49ers will have all season," he says. "Pittsburgh plays really sound defense and they've got a fine runner [Merrill Hoge]. They're capable of upsetting people in a high-scoring game."

Then Walsh and Enberg duck inside an interview room at the Taj. The broadcasters are conducting their usual chats with those players whom they figure will play key roles in Sunday's game. One of the players Walsh and Enberg visit is a rookie running back from Georgia.

The game. First quarter. Dexter hard off left tackle. Thuds into Steeler safety Thomas Everett before getting dragged down. Gain of 11 and a first down. Dexter out of the backfield looking for a pass, gets knocked on his can, bounces back up and snags a flare from Montana. Gain of 11 and a first down. Two Steelers come after Dexter's head on a run to the left. Dexter ducks under both before being tackled from behind after a gain of seven. San Francisco kicks a field goal. Dexter gains more than half the yards on the drive.

New series. Second quarter. Dexter squirts left through Steelers who can hardly see him through the bodies. Gain of six. Dexter cuts up behind a block. Steeler linebacker Hardy Nickerson slams Dexter to the turf. Dexter holds on. Gain of four. Dexter flares out of the backfield on third down, running toward the sidelines. Joe throws behind him. Dexter whirls completely around, hugs the ball, and flops forward for a gain of four yards and a first down. When he comes off the field, Ronnie Lott taps him on the helmet. *Way to go, man.*

New series. Right before halftime. Dexter takes Joe's flip over the middle, and kicks into third gear before diving between two Steelers. Gain of 12 and a first down. Less than a minute to go now. Third down. Dexter sifts through the the line, gets banged by a linebacker, keeps his feet, and makes a leaping grab of Joe's pass to keep the drive alive. The Niners get a touchdown and take the lead.

They win. Dexter has a dominating game—90 yards in 17 carries and 57 more yards on seven catches. Bubby Brister and the Steeler offense score one touchdown. The very first time they have the ball. Then it's September all over again. Zip.

Dexter stood on the sidelines at Candlestick, the clock ticking down in the fourth quarter. NBC filled the frame with a close-up of the rookie of the day. Dexter's hair was rutted by the padding on the inside of his helmet. The diamond stud in his left ear glistened in the late afternoon sun. Up in the booth, Bill Walsh predicted that Dexter would be more respected by and connected with his teammates now that he has proven he can play. Now that he has gone to war and delivered when the platoon was hurting and needed someone to step up and lead them on. "I think this could have been his breakthrough game," Walsh said.

In the locker room after the game, when Dexter took the podium to tell reporters how he finally got out there

on that field and showed a little of what he can do, his re-
lief lit up the room. For half an hour, it was just like
Rocklin again. The words danced out of Dexter's mouth
in his Georgia twang. He was smiling.

Before he left Candlestick, Dexter told reporters
about how he never lost confidence in himself when
everyone else was calling him a loser and a mistake. He
told them how he kept running hard in practice just to
make sure that when he got his chance to play, he would
be ready. And he told them how Sheryl helped him understand that the media reps don't just cut guys into little
pieces because they like to. They have a job to do, so they
do it. Just like football players.

Harry Sydney is standing naked in front of his locker.
A reserve running back and special teams hellion, Sydney is talking about Dexter Carter. Back before the season began, Sydney made a prediction about how well the
rookie back was going to play in his first season in the
bigs. *"He's going to win three games for us this year,"* Sydney
had said.

On this Sunday in October at Candlestick, Sydney remembers his words. He picks up his towel and wraps it
around his waist. He smiles.

"That's one," he says.

Chapter 9

The Breaks
of the Game

*I*t's a Thursday afternoon late in October, three days before a game against the Cleveland Browns at Candlestick. Practice has been going on for about half an hour when George Seifert bellows above the wind.

"LET'S GO, MEN! FIELD GOAL!"

At Seifert's command, the players end their drills and converge out in the center of one of the two grass practice fields at the Taj. As backup center Chuck Thomas bends over to snap the ball, Seifert adds a final thought.

"THIS IS IT, MEN! SUCK IT UP! THE WHOLE GAME COULD COME DOWN TO THIS!"

George Seifert is not a prophet. He's a football coach. But on Sunday at Candlestick, he will legitimately be able to say he is both for a day.

Eight weeks into the NFL season, the whole idea seems ridiculous. That the 49ers could be as close as a field goal at the end of a game against a team like Cleveland? Never happen. After all, these are two teams heading in opposite directions. The Niners, with their win over the Steelers, stand 6 and 0. Only one other team in the league, the Giants, still has a perfect record. In addition, the 49ers boast the NFL's leading offense and both the NFC's second-leading passer, Joe Montana, and second-leading receiver, Jerry Rice. The team of the 1980s is starting the new decade as it ended the last one. On top of the mountain.

And the Browns? There's no nice way to put it. Cleveland stinks. Big time. At 2 and 5, the Browns are off to their worst start since 1984, the last year they didn't make the NFL playoffs. But for owner Art Modell, it's more than losing five of the first seven games and being in last place in the AFC Central that's humiliating. It's *how* the Browns are losing. Blocked punts. Blocked field goals. Missed tackles. A line that can't block for its quarterback or open holes for its running backs.

Cleveland stinks. Big time.

At 65, Art Modell has owned the Cleveland Browns for nearly three decades. For Modell, who once scoured out hulls in a Brooklyn shipyard to help his family make ends meet after his father died, the last five years have been the happiest—and most successful—of his NFL career. Since 1986, Cleveland has played for the AFC Championship three times. Three times in the last four years the Browns have come within a game of the Super Bowl—only to screw things up. One year, Cleveland lost in Denver when a running back fumbled away the tying touchdown near the Bronco goal line as the game was ending. Another year, John Elway led the Broncos on a drive on a muddy field in Cleveland and the Browns lost again. Last year, the Browns got within a field goal of the Broncos before Denver pulled away in the fourth quarter to win 37–21. Art Modell has never liked losing, but even that loss couldn't dim the fact that since 1985 his Browns had put together the fifth-best win–loss record in the NFL.

But this season has been nothing like those glory years. All Art Modell has to do to be reminded of that is to pick up the paper. It's right there in black and white. Look at it. Columnists are calling his team a "mess." Reporters are saying that his "inexperienced [offensive] line leaks" like a sieve, and that this season is already in the tank. Instead of firing head coach Bud Carson, some members of the press are saying, the best thing Art Modell can do to revive the faltering Cleveland Browns is to fire Art Modell. For the owner of the Browns, 1990 is already rotten to the core.

The trendy topic in both the Cleveland and San Francisco press corps during the week leading up to the game is guessing when Modell is going to can Bud Carson. But most football people know that the Browns' real problem isn't its head coach. It's the offensive line. The trouble had all started back in training camp, when starting tackle Cody Risien and tackle-guard Rickey Bolden both decided to retire. Then when guards Ted Banker and Dan Fike weren't ready to come back from knee injuries from the previous year, the Browns were forced to open the season with only one interior lineman—tackle-guard Paul Farren—starting at the same position he had played the year before.

In Cleveland, the offensive line is especially important, because the Cleveland quarterback is Bernie Kosar. At a time when pass rushers are as big and strong as grizzly bears and as quick and graceful as cheetahs, Kosar "runs like a duck," Peter King writes in *Sports Illustrated* early in the week, before the Browns fly to San Francisco. "Bernie's the type of quarterback that you've got to build a barbed-wire fence around," former Browns' coach Sam Rutigliano tells King. "The moment you take it down, he's in trouble."

Adding to the chaos is the fact that Kosar is now working with his fifth offensive coordinator in six seasons with the Browns. When Kosar came to Cleveland out of the University of Miami in 1984, plays were named based on compass directions. At that time, according to *Sports Illustrated*, offensive coordinator Greg Landry "told Kosar to look first at his outside receivers, and then inside." The

next two seasons, that system was changed all around.
New offensive coordinator Lindy Infante used numbers
to name plays and told Kosar to look inside first before
throwing outside. In 1988, Marty Schottenheimer and
Joe Pendry used names *and* numbers. And last season, offensive coordinator Marc Trestman called plays with
numbers and told Kosar to forget the inside–outside
stuff and throw the ball long. All the shuffling around,
Rutigliano tells King, has shattered Kosar's sense of continuity. "People can't grasp how tough this is on a quarterback. But it's like going to college and changing your
major every six months."

For Bernie Kosar in 1990 it all means one thing. Ambush. In seven games, Kosar has been sacked 21 times.
More than 30 of his passes have been batted down. Seven
have been intercepted. With little blocking and no running game, the Browns' offense is a study of inertia.
Cleveland ranks 24 out of 28 NFL teams in total offense
and next to last in rushing. For Bernie Kosar, the good
times—the 1983 national championship in college, the
three AFC Championship games, *decent blocking*—seem
like a lifetime ago. For Art Modell—and for Bud Carson—they *are* a lifetime ago.

Back at the Taj, George Seifert is approaching the
Browns in customary fashion—with sugar and spice.
"Based on what I've seen of them on film, they look
good," Seifert tells reporters early in the week. "They
look efficient. They have as much talent as any club we've
faced. We've got our hands full." Stock stuff from an
NFL coach trying to avoid saying something that will end
up taped to lockers in Cleveland, firing up a bad team to
play over its head and possibly knock off the world champions? Possibly. But Seifert isn't the only 49er who is
more than a little concerned about the Cleveland
Browns.

"They look so good on film," Jesse Sapolu tells Ron
Thomas of the *Chronicle* on Friday. "A little breakdown

here and there is costing them some games, but we're not stupid enough to [forget] that they've been the team that's been playing for the AFC Championship . . . three of the last four years. They've pretty much got the same people, and they're like this sleeping giant ready to explode. We want to make sure that doesn't happen this week."

In the National Football League, only one thing is more dangerous than a team fighting for its life: A team with nothing to lose. A team like the Cleveland Browns.

Forty-five minutes before kickoff, Chet Brooks stands with his hands on his hips near midfield. The rest of the 49ers are at one end of the field warming up. Chet Brooks is warming up too. For five full minutes, Brooks stands silent, watching the Browns. He is watching Bernie Kosar. He is watching wide receiver Webster Slaughter. He is watching three-time Pro Bowl tight end Ozzie Newsome. And he is watching fullback Kevin Mack. But there is one Cleveland Brown whom Chet Brooks watches more than any other. There is one Cleveland Brown whom Chet Brooks is learning to hate all over again standing in the sunshine at Candlestick. The Brown's number is 21. His name is Eric Metcalf.

Brooks and Metcalf played against each other in college, Metcalf at the University of Texas, Chet at Texas A&M. For four years, Metcalf lit up the Southwest Athletic Conference with his speed and moves. "He's outstanding," Brooks said of Metcalf early in the week. "I don't want him being outstanding against me." Almost every day this week, Brooks has risen near dawn, rubbed the sleep from his eyes, and watched films of Eric Metcalf. Brooks has memorized all the moves. The spin. The cutback. The lighting of the afterburner once Metcalf gets in the open field. Watching him on film, Brooks has come to hate Eric Metcalf just like he did back at A&M. He's come to *resent* the threat that, every time he touches the ball, Eric Metcalf can make a cut, explode through a hole and be *gone*. That every time he touches the ball, Eric Metcalf can burn a defense. Burn Chet.

Brooks stands, hands on hips, at the 45-yard line. He is working on number 21, trying to bore his way inside Metcalf's head with his stare, trying to get the second-year back thinking not about what he is going to do, but about what Chet is going to do to *him*. Brooks wants Metcalf to feel his big, cold eyes, like a huge, black anvil plummeting down to squash his talent like a boot stomping on a grape. A play is run. Like a young colt, Metcalf prances into his pattern. The ball is thrown the other way. But Brooks watches his enemy. As Metcalf trots back to his huddle, he sees Brooks. Chet cocks his head up in a greeting, and points his right index finger at Metcalf like a gun. Metcalf returns the gesture. Soon after, both teams head to their locker rooms before coming back out on the field for the pregame introductions. It's time to play the game.

The first half is all San Francisco. Bernie Kosar spends most of his time running from the 49er defensive linemen, who are beating Cleveland's young blockers upfront. The first two times they have the ball, the Browns run a few plays and punt. The third time, Kosar hits wide receiver Webster Slaughter over the middle, but San Francisco rookie Eric Davis shadows Slaughter after the catch and, with a swinging right uppercut, punches the ball loose from behind. Ronnie Lott recovers for the Niners. Eight plays later, Tom Rathman bulls in from the one, and San Francisco is up 14–0. By halftime, the game looks like a 49er rout. It will not end that way.

The Browns start their slow climb back into the game early in the third quarter. On third and eight from the Cleveland 41, Montana throws for Mike Sherrard, who has lined up wide to the right and run a slant pattern over the middle. Montana's pass is catchable, but skips through Sherrard's hands. Cleveland cornerback Tony Blaylock pulls in the deflection and darts up the right sideline. By the time 49ers Harris Barton and Mike Wilson knock him down, Blaylock has rumbled down to the San Francisco 25. Five plays later, the Browns kick a field goal. The 49er lead is 14–3.

Early in the fourth quarter, the 49ers lead 17–3 when, on third and 19 from his own eight, Montana fires for Jerry Rice up the right sideline. The ball is high, and four-time All-Pro cornerback Frank Minnifield is all over Rice. Both of them lunge into the air for the ball, which ricochets into the hands of Cleveland cornerback Felix Wright at the San Francisco 29. Three plays later, quarterback Mike Pagel—who has replaced an ineffective Bernie Kosar—hits Webster Slaughter in the corner of the end zone for a Browns score. Cleveland is now within a touchdown.

With 6:01 left in the game, Cleveland has a first and 10 on its own 34. San Francisco still leads, 17–10. Expecting Pagel to pass, San Francisco brings in its nickel defense. Nose tackle Michael Carter, linebackers Keith DeLong and Matt Millen, and strong safety Chet Brooks are replaced by pass rusher Larry Roberts and defensive backs Eric Wright and Dave Waymer. The San Francisco coaches began substituting Waymer for Brooks in the nickel in training camp when Brooks missed a month holding out and Waymer was proving to everyone that New Orleans had made a big mistake by not protecting him in Plan B. Early in the season, Niner defensive-backs coach Ray Rhodes told Brooks that Waymer was playing in his place in the nickel because Chet wasn't in playing shape yet.

But that was two months ago. Chet is in playing shape now. And Waymer is still in there in the nickel. To Brooks, there's only one way to look at the situation. The game is on. And he is not in the game. At Carter High School in Dallas, Chet Brooks was a football player. In

Dallas, that is the highest compliment that can be paid to someone who puts on a helmet and cleats. Because a football player does it all. Plays hard. Plays hurt. And plays smart. But, most important, a football player plays *every* down.

"Ever since I started playing organized ball, I've always been out there, in the flow," Brooks said, sitting on a sofa in the lobby at the Taj a few days before the Cleveland game. "That's the only way I know how to play football. All the way, every play. That's what a football player does." Then Brooks stopped himself. He looked out from the sofa in the lobby at the Taj. He still wasn't used to what was happening to him. "They got me on the bench, man," he said. "I've never been a role player. I've always been out there, in the middle. When I think about not being out there every play, it hurts—it *hurts*. Because I know I should be in there. The way I see it, I bust my ass on first and second down. I don't have any input who they play on third down. But I know I should be in there. To have something I worked so hard for taken away for no reason hurts—hurts big time. How come I'm not in there? It came down from George. Talk to George, man."

Hurt, angry, and out of the flow, Chet Brooks stands on the San Francisco sidelines as Mike Pagel marches Cleveland toward the 49er end zone—toward a tie. Eight yards to Slaughter. *I've always been out there, in the flow.* Eric Metcalf out of the shotgun for six. *All the way, every play.* Pagel to Slaughter for 12. *That's what a football player does.* Kevin Mack up the middle for five. *I should be in there.* Pagel to Slaughter for 10. *They got me on the bench, man.* Pagel to Metcalf for 19. *Talk to George, man.*

With first down on the San Francisco four, the Niners rush their goal-line defense into the game. Chet Brooks trots onto the field. A few days before, Brooks had talked about a situation just like this one. "The time will come when this team needs me," he said, "and I'll be prepared. I like to win, and I don't win by myself. When the time comes for that one play, when it all comes down to just him and me, I'll forget all this pain I'm feeling having to be on the bench. I won't let the team down. I'll be ready."

Was he? With two minutes left in the game and the Browns four yards from a tie?

On first down, Pagel pitches to Kevin Mack, who tries to run right but is hit for no gain. Second and goal from the four, 1:15 left. Across the line of scrimmage from Brooks, Ozzie Newsome crouches in a three-point stance. *When the time comes for that one play.* At the snap of the ball, Newsome fires off the line toward Brooks. *When it all comes down to just him and me.* Chet backpedals. *I won't let the team down.* Newsome breaks for the corner of the end zone. *I'll be ready.* So does Chet. When Mike Pagel's pass arrives, Ozzie Newsome looks back and dives into the wind for the ball. So does Chet.

After Ozzie Newsome's touchdown ties the game at 17–17, Dexter Carter takes the Cleveland kickoff up the middle of the field to the San Francisco 28. With 1:10 left in the game, the Niners have two time-outs left. On first down, Montana throws for Carter in the right flat. Short. No good. And Mike Sherrard is called for pass interference. Now it's first and 20 on the 18 with 1:02 left on the clock. On the next play, Rice is open down the field, but Montana misses high—his eleventh straight incompletion of the game. Second and 20, 57 seconds left. After Tom Rathman busts up the middle for a gain of six yards, the Browns call time. They want the ball back. And if they can stop one more play—third and 14 from the 49er 24—Cleveland will get another shot to end things once and for all. With 48 seconds left in the game, Montana slides away from center. His protection is perfect. Montana scans the field. Rice has run a post route from the left, drawing his defender deep into the center of the field. At the same time, Sherrard has crossed from right to left, directly into the spot where Rice has led his defender away from. San Francisco had called the play in the second quarter, but Montana, who is having one of the worst games of his career, had missed Sherrard. This time he does not miss.

Sherrard pulls in the pass and lopes down the sideline in front of the 49er bench. By the time Browns Tony Blaylock and Raymond Clayborn twist him to the turf, Sherrard has made it to the Cleveland 41. Later, in the locker room, Mike Sherrard's teammates will say that his play is the one that wins the game. That is not all they will say about Mike Sherrard.

After a 49er time-out, Cleveland puts a blanket defense on San Francisco, forcing Montana to scramble twice. On the ground after the second scramble, Montana burns San Francisco's last time-out. On the sidelines, Seifert, Montana, and quarterback Steve Young click off their options with offensive coordinator Mike Holmgren up in the press box. There is talk of kicking a field goal. But the wind is blowing too hard for that. A play is called. A pass. For Jerry Rice.

Third and one from the Cleveland 32, 13 seconds left. Rice lines up wide to the left and goes in motion to the right. At the snap, Rice shoots upfield and out toward the sidelines. In the playbook, Montana's instructions are simple. If Rice is open, Jerry gets the ball. If not, then Joe dumps the ball out of bounds and the Niners line up and try another play. Against the Browns, Rice is open. Joe throws, Rice catches and ducks out of bounds at the Cleveland 28. First down. Nine seconds left.

This is it, men. Suck it up. The whole game could come down to this.

San Francisco's Mike Cofer, the field-goal kicker, runs onto the field and looks down at the grass. Like a pilot searching for a smooth runway, Cofer hurriedly and automatically scans the scars and gouges in the Candlestick turf. He wants—needs—a level, firm spot from which to launch his kick. Cofer is tamping the turf with his black Nike when Cleveland calls time. The Browns want Mike Cofer to think about this one. They want him to think about how hard the bitter wind is blowing in from San Francisco Bay. They want him to think about how the game is now all up to him.

This is it, men. Suck it up. The whole game could come down to this.

Most of all, the Cleveland Browns want Mike Cofer to think about the kick he tried almost three hours ago at the end of San Francisco's first drive of the game. From 46 yards out. The snap was good and the hold was good. Cofer just missed it. Then, after the ball had thudded onto the grass in the sunshine beyond the south end zone, Mike Cofer had unsnapped his chin strap and trotted slowly to the bench. His head was down, and with every step, he retreated further and further into his own little world—that desolate place where all NFL field-goal kickers go after the snap is good and the hold is good and they just flat miss a kick they are paid good money to make.

When Cofer got to the bench, he sat alone on a cooler of PowerBurst. He sat there for a long time. No one came to offer encouragement. No one came by to tell him that missing the kick was no big deal, that he'd make the next one. No one came by to say those things to Mike Cofer. Because Cofer's teammates knew that if he was going to be any good to the team the rest of the day, they would have to let him sit there alone on the cooler of Power-Burst, listening to a voice. And talking to himself.

You're still good, the voice was saying to him. *It's only one kick. It doesn't have any bearing on the rest of the day. You still belong out there.* Cofer's mind was racing, goading him toward panic, wanting to look only at the negatives. *If you missed that one, you could miss the next one . . . and the next one . . . and the next one. You know that missing field goals is just like getting the shanks in golf. Shank a couple, and all you think about when you take the club back is 'God, I hope I don't shank.' You know what that's like, how that feels inside. Sick. And you missed that first one. You could miss this one, too. That wind—* Cofer snaps himself out of it. Cleveland wants him to think about this kick. Fine. *Find the right hashmark, then the left one, focus on the spot right in the middle—there it is, just hit it right there.* Then, waiting to hear the referee's whistle trill above the crowd and the Candlestick wind, Cofer proceeds to do exactly the opposite of what the Cleveland Browns want him to do. He takes the pressure off his shoulders. *What's the worst thing that can happen?* he asks himself as he stands at the 35-yard line. *I could miss this kick. If I miss, it means I've failed—myself and the team. But the world will not end. I will not be a bad person.* As the referee blows his whistle and San Francisco breaks its huddle to start the play that will decide the game, Mike Cofer thinks of the other possibility. *I could make this kick,* he says to himself. *I could make this kick.*

The two teams settle in around the ball at the Cleveland 28. Barry Helton, the San Francisco punter who also holds for Cofer on field goals, kneels on one knee, fingering the spot Cofer has chosen to kick from. Helton looks back at Cofer. Cofer nods. He's ready. Chuck Thomas snaps the ball. Cofer hops forward on his left foot. In rapid fire, Helton catches the ball, guides it to the ground, and twirls the laces away from Cofer. Cofer lunges forward and lashes his right foot into the ball.

As Mike Cofer's kick makes its way through the wind, Chet Brooks stands with his hands on his hips on the 49er bench. He is frustrated. And he is angry. At himself and at the world. *I should be in there,* he kept saying to himself as the Browns drove down the field for the tie. *Ever since I've been playing organized ball, I've always been out there in the flow. That's the only way I know how to play football. All the way, every play. That's what a football player does.* As the Browns marched down the field toward a tie, Chet Brooks also thought about his anger and about the team. *There'll come a time when this team needs me. When the time comes for that one play, when it all comes down to just him and me, I'll forget all this pain I'm feeling having to be on the bench. I won't let the team down. I'll be ready.* With the Browns marching toward a tie, Chet Brooks raged inside. The game was on. And he was not in the game. He had never felt so angry—or so helpless—in his life.

And then, when it mattered, when Cleveland was on the Niner four and the whole game was on the line, Chet Brooks *was* in there. Just like pee wee league back in Texas, just like at Carter, just like at A&M. The game was on the line and the team needed him. And he had failed. He had gone in there with Cleveland on the four, and he had gotten right up in Ozzie Newsome's face and still Ozzie had dived and pulled down that ball in the back of the end zone and the game was tied.

After the play was over and he was back on the bench, Brooks's teammates had tried to soothe him. "There's nothing you could have done," Matt Millen said, thumping him on the shoulder pad. "Besides, it's not like you got beat by some schmuck. That was Ozzie Fucking Newsome." After Millen was gone, Keena Turner came by and quietly held out his hand for Brooks. It's a universal greeting among football players, the clasping of hands. It's more than affection or male bonding. It's a gesture one comrade offers another when the other guy—or the war itself—is beating them. Brooks reached up to hold Keena's hand as Turner apologized.

"I should have been there," Turner said.

Brooks accepted their pats and their handshakes, but he wasn't buying any of it. Because he knew all he needed to know. He knew he had gone in there when the game was on the line and the team needed him and he had gotten beat by Ozzie Fucking Newsome and the game was tied. Chet had choked. Will Mike Cofer?

Brooks stands, hands on hips, as Cofer's kick knifes out over the trench of bodies at the 28-yard line. He watches it climb end over end into the surly Candlestick wind.

They have done it again. They have played poorly and won with a big play at the end. They are 7 and 0, one of two unbeaten teams still left in the NFL. In the 49er locker room a few minutes after Cofer's kick falls good through the uprights, there is joy.

And then they are numb.

One by one, the word passes from stool to stool. By the time the press descends on them, every 49er has heard the news. On the play that led to Mike Cofer's field goal—the 35-yard pass with less than a minute left to play—Mike Sherrard broke his right leg.

Again.

This was supposed to be Mike Sherrard's year. The year he put all the misery and frustration of three seasons of broken right legs behind him. And he was. He was catching just about every ball that was thrown his way. Whether it was a lob in the back of the end zone or a strafing run across the middle, if a ball was thrown anywhere near Mike Sherrard, he caught it. He was catching everything. He was Venus Fly Trap. Nothing could hurt him now. He had been through enough. He had been down to Hell and come back to tell about it. It was his time now. *His* time. His ankle was feeling the best it had felt since before he first shattered his leg three years ago. It was feeling strong. The days and weeks and months and years of rehabilitation had all been worth it. At last, his right leg was going to let Mike Sherrard last through a whole season so he could see how good he could be.

But that was before he planted his right foot in the turf in front of the 49er bench with less than a minute to go against the Browns. From one side, Cleveland cornerback Tony Blaylock yanked on Sherrard's left leg. This put all of the receiver's weight on his right foot. While Blaylock was tugging one way, another Browns cornerback, Raymond Clayborn, hit Sherrard high, twisting him backwards. With his foot planted in the turf and his body being twisted and stretched in the opposite direction, something had to give. With the clock ticking down, Sherrard got up to run another play—the coaches had called a streak. As he did, he felt it. He was hoping it was just a sprain. But when he tried to run, Mike Sherrard knew what he was feeling was not just a sprain. He knew that it had happened again. He was right. His right fibula had just snapped three inches above the ankle.

While most of the reporters clog the interview room waiting for George Seifert to deliver his postgame address, Mike Sherrard limps down the tunnel to the locker room. Sherrard is leaning on team doctor Michael Dillingham's shoulder. His right foot is wrapped in a beach ball of ice. His mind is filled with the painful, familiar images he has just seen in shades of gray in the tiny X-ray room deep under Candlestick. His eyes are glassy and distant. He is numb. A security guard opens one of the heavy, white double doors into the Niner locker room. Sherrard stops, settles more firmly onto his crutches, and then hobbles through the doorway toward his locker, which is across the room and up a short flight of stairs. As Sherrard inches his way across the room, several pairs of eyes follow him. One pair belongs to the owner of the 49ers.

Eddie DeBartolo Jr. often comes into the locker room after a game. If San Francisco wins, he shakes hands, gives out hugs, and tells everyone how proud he is of them and how much he appreciates all of the effort they have given him out on the field that day. If his Niners lose—which has happened only twice since George Seifert has been head coach—DeBartolo frowns a lot and looks as if he has just been told someone opened the door

at the airport, rolled in a hand grenade, and killed someone in his family.

Before Sherrard came into the room, DeBartolo had
been talking quietly with Carmen Policy, his old friend
from Youngstown and the number-two man in the Niner
organization. Policy was talking, his mouth inches from
DeBartolo's ear. Eddie was bent over listening. When he
saw Mike Sherrard hobble through the double doors,
Policy read the look on his face and stopped talking. The
look on DeBartolo's face told anyone who was paying attention that someone had indeed opened the door, rolled
in a hand grenade, and killed someone in his family.

DeBartolo follows Sherrard and a cadre of trainers
and assistant trainers up the stairs in the center of the
room to the receiver's locker. Sherrard sits down, slowly,
timidly. As he begins the job of unraveling the bandages
from his leg, DeBartolo quietly takes a seat on the stool
next to him. Eddie wears salt-and-pepper colored slacks,
a white button-down oxford shirt, and a purple tie. A
white gym towel hangs from his right shoulder. One
trainer takes over the job of unraveling the bandages on
Sherrard's foot. While Sherrard stares down in a daze at
his broken leg, Eddie DeBartolo reaches out and puts his
hand on his receiver's left knee. Sherrard looks at Eddie.
Eddie looks at Sherrard. Silence. Then, Eddie's eyes start
to well up. He pats Sherrard softly on the leg a second
time. DeBartolo looks like he wants to say something—
like he wants to *do* something—that will erase all of this
and make Mike Sherrard's broken bone one piece again.
But that, Eddie DeBartolo knows, is a fantasy. The stabbing in his heart and the tears welling in his eyes remind
him of that.

When he can't stand it anymore, DeBartolo gets up
and walks over to the edge of the upper level of the locker
room. He rests his elbows on a metal railing. He slumps
his shoulders, drops his head, and stares down at the
floor. Two or three times over the next minute or two, he

looks back at Sherrard, who is still sitting on the stool at his locker in a daze, watching the trainer work on his leg. Eddie DeBartolo is in pain. Maybe not as much—or the same kind—as Mike Sherrard is in. But it's pain nonetheless. Here stands the owner of the greatest football team in America, a towel dumped over his shoulder, sweat bubbling on his forehead, the hurt and disappointment and anger boiling in his eyes. Here stands one of the wealthiest men in America, a sharp and relentless businessman who can buy and sell many good-sized towns.

Here stands a man trying not to cry.

"I hate it when guys get hurt," is all DeBartolo says. Then he turns, leans up against the railing, and looks back at Mike Sherrard.

Around the locker room, the rush of San Francisco's win collides with the disappointment of losing Mike Sherrard. What's left is confusion. None of the Niners really understands why this has happened to Mike Sherrard. All they know is that one minute Venus Fly Trap was making the play that won the game, proving once and for all that he could make big-time plays in the NFL, and the next minute he was hurt again. One minute, Sherrard was finally all he had been working to be—the best possible. The next minute, he was on the outside looking in again.

To a man, the Niners have always believed that all they had to do was work hard and pay the price and they would always get what they deserved. Just now they're not sure that's true anymore. After all, Mike Sherrard had paid the price, and look what happened to him.

Eric Wright is sitting naked on the stool in front of his locker. Mike Sherrard has just limped by him into the trainer's room and disappeared behind a partition. Wright is staring blankly out across the locker room at a clump of reporters who have finished with George Seifert and are now hovering around Eddie DeBartolo. Eric Wright has been where Mike Sherrard is right now.

He was once the best cover man in the league. But that was a long time ago. For the last five years, the cornerback has been fighting a series of injuries. At 31, it's all he can do to just get healthy.

For a long time, Wright sits on the stool in front of his locker. He endures the crush of reporters who swell in around Ronnie Lott's locker. Occasionally, a reporter approaches Wright, who answers in a monotone that curiously has traces of anger and frustration in a word here and there. After awhile, Wright looks out across the locker room at the clot of reporters, football players, and clubhouse personnel milling around. Wright leans down and pulls a towel off the carpet.

"You ask yourself," he says to no one in particular, "when is it going to stop?"

Later, after all of the reporters have gone, George Seifert zips up his bag and heads out through the door of the coaches' dressing room. He is followed closely by John McVay. Another Sunday has ended. But there is no time to savor this win. The Packers are next, and playing in Green Bay is going to be tough. And now, of course, there is the problem of what to do at wide receiver. Seifert and McVay stand in front of the white, double doors leading out of the locker room into the tunnel. They are talking reality. Many people around the league considered the receiving trio of Jerry Rice, John Taylor, and Mike Sherrard the best in the NFL. But now one of those links has been broken, and San Francisco's depth at wide receiver has suddenly thinned dangerously—leaving so many questions.

Can 10-year veteran Mike Wilson step in and spell Sherrard at the third-receiver spot? Is Ron Lewis—a third-round draft pick who had looked good in training camp but then hurt his back and spent the first two months of his rookie season on injured reserve—ready to play in the NFL? Are the ligaments in John Taylor's left knee, strained last week against the Steelers, going to heal so he can play next week against the Packers? Is there a receiver on the practice squad, or on the emergency list of recent NFL cuts and retirees, who can help?

Seifert and McVay push through the doors and walk out into the tunnel. They are still talking reality. Neither one may mention it, but the question has to be somewhere in both of their minds: *How is Mike Sherrard's injury going to affect the rest of the team?*

Will the wrenching exit of one of the team's most popular—and promising—players inspire the healthy Niners to sharpen their focus, to dig in and bring their concentration to an even more intense level? Or will the sudden and premature subtraction of the Venus Fly Trap damage the team's morale—and, by extension, its play on the field—with failure? Neither man knew which it would be.

And although Seifert and McVay would never admit to thinking it—especially to a reporter—the injury to Mike Sherrard had now created another possibility. Did this win, which had come at such a high cost, portend how this season—and their club's bid for history—would go from here on out?

They could only hope the answer was no.

Chapter 10

Doc

When Mike Sherrard broke his leg against the Browns, Dr. Harry Edwards knew that it was time for him to go to work. On a team like the Niners, Edwards knew, an injury such as Sherrard's could mean trouble. The players are bright and inquisitive, and the feelings of respect and commitment that they hold for one another run deep. To Mike Sherrard's teammates—who had watched him go through all those months of rehabilitation, who had watched him fight back so long and so hard, who had shared his pain and frustration, and then his glory at coming back to play football so well again—what happened at Candlestick hurt. It hurt bad. And when people hurt, Edwards knew, they start to wonder if the pain is worth it anymore. They start to wonder if all of their sacrifice and effort and discipline will ever pay off. Or whether they are just working hard for nothing.

Harry Edwards knew what had to be done: He had to keep the players convinced that the pain was worth it. Somehow, he had to keep the team focused on the promise ahead rather than on the torment behind. If he couldn't do that, the Niners could very well lose in Green Bay on Sunday. Lose that game, Edwards knew, and who knows? More losses might follow. Lose enough games and everything—the division lead, the playoffs, the Super Bowl—could all fall apart. All because Mike Sherrard broke his leg. Harry Edwards went to work to make sure that did not happen.

Sometimes he worked in the trainers' room. Other times it was in the players' lounge. He worked in the locker room and out on the field. Sometimes he worked with just one player. Other times there was a small group around him. No matter where he was, no matter how few or how many Niners were in his counsel, Harry Edwards did the same thing. He talked and listened, trying to help everyone through the nightmare of Mike Sherrard.

He knew they were all asking the same questions— questions to which there were no answers. *Why Mike? Why does this have to happen* now, *just when he was starting to get his chance to play? Aren't positive things supposed to happen to the people who deserve them? Didn't Mike work hard? Didn't he pay the price? Is there no justice in the world? Or is life just a crap shoot? And if life is just a crap shoot, then why in the hell are we out here working our asses off trying to put together plans and programs when, in the end, it won't matter how hard or how long we've worked anyway? What did all the hard work and pain and effort get Mike? Does what we're doing matter anymore? Did it ever matter?*

Harry Edwards knew that he didn't have the answers to most of the players' questions. But he knew the answer to one of them. What do the 49ers do *right now?*

"Understand that we have a job to do here," he told the players in the days following the Cleveland game. "If one person falls, somebody has to step into that slot and get the job done. Whether it's [wide receiver] Ron Lewis, whether it's [tight end Wesley] Walls, whether J. T. [John Taylor] or Jerry begin to turn things up yet another notch, or whether it's Brent Jones or Jamie Williams who picks up the slack catching passes. We don't know exactly how we're going to get it done without Mike. But we *are* going to get it done. We have to understand that things like this are part of this business. It's just like in life. Leaders fall, and somebody has to pick up the mantle. Somebody has to take on the challenge and keep this team moving ahead. We want to encourage and support our fallen brother to let him know he is not forgotten. At the same time, we've got to move on. We've got a game to play this week. We cannot sit here and brood to the point where Mike becomes an excuse for us not to do our job."

In his talks with the players, Harry Edwards had now reached the most important part of his message.

"We must deal with the responsibilities that we have taken on," he would say. "We can't go out there and play and then come back in the locker room and say we didn't get it done because we were so distraught and messed up over was has happened. Even in the most desperate of times, we must find a way to meet our responsibilities. I'll tell you the same thing I tell my kids, the same thing I tell my students. Excuses simply do not wash. They never have, and they never will. I don't care what the issue is. By the time you finish with all of the excuses, you are still confronted with the problem. And by the time we get through feeling sorry for Mike and wondering what happened—and, God, how can life and chance be so cruel? —after all, this guy has broken his leg twice before, and he was just coming back—we still have to go out there and face Green Bay—who *kicked our ass* last year at home, *in our house*."

Edwards was blunt with the players. He gave them no room for sentiment. He gave them no time to feel sorry for themselves or for Mike Sherrard. He was trying to help them survive. But he was also trying to do much more than that. He was trying to help them lift themselves up out of a cold, hard, and painful place to somewhere better. He has never known any other way.

Harry Edwards wasn't even old enough to be in school when he saw his first dead body. The day was hot and humid. Fumes from the East St. Louis factories that skirted the Mississippi River hung thick and stifling in the afternoon air. The whistle had just blown at the Monsanto chemical plant where Harry's father and a few of his family's neighbors worked. The workers on the shift that was ending began to file out of the plant. Many started walking across the railroad tracks that ran between Harry's neighborhood and the plant.

Harry knew the tracks well. For the boys in his neighborhood, one rite of passage between childhood and adolescence was hopping trains. Jumping on the side of a moving train was supposed to prove to everyone that you weren't a little kid anymore. It was supposed to prove that you had guts. That you *belonged* with the older guys. Hopping a train was a test of belonging. And for a kid, the price of failing the test was often overwhelming. Before the train came along, two friends—two brothers even—would be just two kids playing on the side of the railroad tracks. They shared just about everything. They were about the same age. They were both black. And their families were both hopelessly poor. They had just about everything in common. But something happened when the Illinois Central Railroad car came and one kid jumped on and the other stayed behind. The two kids who a minute ago shared so much now shared nothing. One had guts. The other was chicken. There was no middle ground. And from then on, the social chasm was practically unbridgeable.

Harry got left behind at the tracks more than once. But he never hopped a train. Because he remembered all of the kids who had fallen beneath the wheels of the train and been killed or mutilated. Those kids had paid a great and terrible price to belong. Harry wasn't sure he wanted to belong to anything or anybody enough to risk getting killed or mangled under the wheels of a train. After what happened the day he heard the whistle blow, he was more sure of that than he had ever been.

Harry was sitting on the side of the tracks when he heard the whistle scream, and then the awful skidding and squealing sounds as the train tried to stop. He went up the side of the tracks to find out what had happened.

He saw his dad. His dad told him to stay away. He said that somebody had been hit by the train. Harry didn't understand what all the fuss was about. He wanted to see what everybody was looking at. He saw.

It was an old man who had worked at the Monsanto plant for years. He had probably walked across the tracks of the I.C. thousands of times in his life. He must not have heard the whistle. Or maybe he just wasn't paying attention. Either way, it didn't matter now. When Harry finally pushed his way to the center of the crowd, he knew instantly why the old woman he stood next to had covered her nose and mouth with a handkerchief. The body on the ground was nothing but a stump. One arm was torn off. The other one was twisted grotesquely. Somebody had put a shirt over the head. The rest of the old man was farther up the track somewhere.

Harry saw his share of dead bodies in Southend, the fetid and festering rathole in East St. Louis, Illinois, that his family called home. Some were like the old man on the railroad tracks. Others were drunks who would lie frozen for days in the alley behind the cut-rate liquor store before anybody would bother to see if they were dead or alive. Still others were women, who had been raped and murdered and then dumped in a lot overrun with weeds and left to roast and rot in the hot July sun for a week or two before the smell got so bad that somebody went to find out what was causing it.

Southend was also full of fights, shootings, and cuttings. It was full of the smell of reefer in the back of the dives where the cool cats and the jitterbugs hung out. It was full of Miles Davis standing on the corner blowing his horn. It was full of Bo Diddly and Little Richard blasting from the radios of beat-up old Buick convertibles, Caddies, and Hudsons driven by men with liquor-red eyes and gold teeth. It was full of softball games that went on all day during the summer. It was full of basketball and

football games that got played in the winter no matter
how cold it was, no matter how deep the snow got, no
matter how muddy or frozen the ground was.

For the black families in Southend—and in the 1940s
and 1950s, when Harry Edwards was living there, Southend was virtually all black—there was never enough
money. And there were almost always too many children.
Fathers felt the burden of feeding all of the mouths at
home, and so they often worked more than one job to
make the money that bought the food and the clothes
and the occasional movie for the kids. The mothers
worked hard to wash the clothes, fix the meals, and raise
the children. But there was always the pressure of too little money and too many children. For the mothers and
fathers, it was a demoralizing, endless struggle, one in
which they often ended up taking out the anger and the
bitterness and the frustration they felt over their
nowhere lives out on each other. That is what happened
to Harry's mother and father.

Harry's father was the grandson of freed slaves. At 16,
he joined a street gang and got caught robbing a store.
He spent eight years in the state penitentiary. Harry's
mother had been raised in a house that was run by her
older sisters. Her mother had died before she was 6. She
didn't get along with her sisters that well, and had no real
life of her own. So in the winter of 1940, when an ex-con
who could read poetry like she had never heard asked
her to marry him, Adelaide Cruise agreed. She figured
that living with an ex-con who said he loved her was
bound to be better than living with her sisters who didn't
seem to care about her at all. At last, she would have her
own life.

The babies started coming almost right away. There
were three—including Harry in 1942—by the time
World War II was under way. During the war, Harry's
father worked two jobs—at a defense plant and a meat-
packing house. Adelaide Cruise Edwards, meanwhile,

raised the children and ran her growing household. She canned fruits, vegetables, and meat when she could find enough to make it worth her while. She made quilts by hand. She got her dress patterns from the Sears catalogs, and sewed them on an old Singer machine. She washed the family's clothes by hand. She made her own soap and her own butter. And she grew collard greens, turnip greens, onions, tomatoes, corn, and other vegetables in the garden she tended every year. Both husband and wife were doing everything they could to keep the family running. Still, it seemed like they were always losing ground.

By 1948, the grinding poverty and struggle to make ends meet was starting to erode everything the family had. There were five children in the family now, and that meant seven people were crammed into a three-room shanty. The savings Harry's parents had built up—about $60—was gone, and all the cows had been sold. His mother remained overweight from her fifth child, and she was no longer canning or sewing. She looked old and tired.

Besides making and having babies and working themselves to exhaustion, the activity Harry's parents did together most often was fight. They fought over her snuff dipping, his tobacco chewing and cigar smoking, and their deteriorating circumstances. Most of the time, however, the subject Harry's parents fought about was money. Over what had happened to what little money they had. Over the fact that there was never enough money. Or that there was never any money at all. Money—from whatever perspective they looked at it— was destroying their lives. Later, in his book, *The Struggle That Must Be,* Harry Edwards remembered that, "as my mother and father surveyed the marital and family wreckage that was so characteristic of my neighborhood . . . , it was inevitable that she would arrive at the conclusion that 'A damn nigger man ain't worth shit!' and he at the opinion that 'You cain't depend on a woman for a damn thing. You should never teach 'em how to drive and you should keep 'em in one dress, in one pair of shoes, and pregnant. You just cain't make chicken pie out of chicken shit.'"

But they did not give up trying. Not yet, anyway.

Harry's father was always scheming up ways to make enough money so his family could have a piece of the good life. There was always another idea. The only problem was that they never worked. Harry's father tried to raise chickens, but the neighbors' dogs got into the cage and that was the end of raising chickens. After that, Harry's father found a partner and opened up a tavern. But a few months later, Harry's father's partner died. And because his father gave away more drinks than he sold, the business soon folded. After the tavern went under, Harry's father tried raising hogs in their backyard. But it soon dawned on him that feeding 15 hogs was almost as expensive as feeding seven children. Besides, the hogs attracted rats. And the last thing Harry's family needed in its rat-infested house was more rats.

Harry's father talked most about politics. He was sure that the Democratic party in East St. Louis was going to someday set them all up for good. Harry's father started dressing in expensive pin-striped suits and fancy shoes. He said it was because he had to go out and meet the people and talk to the big shots. Politics, Harry's father would say, was going to pay off for him—for them— someday, and they would all be on Easy Street. Instead, everything fell apart.

One morning in June 1951, Harry's father left for work. Right after that, his mother said she was going to the store for molasses. She didn't come back for almost a year. During the time his mother was away, she worked at several jobs and, for the first time in a long time—for the first time ever, really—she had her own life. No kids to worry about. No husband to blame her for everything that went wrong. Nothing. Just herself. Back at home, however, things were a shambles. Harry's older sister, Lois, who was 10, had taken over most of their mother's chores. As the two oldest of the seven children, Lois and Harry took turns staying home from school to take care of the babies. In the fall of 1952, Harry's mother came home. Soon after, Harry's father got ill and couldn't work anymore. Adding insult to injury, his mother found out that she was pregnant again. For the eighth time. By the time a baby girl was born, the savings were gone again. And between his father's medical bills and his mother's maternity bills, the Edwards family was deeper in debt than it had ever been. One night in August 1952, Harry Edwards's mother walked off the porch again. The next time she came back, it was to take all of her kids with her. Every one of them went except Harry.

Later, in *The Struggle That Must Be,* Harry Edwards reflected on the disintegration of his parents' marriage and of his family's life in Southend. "I am certain that my mother and father loved each other in the beginning," he wrote. "But as dreams died unfulfilled and even hope faded in the stifling atmosphere created by poverty, ignorance, crushing responsibilities, and increasingly difficult problems, against a background of what I know now to have been virulent institutionalized racism, I think that the time came when for them love was simply not enough. Perhaps it never is in the real world."

Harry Edwards spent the 1960s provoking the white America that had helped to crush his parents' marriage and reduced an entire neighborhood—and, as he would later realize, an entire race of people—into an invisible, unwanted existence in which black people were destined to spend their lives as nobodies imprisoned in a nowhere unless something was done to make things better. In Southend, he had swallowed the grinding poverty and the violence. And he had swallowed the racism. Because then he didn't have a choice. Now as an adult, he was determined to have one.

Long before January 1960, when a black attorney Harry knew loaned him $500 and bought him a train ticket to Fresno, where some relatives enrolled him in college, the black-and-white images of prejudice burned inside him. Harry remembered everything. He could remember the day as a kid when he watched a fat white woman feed the scraps of her hamburger and french fries to her dog. Two feet away, a sign read "NO COLORED SERVED AT COUNTER." That day, Harry was amazed and terrified to see that white people's dogs lived better than the people in his family did—better than the people in every family he knew. That was wrong, he was sure. But it didn't keep it from happening.

In 1954, Harry was in junior high school when the U.S. Supreme Court handed down its first major school-desegregation decision. Legally, the court struck down the "separate but equal" treatment of races. But in Southend, desegregation was a joke. Harry saw that every day. He saw that the only law that mattered to the white teachers and principals at school was the law of black and white. White was right. Black was not. White was everything. Black was nothing. Blacks didn't sit with whites in the lunchroom. Blacks didn't sit with whites in the classroom or in the library. There was even a separate bus to take black athletes to practice.

The only slice of life that the white people decided blacks would be allowed to share with them was on the football field, the basketball court, or the baseball diamond. Those were places that blacks could do some good. For the whites, of course. Growing up, Harry Edwards played the games with the white boys. Football in the fall, basketball in the winter, and track—discus—in the spring. But, in fact, every sport was the same. In athletics, Harry realized quickly, he was allowed into the white power structure and promised that he would no longer be a nobody—that, unlike most blacks in a white-controlled society, he would *matter*—if he played sports with the white kids. What Harry got once he was allowed in, however, was nothing like what was advertised.

One time, Harry saw a black football player dislocate his shoulder and all the white coaches did was order his limp body dragged off into the weeds, because clearly that boy was a wimp. And then there were all of the times that the white coaches dangled the carrot—the prospect of an athletic scholarship to college—in front of a black athlete's hungry mouth to get him to play hard but also as leverage to keep him in line and reinforce who was in charge in this deal. To Harry, there was acceptance in athletics, all right, but it was tinged with haughty racist slurs, cruel innuendos, and insults. Belonging, mattering, he realized early in high school, was all a sham. *Especially* in sports. Sports was advertised as the black man's road to riches, the black man's path to independence—his ticket into mainstream white America. But in the end, Harry Edwards decided, what it came down to was that he was a nigger and was therefore supposed to act like a nigger. And that if he couldn't act like a nigger, then he really didn't belong with white people after all.

Later, when he had earned a string of sociology degrees, Edwards would call sports in America a "plantation system" in which black people were treated like property but incredibly still clung to the assumption that shooting baskets or catching footballs was their surest escape from under the feet of racist white Americans. He was determined to expose the sham for what it really was.

In 1964, after Edwards earned a Bachelor of Arts degree in sociology from San Jose State University, he was awarded a Woodrow Wilson Fellowship. He left California to work on his Master's degree at Cornell University

in upstate New York. Harry Edwards was the first black
graduate student in the department of sociology at Cornell since the early 1950s. In Ithica, Edwards submerged
himself in his Masters' work. But something was missing. He felt somehow dissatisfied with his life. He felt as if
he was neglecting other, more urgent concerns.

Harry knew that in the decade since the Supreme
Court had struck down separate but equal treatment of
the races, the quest of black people toward equal rights
had gathered important momentum. By the mid-1960s,
he wrote in *The Struggle That Must Be,* "Blacks had developed and refined the techniques of nonviolent direct
action, resulting in the elimination of the more blatant
forms and symbols of racist discrimination; television
had for over a decade brought the savagery of racist official and mob violence into the living rooms and con-
sciousness of America; colonialism was in decline, and its
demise, particularly in the continent of Africa, provided
a new source of dignity and pride for Afro-Americans;
and the United States was already engaged in a war in
Southeast Asia that, combined with its long history of racist victimization of minorities at home, placed this nation
at a distinct propaganda disadvantage in its global struggle with international communism for hearts and minds.
All of this accelerated the new militancy emerging in the
Black movement, a militancy that was both fostered and
fed by growing concerns, particularly among young
Blacks, that the gradualism of established civil rights
methods and leadership was too slow."

Harry Edwards had found what was missing in his
life. A cause. The cause of black people. Concerned with
his own "political responsiblities" in the movement of
blacks toward equal rights, he hopped on a bus for New
York City one Sunday morning. He was going to hear
Brother Malcolm. That Sunday morning in Harlem,
Malcolm X railed against the horror that the white man

had committed against the black man. A horror that Harry Edwards had lived in Southend.

" 'Today I'm going to tell you who and what you are so that you will know who and what your enemy is,' " Malcolm X said as Edwards recounted in *The Struggle That Must Be*.

"History shows that you are by nature a beautiful, just and moral Black people whose forebears were stolen from Africa by the white man. . . . The record of history shows that. So it isn't racism, brothers and sisters, when I say to you that this is what happened—that the white man stole us then and keeps us in the situation we're in today. I have the authority of history backing me up. . . .

"He stole our fathers and mothers from Africa, from their culture and brought them to this land in chains. . . . But our people weren't brought right here to this country. They were dropped off first in the Caribbean, where they would break them in, break their spirit to resist enslavement, break their natural will to live free. . . ."

Malcolm X, minister and teacher, was preparing his people for today's lesson. He was going to make them as angry as he possibly could.

"I read in one book, brothers and sisters, where they employed a 'slave breaker' who would take a pregnant Black woman and make her watch as her man was tortured and beaten until he begged the white man to put him to death. . . . And then, with the Black woman watching, that slave breaker would take the tortured and battered Black man and tie him—hands and feet—to four trees that had been deliberately planted in such a way that they could be bent over and secured in this bent position to the ground by ropes. Once the Black man was tied to those bent-over trees, the ropes securing them would be cut and those trees would snap back, tearing that Black man into four different parts—right before his pregnant Black woman's eyes. . . ."

"And then they would take a Black woman that was pregnant and tie her up by her toes, let her be hanging head down; and with her Black man watching, they would take a knife and they would slit her stomach so that the unborn child would fall out and they would stomp its head into the ground. . . . Yes! That Black man was made to stand there and watch this happen to his woman and his *child*. Stand there in chains, bound hand and foot, unable to stop a single thing—and if you think that this isn't true, that I'm not telling the truth . . . then you go and get a book by Spears called *The American Slave Trade*, read *From Slavery to Freedom* by John Hope Franklin, or *Anti-Slavery* by Dwight L. Dumond, or *The Negro Family in the United States* by E. Franklin Frazier. . . ."

Now that he had their attention, Malcolm X was ready to begin today's lesson.

"The slave maker," Brother Malcolm said, "knew that he couldn't make people slaves unless he made both the Black man and the Black woman afraid of him and disrespectful of each other. Because unless the Black man and the Black woman can get together on a basis of mutual love, mutual respect, and mutual understanding, Black people will never get together on anything—least of all on the white man who has worked long and hard to keep us apart and to break the Black family down. . . .

"And so the Black woman had begun to disrespect the Black man even before they were delivered to the slavers in this country, because the Black man was unable to protect her or their children from being raped and murdered by the white man. . . . And not being able to protect the Black woman and being disrespected by her, the Black man soon came to lose his self-respect, to question his status as a man, and to distrust the Black woman—especially after seeing some of the kinds of things that she was forced to do to keep the white man from selling her children away from her on the plantation, or to keep the white man from selling or killing him. . . .

"And so down through the centuries, ever since we were stolen from our African homeland, Black men and Black

women have been at each other's throats—the Black man
attacking the Black woman, the Black woman attacking the
Black man, and the white man alternately attacking both of
us and siding with one against the other one while not being
for either one. . . . He'll have some 'scholars' put out a story
that the Black man hates the Black woman; tomorrow it's a
story that the Black woman shouldn't give a hoot what happens to the Black man. And you *believe* the white man! You
believe him because you're still on the plantation. The
chains have just been taken off your body and placed on
your mind—the white man has a headlock on you! He says
that you should hate your woman, that it's all right to sell
your woman on the street like a piece of meat, that it's all
right to beat, degrade, abuse, and disrespect your woman
and what do you say? 'Yas suh, massa.' Yes! That's what you
say. Because your head is still on the plantation, in chains."

Having whipped his followers into a froth of anger
and then taught them the link between the slavery of
black people long ago and the racism of white America in
the 1960s, Malcolm X was ready to close his lesson with a
call to action.

"Then the white man tells the Black woman, 'Look at
what the Black man does to you. He abuses you, he can't
provide for you, he can't protect you. What kind of a man is
that? You're better off without a man!' And before you
know it, we're at each other's throats. The white man set a
program in motion, geared to keep Black men and Black
women from ever getting together and you bought it; you
swallowed the whole thing—shell, parsley and all; hook,
line and sinker; lock, stock and barrel; the whole en-
chilada—and you loved it so much you cried for the
drippin's. . . .
"Yes. You cried for the drippin's. You loved it so much
that you wanted to be a pimp. Or wanted to be a prostitute.
Some of you even specialized in white men and white
women. A Black person wasn't good enough for you even
though you were nothing but a pimp or a prostitute. That's
what you thought of Black people—that's what you
thought of yourself. . . .

"We will do anything antisocial and immoral that doesn't have any place in a marriage or in the family. The Black woman must understand the Black man and insist that he be a man. Black men and women must stop listening to the white man. Black men must stop *neglecting* and start *respecting* and *protecting* the Black woman. Black men and women must smarten up, clean up, and stand up— together."

In Harlem that morning, the message of Malcolm X hit Harry Edwards like a Southend shotgun blast. His parents, he knew, had been just like the black men and women Brother Malcolm was talking about. They didn't respect each other. They didn't believe in each other. They didn't believe in anything. And so, when things got worse and worse and worse, they went for each other's throats, just like the slaves did.

Half a dozen times over the next few months, Harry Edwards took the bus to New York City and then a cab to Harlem to hear Malcolm X. One time, he was accosted by a thin young boy who tried to sell him his sister—who was seven months pregnant—*like a piece of meat*. During those months, Harry thought about what had happened to his parents and his family. And he realized that, while his parents had simply been unequipped to understand themselves—let alone the world around them—the racism that white America had forced down their throats was just like what had happened to the slaves in Brother Malcolm's story. At just 22, Harry Edwards had already been angry at white America for many years. And now with Malcolm X's words rampaging inside him, he was angrier at the white man than he had ever been.

But his anger still didn't have a shape. It didn't define *his* contribution to the movement toward black equality. That wouldn't happen until February 21, 1965. The day a black man shot Brother Malcolm.

Harry Edwards didn't sleep well at all the night after the assassination. His mind was racing across the social terrain Malcolm X had traveled during his Sunday lectures in Harlem and back to the poverty and racism that had strangled his family in Southend. Back to the carrot—equality—that white people had held out for him if he would play football or basketball with them. And then forward to how angry he was, and about how something had to be done to help black people escape the nothingness in which they had been suspended by white America.

Before he turned out the lights that night, Harry Edwards got out of bed and found a piece of plain white paper. On the paper he wrote an epigram in bold black letters:

BLESSED ARE THOSE BLACK
PEOPLE WHO EXPECT ONLY THE
WORST FROM WHITE AMERICA:
FOR THEY SHALL NOT BE
DISAPPOINTED.

Harry Edwards pinned the piece of paper to his door. It was a reminder that every day when he walked out the door, he was going to do whatever he could to force white America to relinquish its covetous clutches on the rights, dignity, and respect that black people deserved all for themselves. A reminder that it was his responsibility to shatter the stereotype of the black athlete, to delineate precisely how sports actually entraps rather than frees black athletes from the chains of prejudice.

He had so much teaching to do. He had to show an entire race of people how to confront and triumph over the "crackers," "honkies," and "blue-eyed devils" who ruled a racist world. As far as the white man was concerned, Harry Edwards had slammed and locked the doors leading to his mind and his heart. The doors would stay that way for more than 20 years. Until a blue-eyed devil got him to open them up again.

As the 1986 National Football League season approached, Bill Walsh knew he needed special help. In the college draft that year, the Niners had picked up several athletes from small and even remote schools. These football players were going to be depended on heavily to step into the starting lineup as rookies. San Francisco picked Larry Roberts, a defensive lineman from Alabama, in the second round. Tom Rathman, a running back from Nebraska, followed in the third round. Later came Tim McKyer, a cornerback from tiny Texas–Arlington; receiver John Taylor, from Delaware State; and lineman Charles Haley. Haley, Walsh knew, had spent most of his life in a backwoods Virginia town that had only a few hundred people. With its second pick in the fourth round, San Francisco selected Steve Wallace, a 6-foot-5, 276-pound offensive lineman from Georgia. Then there was Don Griffin, a defensive back from Middle Tennessee State, who went in the sixth round. Griffin was extremely quiet—so quiet he hardly ever said a word to anybody. Griffin, Walsh knew, was going to be in for a rude awakening when he met the San Francisco press. All of his new players were.

The year before, Walsh had seen how difficult it had been for Jerry Rice, San Francisco's top draft pick in 1985, to make the transition from life in a small Mississippi town to the fishbowl in the Bay Area. Living on a whopping rookie contract in a huge metropolitan area where the press breathed down his neck every time he dropped a pass, Rice had taken most of his first season just to get himself together enough to hang onto the ball. Now, a season later, Walsh had more rookies coming to his team. If only there was someone who could help this batch of young athletes adjust not only to the pressures and demands of football but also to their their new lives. Bill Walsh went looking for that someone.

Walsh had never met Harry Edwards by the time training camp opened at Sierra College in the summer of

1986. The two had written long letters back and forth for almost three years. They had sent each other long, taped monologues, as well as copies of speeches they had given over the years. Walsh had become quite fascinated with the sociologist's opinions on a host of issues, from the state of college athletics to politics and education. But there were other reasons why Bill Walsh knew about Dr. Harry Edwards. The images were as graphic as they could be.

September 1967. A 25-year-old, part-time sociology instructor at San Jose State University named Harry Edwards compiles a long list of grievances about racism on the campus. At a rally, he and other students cite many examples of racism ranging from all-white fraternities, racially fussy restaurants, and bigoted off-campus landlords to a series of indignities suffered by black athletes in the locker room and on the playing field. Edwards announces that if his group's problems with the situation are not addressed immediately, then the black student association at San Jose State is prepared to "mount a movement on campus to prevent the opening football game of the season from being played—by any means necessary."

When the fear of violence led the campus president to call off the football game, then-California Governor Ronald Reagan was livid. Reagan said giving in to the black students would be an "appeasement of lawbreakers." Edwards, according to Reagan, was "unfit to teach." Edwards, in turn, called Reagan a "petrified pig, unfit to govern."

After tensions calmed, administrators at San Jose State capitulated to the black students and took steps to solve racism problems on campus. By exploiting athletics, the one area of campus life where they had any political leverage, black students made important social and educational gains—not only at San Jose but also at a host of other colleges and universities around the country. Harry Edwards had started teaching.

February 16, 1968. In New York City, nearly 2,000 angry picketers mill outside Madison Square Garden. The mob is on hand to protest the New York Athletic Club's annual track meet because the N.Y.A.C. does not admit black people as members. The police can't handle the crowd, and things are getting scary. Finally, a 6-foot-8, 260-pound black man, the boycott's organizer, picks up the police bullhorn. Harry Edwards tells the crowd that they can "rush the Garden" with his "endorsement," but personally that isn't his bag. He's heading for Harlem to be "with our black brothers." The crowd does not rush the Garden, and the track meet is held peacefully. Soon after, the New York Athletic Club leaves the track-meet business altogether.

October 19, 1968. Two black sprinters, Tommie Smith and John Carlos, bow their heads and raise their fists in a black power salute on the victory stand at the Olympic Games in Mexico City. The salutes culminate a year's effort on behalf of the Olympic Project for Human Rights, a movement to boycott the games by black athletes that had begun in a leaky, converted garage in San Jose the previous year. Harry Edwards lived in the garage.

For most of 1968, Edwards was the boycott's point man. The price he paid was often painful. Edwards came home one day to find that someone had broken into his place and hacked up both of his dogs. Around that same time, someone had slopped sewage on the seats of his car, scratched KKK into the paint, and bombarded his apartment with tomatoes and eggs. Between the fall of 1967 and the spring of 1968, Edwards received more than 200 death threats. He got letters in the mail calling him a "coon," "a nigger," and a "black Hitler." Edwards later learned through the Freedom of Information Act that the FBI was watching him almost everywhere he went. They even had agents in his classroom when he lectured.

In 1968, Bill Walsh knew full well, Harry Thomas Edwards had been one of the hottest names on the FBI's rabble rouser index—a volatile, militant boat rocker who often did not stop rocking the boat until he had overturned it. But Bill Walsh also knew that, to Harry Edwards in 1968, nothing mattered more than the moral struggle of black people. To Edwards, the struggle clearly was too important to worry about one life. Harry Edwards was willing to die for what he believed in. And he continued to carry the struggle through his teaching and organizing at UCLA and then UC Berkeley.

That was exactly the kind of man Bill Walsh wanted. Someone who was willing to pay whatever price it took to accomplish a goal. Someone who was not afraid to tread on untested ground to forge change. Walsh felt an affinity for a man like that. Because, largely undetected under the aloof, mercurial genius image in which the media had cloaked him, Bill Walsh glowed with a sense of urgency to depart from the accepted notion that the only thing a coach or an owner should care about when it came to a professional athlete was how he performed on the field. Walsh was convinced that the mental and emotional life of a player away from the field was as important to winning football games as blocking and tackling. He had seen that so clearly with Jerry Rice. Walsh was curious to hear what Harry Edwards thought of his ideas and his team. So, in the summer of 1986, he invited Edwards to Rocklin for lunch.

Lunch turned into three days, and Harry Edwards spent four of his next five weekends in Rocklin. He listened to the players talk about the pressures, fears, and insecurities they faced as professional football players.

He saw the commitment and the concentration and the close collaboration of people who were totally dependent on one another. He saw that they had a cause, something in which each of them believed and for which each was willing to do anything. Edwards liked that. He could see right away that this was a group that no price was too high to pay to belong. But what really hooked Harry Edwards were the meetings. Here were football players, intelligent, ambitious young athletes, sitting in a classroom, *studying*. Here were football coaches, driven, focused men, *teaching* students. Bill Walsh remembers the first meeting he took Harry Edwards to at Sierra College that summer.

"I could see the effect being there to see up close what sports could be was having on him immediately," Walsh remembers. "His eyes were open in a way they had not been a few minutes earlier. I think Harry realized for the first time that our football ran much deeper than personalities, talent, and contract negotiations. It was a serious business in the fact that men were extremely dependent on each other, and had expectations of each other, and had to work very, very closely with each other. There really was not a lot of room for personalities outside the mainstream. This, I think, was a revelation to Harry. Having been into the classrooms, and in meetings, he saw serious students learning the game of football. He saw that there was effort, thought, and concentration, and the need for people to communicate with each other. And he saw that the very essence of the classroom was in place with a football team. It redeemed the sport in his eyes. Because, through his experiences, he had become somewhat disenfranchised, disillusioned from sports and athletics in general."

Over the next month, Walsh and Edwards outlined a program called "Niners for Life." As head coach, Walsh would make all final decisons. Edwards, on the other hand, would function as a consultant to Walsh and as a mentor to the players. In the beginning, Edwards's chief responsibility was to provide a conduit for communication between the black athletes and the white coaches. To accomplish the task, Walsh granted Edwards complete access to the team. He was allowed to attend meetings and practices. He was in the locker room and on the sidelines on Sundays. And when the Niners went on the road, Harry Edwards went with them.

Harry Edwards had spent his life on the fringes of white America, a frustrated, angry outsider clawing and snarling to be given his rights and dignity and the chance to do what he could do to make a racist society what he thought it should—and could—be. For years, he had been absolutely convinced that no white man would ever have the guts to treat him as his equal. But that is precisely what Bill Walsh had done. Harry Edwards had his chance.

His role was paradoxical. He was brought in by management, but he was not promanagement. He clearly had feelings of commitment and loyalty to the players, but he wasn't proplayer either. He was somewhere in the middle. "In football organizations," Edwards explained one day during the season, "people tend not to want to rock the boat because the balance is so delicate and the relationships tend to be so emotional and intense, depending on whether they won or lost that [week's] game. Somebody has to be able to go in . . . up, down, or sideways, and say, 'This is who we are, this is what we are about, and this is the direction we have to go in.' That is what I do."

In theory, the program Walsh and Edwards set up in 1986 was based on the basic assumption that if a player could cope with his life off the field, then he could perform better on the field. But the two men also were trying to create a mechanism that could help young athletes— especially young black athletes—take responsibility for themselves. At its core, Niners for Life was practical.

Financial counselors were brought in to lay out the business of tax structures and the complexities of income
taxes. Banks sent experts to explain how the athletes
could split their salaries not only to provide them with a
comfortable living while they were playing football but
also to have something left over when they left the game.
Advice on investments, deferred salaries, and real-estate
transactions were all parts of the program.

In addition, Harry Edwards held weekly meetings,
which all rookies were required to attend. These meetings were essentially bull sessions in which players—especially those black athletes who had spent most of their
lives in rural and often poor settings—could search for
answers to a divergent set of questions. Bill Walsh wanted
an open locker room, and this was the concept come to
fruition. No subject was taboo. Nothing was swept under
the carpet to be forgotten about and allowed to fester and
become a bigger problem later on. Players could find out
how to balance their checkbooks and how to handle the
pressures of competition for jobs within the team. They
could talk about how they were supposed to handle the
media, and how they were supposed to act when they
were signing autographs at a supermarket. They could
talk about sex and drugs or the next series of downs.
They could talk about what it was like to play football all
day and then go home and deal with families and wives
and girlfriends who needed their time and their
energy—and how were they supposed to have time for
everybody? And they could ask the questions that every
single rookie was struggling to answer for himself, *What
am I supposed to be doing now that I'm a professional football
player? How am I supposed to act?*

There was more still.

Through the University of San Francisco, Walsh and
Edwards arranged for professors to teach college courses
at the Niners' training facility in Redwood City and later
at the Taj. Classes were held every Tuesday, the players'

day off. One of the original two courses was in finance, investment, and personal budgeting. The other offered instruction in writing and speaking.

A critical element of the Niners for Life program was outreach to the wives and girlfriends of the players. During the five- or six-month-long NFL season, Walsh knew, the women often suffered an overwhelming sense of isolation and detachment. Many times, he knew, the only links a wife or girlfriend had to the team were the wives and girlfriends of other players. But because their men were often competing for the same position, even this outlet was often another wall for the women. So to help connect them to the organization, and community for those who were new to the area, Walsh and Edwards invited the women to hear speakers and counselors discuss the unique problems that football presented to domestic life.

As far as the football players themselves were concerned, a crucial component of Harry Edwards's association with the 49ers was a psychological instrument he developed and put on the organization's computer in 1986. It's not a test per se, but a questionnaire with some 40 items that, according to Edwards, cluster into about 60 different measures of everything from trust, mental toughness, and physical courage to how players handle authority relationships and the degree to which a player has been imbedded in other social groups in which he has been involved. When the athletes were finished filling out the questionnaire—in about half an hour—Walsh and Edwards compared their answers to those of players already on the team. At that point, the two men would have a pretty good feel for how a particular athlete would fit into the organization.

"What we're trying to do is determine what kind of human being we're getting," Edwards explained one day. "The instrument is something that was specifically constructed for the kind of player that the 49ers want. It's not something that would work for another organization unless [it] wanted an identical type of player."

What kind of player do the 49ers want? "We're looking for somebody who's very bright, somebody who has a pretty decent history of positive authority relationships, and of being imbedded in social groups that he is intimately involved with," Edwards says. "The 49ers put a much higher value on intelligence and mental toughness than on innate athletic ability. The coaches want a guy who can go out and get some specific things done for them. If he can do that, he doesn't need to be the greatest athlete in the world."

According to Edwards, one of the chief benefits of his instrument is that when spliced together, an athlete's responses can spotlight a particular skill. For instance, suppose that the coaches are evaluating a college linebacker. No position in the NFL takes more punishment than a linebacker. So the coaches are looking for toughness—both physical and mental. The instrument Harry Edwards developed can isolate toughness—to a highly specific degree. "There might be 15 items, or parts of items, that would give us an indication about how tough mentally and physically a guy is," Edwards says. "When you put those 15 items into the computer, the computer sends out a profile on that guy. That whole section will be tabbed 'Toughness Index,' and we know what we're looking for as far as the score because we already have the measures of guys on the team.

"When it comes to toughness, the 49ers are looking for a guy who is willing to play with pain, for a guy who is willing to cinch it up and support his teammates even when he doesn't feel well—even if he has a slight injury. We're looking for a guy who can take a lick and come back. A guy like Chet Brooks. Chet is solid. He's a 49er in every sense of the word. In terms of courage. In terms of commitment. In terms of going out there when he's hurt or not feeling well and playing his ass off. He's just a solid, solid guy."

In 1986, San Francisco's young black athletes played and played well. Jerry Rice, the second-year receiver from Mississippi Valley State, led the NFL with 1,570 yards receiving and 15 touchdown catches. In just his second year in the league, Rice started on the NFC Pro Bowl team and was named *Sports Illustrated*'s Player of the Year. Tom Rathman, the third-round pick from Nebraska, led the Niner special teams in tackles. Charles Haley had the most quarterback sacks of any rookie in the NFC. Haley also led San Francisco defensive linemen in tackles. For his efforts, Haley was named to most of the major All-Rookie teams. The same was true of Don Griffin, the quiet cornerback from Tennessee. Griffin led the team in tackles, and was named the NFC's Defensive Rookie of the Year by the National Football League Players' Association.

Bill Walsh had given Harry Edwards his shot. And when Edwards came through, Walsh was the first to give credit where credit was due. "The usual scenario for a rookie is to play effectively for five or six games," the 49er head coach told one reporter. "And then, because of injuries or pressure or whatever, performance tends to fall off. But last year, largely due to Harry, we had our young athletes on the field for 16 games, concentrating and making sacrifices."

Harry Edwards does not like to quantify what he does for the Niners, but if pressed, he will admit something. "I don't figure that I actually win games for the team," he said one day. "But I've got to be worth two or three plays a game."

To some of the players, however, he's worth more than that.

It's lunchtime at the Taj. Steve Young sits on the back end of a cart that the 49er trainers use to haul jugs of water and various medical supplies to the practice field. After two seasons in Tampa Bay, and two more before that with the Los Angeles Express of the defunct United

States Football League, Young is in his fourth year as a Niner. He has spent almost all of that time as Joe Montana's backup. San Francisco signed Steve Young in 1987, the season after Montana had surgery on his back. When they were looking for a quarterback who could assimilate San Francisco's complex passing offense, Bill Walsh and Harry Edwards pulled out their trusty 40 items and discovered that Steve Young was exactly the kind of person they were looking for.

Bright, inquisitive, and committed, Young had the intelligence and talent to be a starting quarterback for just about any team in the NFL. But in San Francisco, Joe Montana was the starting quarterback. So where did that leave Steve Young? Instead of languishing on the sidelines, a festering, malignant sore infecting the rest of the team with frustration and anger at not playing, Steve Young helped the Niners win two Super Bowls. Like Chet Brooks, Steve Young is what Harry Edwards calls "a 49er in every sense of the word." Scuffing his white-and-red Mizuno cleats on the concrete sidewalk outside the locker room between practices, Steve Young says exactly the same thing about Harry Edwards.

"When you talk about having harmony in a group like this, that's a tough thing to achieve. Because we've got every kind of difference imaginable—geographic, racial, social, backgrounds, beliefs. So to reach agreement with everybody, that's not easy. From my experience, there are many teams in the NFL who don't reach that harmony—who are incapable of reaching that harmony. And that's one of the real reasons why they don't win. That's where Harry plays a key role."

Young pauses and runs a hand through his short, curly hair. He continues to scuff the sidewalk with his right foot.

"Harry is a mediator," he says. "Somebody who is not directly involved with the team, who can react to specific problems that are many times inflammatory and find solutions to them. Whether it's something with a specific team we're playing or problems with the media, he's somebody who puts everything in perspective so we can attack a problem as a team and find a solution as a team. If you asked him, and if he was honest with you, I think Harry would probably say that, quietly, he resolves a problem every week that no one knows about but that's important to the success of the team. Because of Harry, we don't waste a lot of time and energy figuring out what we should do and how we should feel about things. There are issues that come up that I see affecting teams throughout an entire season that we get over in a 15-minute meeting.

"He's been able to walk a fine line between the management and the players. He's great with the rookies. I think if you asked the rookies on this team about Harry, they'd say they feel very, very comfortable talking to him. That's a great relationship to have with somebody who has access to the owner, has access to the media, has access to the head coach. When somebody goes to Harry with a problem, he's in a unique position to go and handle it in a way that doesn't require going through some bureaucratic hierarchy. I've always enjoyed talking with him about social issues, big issues where he has unique ideas that turn politicians so vanilla they can't approach a problem. It's not a vanilla world. Harry understands that."

Keena Turner agrees with Steve Young about Harry Edwards. In his 10 seasons with the Niners, Turner has seen—and felt—the difference Edwards has made in the performance of the players. But for Turner, Edwards is more than just somebody to talk to, more than a "secret weapon" who helps keep the various working parts of the Super Bowl machine oiled and running.

"What I admire about the guy is the way he can put things in perspective," Turner said one day. "There's nothing we can't talk about. I've read things the Doc has written, and sometimes he uses words and language that I can't even comprehend. [But] I've never left a conversation not knowing exactly what he was trying to say.

"He lives in two worlds. He's this intellectual, but he's also just a guy. My relationship with Doc goes way beyond football. He's been good for *me*."

At Lambeau Field in Green Bay on a cold, breezy Sunday in November, the Niners keep themselves right on course for the NFL playoffs with a 24–20 win over the Packers. It isn't easy. San Francisco comes out flat in the first half. Even with Roger Craig back in the starting lineup for the first time since he hurt his knee in Houston, San Francisco can't move the ball on the ground. Things aren't much better through the air, either. The Niners have made only four first downs by the time Green Bay goes up 10–0 right before the half. With 38 seconds left in the half, Green Bay tries to squib the kickoff along the ground, hoping to get a crazy bounce and pin the Niners deep in their own end of the field. The ball, however, rolls right to running back Harry Sydney, who lumbers up to the San Francisco 41. Three plays later, Joe Montana finds John Taylor in the end zone and the Niners have the momentum.

In the second half, Montana and the offense crank into high gear. Montana throws touchdowns to Brent Jones and, late in the fourth quarter, Jerry Rice. But Montana, who ends up throwing for 411 yards and three touchdowns, isn't the only 49er who has a big day. Charles Haley, the NFL leader in sacks, spends most of the game chasing Packer quarterback Don Majkowski around the Green Bay backfield. Haley makes eight tackles and sacks "Majik" once, one of four times the Niners put Green Bay's quarterback on the ground.

With the win, the Super Bowl machine rolls into Dallas 8 and 0. The Niners have not let the crushing disappointment of Mike Sherrard cloud their thinking or bleed their commitment to getting the job done. Dr. Harry Edwards has gotten them through another week. But there is still a long way to go. And with the Bears, leaders of the NFC Central at 7 and 1, and the Giants, leaders of the NFC East at 7 and 0, still on their heels in the race for the best record in the conference and the home-field advantage in the playoffs, the Niners know they have to keep winning.

They also know that if there is to be any chance of a Three-peat in Tampa, it's going to take more than the wisdom and street savvy of Harry Edwards to get them there. To even have a chance at that, they know that they are going to have to reach down deep and call upon all of the character and strength they can from the magic that makes them who they are.

Chapter 11

One Heartbeat

*I*n a practice at the Taj, receiver Ron Lewis glides deep over the middle, running past a defender like the guy is standing still. The quarterback launches the ball. Lewis runs under it and makes the catch. The guy covering him is burned toast.

Even in practice, no time is a good time to get burned on defense. In the NFL, getting burned usually means six points for the other side. Often, it means the difference between winning and not winning. For a 49er, however, getting beat goes beyond the result of the game. It means that one player has let the rest of his teammates down. For a 49er, that is the worst possible. Out in the afternoon sun, the whoops and warbles of derision come from the guys on the offense. They are part of the penance that Ronnie Lott—Bo to his teammates—is paying for his crime.

"WOOOOOOO . . .

. . . WOOOOOOOOO . . .

. . . Bo *knows* quarterbacks."

As Lewis, a rookie receiver from Florida State University, latched onto the bomb, Chet Brooks pulled up snarling. Brooks, the other safety in the Niner secondary, had nothing to do with the coverage on Ron Lewis. Ronnie Lott was the one who got toasted. To Brooks, though, it doesn't matter who was responsible. Defense is all the same. Us against them. Eleven guys depending on each other to get a job done. Eleven guys who are as strong or as weak as the other 11.

"DAMN, BO!" Brooks hisses as Lott pulls up and watches Lewis run up the field. "CAN'T JUST TALK ABOUT IT, BO!"

If Lott hears Brooks yelling at him, he doesn't show it. Lott's face, in fact, is blank, cold, almost without expression. Inside, though, Bo is burning white hot—angry at himself. After all, he's the one who's always riding his teammates to stay frosty in practice—*C'mon, man*—and to concentrate—*C'mon, man*—and be where they're supposed to be—*C'mon, man*—so they can make a play and hold up their end of the deal. Now, Ronnie Lott has failed to hold up his end. Usually, when Lott blows a coverage or isn't where he's supposed to be to make a play, no one says much to him about it. Because even the coaches know that he's going to be harder on himself than anyone else could ever be. Besides, as Chet Brooks said one day, "Nobody can take a guy's shit out better than Ronnie. The guy is going to the Hall of Fame."

Chet Brooks counts himself among those who look up to Ronnie Lott. "He's a football player, the ultimate warrior," Brooks said in the Taj locker room one day. "Every time he goes out on the football field, he leaves a little piece of himself out there. He'll leave his body out there if necessary. You can't teach somebody to care about something so much, to want to be the best so bad, that they are willing to leave a little piece of their heart out on that field for a cause, for a victory. When you've got a guy like that it inspires every one of us. With a guy like that, if you sell yourself short, not only will you feel like you let yourself down, you'll feel like you let Ronnie Lott down." After practice, Brooks will go back to looking up to Lott. But right now, all Brooks knows is that Bo got burned. He let them all down. It's only practice. So what.

After the play, Brooks waits for Lott 15 yards up the field from the defensive huddle. As Lott shuffles past him, Brooks slaps him on the helmet.

"Can't just talk about it, Bo," Brooks says. Lott runs

past Brooks into the huddle. No one says anything to him when he gets there.

Harry Edwards believes that Ronnie Lott has had it since junior high school. He has seen Lott try to teach others how to learn it. He has seen Lott help people get it back when they've forgotten where they put it or how they once used it. And Edwards has seen Lott demonstrate that there's a difference between having it and doing it.

"I think the thing Ronnie has had an appreciation of, probably since junior high school, is the profound importance of having a commitment to excellence and to doing the job that you are charged with doing."

Edwards is describing Lott's special ingredient one day during the season. "I know that his father was military, and in that life-style you are charged with a particular assignment, and you get that assignment done—without excuses, without rancor. You make up your mind that you have a job to do and that you will get that job done *without concern for the sacrifice*. It's an attitude, and what it means is that you get started on your job and you get it done because that is what *has* to be done. There are no other options. Everybody has a problem with Ronnie. Ronnie is [not] flexible in terms of allowing room for human frailty. But the reason he's a leader, the reason that the guys continue to follow him, is that not only does he hold everyone to that standard, he holds himself to that standard—all the time. Guys like Ronnie Lott set the standard for the entire organization. It all comes back to attitude."

On the 49ers, the players have a name for the attitude. But, most often, when they talk about it or try to remind each other about it, it's not the name that counts so much as the feeling that goes with it. That feeling, they say, is like having one heartbeat.

One heartbeat.

Keena Turner says he has always pictured it meaning "that we're all in it together, kind of like a rowing team. Everybody on the team's got to hit the water at the same time or it's all messed up."

To linebacker Jim Fahnhorst, it means that "there are a lot of Indians behind the chiefs."

Harry Sydney likens it to the sum of the parts being greater than the whole. "It's like a fist," Sydney says. "Five individual fingers make one hand. But when you close those fingers and make a fist, that's more powerful than five separate fingers. Our football team is the same way. We're 45 guys, but we've got an army of one."

To Steve Young, it means that, although "we're a lot of very different people on this team, and although we will always have conflicts and differences that come up, the bottom line is that we don't ever let individual problems and controversies affect the performance of the team. One heartbeat means we're isolated on our goals. It's a reminder of what we're all about: We're a team with a unique destiny. We believe that as a team we have a tremendous amount of talent. There are a lot of teams with talent in this league, and you always think the talented teams are the ones who are going to win. But that's been proven wrong. We've seen a very, very talented Minnesota team the last five years that can't get over the hump. Obviously, if we don't have the people who can make the plays, then the one-heartbeat deal is kind of moot. But put it all together—talent and attitude—and now you've got something unique. That core—the idea that we are all an extension of one another—is why we win. The way we perceive ourselves is why we win. We believe we're first-class, that we're gonna make it happen."

No one really remembers exactly when the heart began to beat. Even Bill Walsh can't remember exactly. Most of the players remember "One Heartbeat" as the battle cry of San Francisco's 1989 season, which ended with the Super Bowl in New Orleans. Other players give the impression that the unique corporate attitude has been around much longer than that. But if the *when* is fuzzy, the *who* is not. Although they are all responsible for the health of the heart, every Niner knows who's really in charge of the checkups.

One year, Ronnie Lott's shoulder hurt so bad he couldn't wash his back in the shower. But he played through the pain and waited until the end of the season to have surgery. In 1985, in a game against the Cowboys, Lott caught the pinkie on his left hand between his shoulder pads and the helmet of Dallas running back Timmy Newsome. With the bone at the end of his finger shattered, doctors told Lott that they'd have to do a bone graft to save the finger. But, the doctors added, even the graft wasn't guaranteed. It might not take. And after two months in a cast he might be right back where he started again. Lott made the decision a warrior would make. He had the end of his pinkie amputated right above the first joint. He has made the Pro Bowl four times since then.

In a 1986 game in Atlanta, Lott gave himself a concussion when he smacked into a Falcon. The next week in Milwaukee, he made 11 tackles and picked off two passes against the Packers. Most of the tackles and both of the interceptions—including the one he ran back 57 yards for a touchdown in the fourth quarter to give the Niners the lead for good—were all accomplished with a hairline crack in his right shin.

By his count, Lott figures he's knocked himself unconscious half a dozen times on tackles. He's dislocated or separated both shoulders. He's pinched a nerve in his neck. He's broken and sprained fingers and torn cartilage in his knee. Ronnie Lott has played through many of these injuries.

Even Roger Craig, who puts himself through brutal workouts in the hills near his home in the off-season—

and likes it—wonders at the whip Lott cracks. "Ronnie Lott is a warrior," Craig says, "and a warrior doesn't come out of the game unless somebody makes him. He sets an example for all of us to follow."

But *why* the obsession?

Fear. Ronnie Lott is afraid.

"If you don't see yourself doing great things, you'll never do anything great," he said once. "A lot of guys don't believe they can do it. That's half the battle. Something inside tells me, 'Ronnie, if you don't play this hard, you'd be just an average football player,' and that scares me."

Ronnie Lott, however, is not scared of the end. He is 31 years old now. He has pushed and punished himself through a decade of football in San Francisco. As wind and clouds bring winter to the Bay Area, Lott knows the sportswriters are right about one thing. He's almost through. For three seasons now, he's heard the talk in the papers. *Too old . . . lost a step . . . can't hit like he used to . . . plays like a coach . . . should be a coach—just get him on the sidelines.*

Ronnie Lott is a proud warrior. But he's not an egomaniac. He knows he can't keep playing the way he does forever. He accepts it. He knows that when he can't strap on the gear and go out on the field and take some guy out, then he'll be the first one to admit that he just doesn't have it anymore. Then it will be time to walk away. But that time is not now. And if there's one thing that he has never been able to tolerate, it's when somebody takes his heart for granted and says that Ronnie Lott doesn't have the guts to get it done anymore.

It happened back in September, before the season opener in New Orleans, when a Bay Area reporter said, "There is a certain spark that hasn't been lit in Lott yet." Ira Miller also wrote in the *Chronicle* that one reason why Lott hadn't played well in the preseason was because he was pouting over the way 49er owner Eddie DeBartolo had treated long-time teammates Eric Wright and Keena Turner in contract negotiations during the off-season. At the Superdome against the Saints, Lott fired himself up for one of the best games of his career. He picked off two passes and forced a fumble. On one play, Lott put Dalton Hilliard, New Orleans's tough runner, on the sidelines to smell salt.

In the locker room after the game, Lott was belligerent when Ron Thomas of the *Chronicle* asked him for his thoughts on the difference between his lackadaisical preseason efforts and his big night against the Saints. "My thoughts were based on your expert, Ira Miller, who said my spark wasn't there," the Niner safety said, glaring at the reporter. "Those things inspire you to play that much harder, because I don't want my teammates reading something like that and saying I'm not giving 110 percent. . . . I read somewhere that I was upset about the way they treated Keena and Eric. I'll do anything for this team. I'll play my heart out for this team, and I'll play my heart out for Mr. DeBartolo. My friendship is one thing, but I'll never let down on my teammates."

A month later, however, at the Astrodome against the Oilers, Ronnie Lott did in fact let down on his teammates. Big time. Warren Moon's two first-half touchdown passes came on routes on which Lott blew the coverage. And that wasn't all. Houston receivers dropped two other balls that also could have gone for scores. Lott blew those coverages, too. When Lott came off the field after one of the plays, Eric Wright did something that doesn't happen very often. He got up in Ronnie Lott's face and chewed out the Ultimate Warrior. Later, back at the Taj, Lott admitted that Eric Wright's words stung him, but that he had stood there on the sidelines in Houston and taken them because he knew his teammate was right. He was absolutely right.

Sitting on the wooden bench outside the locker room at the Taj that day, Ronnie Lott also talked about how what Eric Wright did to him in Houston was one of the ways the players on the one-heartbeat team keep themselves hungry. "On this team, players are not afraid to say, 'Hey, you're not getting the job done,' " he said. "And that's important, because it yanks you up and makes you realize you're not focused. It shouldn't just be the elder statesmen like me or Keena or Eric either. It has to be Charles Haley. It has to be Dexter Carter. It has to be everyone. Because this is our team. It's *our* team."

The one-heartbeat team may belong to the players. But it also belongs to the Prince who pays them.

Chapter 12

The Prince

On the afternoon of March 28, 1977, the owners of the 28 NFL teams gathered at a hotel in Arizona for the league's annual meeting. The big item on the agenda that day was the admission of a new member. Eddie DeBartolo Jr., the son of an Ohio construction magnate, had applied to become the owner of one of the league's most troubled franchises, the San Francisco 49ers. If the league approved the purchase, the 30-year-old DeBartolo would become the youngest owner in the National Football League.

Although Eddie DeBartolo Jr. would be the legal owner of record, it was actually DeBartolo's father who was carrying the deal. Several weeks earlier, Edward Sr. had obtained a letter of credit on behalf of his company, The Edward J. DeBartolo Corporation, which he advanced to his son for the purpose of buying the 49ers. On the afternoon of March 28, the owners met in executive session to discuss Eddie Jr.'s application for ownership. Eddie waited nearby in the hotel. The discussion that day included several key issues. One of those issues was Eddie's father.

In 1977, Edward DeBartolo Sr. was far from a stranger to the NFL. Three years before, he had been considered as head of the new expansion club in Tampa Bay. Although a wealthy Florida attorney, Hugh Culverhouse, was eventually awarded the new franchise,

DeBartolo's financial clout had won him important ad-
mirers within the league's power structure. The reason
was simple. In the NFL, money talks. And Edward J. De-
Bartolo Sr. could speak loudly.

In fact, at the time his son's bid to purchase the 49ers
went before the owners, Edward DeBartolo Sr. was the
biggest land developer in the United States. He had
pioneered both the outdoor shopping center and the
covered shopping mall. In all, some 70 separate com-
panies were under the DeBartolo Corporation's um-
brella, including 34 shopping complexes, four Holiday
Inns, thousands of acres of land, gas wells, several banks
in Florida, and a foreign trade zone in Ohio, one of the
first free-trade zones granted by the federal government.
Edward DeBartolo Sr.'s sports ventures included horse-
racing tracks outside of Cleveland, Chicago, and Shreve-
port, Louisiana. The corporate portfolio also featured
the Pittsburgh Civic Arena, in which Edward DeBartolo
Sr.'s sole personal holding, the Pittsburgh Penguins of
the National Hockey League, played. *Forbes* magazine
later estimated Edward Sr.'s net worth at "well over
$500 million." He was called the richest man in Ohio.

But if the NFL owners had been swayed by DeBartolo's financial clout during the negotiations over the
Tampa Bay franchise, they had also been well aware of
how hard he had worked to acquire it. Like strong perfume, the reputation of Edward J. DeBartolo Sr. pre-
ceded him.

The richest man in Ohio had grown up in a tough
Italian neighborhood in Youngstown called The Hollow.
According to legend, the name came about in the days
before the Great Depression when meat was rare and
stomachs were often empty. The Hollow was the kind of
neighborhood where parents typically lumped kids into
two classes: Good kids were kids who grew up and didn't
go to prison, and bad kids were kids who joined the mob

or didn't want to work for a living. Edward DeBartolo was a good kid. He was a very good kid.

DeBartolo's original name was Anthony Paonessa. He was named after his father, who died of pneumonia two months before he was born in May 1909. When Anthony was two, his mother married immigrant paving contractor Michael DeBartolo, who started a construction business in his adopted country in 1914. Anthony started going to job sites with his stepfather as soon as he could walk.

By the time he was 12, Anthony was bidding jobs and writing contracts for his stepfather, who could neither read nor write English. Although he would later admit he goofed off too much in school, Anthony also took it upon himself to teach Michael DeBartolo what English he could.

In high school, Anthony Paonessa changed his name. He picked Edward as a tribute to both his maternal grandfather and an uncle with whom his mother had lived before she married. He picked DeBartolo because he was grateful for the way his stepfather had treated his mother and brothers and sisters.

After graduating from high school—it took an extra semester because he had been working so much in his stepfather's construction business—Edward DeBartolo headed for Notre Dame. In college, his schedule was grueling. From 11 P.M. until 7 A.M., he worked as a concrete foreman on construction sites all around South Bend. Then he went to classes until noon. After he graduated Notre Dame with a degree in civil engineering, DeBartolo returned to Youngstown and the family construction business.

By 1944, the end of World War II was foreseeable if not imminent, and America's postwar migration to the suburbs was beginning. After years of public contracting, Edward DeBartolo grew tired of begging the city to let him build a gas station here or widen a street there. "I didn't like it," he once told the *Pittsburgh Press*. "You had to gauge your own work according to someone else. You'd get those jobs and if you made a buck . . . , you'd pay taxes and wind up with a yard full of iron . . . dozers, shovels and all that. Then you'd go begging or bidding for another job." Convinced there was a better way, De-Bartolo decided to put his future into his own hands. He formed The Edward J. DeBartolo Corporation. The company was headquartered in a brick building in Youngstown, only a few minutes from where its owner, the thin, restrained man with the 175 IQ and the obsession for 14-hour workdays, lived.

In 1948, the DeBartolo Corporation built its first strip shopping center in a suburban Youngstown neighborhood. More followed, and when the strip centers began to catch on, the company expanded into other areas of the Midwest. By the early 1960s, DeBartolo was ready to try another idea—the enclosed shopping mall. He had a hunch that, with America rushing to the suburbs, those millions of people were going to need places to shop as well as entertain themselves. He put the two together. As he had with the outdoor strip centers, DeBartolo bought land and built his first malls in the Youngstown area. The pattern was always the same. One finished project was used as collateral for the next, and the next, and the next. As roofed malls began to make up a larger and larger percentage of the general merchandise and apparel business in the United States, Edward DeBartolo's hunch proved correct. He had struck gold.

Edward DeBartolo Sr., the NFL owners knew, had started from nothing. But by 1977, they were quite aware, he had everything a businessman could have. He was the king of his world. But the King, of course, was not the DeBartolo who wanted to buy the 49ers. That was his son, the Prince.

Edward DeBartolo Jr. was born in November 1946, two months after the San Francisco 49ers played their first game as a member of the eight-team All-America Football Conference. At an early age, it was clear that Edward Jr. was quite unlike his father in two obvious ways. Edward Sr. was thin and soft-spoken. Edward Jr. was stocky and as quiet as a flurry of right crosses to the chin. Nevertheless, father and son did share certain similarities. Both, for instance, had volatile tempers. Both were short. Both were relentless and intense in everything they did. Both were feisty and competitive. And both worked for The Edward J. DeBartolo Corporation.

Eddie Jr. started in his father's company at the very bottom. He mopped floors, cut grass, and picked up cigarette butts at one of the malls his father's company owned. Later, when it was time for college, Eddie Jr. chose Notre Dame just as his father had. In 1968, Eddie graduated from Notre Dame and returned to Youngstown, where he embarked on an executive-training program that took him into each department in his father's corporation. In 1971, Eddie Jr. was appointed vice-president of the company. Five years later, he was named executive vice-president. Eddie DeBartolo Jr. was now almost 30. He was an executive in the one of the most influential corporations in the United States. He was married to his high school sweetheart. He lived in a big house. He played golf at the country club. And he made more money in a year than some people can even imagine making in their lifetimes. Still, something wasn't right. Eddie finally discovered what it was.

He realized that, even though he was bright and creative and relentless, he had always been Edward DeBartolo Sr.'s son. He had never been *Edward DeBartolo Jr.* His father had always joked that he was "the Prince," but the joke wasn't funny anymore. In fact, it almost hurt. The King's robes cast such a long shadow that the Prince had never been able to distinguish himself from his father or his father's accomplishments. He had no identity of his own. He had always tried to fill his father's shoes, to carry on the construction empire that the King had forged with his drive and his smarts and his guts. The Prince's dilemma had always been the same. How was he supposed to improve something that was already the biggest and the best around? How could he add to a magnificent setting of stones that was already perfect? What was he supposed to be doing that his father wasn't already doing from 5:30 A.M. until 8 P.M. every day of the year including Christmas? Where was the challenge in that?

Eddie Jr. was in a situation he loved but at the same time couldn't stand. He loved his family, and he loved his father and his father's business. But he was suffocating. His situation was, as *Sports Illustrated* once put it, "like making the white pages or inheriting England." The Prince knew that he needed something that he could do on his own.

One morning in February 1977, Edward Sr. took a phone call from one Joe Thomas. Thomas had been fired the month before as the general manager of the Baltimore Colts. Thomas had helped build the Colts into a winner. And he'd done the same thing in Miami with the Dolphins, who won two Super Bowls. Out of a job, Thomas wanted back into the NFL. He knew the 49ers were on the block. He also knew of one man who might be interested in buying the team. Ten years before, Thomas had met Edward Sr. in Chicago. That day, the two had a long conversation about the football business. DeBartolo had been impressed with Thomas, and the two men had kept in touch over the years. Now in February 1977, DeBartolo told Thomas he would buy the team if Thomas would be the general manager. Before the negotiations for the purchase of the 49ers had even begun, Joe Thomas had signed a contract.

In training camp, Joe Montana (far left) signs a contract that makes him the NFL's highest-paid player. For most of the season, while the running game sputters, Montana carries the Niners.

Two reasons why the Niners win: VP John McVay (left) brings big-time talent to the field, while Dr. Harry Edwards, the volatile sociologist from Berkeley, monitors the chemistry of the locker room.

Head coach George Siefert on the sidelines during the last preseason game, a blowout loss to Seattle. Seifert is starting to show the stress of a month of hold-outs, injuries, and mistakes.

In New Orleans, the Saints shut down the best receiver in football for most of the night. But down by two with :31 left, Jerry Rice gets loose over the middle and the Niners pull out a win.

Photo by J. Richard Faulk, Jr.

Niner fans—The Faithful—used to think Eddie DeBartolo, Jr., was a spoiled rich kid who was messing up their team. Four Super Bowl wins changed their mind. Here, at halftime of the regular season home opener against Washington, the 49er owner thanks the fans for their support and . . .

Photo by J. Richard Faulk, Jr.

. . . with the franchise's four Super Bowl trophies glinting in the sun, pledges to bring a historic third-straight NFL title home to the Bay Area.

Steve Wallace (right) is the feistiest of the Niner offensive linemen. In September, Wallace shuts down Washington's Charles Mann. Montana has a huge game and the Niners win big.

Montana meets the press. Montana is sick of reporters who always want him to talk about why he's so great. Montana doesn't like talking. He just wants to play.

Already missing four starters, the Niners lose another one early in the Pittsburgh game when John Taylor takes a hit on his knee.

Trainer Lindsy McLean (left) and team physician Michael Dillingham (center) look at Taylor's X-rays on the sidelines. Dillingham sometimes dreams about Niners getting hurt. He will have nightmares for the rest of the season.

The Niners huddle before the Green Bay game. A week after losing receiver Mike Sherrard to a broken leg, the players feel they must pull together and beat the Packers or risk losing their momentum.

When the offense comes out flat, the defense keeps the Niners close. Here, Charles Haley belts Packer quarterback Don Majkowski.

Photo by Jeff Bayer

John Taylor's score right before halftime ignites the offense and the Niners get a tough win. Taylor doesn't get the ink Jerry Rice does, but coaches around the NFL know JT is just as explosive.

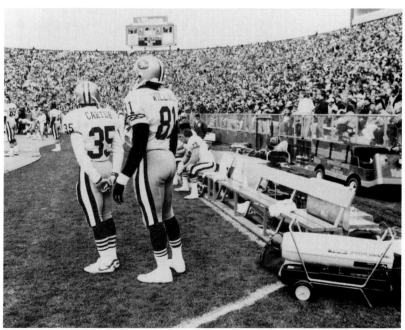

Photo by Jeff Bayer

Tight end Jamie Williams (right) took Dexter Carter under his wing until the Niners' number-one draft pick could get his act together. The two friends are shown keeping warm as the clock winds down in Green Bay.

Pat Terrell of the Rams (with ball) celebrates after picking off a Montana pass at Candlestick. The Niners give the ball away six times, and lose for the first time all season.

Jim Burt (left) and Matt Millen leave the field muddy and beaten. The mood is grim. It won't stay that way for long. The Giants are next.

On the afternoon of March 28, 1977, the owners of the National Football League voted unanimously to approve the transfer of the majority ownership in the San Francisco 49ers to Edward DeBartolo Jr. As the deal was structured, the figures put DeBartolo's purchase of 90 percent of the 49ers at $17 million. The remaining percentage of the team was still held by Franklin Meuli, who also owned the Golden State Warriors of the National Basketball Association, and the Morabito sisters, widows of the two brothers who had run the team in its early years.

The Prince was now on his own.

For most of its 41 years as a professional football franchise, the San Francisco 49ers had been nothing to speak of. There had been winning seasons and some very fine players over the years, but it always seemed that, in the end, when the Niners got close to something good, they always found a way to disintegrate. In 1957, two events symbolized the team's jinxed life. On October 27, before halftime of a game at Kezar Stadium against the Chicago Bears, Tony Morabito, the trucking executive who owned and founded the team, had a heart attack in the stands. Morabito did not live to see San Francisco play in its first NFL playoff game at Kezar that December against the Detroit Lions. After three quarters, the Niners led, 27–7. But three interceptions and two fumbles later, Detroit won 31–27. The Niners didn't make the playoffs again for 13 years. And even then they lost.

Although the team had regularly been stocked with a long list of star players—from Y. A. Tittle, Frankie Albert, and Joe Perry in the early years to John Brodie, Gene Washington, Jimmy Johnson, and Dave Wilcox later on—the Niners had always seemed to find a way to get just close enough to decency that the fans who followed them found it excruciating to get their hopes up every year only to have their heartstrings snipped by another 49er failure. To protect themselves, 49er fans girded for disappointment with a name. They called themselves the Faithful. For years, faith was offered but rarely repaid.

In the decade before Eddie DeBartolo bought the team, the Niners had gone even farther downhill. Since winning the NFC West title in 1972, only once had San Francisco won more games than it lost in a single season. When he bought the team, Eddie DeBartolo promised the Faithful he was going to make things better. He promised them that he was going to make their Niners into a winner, a team they would all be proud of. But things did not start out particularly well.

The Prince did not know San Francisco. And he had no idea how particular the Faithful were about their team. At one of his first press conferences as owner of the 49ers, Eddie DeBartolo Jr. casually declared, "You can be assured I'll get Frisco back on track." The Prince did not know he had irritated the Faithful, who considered his abbreviated reference to their home an insult of epic proportions. And then as Joe Thomas, DeBartolo's new general manager, began to make changes in the organization, some of the Faithful resisted. The Prince did not like such second-guessing. "Doesn't anybody around here realize we're running a business?" he snapped one day. "This is not a play toy. . . . We're not here to placate personalities." The Faithful did not like that kind of talk. And they bristled even more when, at a Chamber of Commerce luncheon, the Prince sniped: "I'm here to stay whether you like it or not."

On the street, it didn't take long before much of San Francisco had decided that the Prince was a snotty rich kid from the East who had no idea what San Francisco was all about or what he was doing with the city's beloved 49ers. The people of the city listened to the things the Prince said, and they listened to the way he said them, and they drew the conclusion that he clearly had no tact and was stuck on himself in the most annoying way. In the beginning, the Faithful were not the only ones who did not like their new Prince.

To the beat writers who covered the Niners, DeBartolo was too cocky for his—or their—own good. His brash manner made him seem obnoxious, and his phalanx of bodyguards made him look pretentious. Some reporters even looked at Eddie Jr.'s bodyguards and wondered if the old story about the DeBartolo family's links to organized crime were true. For the sportswriters, however, what matters came down to most was that they simply didn't think the Prince had what it took to turn the Niners around. He was a rich, naive kid, and they just didn't think he could cut it in the big time. They knew he was going to fall flat on his face. They just knew it.

For his first couple of seasons in San Francisco, the beat reporters had their own name for the Prince. They called him the Little Twerp and it was not because he was only five feet, seven inches tall. As bona fide experts on the game of professional football, the reporters were confident that, in time, the Niners would turn out just as bad as they always had. Then the Little Twerp would have to admit that he was in over his head, and that would prove to everyone that they were right. In the beginning, it looked like they would be.

Joe Thomas was determined to start over in San Francisco. Like Eddie DeBartolo Jr., Thomas had something to prove. Getting fired by the Colts had stung his considerable ego. Thomas burned to show the Colts that they had been wrong about him. He began by giving his new club a thorough housecleaning.

Shortly after taking command, Thomas fired San Francisco's popular head coach, Monte Clark, who the year before had directed the team to its first winning season since 1972. Joe Thomas was only warming up. He dismantled the staff, and ordered all of the photographs of the former 49er greats that hung on the walls at the team's offices in Redwood City taken down. He said he wanted them all burned. A public-relations assistant took them home and hid them in his basement instead. Thomas also told beloved 49er greats like Y. A. Tittle and Hugh McElhenny that their days of special privileges were over. He eliminated the children's section at Candlestick. He wiped out the cheerleaders. Joe Thomas even canceled the 49er Christmas card.

In two years, Joe Thomas turned a bad team into a horrible one. In 1977, the Niners were 5 and 9. The next year, things fell apart completely as they won two and lost 14, including nine in a row to set a new franchise record. Of the two drafts Joe Thomas was in charge of, not even one of the players lasted in San Francisco longer than a season.

To Eddie DeBartolo Jr., the losing was intolerable. Every other week, it was the same grim routine all over again. If the Niners were playing at home, Eddie and his wife, Candy, would fly to San Francisco. Almost every week, they watched Eddie's Niners get *embarrassed*. Then, Eddie and Candy would catch a red eye flight back to Ohio so Eddie could be at work on Monday morning to continue his duties as an executive in his father's corporation. The Prince was consumed with frustration. He had waited his whole life for a chance to do something he could call his own. And now that he finally had that chance, everything was going wrong.

Carmen Policy remembers what the losing was doing to Eddie DeBartolo. There was so much pain. Policy has known Eddie since the two met at a cocktail party in the early 1970s. That night, Policy remembers, "the chemistry" between them worked and the two became friends.

A few days later, Policy got a phone call from a secretary at the DeBartolo Corporation. A Youngstown attorney, Policy knew what the young woman was calling about. He had recently filed a lien for a client on a mall the DeBartolos were building. The secretary wanted to know if the Carmen Policy that Mr. DeBartolo had had the pleasure of meeting at the cocktail party was the same Carmen Policy who had filed a lien against the DeBartolo company. Policy said he was. The secretary said that Mr. DeBartolo was scheduling a meeting to discuss the project with his staff and would like him to attend. Policy said he would be there. When he hung up the phone, Policy figured that his budding friendship with Eddie DeBartolo was not going to last much longer. He was only a young lawyer, and Eddie DeBartolo was a young lion. Policy figured there was a good chance he would be eaten alive.

At the meeting a few days later, Policy explained his client's side in the matter. A chief of construction representing the DeBartolos explained the company's position. Eddie didn't say too much. He just listened. Finally, he had heard enough.

"I really think, after hearing all of this, that Carmen's client's right," Eddie said. "They have the money coming."

Two days later, The Edward J. DeBartolo Corporation cut Policy's client a check. Eddie had not eaten Carmen alive. A friendship was just beginning.

Carmen Policy sits cross-legged on a green hotel divan. It's the night before a road game. The 49ers' executive vice-president of front office and league relations is thinking back to 1978—and to what the losing was doing to Eddie.

"Every loss on the field was like a personal rejection of him. Every loss on the field was a personal failure by him. A loss on the field was like having someone in his family injured."

Policy pauses for half a minute, staring down. "Eddie will never be a good loser," Policy decides, finally. "He never accepts a loss. He has learned to handle them. Before, he couldn't accept or handle them."

Back in 1978, losing wasn't just something that was happening to Eddie DeBartolo. It was changing his whole life. He was not himself. If the 49ers lost on Sunday, it would be Wednesday before the door to his office was open again. And even when it was, Eddie was not always pleasant. Eddie had always been a worrier. About everything. Take popcorn.

When his three daughters were little, Eddie was scared to death when they made popcorn. He'd stand there and pick out every unpopped or small kernel. If he missed one, Eddie was sure that one of his girls would choke on it. Eddie worried about his girls at dinner, too. He stared at them while they ate, terrified that they weren't cutting their meat small enough. And no hard candy—that stuff was made to gag little girls. Or balloons. Balloons were bad, too. Eddie just knew that if he let his girls play with balloons, he would leave the room one day and when he came back he would discover to his everlasting horror that one—or all—of his girls had inhaled a damn balloon. Balloons were bad. No balloons.

Back in September, at the beginning of the quest for Three-peat, Eddie worried himself sick about what happened at a pub one night in Berkeley, a college town near San Francisco where one of his daughters goes to school. The way Eddie heard it, an Iranian gunman had barged into a pub, shot up the place, and taken hostages. Later, the guy made all of the white women with blond hair strip from the waist down. Even after Eddie's daughter told him she was nowhere near the pub that night, Eddie was still worried. *Is everything all right?* the Prince frantically asked his daughter. *Where were you that night? Did you ever go there?* Eddie told his daughter that he wanted a list of all the places at which she ate. That way, at least he could concentrate when he worried about her.

Eddie had always worried. And if he had to rationalize why he worried or how much he worried, then perhaps all of the worrying got him somewhere. Now that he owned the 49ers, though, worrying wasn't getting him anywhere anymore. The losing was ruining everything—even Eddie's and Candy's marriage wasn't as good as it had been.

Adding insult to injury was the way the Faithful treated their Prince at times. During one game at Candlestick, somebody threw a full can of beer down at him from the stands. The can conked DeBartolo right on the head. At another game, a fan spit in his face. "I was so steamed and so frustrated," DeBartolo once told *Sports Illustrated*. "I didn't know what to do. . . . All I could think was, 'What the hell am I doing here? I could be back in Youngstown playing golf.' "

Toward the end of San Francisco's nine-game losing streak in 1978, the press had become rabid. Many were calling for Joe Thomas's head. During one game that the Niners were losing, as usual, fans in the upper deck at Candlestick unfurled a banner that read, "BLAME JOE THOMAS." In the left corner of the banner, there was an axe. When security guards ordered the fans to roll up their message—according to the *San Francisco Chronicle*, the guards were acting on orders from "someone in the box of 49er . . . owner Eddie DeBartolo Jr."—most of Candlestick booed. The paying customers had made it quite clear how they felt about the man who was wrecking their Niners.

But the Prince was not about to give up on Joe Thomas. Because, as his father the King had taught him, he believed that the cardinal rule of running a successful organization was to treat employees like family, pay them like royalty, and fire them only for disloyalty. To Eddie DeBartolo, Joe Thomas was still family. Early in November, with his team in the throes of what would become the nine-game losing streak, the owner of the 49ers issued a public statement. DeBartolo announced that he had given Joe Thomas a four-year contract extension. The Prince wanted his embattled general manager to be family for a long time. It wasn't until a Monday several weeks later that Eddie DeBartolo changed his mind. When he finally realized that he was going to have to do what his father had always done in the construction business when a project didn't work out. Back up the truck and start over.

Shortly after 11 A.M. on November 27, 1978, Dan White, a former member of the San Francisco Board of Supervisors, walked into the second-floor office of Mayor George Moscone at city hall in downtown San Francisco. Seventeen days before, White had resigned from his seat on the board, claiming that his $9,600 salary wasn't enough to support his wife and baby. Five days later, however, White changed his mind and asked Moscone to reappoint him. But Moscone had already set the wheels in motion to find a successor. Board meetings were held to discuss what to do. There were heated debates over whether Dan White should be allowed to have his seat on the board back. One of the most vocal opponents of White's reinstatement was Harvey Milk, San Francisco's first gay supervisor. Eventually, the board ruled that White was out for good.

In the den adjoining the mayor's ornate office that November morning, Dan White fatally shot George Moscone four times. White then left the mayor's office through a side door and walked quickly to the other side of city hall. There, in the office he had once occupied, he shot and killed Harvey Milk. Thirty-five minutes later, Dan White turned himself in.

That night, the 49ers were scheduled to play the Pittsburgh Steelers at Candlestick on ABC's "Monday Night Football." But the football game was the least of Joe Thomas's worries. When he heard about the assassinations, Thomas spun into a panic. He told Eddie DeBartolo that he wanted the game canceled because he was afraid someone would try to shoot him, too. "I knew then," Eddie DeBartolo would say later, "that I had to make a change."

Early the following year, DeBartolo fired Joe Thomas. The new coach of the 49ers was Bill Walsh, who, in just two years, had turned the football program at Stanford University completely around. He had turned a loser into a winner. That was exactly what Eddie DeBartolo wanted him to do for the 49ers.

Five months later, Bill Walsh drafted a quarterback from Notre Dame named Joe Montana. In the eleventh round, Walsh picked a receiver from Clemson named Dwight Clark. In 1979, the Niners endured another long and horrible 2 and 14 season. But Eddie DeBartolo Jr. knew it was going to take time. And his team, he could see, was finally getting some good players. They were going to get better. He was sure of it.

By spring 1985, the Prince had been proven right twice. His Niners had gotten better. In January that year, San Francisco blitzed Miami to win its second Super Bowl in four seasons. The losing was all ancient history now. So was the "Little Twerp" label. Two Super Bowls had proven that he could cut it in the big time, that he most certainly was not in over his head. But there was something else now.

After the Niners beat the Dolphins, the now 38-year-old owner of the 49ers took a walking tour around his club's home stadium. DeBartolo was appalled. Candlestick, he could see, was a dump. The bathrooms were small and dingy. The same was true of the locker rooms and the concession areas. There were none of the dozens of luxury boxes he dreamed about—boxes that almost all of the other clubs had or were building in their stadiums. Parking was lousy, too, and fans always had a tough time getting to Candlestick, which sits on an outcropping of land at the edge of San Francisco Bay. Something, De-Bartolo realized, had to be done about Candlestick. His football team—his world champions—deserved better.

But there were two problems. First, the team's lease with the City of San Francisco bound the Niners to Candlestick until the year 2000. Second, the owner of the San Francisco Giants baseball team, Bob Lurie, had already been complaining about Candlestick for years and nothing had yet been done. When Lurie complained to the politicians in the city, DeBartolo knew full well that the answer Lurie got was always the same. *"Sorry, but the budget's tight and there just isn't enough money in the kitty right now."* Lurie, in fact, had been at it again in the wake of the Niners' latest Super Bowl win. On the last day of February, the Giants' owner announced that his team would not play at Candlestick after the 1985 baseball season. Lurie was sick and tired of Candlestick and he wanted out. Eddie DeBartolo Jr. knew full well that his lease with the city afforded him no political leverage whatsoever. Legally, he was locked in until the end of the century. He thought about the situation some more. Then he got an idea. He was going to drop a few bombs to see what might be shaken loose in the chaos.

The day after Lurie's press conference, Bill Walsh told a San Francisco radio station that the 49ers were unhappy with Candlestick. Walsh added that it made sense for both the Giants and the 49ers to work together to find a new stadium to play in. This was the first bomb. Up until this point, the 49ers had admitted that they had some problems with Candlestick, but that the problems were certainly things they could live with if a few minor improvements were made. Now, according to Bill Walsh, the team's official position had changed. San Francisco Mayor Dianne Feinstein was reeling at the news. First, it was the Giants who were leaving San Francisco. Now, there was the possibility that the 49ers—*the Super Niners*—might be taking off, too. Feinstein realized that she

had to do something—and quickly—or she just might go
down in history as the mayor who lost the 49ers. Nobody
had to tell Dianne Feinstein that that would be political
suicide.

Several days later, San Francisco was still buzzing in
the aftermath of the bomb Bill Walsh dropped. But, as
the city would soon see, that was only a small explosion
compared to the charges that Eddie DeBartolo Jr. was
about to detonate. In the space of a week, the owner of
the 49ers called Candlestick a "pigsty" and a "piece of
shit." He railed at the unsafe and unacceptable conditions at the stadium. He said he would move his Niners
elsewhere if something wasn't done. This was blitzkrieg.

"I don't know whether they can put enough money
into Candlestick to make it viable," DeBartolo told the
San Francisco Chronicle. "[Mayor Feinstein has] got to
show me they can. I really don't think that the thing can
be worked out, no matter how many dollars are put in
there. It probably would be easier to build a new stadium.
. . . When I walked through that place, alone, without
any fans there and without any players on the field or
anything else, and you look at that pigsty, then you really
know how bad that thing is. . . . The place has deterio-
rated so badly, in my humble opinion, they're in default
on the lease. . . . We'd just as soon stay within the boundaries of San Francisco, but if it can't work out, it can't
work out."

When a reporter suggested that his family was
wealthy enough to build its own stadium, DeBartolo continued his bombing run. "Forget all this crap about how
much money Edward DeBartolo has, or Edward DeBartolo Jr., or the DeBartolo Corporation. We have that
money because we worked hard for it, and I'm not going
to give it away when all these [other] teams are getting
things from cities that make their franchises a viable competitor. We deserve it [stadium improvements]. We've
been good for San Francisco."

In the *Chronicle,* Dianne Feinstein tried to sidestep the flak by saying only that she was "surprised" by what De-Bartolo had said about Candlestick. Other city officials, however, were not restricted by Feinstein's political considerations. One called what Bob Lurie and Eddie De-Bartolo were doing to Dianne Feinstein "Chinese water torture." Whatever it was, it worked.

Two days later, Dianne Feinstein flew to meet with DeBartolo in Phoenix, where the 49er owner was attending the NFL meeting. At a press conference on March 13, the mayor smiled, put her arm around the Prince, and reported that the city and the team had reached agreement on a plan in which the city was going to spend $25 to $30 million for a major facelift of Candlestick Park. The renovation was to feature the addition of some 10,000 seats; an expansion of the locker rooms, rest rooms, and concession areas; as well as parking improvements and a paint job. As the mayor spoke, Eddie DeBartolo smiled. The Prince had good reason.

Two key aspects of the deal were especially pleasing to the 49er owner. First, he was going to get more than 100 luxury boxes. Around the league, the Prince knew, teams were making millions leasing boxes out to politicians, CEOs, and other high rollers. The Prince badly wanted to get in on the action—so badly, in fact, that he agreed to spend $2.25 million up front to get construction of the first boxes going right away. There was also the matter of the parking and concession revenue. Under the terms of the team's original lease, the 49ers received no revenue from food and beverages sold at Candlestick during 49er games. Not a dime. The same was true of parking money. This fact had bothered DeBartolo for some time. "We're the reason those cars are out in the parking lot," he said once. "We're the reason people are buying hot dogs and beer. We deserve some of that money." Under the terms of the new lease—which was not finalized until August 1985, following several months of negotiations—the team would soon be entitled to 58 percent of the gross parking revenues at the stadium. The 49ers would also pull in 85 percent of the funds earned through concessions sales during football games.

To some in San Francisco, the Prince had thrown a tantrum. He had acted like a spoiled rich kid who always wants his way, and they let him have it with both barrels. In the *Chronicle*, Lowell Cohn blasted "Little Prince Eddie," who had "balled up his tiny fists and held his breath and stamped his feet" until "Lady Dianne" gave him a "new castle."

But even those who didn't appreciate the way DeBartolo went after what he wanted had to admit that his timing could not have been more perfect. "I thought he was a little bit inappropriate," remembers Quentin Kopp, the San Francisco supervisor who chaired the committee that negotiated the final deal with the 49ers on behalf of the city. "It was so stark. It came out of the blue. They had just come off this marvelous season, a Super Bowl, at Stanford. The whole area was upbeat, and boom, all of a sudden, Candlestick is a pigsty . . . and by God, he's going to break the lease and move the team out of Candlestick if something isn't done. Eddie DeBartolo is no saint . . . , but to put it in the vernacular, he scared the shit out of Feinstein. He knew exactly what he was doing.

"During the negotiations [that began shortly after Dianne Feinstein's press conference in Phoenix], I was skeptical," Kopp adds. "I remember at one of the meetings, he started making threats about breaking the lease. He said, 'I'll spend $20 million if I have to to get out of this lease.' I felt it was all just a negotiating ploy. I felt he was posturing. He and Carmen played this bad guy–good guy routine. Eddie would fly off the handle and Carmen would always bring things back to center. Carmen was a firm negotiator. And let me say one thing. Eddie DeBartolo put his money where his mouth was."

Money.
With the Prince, that's what it always comes down to.

The Prince loves to spend, especially on his football team. His player payroll is the highest in the National Football League—almost $27 million in 1990. That's more than some teams spend in two seasons. No problem. How can he not pay Joe Montana $4 million a year? Joe is the greatest quarterback around. Besides, Joe is family. So are Roger and Ronnie and Jerry. And so is Jeff Fuller, who still can't use his right arm because he got hurt playing football for the Prince in 1989. The day it happened, the Prince followed Fuller's ambulance to the hospital. Then he sat in Fuller's hospital room. He watched his football player cry. He cried. Later, the Prince couldn't stop thinking that he wasn't doing enough for Jeff Fuller. So he's sending him something— one-hundred thousand somethings every year for as long as Jeff Fuller wants them.

The Prince believes that everyone should be treated with respect. In fact, he demands it. He can't stand what happens on other teams, where one guy matters three times as much as another guy, and some guys hardly matter at all. That's why he has a one-heartbeat team. Everybody is as important as everybody else. The Prince demands a great deal from his people. He wants things to get done.

He gives them what they need to get things done. He takes care of his family. In the NFL, this means money. The Prince does what he can. Because he's the Prince, he can do a lot more than some. Most of the time, no price is too high to keep a 49er where he belongs. After his team won its second-straight Super Bowl in 1989, it looked like either the Phoenix Cardinals or the New York Jets were going to ask 49er offensive coordinator Mike Holmgren to become their new head coach. The Prince knew Holmgren works magic with Joe and Jerry and J. T., so he decided to give Mike Holmgren a raise to see if that might keep him happy. It did. Mike Holmgren makes more than some head coaches in the NFL. And he gets to keep coaching for the Prince.

There is also Steve Young, Joe Montana's understudy. Young is good enough to be playing in front of some other understudy. But Joe is Joe and there has never been anyone like him. So Steve Young stands on the sidelines. He wig-wags the plays in to Joe. Every once in a while, Joe has to come out of the game and Steve Young gets to go in. Most of the time when he's in the game, Steve Young is good. He is very good. The Prince wants Steve Young to know he appreciates the sacrifice he is making to stay with the one-heartbeat team. So he pays Steve Young more than anyone else on the Niners except Joe. More than Jerry. More than Ronnie Lott. And more than Roger Craig. Steve Young makes a lot more than George Seifert. To the Prince, it's worth it. Because that's the way you treat family. Like royalty.

Some of the other owners don't like the Prince because he has so much money to spend. They say he's got an unfair advantage over them because his father, the King, owns a company that's a bottomless well. All the Prince has to do, they say, is dip his bucket down in there and bring that pail up and he's got all he needs. The Prince doesn't care what the other owners think. He says they've got no business telling him how to run his team. Besides, it's not like he spends because he has to. He wants to. For a 49er, nothing is ever too good.

There's the Taj. The Taj has everything a football team could ever need to get ready to play. There's the single hotel rooms on the road. There's the charter airplane big enough so every player can have two seats. There's what happens when a 49er gets injured on the road and has to stay behind in a hospital: He gets to fly back to San Francisco in the Prince's company jet. There's the little things. When the wife of a 49er has a baby, the Prince sends flowers that usually weigh 10 times what the baby does. There's what happens when the Niners win their division—or when Easter rolls around. The Prince buys roses for every player and staffer to take home to give to his wife or his mom or his girl. There's what happened one Christmas. The Prince bought Neiman-Marcus gift certificates for every 49er's wife or girlfriend. The women are family, too.

The Prince loves to thank his family for all they do for him. In 1989, after his team won its third Super Bowl of the decade, the Prince flew all the players, their wives, girlfriends, dates, or just friends, plus the whole office staff, to Youngstown to celebrate. The Prince put everyone up for two nights at the Holiday Inn. Why the Holiday Inn? Because the Prince owns it. There was a fabulous gourmet dinner. The Prince hired the head chef from the Mayfair House hotel in Miami. He hired the pastry chef from the Beverly Hills Hotel. There were other chefs. There was a lot to eat—enough for 750 people. The menu included pasta, imported lobster, salmon, and an assortment of chocolates. Everything was served by models the Prince brought down from New York and trained to serve his guests. Jeffrey Osborne was there to sing. That was only the second night. The night before, the Prince closed his restaurant, Paonessa's, to the public and served dinner to his football family. When the players finally made it back to their rooms, the Prince's staff had left CD players, perfume, cologne, chocolates, and bottles of champagne. They did not forget fruit baskets.

The next year, the Prince had a problem. When his Niners won another Super Bowl, he had to figure out a way to do something nicer, something more memorable to thank them with, than he had the year before. So he treated everyone in his football family to a week in Hawaii. Meals were on him, and yet the Prince gave each player $600 to spend on food anyway. Then the Prince decided that he hadn't done enough. So he gave all the players another $500. Huey Lewis & the News sang at dinner. Huey is a Niner fan. Big time. Huey is family. The Prince had outdone himself.

He always does.

The bottom line.

Does the one-heartbeat team win because the Prince spends so much money? Jim Finks does not think so. Finks is the president and general manager of the New Orleans Saints. Back in 1968, some years after he'd played quarterback for the Pittsburgh Steelers and swatted baseballs in the Cincinnati Reds' farm system, Finks served on the first NFL negotiating committee that met with the players' association. Before he hooked on with the Saints, in 1986, Finks worked for 10 years in the Minnesota Vikings' front office. While he was in Minnesota, the Vikings went to the Super Bowl twice. After the Vikings, Finks was an executive with the NFL Management Council. Then he spent a decade building the Chicago Bears into a Super Bowl winner. In 1989, when the NFL was looking for someone to replace Pete Rozelle, who was retiring as commissioner, Finks was one of the leading candidates. Jim Finks knows football, knows the NFL.

Finks does not think the Prince—or any other prince—can buy a championship in the National Football League.

"There's no question that you've got to have the resources to compete in this league," Finks said one day during the quest. "But can you buy a championship in the National Football League? The answer is no. The 49ers were winning back in the early eighties when their payroll was one of the lowest in the league. I think they win Super Bowls because they've got leadership that starts at the very top. A lot of funny things can happen if you don't have leadership."

The King could not have said it better.

Chapter 13

Day and Night

I. Day

And it shall come to pass, that he who fleeth from the noise of the fear shall fall into the pit.

As a boy, one of Jesse Sapolu's favorite parts of the Bible was the Book of the Prophet Isaiah. In the Bible, Isaiah had visions through which God showed him the punishment, war, murder, and bloody rebellion that would take place in Judea and Jerusalem in the days ahead. Isaiah himself passed through horrible, wrenching trials. Pain and conflict were his constant companions. To Jesse Sapolu, Isaiah was an inspiration. Because Isaiah never let any of the visions or the violence or the calamities get to him. Isaiah never ran from the noise of the fear.

If any of Mike Sherrard's teammates knew what it was like to face the noise of the fear, it was Jesse Sapolu. In fact, the 49er center could top his teammate's three broken bones. By one. Three times between summer 1984 and summer 1985, Sapolu broke the same bone in his right foot. Then, when his right foot stopped breaking, he broke his left leg. For three entire seasons, Jesse only made it out of training camp on crutches. During those painful three years, when the one thing he wanted more than anything in the world was for God to heal him so he

227

could walk out on the football field again, Jesse Sapolu faced the noise of the fear. And somehow he did not fall into the pit.

The first time Jesse Sapolu broke his foot, he was working out on the Astroturf at Cook Field in Honolulu. It was a summer day in 1984, one week before training camp—Jesse's second as a 49er—opened at Sierra College. He was running sprints between the goal line and the 10-yard-line when he stopped and planted his right foot to run back the other way. As soon as he pivoted, the fifth metatarsal, a long bone on the outside of his right foot, gave way under his 260 pounds.

For Sapolu, the noise of the fear was deafening. It sounded like thunder. Inside his head and his heart, the thunderclaps were cracking, black and angry, leaving him with doubt and confusion. He could not hear. He could not think. He could only feel. And Jesse did not like what he was feeling. He felt out of control, like someone had strapped him into a bobsled at the top of an icy mountain. Then someone had tied his hands and his feet and let off the brake. On his bobsled, Jesse was hurtling down the mountain, toward a gaping, ugly crevice, and there was nothing he could do to stop himself. Except plead with the Lord. *Why now, Lord?* Jesse said in his prayers after he got hurt. *My career is just getting started. You let me start two games my rookie year, which was a hard thing for an eleventh-round draft pick to do. Now this. All of a sudden, everything wrenched to a stop. Why? Why? WHY????*

For Jesse Sapolu, God's answer was always the same. The thunder got louder.

Jesse had never been hurt. At Farrington High School in Honolulu, he had been an all-state lineman who played both ways in football, who played center and forward in basketball, who wrestled and threw the shot put and discus in track (his senior year, Jesse finished second in the state in the shot put). *He had never been hurt.* At the University of Hawaii, he had started three seasons and been named All-Western Athletic Conference at guard and center. *He had never been hurt.* And during his rookie year with the 49ers in 1983, he had played in all 16 regular season games as well as the playoffs against Detroit and Washington.

For Jesse Sapolu, being hurt was something new. And he was afraid. Of not being able to play a game he loved. And of what God meant by putting the injury in his life. He wondered. Was he supposed to quit football and do something else? Or was the injury just an obstacle he was supposed to overcome?

By the second half of the 1984 season, Jesse was miserable. The 49ers were on their way to the Super Bowl. Everybody could see that they were the best team in the league. And Jesse wanted desperately to be part of it all. He had never played in a championship game. Not in high school. Not in college. Never. Now his team was heading straight for the biggest championship game of all and he couldn't even walk on the field. In early November, the 49ers asked Jesse if he was ready to come back. Jesse knew he wasn't. He knew that the four-and-a-half-inch-long bone in his right foot—the one that had snapped in the middle when he was running in Hawaii—wasn't strong enough yet. But he wanted to play. He wanted to be out there on that field, to be part of something special, to show his friends back in Hawaii and his family in Los Angeles that *he* was something special. He wanted those things so badly it hurt inside. Jesse said he was ready.

He managed to make it through one game, a 41–7 49er blowout in Cleveland. Jesse played the whole fourth quarter, at both guard and center. Three days later, on a pass play in practice back in Redwood City, a 320-pound lineman named Louie Kelcher lumbered off the line and stepped on Jesse's right foot. The fifth metatarsal bone splintered again. This time, the noise of the fear thunderclapping inside Jesse's mind was even louder. He wanted to play so bad. He wanted to be a part of what he knew was a team that was going to the Super Bowl. But the fifth metatarsal bone just wasn't going to let him. Jesse knew that he had come back too soon. But nobody else did. They just thought Jesse was jinxed.

San Francisco's march to the Super Bowl in 1984 was the most painful time Jesse Sapolu had ever been through in his life. With Joe Montana throwing, Dwight Clark catching, Wendell Tyler and Roger Craig running, and a defense led by four defensive backs who would make NFL history by playing in the same Pro Bowl game together, there was little doubt that the 49ers were on their way to their second NFL championship of the 1980s. And even in a sport where the bonds between the men who go to war together are sometimes so deep they defy words, it was easy to describe what Jesse Sapolu felt like. He was not one of the boys anymore. He was an outsider. He was *invisible*.

On the outside, he was rooting for his teammates to achieve the greatness of which he knew they were capable. But on the inside, the noise of the fear rendered Jesse's cheering hollow. Jesse was glad for his teammates, but his heart wasn't in it. The noise of the fear began to work on him slowly, turning him into a person he did not know and did not like. With the thunder and the doubt and the pain booming inside him, Jesse retreated into a world of silence and self-pity. He became irritable, selfish, and angry. Often during the winter of 1984, Jesse would find himself sitting on the bed in his room at home staring at the wall. *Why did I have to go running that day?* he would ask himself over and over. Sitting by himself in the bedroom, Jesse told himself a million times that if he hadn't gone running that day, he wouldn't have broken his foot and he wouldn't have been hurting like he was right then. And if he wasn't hurting like he was right then, he would have been getting ready to play in the Super Bowl.

Jesse's second injury was hard on his family, too. Especially Melanie Ann, his wife. Sometimes, when she found Jesse sitting in the bedroom staring at the wall thinking about why he had to go running that day, she would try to help her husband listen to the thunder. She would say something soft, and she would touch Jesse gently. Or she would say nothing and just put her arms around him as if just by her touch she could make all the pain and anger and disappointment that was raging inside him go away. But she couldn't do that. Because Jesse didn't want comfort. He didn't want love. He wanted to play football. And so, when Melanie Ann would try to help him listen to the thunder, Jesse would glare at her and tell his wife to just leave him alone. Then, a little while later, he'd feel bad and he'd find her and apologize.

"It will never happen again," he would say.

But in two days, Jesse would be sitting on the bed staring at the wall thinking about why he had to go running that day—or about how his team was going to the Super Bowl and he wasn't—and Melanie Ann would put her arms around him and Jesse would grunt about how he wished she would just leave him alone. The noise of the fear was leading Jesse Sapolu closer and closer to the edge of the pit.

When the Niners bombed Miami in Super Bowl XIX, Jesse Sapolu snapped himself out of his funk. The Super Bowl was finally over, and the writers were all writing about how, with two Super Bowl wins in four years, the 49ers were a dynasty. All the talk made Jesse realize something. *If this team is a dynasty, there will be more Super Bowls.* Jesse Sapolu decided right then that playing in the Super Bowl would be his goal. All he had to do was ask God to heal him and then he would work his butt off. If he did those things, then he'd be ready when training camp rolled around for the 1985 season. Jesse Sapolu would no longer be on the outside looking in. He would be one of the boys again. He would be able to play football.

The next year, 1985, Jesse didn't make it out of training camp. Late in a morning practice on the second Monday of camp, Jesse pulled back from the line to block for a pass. This time, when the fifth metatarsal bone on the outside of his right foot broke in two, Jesse Sapolu told himself it was the end. He couldn't go through it all again. The time in the cast. The endless string of days spent sitting on the bed staring at the wall and wondering if he would ever be able to play football again. The excruciating agony and doubt over whether all of the effort and the waiting and the rehabilitation was going to be worth it in the end. But this time, there was a new sound added to the noise of the fear. And this new sound hurt more than any of the others.

Shortly after he broke his foot for the third time, Jesse began to hear the talk. Some of it was coming from the press. But it was also coming from behind his back, from people back in the islands and in Los Angeles—people he thought were his friends. *"Who does he think he's fooling?"* they were saying. *"He can't play." "Why doesn't he just give up, retire?" "He's just hanging around sucking the bucks out of the 49ers." "I don't know why they don't wise up and cut him."*

Jesse listened to the talk. In fact, the talk was one of the reasons he had tried to come back so soon after the first time he broke his foot. He wanted to be out there playing. And because he wasn't, Jesse felt like he was letting people down. As one of the few Hawaiians ever to play in the NFL, Jesse knew that his family and friends back in the islands and down in Los Angeles were all counting on him to make them proud. Jesse felt the burden. He wasn't just playing for himself. He was playing for all of Hawaii, all of Western Samoa, *all Polynesian people*.

And then there was the team. The 49ers were paying him good money for nothing. He was a prospect. That much he knew. The coaches said he was explosive and intelligent and a hard worker who had the right attitude and all the talent he would need to have a long career in the NFL. But what good are attitude and talent if a guy can't ever get out of training camp? Jesse felt like he was hiding. People were counting on him, and he was disappointing them. They were putting their faith in him and he was off hiding in the pool or the trainers' room, pulling down the bucks for doing nothing. Jesse wanted to play—wanted it more than anything he'd ever wanted in his life. But the people talking behind his back thought just the opposite. *"Who does he think he is?"* they sniped. *"Who does he think he's fooling?" "He can't play." "Why doesn't he just quit?"*

To Jesse, the sound of the thunder was so loud, it was all he could hear. There was no escaping the roar.

On the second Monday of training camp in 1985, in the moments after he broke his foot for the third time, Jesse Sapolu decided it was time to flee the noise of the fear. The frustration and the doubt were too much. The thunder was too loud. All he wanted was quiet. Quiet. While trainer Lindsy McLean was packing his foot for the trip to the hospital and surgery—this time, doctors would insert a three-inch screw in his foot to help strengthen the fifth metatarsal—Jesse decided he had come to the end. *The 49ers,* he thought to himself as McLean wrapped his leg in ice, *have been so patient with me. They've been so good to me. But they have to be tired of waiting to see whether I am ever going to be able to play. I'm gonna call it and they can put their faith in somebody else.*

Jesse Sapolu was sitting in a golf cart. He was on his

way down to the parking lot at Sierra College. He was on his way to the hospital when 49er head coach Bill Walsh stopped by. Jesse tried to flee the noise of the fear.

"Coach, I think I'm gonna call it," he said to Walsh.

"Don't be silly," Walsh answered. "You're still a young man. You can still have a long career. I want you to get some rest. Then I want you to try again."

Suddenly, everything was quiet. The 49ers, Jesse realized, were not tired of waiting for him. They weren't sick of his hanging on and sucking the bucks out of them. After two years of nothing but broken bones and frustration, the team still believed in him. Bill Walsh said so. Riding in the golf cart down to the parking lot for the trip to the hospital, something happened inside Jesse Sapolu. A thought flickered across his mind that made him feel warm, made him feel strong. It almost made him laugh.

I still believe in me, too, he thought.

It didn't make any sense, Jesse would say later. There he was, sitting in a golf cart on his way to the hospital for the third time in a year to fix the same broken bone in his foot. After two years of effort, misery, pain, and frustration, there he was sitting in a golf cart with the fifth metatarsal bone on the outside of his right foot broken in two and another year of rehabilitation ahead of him. And he was feeling warm inside, at peace, almost laughing to himself. How could that be? Because this time, Jesse knew, there would be no noise, no fear, no thunder. Bill Walsh had just paved over the pit with patience.

Jesse Sapolu changed in that golf cart at Sierra College. When Bill Walsh told him that he wanted him to get some rest and come back and try again, Jesse stopped listening to the talk. About how he was jinxed and how he should quit trying to fool the 49ers into thinking he would ever play in the NFL. Jesse Sapolu stopped listening to other people and started listening to himself. By accepting that he might never play football again, he stopped *being afraid* of never playing football again. By accepting the end, he was no longer afraid of it. And by accepting that he played football for himself and for his family and for God and not for the people who were talking behind his back, Jesse Sapolu found the strength and the purpose he had been searching for.

"I felt peace when I was finally able to let go of all the anger and the hate I felt inside, of trying to prove people wrong," Jesse said one day at the Taj. "I felt peace when I was finally able to stop trying to prove myself to other people and start worrying only about being the best football player I could be."

Jesse Sapolu was 24 years old when he broke his right foot for the third time. He had just been through enough pain and suffering for a whole lifetime in just one year. The cost had been high, but he had just learned a lesson that was invaluable.

He had learned how to survive.

But even as the light of a new way of life was dawning before him, darkness was about to return. There would be another broken bone in his future. And the voice who had first shown him how to survive would soon be silenced.

Jesse Sapolu sits crying. He's a five-, or six-, or eight-year-old kid growing up in Hawaii. One of the older kids in the neighborhood has just beaten him up again. So Jesse sits crying. His dad hears him.

"What's wrong, son?" Pa'apa'a Sapolu says.

"One of the older boys hit me."

"If you can't play with the big boys, don't play with them. Because they're just playing thinking you can take it."

Sometimes, Jesse stops crying. Other times, he keeps right on going. And gets mad at his dad.

Years later, Jesse Sapolu is talking about what his dad was trying to teach him those times he found his son crying after one of the older kids had hit him. "When my dad talked to me like that, he was telling me how life was going to be," Jesse decided. "In a way, it developed a certain character in me. Because I wanted to be able to say I played with the big boys."

Pa'apa'a Niu Sapolu, Jesse's father, was born in Western Samoa, a chain of islands between Hawaii and Australia, in 1921. His own father was a minister, and from the time he was little, Pa'apa'a harbored the same dream his dad had when he was little: To share the love of God with others. When he was in his mid-20s, Pa'apa'a enrolled in a theological college in Western Samoa. In 1950, a year after he had married Lila Manase, the daughter of a minister, Pa'apa'a graduated and took his wife on a Christian mission to Papua, New Guinea. The Sapolus spent almost seven years in New Guinea. Their first child, Esther, was born there in 1953. A second daughter, Va'aipu, was adopted in 1959, the same year a third daughter, Ata, was born. Nineteen fifty-nine was also the year Pa'apa'a received the call he had been waiting for. A church in Western Samoa needed a minister. At the time, Lila was pregnant with Ata. And going home meant a week on a ship. But the Lord was calling, so the Sapolus took the ship. They stayed 11 years on the Western Samoan island of Toamua. On March 10, 1961, Manase Jesse Sapolu was the fourth and final child born to the Reverend and Mrs. Pa'apa'a Sapolu.

In 1970, Jesse was in third grade when the church gave Pa'apa'a a year off and he and Lila moved the family to Los Angeles in search of better schools for their children. But after his year's vacation was up, Pa'apa'a got another call, this time from a church in Hawaii. The Sapolus moved again. They spent 12 years in Hawaii. Hawaii is where Jesse Sapolu grew up.

At home, Jesse remembers that discipline was the law of the land. Forget to take out the garbage, and pay the price. Go down to McDonald's on your skateboard when you are supposed to be picking up leaves in the yard, and pay the price. Decide that goofing off is more important than doing your homework, and pay the price. Get caught watching NFL games on television when you are supposed to be in Sunday school, and pay the price. And talk back to your dad?

"That," Jesse remembers, "would be your worst nightmare. You didn't talk back to my dad." Jesse and his sisters can still remember some of the spankings they got when they talked back to Pa'apa'a Sapolu.

Of course, life in the Sapolu family wasn't all discipline. Jesse remembers that there was also plenty of love—even if he had to share it with the rest of the kids in his church. All through high school, the routine was the same. It didn't really matter whether Jesse was playing football or basketball. On Friday nights, Lila, Esther, Va'aipu, Ata, and usually a cousin or two would all pile in cars and go to Jesse's games. Pa'apa'a Sapolu would go to a different game. Because, most of the time, there would be another kid who went to the church—but to a different high school than Jesse—who was playing at the same time. So there was a choice to make. And Pa'apa'a made the choice that he felt he had to make as the spiritual leader of his church. He would go to the other kid's game instead of Jesse's. It was duty. It was love. "My dad wanted to make sure that he showed the other parents that he was just as interested in their kids as he was in his own," Jesse once explained his dad's choice. "He wanted to show people that he loved everybody equally. And he did. My dad loved everybody."

Jesse says Pa'apa'a did enough to make sure he knew his dad loved him, so Jesse got used to his father not watching his games. From high school through college, Pa'apa'a Sapolu sat in the bleachers for only a handful of

his son's games. During Jesse's rookie season with the
49ers, Pa'apa'a made the trip up from Los Angeles—
missing a Sunday service—just once, against the Dallas
Cowboys. The Cowboy game was the last weekend of the
season, and San Francisco needed a win to capture the
NFC West title. For Jesse, it was like high school all over
again. His mom was there. So were two of his sisters. And,
for one of those rare times, so was his dad.

For Jesse, it was a special night. The Niners whomped
the Cowboys, 42–17, and won the division. After the
game, Jesse and his family went out for a quiet Chinese
dinner. At one point during dinner, Pa'apa'a turned to
his son and admitted two things. "Son, I really didn't
think you guys could beat Dallas. But your guys impressed me tonight." Pa'apa'a Sapolu told his son how
proud he was to be there to watch his son play. Jesse
couldn't remember ever being as happy as he was right
then.

But then, of course, his fifth metatarsal bone kept
breaking, and Jesse Sapolu was as miserable as he could
ever remember being. And by the summer of 1986,
Pa'apa'a Sapolu was also having his own health problems.
He had high blood pressure and diabetes, and as Jesse
was getting ready to go to training camp, his dad's condition worsened. Pa'apa'a was not so sick that he had to go
to the hospital—not yet—but he was sick enough that he
could no longer carry out his responsibilities at the
church. So he resigned.

Jesse says his dad was as ill as he was because he didn't
follow the doctor's exact orders when it came to his medication. "My dad was one who just wanted to live life and
be happy," Jesse remembers. "He believed that 'When it's
my time, it's my time.' He was from the old school, and he
didn't believe in all the medication and the things the
doctors wanted him to do to help his diabetes." Pa'apa'a
Sapolu believed that things such as how long a person

lives should not be left up to doctors. Things like that, he believed, should be left up to God.

During the fall and winter of 1986, Jesse Sapolu and his dad talked a lot about the things in life that should be left up to God—and those that should be left up to people. It was football season again, but Jesse was not playing football. He was on the mend from another injury, this time to his left leg. It happened on a running play in a morning scrimmage in Rocklin. Jesse fired off the line, made his block, and went down in a pile of players. While he was down, a teammate fell on his leg. Like walloping a piece of kindling with a two-by-four, the weight of his teammate's body snapped Jesse's fibula, the larger of the two bones in the leg, just above the ankle.

For the fourth time in three years, Jesse had a choice to make. Quit. Or try again. A year before, sitting in the golf cart after he'd broken his right foot for the third time, Jesse had changed, gotten stronger, accepted the fact that football was finite. And although the fourth broken bone brought no thunder, and the noise of the fear was not nearly as bad, Jesse Sapolu was still wondering what to do. *Is it time to quit?* he asked himself. *Is God trying to tell me something? Maybe it's time to move on and do something else with my life.* Jesse was looking for a sign, an omen, that would tell him whether he should try to come back one more time. He got two.

The first came at the hospital in Davis after he broke his leg in the pileup. Bobb McKittrick, the 49er offensive line coach, paid a visit to Jesse's room.

"I want you to go home and relax," McKittrick told his young lineman. "Take all the time you need. But if you feel like your leg is going to be well enough for you to come back and play, then I want you to come back. Because I know you can play in this league."

McKittrick's visit made Jesse feel better. After three seasons of broken bones, the team *still* was willing to wait for his talent to come to fruition on the field. Jesse still

wanted to play. Because, like the last time he broke his
foot, he knew inside that he *could* play in the NFL. It was
just a matter of enduring the pain of being hurt again.
But, now, with another broken bone, he wasn't sure anymore. And before he could be sure that trying again was
the right thing to do, there was one other person he had
to talk to.

Shortly after McKittrick's visit to his hospital room,
the 49ers gave Jesse permission to spend the early part of
his rehabilitation time in Southern California. Although
his dad's diabetes and high blood pressure were acting
up, Jesse and his father could still talk. One of the topics
Jesse kept returning to day after day was the backbiting
—the snide little comments people were making behind
his back. One day, when Jesse brought up the subject,
Pa'apa'a interrupted his son. He saw the anger and the
resentment consuming Jesse, and that was not the kind of
son he had raised.

"Son," Pa'apa'a said, "you have to be at peace with
yourself. If you really feel like you can come back from
this injury, then I want you to try. But you must be the
one to make the decision." For Jesse, hearing the words
from someone he respected such as his dad, "was like a
signpost telling me that I'm supposed to try this road one
more time." He was not going to quit. He was going to try
again.

Pa'apa'a Sapolu died on November 11, 1986, more
than nine months before his son would finally make it out
of training camp to play football for the first time in four
seasons. The day of the funeral, more than three months
after he'd broken his leg in the pileup, Jesse was still limping. He was in pain. But there was no way he would miss
carrying his dad's casket.

After the service, Jesse was riding in the hearse at the

head of the funeral procession. At one point, the driver picked up his walkie talkie and called back to the policeman who was trailing the procession.

"What's the count?" the driver asked.

"Sixty-one," the cop replied.

Jesse was highly offended. After all, here he was on his way to the cemetery to bury his dad, the man who had taught him how to love and how to survive, and all the driver of the hearse cared about was how many cars were in the funeral procession. Later at the reception, Jesse still burned over the comment. He mentioned it to a friend. The friend, however, saw the incident in an entirely different light.

"How many cars were there in the procession?" Jesse's friend asked after he had had Jesse repeat the conversation.

"Sixty-one."

Jesse's friend paused. Both of them knew that 61 was not just the number of cars in Pa'apa'a Sapolu's funeral procession. Both of them knew full well that 61 was Jesse's number with the 49ers.

"You know what I think?" Jesse's friend said, finally. "I think it means your dad is going to protect you from now on."

Jesse thought about that for a minute. In a way, what his friend said made sense. His dad had spent most of his life serving the Lord. And there was no reason to think that just because he had now passed away that his spirit could not somehow remain alive to help those he loved most. At the reception, though, Jesse was still mad at the hearse driver, so he let his friend's theory go. But by that evening, when the family piled out of the car to go in the house after the reception, Jesse had decided that his friend was right. His old man was going to protect him. Of that, there was no doubt in his mind. Because he had just passed the signpost. Those 61 cars.

Jesse Sapolu made it back. In 1987, he played in 12 of San Francisco's 16 regular season games. When left guard Guy McIntyre went down with an injury in New Orleans right before Halloween, Jesse filled in. The next week, against the Rams, he was in the starting lineup for good. In 1988, Bill Walsh's last year as head coach of the 49ers, Jesse started every game as San Francisco survived a rocky regular season and marched through playoff games with Minnesota and Chicago to earn a trip to the Super Bowl for the third time in eight years. On January 22, 1989, Jesse Sapolu was standing in the tunnel at Joe Robbie Stadium in Miami, waiting to be introduced before the biggest game of his life. With a whole stadium—and more than 110 million television viewers—waiting for the game to start, Jesse flashed back to what his friend had said the day of his dad's funeral more than two years before.

You know what I think? I think it means your dad is going to protect you from now on.

Jesse started to cry. It didn't even make sense. His dad had hardly ever been there to watch him play. He had always been at some other kid's game. But Pa'apa'a Sapolu had seen Jesse go through three years of broken bones and frustration. He had seen all of that. His dad, Jesse knew inside, had also been the one who taught him how to survive. How to find peace in his heart and his life and how to let God take care of everything else.

But to Jesse, standing there in the tunnel waiting to play the Cincinnati Bengals for all the marbles, it didn't matter that his dad had never been there to watch him play. It didn't matter that there were 61 cars in his dad's funeral procession and that he thought that meant his dad was going to protect him from now on just as he protected all of the people in all of the churches in which he had ever preached. To Jesse, none of that mattered at all right then. Because Jesse didn't want his dad protecting him. He wanted him there at Joe Robbie watching him play football. To see for himself that his son could play with the big boys.

October 28, 1990. The game between the 49ers and the Browns had just started at Candlestick. As NBC opened its broadcast, the network flashed the customary graphic of the starting offensive line unit of the San Francisco 49ers. Play-by-play man Charlie Jones ticked off the names one by one. When he got to the center, Jones told a national television audience that Jesse Sapolu was "having an outstanding year—an all-pro year." In fact, the All-Pro Team· for the National Football League would not be announced for more than two months yet, but would this year, his second full season at center, be the year Jesse Sapolu made it?

"Maybe," Jesse said a few days after the game. "Maybe."

But there was more to his answer than that. The laughing brown eyes and the smile betrayed a deeper feeling. All-Pro would be nice, Sapolu's face said. To have the recognition as one of the best players in the NFL at his position would be a very proud moment indeed. But was being named All-Pro *important?* The face said no. At least not now.

Deep down inside, number 61 already had something that the All-Pro team couldn't give him. At the halfway point in the drive for Three-peat, Jesse Sapolu already had the knowledge that he was doing everything he possibly could to help his team win the little battles in the larger war. He was doing the best he could. God would take care of the rest. To Jesse Sapolu, that was all that mattered. He was at peace.

He was having the best year of his life.

II. *Night*

As the quest reached late October, Chet Brooks knew exactly what kind of season he was having. It was not the kind of season Jesse Sapolu was having. It wasn't even close. For Chet Brooks, the starting strong safety for the Niners, four words covered what kind of season he was having. No matter what time of day it was. No matter what day of the week it was. Whether he was dressing or whether he was undressing. Whether he was reading the sports page at his locker or whether he was coming off the field right after practice.

"What's up?" someone would ask Chet.

And he would answer, "Same shit. Different day."

The words were simple. It was impossible to miss their meaning. But for Chet Brooks, the four words had to do with far more than just living through the same stuff on different days. They had to do with Chet not being out there, in the flow like he always had been. They had to do with Chet getting beat for a touchdown by Ozzie Newsome in the back of the end zone at Candlestick with the game on the line and the team depending on him to come through. They had to do with bad timing and frustration and why lousy things happen to good people in the world. And they had to do with commitment and sacrifice and why a 24-year-old man devotes much of his life to playing football on a field better than anybody else, and if he can't do that then the man doesn't quite look at himself in the mirror the same way anymore.

Chet Brooks's four words had to do with all of those things. But more than anything, the words had to do with a difference. The difference between this season and last. With the fact that this season has been nothing like last season.

In 1989, Chet Brooks became a star. In just his second season in the National Football League, Brooks managed to do what many said an eleventh-round draft pick with a bad right ankle and a bad left knee couldn't do: make it in the NFL. While San Francisco's explosive offense was getting most of the attention in the press, the 49er defense was actually the foundation upon which the Niners' second-straight Super Bowl season was built. And if defense led to the mugging of the Broncos in New Orleans, then Chet Brooks was most certainly one of its ringleaders. Because from the Hoosier Dome in September to the Superdome in January, Brooks had been out there, in the flow, in the middle of it all.

To Brooks, it didn't matter who the guy was. Eric Dickerson. Randall Cunningham. Dave Meggett. Thurman Thomas. Herschel Walker. Superstar or second-string, if a guy came in his direction, most of the time the guy got up trying to remember the license number of the truck that hit him. Brooks finished the regular season with 76 tackles—second only to linebacker Michael Walter. Brooks also picked off three passes, including one in the NFC divisional playoff game against the Vikings and another against the Broncos in the Super Bowl.

But Chet Brooks did more than make big plays in 1989. He made big plays when the team needed big plays —times when the team was depending on someone to come through and be a leader. When Ronnie Lott was out for five games with a bad ankle, it was Chet Brooks who stepped into the hole and started dishing out the big hits in the Niner secondary. And when Jeff Fuller, the Niner starting strong safety, was hurt playing New England, it was Chet Brooks who stepped up and started dishing out the big hits on San Francisco's march to New Orleans. For Chet Brooks, 1989 had been the breakthrough season he'd been working for since his junior year of high school back in Dallas, when the Division I recruiters started coming around. Until 1989, about all anybody in San Francisco knew about Chet Brooks was that he went to the same school Jeff Fuller did. John Madden changed all that.

A week before the Super Bowl against the Broncos, the former Raider coach unveiled the members of his coveted All-Madden Team on CBS. There were 22 players on the roster. Marquee names mostly. Tim Harris of the Packers. Richard Dent and Dan Hampton of the Bears. Reggie White and Jerome Brown of the Eagles. Lawrence Taylor and Leonard Marshall of the Giants. Ronnie Lott and Matt Millen of the 49ers. But right up there in bright lights with the big shots was Chet Brooks, the eleventh-round pick from Texas A&M. The guy with the bad right ankle. The guy with the knees of an old man. The guy who had to take the ribbing from his buddies back in Dalls when the 49ers made him the three hundred third player picked in a draft of 336.

"Hey, Chet, whaddya gonna do, man?" his buddies teased. *"Eleventh rounders don't make it in the big league. Everybody knows that. What makes you think you're different?"*

The talk—and the implication that he wasn't good enough to play in the major leagues—had rankled Brooks big time. "I've always been a fighter," he said at the Taj one day. "If somebody said, 'You can't do something, I'd do it just to prove a point. Not being drafted until the eleventh round was like telling me that I couldn't play football in the NFL, that I wasn't good enough. That motivated me, because I knew I could do the job."

But if the talk bothered Brooks, he also knew the talk wasn't without foundation. He knew that most of the time guys from the eleventh round *don't* stick around in the NFL. He knew that most of the time guys who get drafted that low get cut by two or three clubs and then end up coaching at some backwater college or teaching PE or sitting around the gym telling tall tales about the high school glory days when they were better than everybody else and everybody else knew it. Chet knew that no matter how determined he was to prove himself—to prove that he was a better football player than the three hundred third pick in the draft would indicate—the odds were against him. The odds, he knew, dictated that football players drafted in the eleventh roung generally don't do what he did to Thurman Thomas of the Buffalo Bills at Candlestick on a December day in 1989.

Ever since he walked onto the football field at Willow Ridge High School in Missouri City, Texas, Thurman Thomas had been one of the finest running backs in the country. A Parade All-American and all-state player during his senior year in high school, Thomas got even better at Oklahoma State University. In four seasons, Thomas chewed up more yards on the ground—4,595—than any running back except Nebraska's Mike Rozier ever had in the Big Eight Conference. As a sophomore, Thomas ran for 1,650 yards and was named a first-team All-American by the Associated Press. As a senior, Thomas finished seventh in the voting for the Heisman Trophy. In 1989, his second year with the Bills, Thomas gained more yards running and receiving than anyone in the NFL. That year, Thomas played in Hawaii in the Pro Bowl with the premier players of the National Football League.

But at Candlestick on December 17, 1989, Thurman Thomas was just another running back. Chet Brooks was the reason. Once, after Thomas had faked Brooks out for a nice gain, Chet heard someone yelling at him from the Bills' bench.

"PICK UP YOUR DRAWERS, CHET," the voice sneered. "PICK UP YOUR DRAWERS."

Brooks lost it.

"Your ass is mine," he hissed at Thomas as the two players walked back to their huddles.

On the next play, Brooks thundered into the Buffalo backfield and knocked Thomas down for a 5-yard loss.

"That," Brooks barked, "was *my* turn."

Brooks made seven tackles against the Bills that day. He knocked down a pass. And in the fourth quarter he picked off a pass that killed a Buffalo drive and put the game away for the Niners. On the stat sheet, Chet Brooks had led San Francisco to a 21–10 win. But out on the field, everybody who watched him knew how Chet had taken over the game with his hitting and his will. And *that,* Brooks knew, was the kind of thing a guy drafted in the eleventh round generally doesn't—can't—do in the NFL. It just isn't done. But Chet Brooks did it, and his name was right there on CBS, on the All-Madden Team at the end of the year.

For Brooks, though, just being on Madden's team wasn't the best part about the whole thing. It wasn't the trophy he got, or the sweat jacket with the All-Madden logo on it. What meant something to Chet—because it showed all of America that he *was* good enough to play in the major leagues—was what Madden said about him when he announced the team.

"When Chet Brooks hits you, you're stopped," Madden had said as the images of Brooks slashing in to attack a running back and dropping deep to pick off a pass filled the screen.

When Chet Brooks hits you, you're stopped. As people listened to the words, they pictured Madden up in the booth, waving his arms and hollering, his face getting redder and redder, as if he was about to burst several blood vessels. And as they pictured Madden getting so worked up, they realized that the guy he was getting all worked up over was Chet Brooks. And then they thought about Chet Brooks in a way they'd never thought about him before. This wasn't just some guy from the eleventh round anymore, a throwaway pick who'd gotten lucky and had a couple of good games. Chet Brooks was a thunderous, big-time hitter, a rough, tough football player, the kind that John Madden, the football player's football coach, could get all worked up over—worked up enough to name him to the All-Madden Team and say on national television, "*When Chet Brooks hits you, you're stopped.*"

For Brooks, such success was sweet vindication. He had been telling people all along what he could do in the NFL if he got the chance. Ever since he was four, he had badgered the older guys in the neighborhood to let him play tackle with them on the streets in Dallas. In 1989, when he finally got his shot, Brooks had done exactly what he said he could.

But then the season for the ages was over and the next one was starting. And Chet Brooks thought he should be making more money. So he held out during a month of training camp while his agent tried to convince John McVay and Eddie DeBartolo to bend the 49er policy of not renegotiating player contracts before their terms were up. In the end, Chet got the raise he was looking for—a bump up from the bargain-basement $90,500 he made during his All-Madden year to a reported $400,000—but the month he missed put him behind. First, Dave Waymer was playing in his place in the nickel defense because he had missed most of camp and wasn't in game-shape yet. Then, when Chet was in game-shape and getting his timing back to deliver the big hits just like he did last year, Waymer, the 10-year veteran from New Orleans, was sprinting around the field like a rookie and Brooks was still on the bench when the nickel team went into the game.

Chet was frustrated by the whole thing. After all, ever since he was four years old, he had always been out there on the field, in the flow, every play. Now he wasn't. But he wasn't complaining publicly. Brooks wasn't griping to the press. Mostly because he didn't want his unhappiness to become a distraction to the team. But it was also because he figured that he would just keep hitting and eventually things would work out in his favor. "The cream always rises to the top," Chet said one day early in the season.

And that's always the way things had worked out for Chet Brooks. He had risen to the top. He had hit the hardest and he had hit the longest. He had always been the one standing at the end of the war when all the fighting was over. It had always been that way, and there was every reason for him to think that as long as he kept hitting, it would always continue to be that way.

But little did Chet Brooks know that when the cream rose to the top in 1990, it would be Ozzie Newsome who would be sitting at the top of the vat of cream looking down at Chet. And Chet would be gasping and sputtering to stay alive in the wake of that humiliating touchdown in the end zone at Candlestick three days before Halloween. Ten months after John Madden told America that *when Chet Brooks hits you, you're stopped,* 10 months after he had finished the best season of his life with an interception in the Super Bowl, Chet Brooks's cream had not only *not* risen to the top, but it had spoiled.

When Chet Brooks thought about the way things were going for him during the early stages of San Francisco's quest for Three-peat, it seemed like such a long fall in such a short time. One year, he had been everything he had ever wanted to be. The next year, he was nothing. For Brooks, being everything one minute and nothing the next was a completely new experience. But in one way, it was very familiar. Because it had happened before. To his best friend in the world.

"Chet, I can't move. I'm cold."

Jeff Fuller lay frozen on his back on the grass. His eyes were as big as quarters. His voice was a whisper.

"Chet, I can't move. I'm cold."

It was October 22, 1989. On the second play of the 49ers' game against the New England Patriots, Jeff Fuller had darted in from free safety, up into the hole off the left side of the line of scrimmage. There he met John

Stephens, a 215-pound New England running back. Fuller lowered his head to make the tackle and thumped—*BMMMMPP!!!*—into Stephens. John Stephens went down. So did Jeff Fuller. Stephens got up. Fuller did not.

Chet Brooks figured Fuller was just dinged. Seconds behind Fuller to the point of the collision, Brooks was stoked. *Yeah, Jeff, way to knock this guy's shit out,* he was thinking, not knowing that the force of the tackle had just severed nerve endings—the nerves that control the use of the right arm—in Jeff Fuller's neck. Brooks reached down to help Fuller up. What he saw and heard when he looked down into Fuller's helmet made him wish for the first time in his life that he was anywhere but a football field.

"*Chet,*" Jeff Fuller said, "*I can't move. I'm cold.*"

The words came out in a whisper, a hoarse, scared panic that did something to Chet Brooks inside that nothing or no one had ever done to him before. It made him wonder. *What am I doing out here?* Brooks was asking himself as the number of trainers working on Jeff Fuller grew and grew. *What am I doing out here? What does football mean?*

"I just froze," Brooks remembered later. "I couldn't say nothing. I motioned to the sidelines [for help]. But I never took my eyes off Jeff. I just kept looking down into his eyes. They were racing a million miles an hour, like he was searching for something. I'd never seen nothing like that look before. I'd seen people get hurt before, but this was worse than somebody getting hurt. This was Jeff."

Jeff.

In 1988, his rookie year with the 49ers, things had not gone Chet Brooks's way for the first time in his football life. In 1987, the 49er defense had allowed the fewest yards of any defense in the NFL. The secondary was full of stars. Ronnie Lott, Jeff Fuller, Don Griffin, and Tim McKyer were the starters, and that meant that Chet was playing only a few downs in the nickel and on special teams. Late in the year, he hurt his left knee. He finished the year on injured reserve.

For Chet, the situation was the most frustrating he had ever been in. He was a football player, and football players don't play 10 plays in practice and then take a knee and watch the other guys do it for the rest of the day. Chet wanted to play, wanted to prove to everyone— including himself—that this eleventh-round draft pick had the stuff to make it in the NFL. But with Ronnie Lott, Jeff Fuller, and the others manning the secondary, there just wasn't room for Chet. Not yet. Chet was ready to explode. Fortunately, there was someone he could talk to. There was one person who knew how frustrated, how lonely, and how ready to explode he was. *Jeff.*

Fuller and Brooks had everything in common. Both were from Oak Cliff, a middle-class neighborhood in Dallas. Both had been playing football—first in the street, then on sandlot fields, and later in organized games with uniforms and everything—ever since they were old enough to run. Both had played football in the defensive factory at Texas A&M in the relentless Southwest Athletic Conference. And now in 1988, both were playing defensive back in the NFL for the San Francisco 49ers. Fuller had arrived in San Francisco four seasons before Brooks. And if he had empathy for what Chet was going through, it was because he had been through the frustrating times himself. In 1984, Fuller's rookie season in San Francisco, all four members of the Niner secondary—Lott, Carlton Williamson, Dwight Hicks, and Eric Wright—went to the Pro Bowl. It was the first time in NFL history that all four members of a secondary had played together in the same Pro Bowl game. It took Jeff Fuller three seasons to make it into the starting lineup. Jeff Fuller knew about being patient, about waiting for his turn to play.

But knowing that someone else knew what he was going through and having someone to talk to about his problems didn't make Brooks's frustration go away. Nothing could change the fact that Ronnie Lott was still around, not playing cornerback anymore like he was when Fuller came up, but playing free safety. Nothing could change the fact that Jeff Fuller was now a fixture at free safety. And nothing could change the fact that both starting cornerbacks, Don Griffin and Tim McKyer, were holding out, and that former Pro Bowl cornerback Eric Wright was nursing a painful groin injury. With only room for two safeties on the field at the same time, and with gaping holes at both corners, it meant that Chet Brooks was spending his practices doing one of two things. Filling in at cornerback. Or down on one knee watching Ronnie Lott and Jeff Fuller play safety.

Brooks had never sat anywhere on any bench and watched anybody play football. And Brooks had never been bashful in his life. So, faced with the possibility of not getting a chance to show what he could do in his first season as a professional football player, Brooks confided his fears and his frustrations to his best friend in the world. *Jeff.* "He would always tell me," Brooks said one day at the Taj. " 'I know what you're going through. I've been there. Just be patient. Your time will come.' How was I supposed to know—how was anybody supposed to know—that my time would come when he got hurt and couldn't play?"

Brooks was at his parents' house in Dallas on that April day in 1988, the second day of the National Football League's college draft. In the weeks before the draft, a host of NFL teams had called and asked him to come work out for them. The Raiders were the most interested, going so far as to ask him if he'd consider switching from his last college position—strong safety—back to his first—cornerback. Brooks didn't really want to play corner, so he told the Raiders he didn't know if he could do that. "I don't know how I'll recover from this."

This was a broken ankle he'd gotten on a blind-side cheap shot against Texas in the last regular season game of his college career at A&M. The play was a run to the opposite side of the field, and Brooks had no chance to do anything about it. So he let up, quit running. Just after he had planted his right foot in the Astroturf, a Longhorn receiver raced in from his blind side and dove at his knee. Chet went down. He was mad. He whirled around and barked at the ref.

"ARE YOU GONNA CALL THIS BULLSHIT?!"

There was no call. Then Chet tried to walk. He fell down before he could take a step. He still has five screws and a plate in his leg.

The broken ankle was what scared a lot of the NFL clubs away. A lot of the scouts who watched him on film thought Chet Brooks was a great ballplayer. But none of them could be sure how his broken right ankle would mend. None of them could be sure whether he would be able to run the way he used to run. None of them could be sure whether he would be able to keep up with the speed merchants who catch passes in the NFL. Brooks, on the other hand, knew his leg would heal. But what he didn't know about—and what most of the NFL scouts were even more afraid of than his broken right ankle—was whether his left knee would hold up.

The scar is about six inches long. It snakes its way up from below the kneecap, up over the top of the knee, ending before it reaches the thigh. Chet calls it his "conversation piece." The injury that left the scar behind is a dislocated kneecap that he suffered in a game against Baylor his sophomore year at A&M. He was covering a receiver on a post route when he planted his foot in the turf. The next thing Chet knew, his kneecap was facing

sideways and he was in the hospital listening to some doctor telling him how he would be lucky to walk normally
again let alone play football. Chet remembers thinking
how full of bullshit the doctor was for telling him he was
never going to play football again.

But Brooks also remembers how much the whole
thing scared him. Sitting there in the wheelchair listening
to the doctor, Chet Brooks realized that he had come to a
critical point in his life.

"I couldn't call my mother and ask her for help," he
said later. "My life was up to me now. I had a choice. I
could quit. Or I could move on. I was young, and I still
wanted to play. And I've never been a quitter." Brooks
thought about things for about five minutes. He decided
to move on.

At A&M, the decision looked like the right one. When
he was healthy, Brooks was a force, a reckless hitter who
forced offenses to make mistakes. As a junior, Brooks
made the All-Southwest Conference team. And as a
senior—when he was moved from cornerback to safety
—the Associated Press named him honorable mention
All-American. But then, against Texas on Thanksgiving
Day 1987, in his final regular season game as an Aggie, a
Texas Longhorn raced in from Chet's blind side and
splintered his ankle in two. Chet knew deep down that
the ankle was no problem. It would heal. But the NFL
scouts weren't so sure. About the ankle, or the knee he'd
hurt two seasons before.

And the scouts were the ones who were going to have
most of the say about whether Chet Brooks was going to
get a chance to become a professional football player.

One play from a game during his junior year typifies
the kind of football player Chet Brooks was at Carter
High School in Dallas. It was in 1983. The opponent was
Kimball High School, Carter's bitter neighborhood rival.

Games between Carter and Kimball are like the fights between two tough guys who want the same girl. Long, bitter, and vicious. On the Astroturf that winter day, Chet Brooks was all of those things—and more. That winter day, Chet Brooks made a statement to everyone in the stands: He could play football better and harder than anybody on the field.

The play came on Kimball's first series. Chet lined up at right cornerback. At the snap of the ball, a running back slashed to his left, toward Chet's side of the field. As the runner reached the corner, it was just him and Chet.

"I'll never forget that hit as long as I live," remembers Alex Gilliam, then an assistant coach at Carter. "Chet penetrated the line of scrimmage and hit that poor kid with one of the most crushing hits I've ever seen given out on a football field by a defensive player. They could hear the thud all the way up in the press box. The ball went one way, and the runner went down. And he stayed down. They carried this kid off the field. He was through for the day."

And so was Kimball. "That one play totally destroyed the confidence of the whole Kimball team," Gilliam remembers. "Whenever they got the ball that day, they went backwards."

As he watched Chet knife in, hit those poor kids from Kimball, and then stand straddling his fallen and overmatched prey, talking noise—*your ass is* mine—Alex Gilliam realized that there was something special about what Chet Brooks could do on a football field. Something unnerving.

"I was frightened by what Chet did to Kimball that day," Gilliam remembers. "We beat Kimball 52–0, and Chet put a running back and a quarterback out of the game. They had to take them to the hospital. And the other quarterback was so jittery he couldn't do anything. He didn't want to be out there with Chet."

Gilliam has never forgotten how Brooks intimidated the whole Kimball team. And he has never forgotten the look in Brooks's eyes that day, either. "Chet flat out intimidated [those] guys just by looking at them," Gilliam says. "His eyes were cold and big, full of murder. He was like an assassin. Whether it was football or basketball, Chet played athletics one way—wide open. He played in a vacuum, and when he took an athletic field, nothing mattered but the complete destruction of the opponent."

On that winter day against Kimball, Chet Brooks, Assassin, picked off three passes and made 12 unassisted tackles. He had convinced Alex Gilliam that "this boy had something extra special to give to athletics."

But could a guy from the eleventh round make it in the big leagues?

In the weeks before the 1988 NFL draft, the 49ers had not been one of the NFL teams interested in Brooks. Tony Razzano, the 49ers' director of college scouting, had seen Brooks on film. And Razzano, a scout in professonal football since 1963 and the man who talked Bill Walsh into drafting Joe Montana in 1979, had seen immediately that Brooks had everything—size, speed, strength, instinct, and the kind of cold, mean approach to playing football that coaches can't teach. But, Razzano also knew, the kid had been through two major injuries. The 49ers had not invited Chet to work out for them. The 49ers, in fact, didn't enter into Brooks's picture until Ray Rhodes, San Francisco's defensive backs coach, called just after the sixth round of the draft.

"Chet," Rhodes said on the phone, "you look like a helluva ballplayer. I'm trying to get you."

"Okay," Brooks said.

Chet sat down to watch the draft. Two rounds went by. Ray Rhodes called again.

"I'm still trying to get you," he told Chet.

"Okay," Brooks said.

But Chet was tired of waiting. So he went out to play basketball while the draft wound itself up without him. A couple of hours later, Brooks wandered back into the house. The TV was still on, and the talking head was reviewing the day's selections. The phone rang.

"Chet," Ray Rhodes said, "we got you on the eleventh round." Rhodes paused, then added, "Where were you?"

"I was out playing ball," Chet said.

Brooks paused, then added: "Coach, I'm gonna make your team."

"I believe you, Chet," Rhodes said. "You look like a helluva ballplayer."

"I'm too frustrated to talk, man."

It's a cold and windy Sunday afternoon at Candlestick, three days before Halloween. Fifteen minutes ago, Mike Cofer's kick beat the Browns. Inside the 49er locker room, the players are dressing slowly. They are all trying to deal with what has happened to Mike Sherrard. Chet Brooks is trying to deal with Ozzie Newsome.

Brooks is standing in front of his locker. He is already dressed, and is packing a black athletic bag when a reporter asks him what happened with Ozzie Newsome in the back of the end zone. Brooks doesn't answer. The reporter repeats the question.

"I'm too frustrated to talk, man," Brooks mumbles. Then he swings the suspenders of his black overalls on over a black L.A. Gear sweatshirt. Across the front of the sweatshirt, there is a word written in neon pink, blue, and green, a word that couldn't be more ironic as far as Chet Brooks is concerned: *Unstoppable*.

The word is ironic, of course, because Chet Brooks can't stop anybody. Especially Ozzie Newsome. Ozzie's the cream. The *unstoppable* cream. Chet is just out of the flow. Brooks bends over to zip up his bag. A reporter asks him to describe his frustration. Brooks straightens up, grabs the straps of his bag, and starts off across the locker room.

"It doesn't get any worse than this," he says.

He was wrong.

Chet Brooks hurt his knee on a pass play at the start of the second quarter against the Packers in Green Bay. He was in man-to-man pass coverage against a Packer running back named Keith Woodside. When Woodside flared out of the backfield, Brooks turned and planted his left foot in the cold grass to run with him. Don Majkowski, the Packer quarterback, got sacked on the play. So did Chet. He felt it as soon as he pushed off to cover Woodside.

"You okay, Chet?" Ray Rhodes asked when Brooks took himself out of the game.

Chet knew he was hurt. But he'd been hurt before. Besides, to a football player, pain is just another distraction. It's part of the game. It's not something that keeps you off the field, out of the flow. So he tried to ignore it.

"Yeah," Brooks said to Rhodes. "I'll be okay in a minute."

But he wasn't. When Michael Dillingham was through looking at him in the locker room, Chet was done. In the second half, while Joe Montana was bringing the Niners from behind against the Packers, Brooks was standing on the sidelines in brown sweat clothes. He was cold. And his left knee hurt badly.

Back in the Bay Area the next morning, Brooks sits in a small, sterile room at Sequoia Hospital in Redwood City. The procedure Dillingham performed is known as a magnetic resonance imaging test—a sort of high-tech X-ray commonly referred to as an MRI. As far as Dillingham was concerned, the MRI results were conclusive. Chet Brooks needed arthroscopic surgery immediately. As Dillingham explained that morning, when Chet made his cut to cover Keith Woodside he had suffered a tear in a ring of cartilage that runs around the kneecap. The result was that a little flap of cartilage was now floating at the front of Chet's knee, still attached to the cartilage like the lid of a bucket. Without surgery to remove the flap, Dillingham said, the flap could catch and rip even more.

But Brooks is adamant. No surgery. At least not right now.

"I just want to be sure surgery is necessary," he tells Dillingham. "Maybe all it needs is a little rest. Besides, everybody is dinged up by this time of the year. I can play hurt."

Dillingham is not pleased. But he knows there is nothing he can do. He's read his patient the medical bill of rights. And surgery, he knows, is a decision that's not his to make. Dillingham wraps Brooks's knee in some ice and Chet leaves.

Sunday evening, six days later, Texas Stadium, Dallas. Chet Brooks has been waiting all year for this game. For the Cowboys, in Dallas, at *home*. Unlike some professional athletes, who leave their hometowns for the NFL and never look back, Dallas will always be home to Brooks. His mom and dad don't live in Oak Cliff anymore, but they still live in Dallas. So does Jeff Fuller, and so does Chet. In fact, in the off-season, he still works out at the President's Executive Health Club downtown. He still plays basketball at all of the old recreation centers. He still runs on the hard, bumpy field at Carter High School, and he still lifts in the Carter weight room. "It reminds me where I came from," Chet says. "I don't ever want to forget that because it's part of who I am."

For Brooks, playing in Dallas is always special. But this homecoming, 11 days before Thanksgiving, is nothing but torture. His left knee doesn't hurt that badly anymore, but it's still too weak. Michael Dillingham is still insisting that arthroscopic surgery is his best—indeed, only—alternative for a complete recovery in the long run. But Brooks still isn't sure. His knee's already been under the knife once too often. And, he knows, every time the doctors cut in there it's only another step toward life as a permanent gimp. Toward life without football. And he is not ready for that. Not yet.

Forty minutes before kickoff, Brooks wanders out onto the field toward the 49er bench. He is wearing his sweatshirt that says *Unstoppable*. Brooks reaches the bench and stops. For several minutes, he explores the action out on the field. Quarterbacks throwing, receivers catching, defensive players backpedaling to cover receivers. His eyes flit from one scene to another. He can't watch one play—or one player—too long, because then he starts thinking. About how that guy's getting ready for a football game. And about how he, Chet Brooks, is not.

"Maybe you should have stayed at the hotel," someone says to Chet.

Brooks just keeps staring out at the field. His big eyes are dancing all over the place. He says nothing.

"It probably doesn't help knowing that this is only one game, and that you'll be back out there before too long?"

"It don't help tonight, man," Chet says. "It don't help tonight."

Then the 49er defensive backs begin a pregame drill. The players pair off—one plays receiver, the other defensive back—and they run along the sidelines. After five yards or so, John Gruden, a coaches' assistant, rifles a ball toward them. When the ball arrives, the player playing defensive back bats it away just like it was a real play in a game. Ronnie Lott and Johnny Jackson run the drill. Then Eric Wright and Darryl Pollard. Then Don Griffin and Dave Waymer. Waymer is the receiver, and when the ball arrives, Griffin bats it away. The ball caroms a full 10 yards before coming to rest at Brooks's feet.

Instinctively, Brooks reaches down and picks up the ball. He holds it for a few seconds, rubbing his hands over the brown leather. Over the white laces. Over the wet

spot blotching the name of the NFL's first-year commissioner, Paul Tagliabue. Then it hits him. *This is a football.
A part of the game.* And tonight, he isn't going to be part of
the game. Not tonight. Suddenly, it's like he's holding
something poisonous. Brooks flicks the ball to the
ground. He bites his lip. Then he stuffs his hands into his
overalls and shuffles quickly back into the locker room.

On that warm and humid Sunday night in Dallas, the
Niners trample the Cowboys, 24–6. San Francisco trails
by a field goal early, but the game is never in doubt. With
Jesse Sapolu and the offensive line dominating the line of
scrimmage, Joe Montana and Jerry Rice have great
games. Rice catches 12 Montana passes for 147 yards and
a touchdown. Even San Francisco's running game, which
has not been clicking this season, cranks up.

In the second half, the 49er offense holds the ball for
24 of 30 minutes. Twenty-two of 40 plays are runs, and
the Cowboys don't even get a chance to get back into the
game.

In recognition of the outstanding job he does of protecting Joe Montana and opening holes for the 49er running backs, Jesse Sapolu is awarded his second game ball
in three weeks. The only thing Chet Brooks gets is a
sleepless flight back to San Francisco. And a feeling that
Michael Dillingham is right about his knee.

Chapter 14

Stealth Quarterback

*T*he game in Dallas already had ended when Leigh Montville, a writer for *Sports Illustrated,* walked up the tunnel toward the visitors' locker room at Texas Stadium. Montville was in Dallas working on a big story about Joe Montana. The rest of the world wouldn't know about it for more than a month, but the magazine had already picked Montana as its Sportsman of the Year. Other NFL players had won the award before, but they had always shared it with somebody else. Montana would be the first to win it by himself in the 37 years the award had been given out. Montville's story would be titled "An American Dream." In Dallas, Montville got a glimpse of the dream.

As he waited at Joe's locker, someone came by to tell Montville that Joe would be talking to the press in another room. Montville went to that room. Joe was standing on a bench, 10 microphones and four cameras in his face, tape rolling. He was wearing gray gym shorts, his red-and-white striped game socks, and a T-shirt. The T-shirt used to be white, but now it was almost pink. During the game, the red from Joe's jersey bled from all the sweating he did against the Cowboys. Yes. Joe sweats. Dreams are not always perfect. Up on the bench in front of the press, Joe was standing with his arms crossed. There was a little blood on his right elbow. Joe was saying how he played "just average" against the Cowboys. Twenty-seven of 37 for 290 yards and a touchdown in an easy win—his teams' ninth straight of the season—is "just average" to Joe. To Joe, dreams are never perfect.

Montville watched Joe. He decided that Joe looked like singer Barry Manilow. That's a coincidence. In college at Notre Dame, some of Joe's teammates used to call him Joe Montanalow because they thought he looked like Barry Manilow, too. In front of the press, Montville noticed, Joe smiled shyly and his words seemed to come easily. But he didn't really say much. He never does.

Joe talked to the press for exactly seven minutes. Then, Joe's guard, a taciturn man named Jimmy Warren, moved in and Joe was soon gone. Montville followed Joe. Outside, police officers on motorcycles were waiting to lead the buses to the airport. Like it always is on the road, the engines were idling by the time Joe ran toward the bus. Like it is anytime Joe goes anywhere, people were yelling and screaming his name. They were holding out pieces of paper for Joe to sign. They wanted a piece of the dream. Joe did not stop. He got on the bus. He walked to the last seat. He sat next to Ronnie Lott. Ronnie gave Joe a beer. Joe sat down. The motorcycles rolled. The buses rolled. Somehow, Montville noticed the number on the back of Joe's bus. The number was 711. Sometimes, dreams are perfect.

Back in January, before the Niners beat the Broncos in the Super Bowl, another writer, C. W. Nevius of the *San Francisco Chronicle,* wrote a column about Joe Montana. Nevius started his column by describing what it's like to try to catch a piece of Joe's dream.

"He is the stealth quarterback," Nevius wrote. "During the week, he is rarely seen or heard. Our screens do not seem to pick him up.

"Joe Montana appears suddenly on game days, displays a dazzling array of skills, and vanishes. . . ."

That's how reporters see Joe Montana. In bits here, in pieces there. Never for very long. Sometimes not at all. Catching the dream is like piecing a puzzle together. It's important to start with the edges.

Joseph C. Montana was born on June 11, 1956, in New Eagle, Pennsylvania, a small, blue-collar town in the rugged valley country of western Pennsylvania. He grew up a little south of there in Monongahela, another small town on a curve of the Monongahela River south of Pittsburgh. He lived in a two-story frame house in a middle-class neighborhood. Most of his friends also lived in two-story frame houses in middle-class neighborhoods. It was usually like that in western Pennsylvania. Nobody's house was any better than anybody else's, because they were all pretty much the same.

When Joey was growing up, western Pennsylvania was still the kind of place where, when boys got old enough, they followed their fathers into the steel mills or the coal mines or the factories. Many of the families were Italian or German, so the parents were the children or even grandchildren of immigrants. In many families, it was traditional for the son to carry on the father's work. In many cases, in fact, it was *expected.* Life was simple and often hard. But that was the way the parents wanted it. Because the parents believed that hard work taught kids everything that was important for them to know. It taught them sacrifice. It taught them discipline and regimentation. And it taught them how to survive.

Life went on like this until the oil embargo in the early 1970s, when the steel business went to hell and heavy industry moved out of the Monongahela Valley. When that happened, fathers and mothers lost their jobs, and many families lost their houses. Some people even lost their families. Life was harder than before. Much harder. But there was no point in quitting or getting depressed. That only made things worse. The only thing to do was to keep working hard at whatever could be found. Pay the mortgage. Feed the family. Raise the kids. The idea was to keep moving forward. Somehow.

Back when Joey was growing up, kids didn't use drugs or drive fancy cars. Most of the time, they simply didn't have the money for those things. In fact, a lot of the kids who lived in the two-story frame houses in the middle-class neighborhoods didn't have dreams about doing anything else with their lives besides getting older, going to work, getting married, having a family, and getting old. It was a simple and natural progression that had been repeated for generations. Many of the kids didn't bother to question it. The only possibility they saw for their futures was the same one their fathers, mothers, grandfathers, and grandmothers had seen when they looked at their futures. Make a living. That's what life was all about. Joey, though, never worried about making a living. He and his dad were too busy playing ball.

Joey played all sports, each in their season. Baseball and basketball in the spring and summer. Football in the fall. Basketball in the winter when football was done. Basketball was his favorite sport. Joey loved to practice basketball. He could practice basketball all day. A lot of times, he did. But it was football that got all the college scouts drooling. Joey started playing when he was eight. The kids were supposed to be nine to play, but his dad faked his age and he got in. By the time Joey got to high school, it was all there. He could take the snap and be back to pass just like that. He could flush out of the pocket to his left or to his right, scrambling and dodging, buying time where there was none until one of his guys could get open and he could get them the ball. He could roll left and throw right. He could roll right and throw back to the left. He could get things done when the pressure was on. And he could win. He could do that best of all.

Every Friday night, between the time school started in

the fall until sometime around Thanksgiving, good, disciplined kids played clean, hard football in the mud
under the lights and in the shadows of the smokestacks all
across western Pennsylvania. Joey was one of those kids.
He was a good, disciplined kid. He didn't smoke, he
didn't drink, and he didn't get into trouble. Mostly, he
played ball and ate the ravioli his mom cooked in big,
steaming batches on the stove. That was the best. Playing
ball out in the backyard with his father, and then coming
into the kitchen and smelling the ravioli his mother had
on the stove. That was the best. But then Joey went to college and everything changed.

For one thing, he married his high school sweetheart.
They were together less than three years. Both of them
were just too young. Things were not the same on the
football field either. As a senior at Ringgold High School
in Monongahela, Joe had been named a Parade All-
American. He had been a hotshot—*the* hotshot. But at
Notre Dame, everybody was a hotshot. The year before
he got to South Bend, the Irish had won the national
championship under Ara Parseghian. Joe was no longer
the big fish in the pond. He was a hatchling, and there
was a whole ocean of bigger fish all around him. He was
either going to learn to swim or he was going to be eaten.
He had two choices.

Joe didn't play at all on the varsity team his first year.
In fact, he hardly played in the freshman games. But lack
of playing time wasn't the hardest part of Joe's first year
at college. He missed home. He missed his best friend.
Joe would call Joe Sr. three or four times a week. Every
once in a while, Joe Sr. would make the eight-hour trip
from Monongahela to watch Joe throw a few passes in a
scrimmage. Then he'd have something to eat with Joe
and be back on the road because he had to be at work the
next day. Other times, Joe Sr. would show up at 1 A.M.
and take Joe and his roommates out for big stacks of pan-
cakes. Once, when things got so crazy that he couldn't

stand it anymore, Joe drove home in the middle of the night. He wasn't sure where things at Notre Dame were headed anymore, and he needed to hear what his dad had to say. Joe Sr. told him to keep trying and things were bound to get better.

In Joe's sophomore year, things did. He came off the bench and won two games in the fourth quarter. In one, Notre Dame was losing 14–6 with a little more than five minutes left. Joe played one minute and two seconds. He ended up with 129 yards passing, and Notre Dame won 21–14. Later, that game would be the first entry on a list made up by the sports information department at Notre Dame. The title of the list would be "Joe Montana's Comeback Statistics." Joe still had doubts about how good he was: He would have them right up until the end of his college career. But at least now he thought he knew where things were headed. It looked like he was finally learning to swim with the big fish. But as a junior, Montana separated his shoulder and missed the whole season. The next year, he was right back where he started. On the bench.

He would not stay there for long.

It's New Year's Day 1979 in Dallas. The game is the Cotton Bowl between Joe's Fighting Irish and the Cougars of the University of Houston. It's Joe's last game for Notre Dame. The day is frigid. A freak ice storm has made everything frozen and brittle. By the fourth quarter, things look bad for Notre Dame. Houston is ahead, 34–12, and Joe is in the locker room under a bunch of blankets. His temperature is 96 degrees. The doctors start feeding Joe hot chicken bouillon. Every five minutes, a Notre Dame coach runs into the locker room from the bench to check on Joe's temperature. With 7:37 left in the game, Joe runs onto the field and into the huddle.

Six seconds left. Joe has brought Notre Dame back. His Irish are losing by only six points. They have the ball at the Houston eight. The coach calls "91," a quick out in which a receiver fires off the line and cuts quickly to the sidelines. Joe takes the snap and fires. But the receiver slips and Joe throws the ball away. Only two seconds left now. Joe looks over to the sidelines for the play. The coach turns his back to the field. This means Joe is supposed to call his own play. Joe is cool. He calls the 91. Joe looks at his receiver in the huddle. The receiver looks jittery, nervous, afraid. Joe sees this. Joe is cool.

"Don't worry," he says to the receiver, "you can do it."

The receiver moves out to his position. Joe takes the snap. There's a guy right in his face. Joe is cool. He throws a bullet, hard and low, for the sidelines. His receiver doesn't slip. He dives for the ball—the ball is out of bounds—and catches it. His feet are in. Notre Dame wins by a point. The game makes the list. Joe is cool.

Joe has always been cool. At the Super Bowl against Cincinnati in 1989, the Niners are standing around on the field waiting to start their winning drive against the Bengals. At the time, the Niners are behind 16–13 with only some three minutes left in the game. Joe is cool because of what he says standing around waiting to get the game started again.

"Hey, check it out," he says to tackle Harris Barton.

"Check what out," Barton answers.

"There, in the stands, near the exit ramp. There's John Candy."

Then Joe led the Niners down the field and they won the Super Bowl. Joe threw the winning pass. Of course. Joe loves to win. But, when it comes right down to it, Joe just loves to play. He never wants to stop. He loves it so much. He's always been this way. When he was a kid, he was playing with his aunt's dog. The dog wanted to stop playing. He didn't. His aunt's dog bit him. That's why he has a scar over his lip.

With the Niners, Joe has had all the injuries that quarterbacks get in the NFL. Broken collarbone. Concussion. Torn cartilage in his knee. Sore elbow. Tendonitis.

Bruised sternum. Sprained ankles. Bruised ribs. Sprained knuckle. Torn hamstring. Ruptured disc in his back. He keeps coming back. Joe loves the game. Joe loves to play.

"He's at home in the locker room," Harry Edwards says. "Anyplace else he is, he's away from home. I don't care where it is. I don't care if it's at home with his family. I've never known a guy who was more comfortable, who fit in more with the guys, who loved the game, the atmosphere, the camaraderie, the smells, and the spirit of the game more than he does."

Joe never wants to quit playing, because he loves the game. There are many reasons why Joe loves the game. Pick one.

Joe loves bicycles. One year in training camp, when the guys on defense were in a meeting, Joe put all of their bikes up in trees. Another year, Joe got a long chain and locked them all together. In training camp, the Niners stay in the dorms at Sierra College. The dorms are across the campus from the cafeteria. It's even farther to the locker room and the field. In the sweltering summer heat, the Niners don't like walking anywhere they don't have to. So many of the players rent bikes to ride across campus to the cafeteria and to practice. Every year, a guy rents each of them a bike for $25 a week. Joe never rents a bike, but he rides one every day. The rookies never know what's happening. They ride their bikes from the dorms to the locker room up by the practice field. Then when they come out of the locker room after practice, they go to ride their bikes but they're gone. All the veterans know where the rookies' bikes are. And they know who took them. Joe did. But the rookies don't. Joe likes it that way. Joe loves jokes.

Training camp is Joe's playground. One of his favorite jokes is putting saran wrap across a toilet seat in a dorm bathroom. He puts a sign, "Out of Order," on the one toilet in the dorm hallway. Then Joe stretches saran

wrap across the other toilet. For days—maybe weeks—
Joe watches his victims. Joe knows that everyday after
lunch, a teammate comes back from the cafeteria, goes to
his room, maybe gets the sports page from *USA Today*,
and heads for the bathroom. By this time, all of the other
players are in on Joe's joke, and so they stay away from
the toilet with the saran wrap. Like clockwork, the player
wanders into the bathroom. He isn't paying attention to
what he's doing. He's reading the sports page. He sits
down to go to the bathroom. By the time he's figured out
that something's not right, Joe has already claimed
another victim. Joe hears his teammate hollering, or
maybe he hears about it later. Wherever he is, Joe grins.

Joe likes other kinds of jokes, too. He likes to sneak up
behind the secretaries at the Taj and scare them. He likes
to plant stink bombs in the players' lounge and then slink
out and watch his teammates gag on the smell. Joe is the
one who started calling Tom Rathman "Woody" after the
loopy bartender on the television show "Cheers." Sometimes, Joe's jokes involve gadgets that are more expensive
than saran wrap. At the end of practice one day during
the week of the Packers game in early November, George
Seifert called the Niners together in a circle on the practice field like he always does at the end of the day. Seifert
started talking. As usual, the Niners' head coach was intense and serious. Suddenly, a snippy and sarcastic voice
could be heard from within the circle of football players
around Seifert.

"Fuckin' jerk."

Everyone looked around. It was Joe. He had a small
pretaped beeper that cusses. Everyone was laughing. Joe
pressed a button and George Seifert was a "fuckin' jerk."
Only Joe could get away with that. Besides, he was only
joking. Joe loves jokes.

But Joe doesn't love everything about football. Joe
doesn't love reporters. Reporters want to know everything about Joe. They want to know what he thinks about
out there on the field in the huddle, what he thinks about

when he walks to the line of scrimmage and is scanning the defense, what he thinks about as he drops back to pass, what he thinks about as he is releasing the ball, what he thinks about as he sees the ball fly toward Jerry Rice, what he thinks about as Jerry Rice pulls in his pass and turns on the afterburner for the end zone, what he thinks about as he is running to the sidelines after he has thrown a touchdown pass to Jerry Rice. Reporters want to know how much money Joe makes. They want to know what Joe and his wife, Jennifer, do on vacation. They want to know Joe's golf handicap. In the end, the reporters all want to know how—and why—Joe is able to do the things he does on the football field. Joe does not want to tell them. Joe can't tell them.

Joe is not a rocket scientist. This does not mean that Joe isn't bright. Joe is bright. But playing quarterback is not like solving homelessness or devising a complicated algorithm. For Joe, playing quarterback is like standing in the middle of the freeway throwing a football into the blur of the headlights screaming at him from every direction. Joe is not thinking out there. He is reacting.

Reporters want to know how Joe does it. They want to know how Joe stays alive out there, out on the freeway. They want to know deep, personal things about the man who does things they have never seen anyone do before. So they wait for him after the game at his locker, dozens of them with their cameras and their notepads. Joe doesn't always come to his locker. Sometimes he stays in the trainers' room where the reporters can't go. Sometimes he has Jimmy Warren go out to his locker and bring him his clothes. Other times Dwight Clark brings Joe his clothes. Clark used to be a 49er with Joe. Clark is still Joe's friend.

Sometimes, though, Joe does come to his locker. When he appears, the reporters push and shove and elbow one another. They all want to get close enough to snatch a piece of the dream. They shove their microphones and their questions at him. Joe does not like this. He talks quietly. His voice is mechanical. His eyes are empty. Joe feels trapped. He tries his best, but he is always afraid of sharing himself, because he is never quite sure which reporter might use what he shares against him. So he says as little as possible. That way he can't get hurt. The reporters often leave the locker room and say that Joe is a bad interview. They say they don't understand how Joe can do the great things he does as a quarterback and not be able to talk about it afterward. What they do not realize is that Joe has no idea why he is as great at playing quarterback as he is. He does it. He can't explain it. He doesn't want to.

Joe doesn't have to explain about tape. Tape requires no explanation. Joe loves tape. Every day before practice, Joe does the same thing. He stands under the portable yellow goal post at the Taj. He looks up and judges the wind. Then he lobs an inch-and-a-half-wide roll of tape up into the hollow end of the goal post. Before practice, Joe plays for Team Tape. There are three players on the team—Joe, Steve Young, and Steve Bono. The three Niner quarterbacks. Team Tape plays before practice every day. Joe does it better than anybody. He does it with touch. He does it with concentration. But he does it. He puts it in. That's what counts.

Before the Super Bowl in New Orleans, Jamie Williams remembers watching Joe. It was Jamie's first Super Bowl, and he was anxious to see how the big boys got ready for the big game. So Jamie watched Joe. For a long time, Joe did the same thing. Tear some tape. Wad it up. Put it down by his locker. *Tear, wad, down, tear, wad, down.* Jamie Williams was horrified. *Oh, no,* he thought, *Montana is nervous. The Man is nervous.* Jamie went back to his locker and tried to keep himself from getting nervous. But it was impossible. This was Joe's fourth Super Bowl.

And if Joe was nervous. . . . A little later, right before kickoff, Jamie looked over at Joe. Joe was throwing the balls of tape at Harris Barton. Joe was not nervous after all.

Joe always seems to have perfect timing. One day, Jerry Walker, the 49ers' public-relations director, was cleaning out his car. Walker found a letter that had fallen down behind the seat. It was addressed to Joe. It was almost a year old. Walker read the letter. A girl wanted a picture of Joe with his signature. Walker had Joe sign a picture, and he put it in the mail. A week or so later, Walker was going through Joe's mail when he saw an envelope with the same name and the same handwriting. Walker opened the letter. It was a note from the girl. Joe's picture got to her exactly on her birthday and she was writing to thank Joe for being so thoughtful to time things so perfectly.

Joe has heart, too. In the middle of September 1986, the headlines in the San Francisco newspapers displayed important news. There was the hotel union strike. There was the rebirth of Market Street. There was the day-care center that was supposedly using electric stun guns to discipline kids.

Then there was Joe's back. In the first game of the season, Joe took the snap and ran to his left at Tampa Stadium. Joe was looking for Dwight Clark, who was running a pattern back over on the right side of the field. Joe jumped, twisted, and threw. He felt something in his back and came out of the game. Eight days later, Joe was in the hospital. A surgeon made a four-inch incision in his back and fixed a herniated disc. Many people—including some of Joe's doctors—were saying that Joe wouldn't ever be able to play football again. Many people were saying that Joe wouldn't *want* to play football again, that what Joe would do is take the money he had coming to him—around $1 million a year back then—and go sit on a beach somewhere. All of those people were wrong.

On November 9, 63 days after the doctor cut into his back, Joe completed 13 of 19 passes for 270 yards and three touchdowns against the St. Louis Cardinals. The Niners won big, and Joe was back. He couldn't stay away. He couldn't just take the money and run. Because he doesn't play the game for money. He plays the game for the game. A reporter once asked Ronnie Lott what makes Joe so special. Lott thought for a moment. When he answered, his voice was shaking.

"No one can measure his heart," Lott said. "No one will ever be able to put that into words."

But the writers always try. There are many reasons why the writers call Joe the greatest quarterback who ever played the game. These reasons, of course, revolve around the things Joe has done on the football field. The last-minute comeback wins. The two Super Bowl wins, the NFL MVP award, and the Super Bowl MVP award— all after having a doctor dig around in his back. Joe has done things no one has ever done before. Things no one may ever do again. His career has indeed been an American Dream. But when the writers look for reasons why Joe is the greatest quarterback around, they should look not only at *what* he has done but also at *how* he has done it.

Joe knows how to make something out of nothing. Joe knows about possibilities. What is impossible to everyone in the stadium is possible to Joe. What is hopeless for everyone in the stadium is swelling with hope for Joe. What is empty to everybody is full to Joe. People cannot do what they cannot see. Joe knows this. He does things that other people cannot even see as possibilities. He does them because he is able to imagine that he can do them. He *expects* to do them. To Joe, something is possible because it has to be done. That is the secret that lies at the center of the dream.

As the quest moves later into November, the Niners are clinging to the dream tighter than ever. They are winning because they have to. They aren't blowing teams away like they did at the end of last season, but they are winning. The Super Bowl machine rolls on. And this season, more than ever, Joe is the show. So far this season, San Francisco has hardly had a running game at all. The offensive linemen and the running backs say it's because the coaches aren't calling enough running plays. The coaches say it's because they have a quarterback like Joe and receivers like Jerry Rice, John Taylor, Brent Jones, and Mike Sherrard, so why should they bother to call running plays when the Niners can pass it better than anybody? Whatever the reason, by the end of November, roughly three of every four San Francisco plays have been passes by Joe. Joe is the show. Especially close to curtain.

Four times the Niners have come from behind to win games in the fourth quarter. Joe has thrown a clutch pass in each of those games. In New Orleans, the guys up front couldn't keep the Saints out of the backfield and Joe was running for his life. But when the clock was ticking down, he found Jerry over the middle and Mike Cofer kicked the field goal that won the game. In Houston, the Oilers had the Niners down in the fourth quarter when Joe found John Taylor on a short ball that Taylor turned into the winning points. Against Cleveland at Candlestick before Halloween, Joe had a horrible day. He ended up completing only 17 of 37 passes for 185 yards. He also threw two interceptions. But he had the magic when it counted. On that final drive, when the game was tied and the Niners needed somebody to make a play, Joe made two. The pass to Mike Sherrard that took San Francisco into Cleveland territory, and the little flip to Rice that set up Mike Cofer's winning kick. And in Green Bay three weeks later, the Pack was playing San Francisco tough. But Joe threw a pass and the Niners pulled out another win.

Joe has had big games this season, too. Against the Redskins at Candlestick in September, he bombed Washington for 390 yards and two touchdowns. In Atlanta a few weeks later, Joe exploded for 476 yards and six touchdown passes. In a season when the Niners aren't running the ball, Joe is carrying the offense. Some reporters, in fact, are even writing that, at 34 years old, Joe Montana is having the best season of his career.

For San Francisco, it's a good thing. The Giants are next, and the Giants have been killing everybody. For the Niners to win, Joe is going to have to be as good as he has been all season. Because the game is going to be rough and ugly and close.

Blood feuds always are.

Chapter 15

Blood Feud

*E*ight-thirty in the morning and already Chet Brooks is late.

He has only six days—not much time—until Monday night. Until Dave Meggett. Until the biggest game of the season. Giants and Niners at Candlestick. Brooks winces as he strains with the 275 pounds on the leg press. The weights are heavy. His knee is weak. He has only six days. He does another set.

Less than three weeks ago, Brooks finally took Dr. Michael Dillingham's advice and had arthroscopic surgery to repair the damage he had done to his left knee in Green Bay. Brooks was on the table for 45 minutes. He watched Dillingham's every move on a monitor. Dillingham entered his knee in three places and removed the flap of cartilage that had torn. Then the countdown to Monday night began.

Six days before the game, Brooks has already picked out the Giant that he is going to hate this week. *Meggett. Monday night. Got somethin' to deal with.* He has already spent hours watching film of New York's dangerous running back. Meggett bulling his way up the middle on a touchdown run. Meggett taking a swing pass and juking the defenders out of their jockstraps. Brooks transfers himself to the screen. He imagines Meggett doing those things to him. He gets angry. In his head and in his heart, Brooks is ready for the Giants. It's his body that's the question. Six days before the game, it's just a matter of time. Does he have enough?

As Brooks works his knee to get ready for the Giants, the Stones come on the radio. Someone cranks it up. Inside the weight room at the Taj, the sound of guitars and drums and Mick ricochets crisply through the empty morning. Mick is singing his life. Something about being stuck between a rock and a hard place. On one hand, Brooks wants desperately to play against the Giants—"These are the games football players live for," he says this morning—but, less than three weeks after surgery, his knee may not be strong enough. Brooks is stuck between wanting to play and not having enough time to get ready to play.

The Stones fade. Brooks gets up out of the leg-press machine and walks into the trainer's room. He sits on a table. He dangles his legs off the edge at the knees. He straps 25 pounds to his left ankle. As he lifts his leg, he winces. The weights are heavy. His knee is weak. There are only six days. He does another set.

Chet Brooks isn't the only dinged Niner who has shown up for medical treatment this Tuesday morning, the players' one day off this week. Michael Carter arrived a few minutes after Brooks. Last October, San Francisco's six-foot-two, 326-pound Pro Bowl nose tackle hurt his right foot against the Jets. After the Super Bowl, the foot was still weak, so Carter had a bone grafted from his hip to help strengthen it. The months of rehabilitation went by slowly, but Carter didn't push it. He figured that if he was ready, he was ready. But if it took another year, it took another year. And if his foot never healed well enough to let him play like he used to, Michael Carter had accepted that, too. This season, Carter missed most of training camp and the opener in New Orleans. But although he's been playing ever since, Michael Carter's right foot has needed frequent rest and the electrical stimulation he has come for this morning.

Charles Haley limped in around nine. Two days ago,

right before halftime of the game against the Rams at
Candlestick, the NFC's sack leader bruised his left knee
when Michael Carter fell on him after a running play.
Haley had to be helped to the locker room. But then in
the third quarter, pride and guts took over, and Haley
put himself back in the lineup. This morning, six days before the blood feud with the Giants, Haley is paying for
his valor. He can hardly walk. As he gimps into the
trainer's room, it's clear he's in pain—and in a foul mood.

As Haley hobbles past trainer Lindsy McLean, Chet
Brooks looks up from the machine that is shooting so
many amps of electrical current into his knee that the
muscles twitch and bubble like hot lava.

"Calm down any?" Brooks asks, referring to the
throbbing in his teammate's leg. Haley shakes his head in
the exaggerated way a little boy sometimes does when his
mom asks him if he has brushed his teeth yet. *No.* Mc-
Lean follows Haley—at a respectful distance—to a training table. Haley sits up slowly, painfully. When McLean
informs Haley what this morning's treatment is—time in
the whirlpool, electrical stimulation, resistance work with
a trainer gently flexing the sore knee, then massage and
some ice—Haley is not thrilled.

"Man, I don't want to do any of that," he whines, glaring at McLean, a quiet, red-headed man who, as a trainer
for the 49ers since 1979, has been glared at by hundreds
of hurt, angry football players. Later, however, Charles
Haley does everything Lindsy McLean asks of him. Haley
also takes a phone call from Ronnie Lott, his closest
friend on the team. As he and Lott talk, Haley's angry
glare gives way to a huge, toothy grin. And his voice no
longer reeks with pain and torment. Out in the weight
room, Chet Brooks can hear what Haley is saying on the
phone to Ronnie Lott. He is laughing.

Later today, Michael Dillingham will perform a
magnetic resonance imaging test—a more sophisticated
form of X-ray—to assess the condition of Charles Haley's

knee. Tomorrow, George Seifert will tell reporters that the doctors have found nothing serious enough to prevent Haley from playing against the Giants. Haley himself, on the other hand, will say that his knee is still so sore that there's a chance he won't be able to go Monday night. The reporters print what Haley says, but some don't believe him.

"The guy's like Ronnie Lott or Roger [Craig]," one reporter says. "You'd have to cut off his nuts to keep him out of this game."

It all started, this blood feud between the 49ers and the Giants, back in 1981, the year New York came to Candlestick for a divisional playoff game. San Francisco had just won its first NFC West title in nine years. The week before, the Giants had just appeared in their first playoff game in 18 years. The final score that day was 38–24, 49ers. Three weeks later, San Francisco won its first Super Bowl by beating the Cincinnati Bengals 26–21 at the Silverdome in Pontiac, Michigan. In 1984, it happened to the Giants again. In the NFC divisional playoff at Candlestick, the 49ers beat New York, 21–10. Three weeks later, San Francisco bombed Miami 38–16 in Palo Alto to become world champions for the second time in four seasons.

In 1985 and 1986, the Giants got even, throttling San Francisco in playoff games at the Meadowlands in New Jersey. During the week before the wild-card game in 1985, Ira Miller of the *Chronicle* quoted Joe Montana as saying he didn't like Giants quarterback Phil Simms because Simms was too cocky. Montana later said he thought his comment was off the record. But the damage had been done. New York throttled San Francisco 17–3, keeping the Niner offense out of the end zone for only the second time in Bill Walsh's seven seasons as coach. The next year, things got even uglier. Just before halftime in a game New York would eventually win 49–3,

Giants nose tackle Jim Burt barged through the line and knocked Joe Montana unconscious. Three weeks later, it was the Giants, not the Niners, who were world champions of the NFL. After so many bitter defeats at the hands of the 49ers, New York felt vindicated. Finally. The feeling would not last very long.

Over the next three seasons, San Francisco beat New York three times in a row. One game, at the Meadowlands in September 1988, ended 20–17 when Montana hit Jerry Rice with a 78-yard score with less than a minute left in the game. For New York, the 1988 season went down to the final week. If the 49ers could beat the Rams at Candlestick, then the Giants would be in the playoffs as a wild-card team. But if the Rams won, New York was done. With the Giants' season depending on them, the Niners lost big, 38–16. Phil Simms was disgusted. "The 49ers lay down like dogs," Simms said of what he regarded as a half-hearted effort against Los Angeles. A month after losing to the Rams, San Francisco beat Cincinnati 20–16 for the franchise's third Super Bowl win in eight seasons. The Niners were on top of the mountain again. And the Giants felt the hate like it never went away.

For the Giants, however, things with the 49ers had never been worse than last year. On a Monday night at Candlestick late in November, New York lost to San Francisco again, 34–24, after spotting the Niners a 24–7 lead, fighting back to a tie, and then giving it all away on a penalty and an interception at the end. To the Giants, though, the thing that cut even deeper than the score was what happened to Lawrence Taylor. One play brought 10 years of hate to a boil.

The play was a sweep in the second quarter. The Giants trailed 17–7, and San Francisco had just started a drive at the New York 35 following an interception. As Roger Craig ran to the right side of the field, away from Taylor, 49er tight end Wesley Walls homed in from behind and dove at Taylor, trying to knock the linebacker's legs out from under him. Taylor and Walls fell to the turf. The impact of the fall caused Walls to roll against Taylor's leg, bending it back the wrong way. Lawrence Taylor then did something his teammates had never heard him do before—he screamed—and then left the game on a cart. After X-rays were taken at halftime, the Giants announced that Lawrence Taylor had suffered a severe sprain of his right knee. Later, another X-ray would reveal that he had cracked a bone in his foot.

The players from New York are competitors who hate to lose football games to anybody in the NFL. But there is one team the players from New York hate to lose to more than anybody else. On that night at Candlestick in 1989, the Giants had just lost to that team. And, to a man, they were stinging.

"What did I learn from this?" Phil Simms asked caustically, repeating a question by C. W. Nevius of the *Chronicle*. "The same thing I always learn from something like this. That I hate to ————ing lose."

The Giants were also furious at what they believed to be Wesley Walls's cheap shot on Lawrence Taylor. In his book, *No Medals for Trying*, which chronicled one week in New York's 1989 season, Jerry Izenberg captured the reaction of Giants' defensive coordinator Bill Belichick as the coach and his defensive staff were watching films of the game at the Meadowlands the next day. "Next time we play these sons of bitches, we've got to build up some hate. Look at that! Did you see it? These are the worst cheap-shot, career-ending bastards in the league. Just look at that."

The next time is almost here. When it arrives, the hate will be flashing on both sides.

On Wednesday afternoon, five days before the game, Jim Burt stands on the red brick walkway outside the

locker room at the Taj. He is talking about the hate. Burt
came to San Francisco last season after playing eight
years for the Giants. And so, more than anyone else in
San Francisco, Jim Burt knows what it feels like for
Giants to hate 49ers.

"I'll admit [it] right now," Burt tells more than a dozen
reporters. "In '81 and '84, I developed some hate towards
the 49ers. The 49ers were always the darlings; they always beat us in the playoffs. They beat us in '81 and '84.
[And] the '88 game when Jerry caught that pass, that
stuck us pretty hard—especially on the defensive side.
You work all year to get to those guys, and then you lose.
When that happens, you develop some hatred. If you get
beat by someone all the time, you're going to start saying,
'We've gotta figure something out to beat these guys.'
The Giants want to go out and be the number-one team,
[the team] that everyone talks about. And the 49ers want
to stay the number-one team. That's basically where
we're at."

Burt then tells reporters that he has been talking to
some of his old teammates in New York. After last year's
bitter loss at Candlestick, he says, the Giants' nerves are
rawer than they have ever been. "My inside information
tells me that they are extremely, extremely, fired up
about this [game], especially on the defensive side," Burt
says. "The coaches have really got them revved up. I
mean, they're showing them films of someone cut blocking, and they're rallying on that. They're going to come
after us, and they're going to be really fired up. But that's
the way it is every week for us."

A reporter asks Burt about the stories that Lawrence
Taylor is getting old, that he's lost a step, that he's not the
dominating force he used to be. Early in his career,
Lawrence Taylor redefined the position of linebacker in
football. At six-foot-three and 243 pounds, Taylor was
strong enough that he could bull by—or through—270-
pound tackles on his way to the quarterback. And he was

fast enough that he could drop back in coverage and run with the backs looking to catch the ball and go the distance. Taylor was mean. And he was tough—nobody was as tough as L. T. He could play through pain better than anybody. Neither broken bones nor pulled muscles could keep him off the field on Sunday. L. T. was larger than life. He was Superman. But as the blood feud draws closer, one of the week's big theories is that after 10 seasons in the NFL, Superman has finally come down to earth. Jim Burt says this is hogwash.

"L. T. hasn't slowed down," Burt says. "L. T. is 245, but tackles nowadays are 300 pounds. This is a big game, Monday night, highly publicized. L. T. is the type of guy who, when he's on Monday night or Madden's doing a nationally televised game, he comes up with big plays all the time. On Monday night, L. T. will be out there, and he'll be making big plays."

In five days, Jamie Williams will be one of the 49ers whose job it will be to keep Lawrence Taylor from making big plays. So far in 1990, the 49er tight end has had a quiet year. Going into the blood feud, Williams has caught just five passes for 24 yards. He has only one touchdown catch—and that was way back in preseason against the Broncos, so it doesn't really even count.

But catching passes is not really what Jamie Williams does best for the 49ers anyway. What he does best is block. "Jamie is the best-blocking tight end in the league," 49er offensive coordinator Mike Holmgren said one day early in the season. Bobb McKittrick, the 49er offensive line coach who's been teaching blockers in the NFL since 1971, said the same thing. "I haven't seen anybody better," McKittrick said. "He's strong. He's got great technique. He's big enough to be a problem. And he's tenacious. He's got the ability to stay with a guy for as long as it takes to get the job done."

On Monday night against the Giants, however, Jamie Williams knows that getting the job done is going to be especially difficult. He's well aware that after 11 games New York boasts the NFL's stingiest defense. And he knows that, despite all the talk claiming that Lawrence Taylor has lost a step, L. T. minus a step or two is still a better linebacker than most linebackers are with all of their steps.

"The guy is as good as there is," Jamie says after practice on Wednesday. "The guy can do it all. He's fast, he's strong, and he's savvy. He knows how to make plays that other guys can't. He does things you won't see other linebackers do to get out of a block.

"My thing," Jamie decides, "is to try to neutralize him. I think if I can go in and keep him frustrated a little, keep his mind occupied with eating me up instead of with what the rest of the guys are doing, then I'll be helping the team."

The Giants, Jamie Williams knows, are a vicious bunch who will stop at nothing to win the blood feud. But he's ready. Because if the Giants are feeling the hate, so is he.

As the New York Giants' third-round pick out of the University of Nebraska in 1983, Jamie Williams thought that he had made a good impression on the coaches in his first NFL training camp. He knew he'd made some mistakes. But all rookies make mistakes. He thought that he had caught the ball well and blocked well. He thought that he had played hard and showed everyone that he was willing to learn how to get better. The Giants, he thought, needed players like him. After all, the season before he was drafted, the Giants lost more games than they won, and the head coach was fired. Jamie figured the new coach, Bill Parcells, would need talented young players who would get better and better the more they played. He was wrong.

That year, right before the season started, Bill Parcells cut him. Jamie would remember the words for a long time. *We're not quite sure you have what we're looking for in a tight end, not sure you fit in with what we're trying to do here, so we're letting you go.* Suddenly, Jamie's dream—to be a professional football player, to be *somebody*—was dead. Just like that. He'd been working to make the dream a reality ever since he started playing ball in the streets as a kid back in Davenport. He kept working at it in high school, running through the snow in the dark to lift weights before class. And while he built up his body, he made sure to study and get the grades so someday he might get a shot at a scholarship and be able to go to college. Growing up, football had been more than a game to Jamie Williams. It had been his chance to be somebody. But the New York Giants fixed that.

At first, when Bill Parcells told him he was being released, Jamie couldn't believe what had happened. *Me? Cut? Whaddya mean? I've never been cut from anything.* In high school, he had always been a starter and an all-star. And as a senior at Nebraska in 1982, he had been named first team All-Big Eight and an honorable mention All-American by the Associated Press. Now he was none of those things. Now he felt like Bill Parcells had just cast him into a black hole, a sterile and endless vacuum where there was nothing to hold on to, nothing to look at, nothing to smell, touch, hear, or taste. There was nothing. There was no one but Jamie.

Then when he returned to Nebraska and thought more about things, Jamie got angry. Because while Bill Parcells had not come right out and said so, Jamie finally understood what the Giants' coach had *really* been trying to tell him. *They're not just saying I'm not good enough to play on their team,* he realized. *They don't think I'm good enough to play in this league. I'm not worth keeping because I'm nothing.*

In the days and weeks after he was cut, Jamie put the words together with other things that had happened to him in training camp. And he began to hate the way the New York Giants had treated him. Mostly, he remembered the little things. The snide comments some of the coaches had made to him. About his long hair. About his thing for comic book superheroes. About how he was an "individualist" who liked to do things his own way instead of doing things the way the New York Giants wanted them done. Jamie had always felt that coaches had a responsibility not only to make their players better on the football field but also to support them and help them become better people off the football field. The New York Giants' coaches, Jamie decided, did not believe the way he did. Not at all.

But if being shocked and humiliated and angry had been the extent of the damage done to him by the Giants, then Jamie Williams probably would have been able to leave the whole thing behind him long before. But it wasn't. Because after he was through being shocked and humiliated and angry, Jamie did something he had never done before in his life. Something he would swear later he would never do again. He doubted himself. *Am I as good as I think I am?* he wondered. *Am I good enough to play in the NFL?* He thought he was. He thought he could catch and block and play just as hard as any tight end in the league. But after the Giants cut him, he wasn't sure anymore. He wasn't sure of anything anymore.

Several weeks after the Giants let him go, Jamie hooked on with the St. Louis Cardinals. He hardly ever played. He got cut after four games. But before Jim Hanifan, the Cardinals' head coach, let Jamie go, Hanifan made a point to tell the young tight end that the reason he was letting him go was not because he couldn't play the game. It was because he needed the help of the defensive player who would be replacing Jamie on the Cardinals' roster.

"Don't quit," Hanifan said to Jamie. "Don't give up. Because you can be a starter in this league. This isn't the place. But you'll find that place."

The next season, a year after he was cut by the Giants,

Jamie Williams won the starting tight end job in Houston. The first person he thought of when the coaches told him was Jim Hanifan. The second was Bill Parcells.

Five days before the Giants come to Candlestick, 1983 seems like a long time ago. Jamie Williams knows that. He got over the hurt and disappointment of being cut a long time ago. He played five years in Houston. And last year with the 49ers, he even got a Super Bowl ring. He knows he's somebody. But Super Bowl rings have nothing to do with what happened between Jamie and the Giants seven years ago. That was different. That was personal. He will never forget. Especially now.

Five days before the renewal of the blood feud, Jamie Williams is doing something that would have revolted him back in 1983. He is *trying to remember* what he felt like when he was cut by the Giants. He is trying to call up the powerful feelings that tore through him then. He wants to feel the pain, the doubt, and the frustration. He wants to hurt and to hate. Because he is going to use it against the Giants. To destroy the destroyers.

But Jamie Williams knows that hate alone will not be enough. He knows he will need more help. And he has it. He has friends in power.

One friend is a freelance photographer who was bitten by a common house spider that had been nuked by radioactive laboratory waste. After the souped-up enzymes from the spider's blood get transferred into his, the photographer can dodge bullets and sense danger before it's there. The other friend is a brooding warrior from an imaginary age 12,000 years ago where magic is real and men take revenge with swords. Jamie Williams needs them both to play in a football game. Especially a blood feud. This week, Spiderman and Conan the Barbarian will help Jamie Williams destroy Lawrence Taylor and the Giants.

Jamie started using the two comic book characters to

get himself ready to play football when he was with the Oilers. It has continued as a ritual for Jamie to gather strength to fight in a war in which pain and suffering don't come just from the enemies on the other side of the ball. "Having alter egos is the only way I can deal with the complexities of surviving in this type of society," is the way he explained it one day at the Taj. "I see guys getting hurt and cut from the team. I see coaches lose their jobs. That stuff hurts. It's tough to take. This is a cutthroat business. I have to make it surreal to survive. Spiderman and Conan are my way of giving myself mental armor.

"I identify with Spiderman because he has problems like everybody else. He can't pay his bills. He argues with his girlfriend. Normal stuff. But he still goes out and saves the city. He's just this guy. He works at a newspaper. But he can do special things. He has a cause to his life. Spiderman takes it personal when he saves someone's life. I see a lot of myself in him. I have bills. I have a family. I have responsibilities. But I still have a cause to my life. I still have to show up and perform for this team. I take that personal. To me, it isn't enough just to come out here, run around, and get a paycheck. These guys are counting on me. *I'm* counting on me. So I've got to make something happen. I've got to save the day."

But *two* superheroes? If Spiderman is so quick, so strong—so *superhuman*—then why is Conan necessary? Because, Jamie explained, Spiderman always plays by the rules. And professional football is a war that's not always played by the rules. It's at these times—when a linebacker starts kneeing him in pileups or swearing at him to get him off his game—that Jamie sheds his Spiderman personality and becomes the remorseless mentality that worries only about where his God, Crom, is after a battle is over. When Conan needs *somebody* to count the bodies. "Conan doesn't look for help," Jamie said. "He fights by himself. He might have twenty guys coming at him, he may be backed up against the wall with only a sword, but he isn't afraid to fight. He has total confidence. When there's no way for him to get away, when he's cornered, he faces the onslaught and wins."

Long before he left Houston, Jamie had the routine down. Early in the week of a game, he picks out a couple of comics. He has hundreds. He buys more every month. Usually it's a Spiderman and a Conan. Sometimes, however, it's two of one or the other. Sometimes, he'll choose a Spiderman comic and a Conan novel. Whatever the combination, the intent is the same. Feed off the good and become enraged at the evil. Submerge into a pretend place and time where two things exist—good and evil— and there is no choice as to which one must win out.

By Wednesday afternoon, five days before the Giants come to Candlestick, Jamie Williams has selected this week's reading. The first is a Spiderman adventure in which a bloodthirsty supervillain known as Hobgoblin is toasting people right and left. The people are in danger and they need help. Spiderman is their only hope. The other is a Conan saga, *The End Must Come.* From now until the game, Jamie will gorge himself on the brutality and the injustice being wreaked on good by evil. He will read at night before he goes to bed. He'll read at the hotel the night before the game. And he'll read again the day of the game and in the locker room right before he takes the field. Good versus evil always fires him up.

Jamie knows that against the Giants, he will need to be more fired up than he has ever been. Because he will be playing against Lawrence Taylor. But no matter how well he plays against L. T., Jamie Williams cannot come even close to saving the day by himself. No one can do that. But he has do his part. Or everything could go to hell.

Hell. That had come to earth in San Francisco last Sunday, and no one in a 49er uniform would ever forget it. On a cold, windy, rainy, and miserable Sunday at Candlestick, the 49ers got a taste of their own medicine from the most offensive of enemies. The Los Angeles Rams.

Most of the day, the rain fell in thick sheets and the wind cut holes in faces and hands if they weren't shielded. Afterward, most of the players shrugged off the storm's effect on the game. But anyone who watched John Madden's chalkboard diagram of the Fuji blimp being yanked like a cotton ball across the angry gray sky overhead knew that such talk was only macho pride. Because down on the field, the wind and water were making it very hard to play football.

The Rams, winners of only three of their first 10 games of the season and a team destined to miss the playoffs entirely after being picked by some forecasters to win the Super Bowl, take control of the game early. In the first quarter, San Francisco loses the ball twice on fumbles and once on an interception, and the Rams lead, 7–0. By halftime, the 49ers have fumbled the ball to L.A. twice more, and the Rams are in control 21–7.

In the third quarter, the Niners look like they are ready to play like the team that tied an NFL record by winning its eighteenth straight game the week before against Tampa Bay. Running back Harry Sydney grabs a Joe Montana pass and threads his way into the end zone for one score. And right before the end of the quarter, Mike Cofer's 42-yard field goal closes L.A.'s lead to 21–17.

But that's as close as San Francisco would get to the Rams. And, aside from the tricky L.A. nickel defense, the wind was the biggest reason. In the third quarter, when Rams quarterback Jim Everett was throwing into the wind, he completed only two of five throws for 21 yards. L.A.'s only first down came on a penalty. But in the fourth quarter, when Everett had the wind at his back, things turned around. Everett was five for five for 63 yards, and the Rams made three first downs through the air. With 13:08 left to play and the game still on the line, the Rams started a drive at their own 10. With the wind at his back, Everett promptly drove the Rams 90 yards in 17 plays for the touchdown that put L.A. in command 28–17. Joe Montana and the 49er offense got the ball back with just 2:31 left in the game. On first down, Montana threw deep into the wind for Jerry Rice. The ball died and L.A.'s Vince Newsome intercepted. It was the Niners' sixth turnover of the day. It was their first loss of the season.

They had lost the way they usually win. With a long drive and big plays at the end. After the game, the Rams gloated. As they ran up the tunnel to their dressing room, they pounded gloved fists on the wall outside the 49er locker room. And they shouted:

"LOSERS . . .

. . . LOSERS . . .

. . . WE BEAT YOUR ASSES . . .

. . . HOWZ IT FEEL, LOSERS?"

To the 49ers, it felt pretty damn bad.

But if the Niners had fallen from perfection, they were not the only ones. That same Sunday in Philadelphia, the Eagles pushed the New York Giants all over Veterans Stadium. The Giants scored the first touchdown of the game, but it was all downhill after that. Two interceptions and a dominating game by Eagle quarterback Randall Cunningham paved the way for a 31–13 pasting. That day the Giants are humiliated on both sides of the ball. Lawrence Taylor has one solo tackle, one assist, and no sacks. Superman gets into three footraces with Randall Cunningham. Cunningham wins the first two. On the third, L. T. manages to get the quarterback down—by ticking Cunningham's foot as the Philly quarterback motors by him.

Phil Simms, too, has his share of problems. Against the Eagle defense, the NFL's top-rated quarterback completes only 17 of 40 passes. Simms is sacked twice, and he throws those two interceptions—one of which is returned for a Philadelphia touchdown. As Simms leaves the field after the game, the Philly fans swarm over the entrance to the tunnel leading to the Giants' locker room, howling a dictionary full of epithets at the bum from New York. Simms could have ignored them. Football players do it all the time. But fresh from his team's first loss of the year, Simms is in no mood to put up with a bunch of jerks from Philadelphia. Simms pauses and stares up at the mob. He points at them. Then he gives them the finger. Both fingers, in fact. On a day that started good and went rotten after that, it was the only revenge he could get.

By 2:30 in the afternoon of December 1, San Francisco's final full-length practice before the blood feud has been over for more than an hour when Chet Brooks follows George Seifert down a hallway into a meeting room at the Taj. Seifert opens the door and remains in the hallway until Brooks goes in. Then Seifert closes the door behind him. Both men sit down. The discussion is short.

"How are you feeling?" Seifert asks his safety.

"I feel good," Brooks answers, quickly.

"Do you feel like you can play?"

"Definitely. I'm ready to go."

"Well, it's not set in concrete, but at this time we're not sure we want to push it."

Brooks stares coldly at Seifert, who pauses before speaking again.

"We'll need you there at the game to help coach," he says.

"I'll be there."

There's nothing else to say. The choice has been made, and there is nothing Brooks can do to change it. So he stands up to leave. Seifert does not stop him. Brooks opens the door and walks back up the hallway into the locker room. There are only a handful of players left at the Taj. There are even fewer reporters. Hardly anyone is around to see that the look in Brooks's eyes is the same as it was that night in Dallas when he was holding the football in warm-ups and realized that he was not going to be playing football. The look is simple, but like a prism it reflects a splintering set of emotions. Anger. Frustration. Disgust. Detachment. Determination. They are all there.

Brooks has practiced exactly two times since his surgery. George Seifert has decided that it is simply not enough time. He's decided that Brooks's left knee is simply not ready to go. Privately, Seifert had pulled for Brooks to make it in time for the game. Having coached defensive backs for so many years, Seifert *likes* defensive backs. But difficult as it was, Seifert had watched Brooks run and cut and jump and he had accepted the fact that his ballplayer was not ready to take part in the blood feud. The team would have to get it done without him.

Acceptance, however, was not one of the emotions reflected in Chet Brooks's big cold eyes that afternoon at the Taj. Tolerance? For this game perhaps. But only because yesterday morning, Ray Rhodes, San Francisco's defensive backs coach, came down with stomach pains and was rushed to Stanford Hospital for an emergency appendectomy. That's why Seifert asked Brooks to be at the game. There will be a three-way phone hookup linking Rhodes's room to the coaches' booth at Candlestick to the sidelines. Chet Brooks will be asked to put on a headset and help put the secondary in the right formations. That's why he's going to the game. If the team didn't need him to coach, no way would he be there. No way. Chet Brooks doesn't show up unless he can hit somebody.

So on Monday night, he will be making an exception to that rule. And to Brooks, there really is no other choice. He knows that if the Niners are going to win the blood feud, they are going to need his help. And if one thing means something to Chet Brooks, it's giving everything he has for the good of the team. So he will be there on the sidelines to help his boys fight the blood feud. He will help coach. But he won't like it. And he will never accept the idea that his knee isn't ready. That won't come until long after he is gone from the game and the locker has somebody else's name on it.

At 3:30 the next morning, Colleen Burt is asleep. Her husband, Jim, however, is wired. He's been this way the whole week. He's downstairs watching another old movie on TV. In a few minutes, "SportsCenter" comes on ESPN. Jim saw the show five hours ago, but that doesn't matter. He can't sleep, so he'll watch it again. After that, he will trudge back up to bed. He will try to sleep. He will toss and turn. He will tamp the pillow. He will turn the pillow over. Nothing works. Finally, around 5:30, he will look at the clock. He will look over at Colleen. Then he will think to himself, *The hell with this.*

This means he has given up on sleeping and is about to do what he has done almost every day this week. He will put on his sweat clothes and his Nike high-tops and drive over to the Taj. There he will watch films of the New York Giants. He will lift weights. Then, when the rest of the coaches and players get there, he will watch more film, take in some meetings, and practice. Then he will drive home, play some catch with Jimmy Jr., and have dinner with Colleen and the kids. After dinner, they will all talk and watch a little TV. Then it will be time for Jim to go to the hotel with the rest of the team. After some meetings and something to eat, Jim Burt will go up to his room.

He will not be able to sleep.

That won't come until Wednesday. When he has had time to calm down from the blood feud. When he has had time to recover from eight years of memories that have welled up and shouted in his dreams.

Jim Burt signed with the New York Giants as a free agent in 1981. That year the Giants got a new defensive coordinator, a New England Patriots' assistant named Bill Parcells. That year the Giants made the playoffs, but lost to the 49ers at Candlestick and their season was over. Two years later, after a losing season, the Giants promoted Bill Parcells to head coach. The team's first season under Parcells was rocky. More than half the players spent time on the injured-reserve list, and the Giants led the NFL with 58 turnovers. New York won only three of 16 games in 1983, and nobody knew where things were headed.

But the Giants were headed in the right direction. In 1986, New York roared to the top of the mountain in the National Football League. New York didn't lose a game at Giants Stadium all year. Lawrence Taylor was named the league's Most Valuable Player. Bill Parcells was hailed as the coach of the year in all the national polls. At the Rose Bowl in Pasadena, the Giants slaughtered Denver 39–20 to win Super Bowl XXI. That season, Jim Burt made the All-NFL Team and the NFC Pro Bowl squad. In six years, Burt had gone from a long-shot free agent to one of the NFL's best nose tackles. In six years, Jim Burt and Bill Parcells had worked together to take the New York Giants from a team without much talent or depth to winners of the biggest prize in the game. Standing at the top of the football mountain, the Giants could see a long way in every direction. Very few of them were looking down.

The next season, Jim Burt hurt his back. He missed half the season—and even in the games he played, he wasn't very effective. After the season, he had surgery. In 1988, Burt came back and started all 16 regular-season games at nose tackle for New York. In the off-season, he signed a new contract that included both a raise and a signing bonus.

The next year, the Giants got rid of him.

The problem was his back. After two major surgeries —the first was done to fix a herniated disc in 1983—the Giants were becoming convinced that Burt's ability to stay healthy was coming to an end. This conviction solidified in the spring of 1989, when Burt sat out the Giants' minicamp with a sprained muscle in his back. Officially, as Giants' general manager George Young told *Newsday,* the team was "very nervous" about the condition of Jim Burt's back. Privately, however, Bill Parcells had already decided that his nose tackle was through.

Three days before training camp opened that year, Parcells called Burt into his office at Giants Stadium. Parcells, Burt remembered later, informed him that he had failed his preseason physical. To Burt, this didn't make sense. *How could I fail my physical when I never even took a physical?* he wondered as he listened to Parcells tell him how worried the team was that he would hurt his back seriously—maybe even permanently—if he continued to play.

"So you're cutting me," Burt said to Parcells.

"No," Parcells answered. "I'm asking you to retire."

At first, Burt was "pissed off" as he listened to Bill Parcells tell him he was through as a Giant. Burt still wanted to play football. And his back felt much better than it had in minicamp. But Burt and Parcells were friends. And if Parcells said there was something so wrong with his back that he was asking him to retire, then something must really be wrong with his back. Ever since the Giants started winning, the coach and his nose tackle had been bluntly honest with each other. The two would go back and forth all the time. They were kidding. But they were serious.

"I brought you here," Parcells would say, baiting Burt. *"I gave you a chance. You would never have been anything without me."*

"Yeah," Burt would shoot back, *"if you didn't give me a chance somebody else would have. If I ever go somewhere else, I'll haunt you. You know me. I'll do anything I can to beat you."*

It had never really mattered how much of what was said between the two was joking and how much was serious. Because Jim Burt was a Giant, and that's always the way he wanted it to be. Then Bill Parcells called him into his office and everything changed. That summer day, Burt remembers asking Parcells the same question about 20 times.

"So, you're cutting me."

And he remembers getting the same answer from Parcells every time.

"No, I'm not cutting you. I'm asking you to retire."

Only once—maybe twice—did Burt take things a step further.

"What happens if I don't want to retire?" he asked Parcells. Parcells didn't waffle.

"We aren't going to ask you back."

By the time he left Bill Parcells's office, Jim Burt had pretty much accepted the fact that his time had come. Football had been fun. But as he left Parcells's office, something still didn't make sense. Two days before, Burt had been talking with Russell Warren, the Giants' team physician. What Warren had told him about his back was nothing like what Bill Parcells had just told him about his back. Jim Burt remembered Russell Warren's words.

"Jim, your back is as good as it's been since your operation. You should be playing."

Suddenly, Burt knew what was happening. He was being forced out. Out of the organization he grew up with. Out of the organization he had helped build from the ground up. Out of football. Three days before the season was starting, he was being told he could no longer be the only thing he had wanted to be ever since he was old enough to walk—a football player. Inside, Burt raged at Parcells. *If he wants me out, why doesn't he just come out and say it?* he asked himself. *I always told him, "When it's my time, tell me and I'll listen."* Burt felt that he had always been honest with Parcells. And now Parcells was betraying him. Burt went home and thought about things. The more he thought, the angrier he got. After playing eight seasons in the NFL, the end had come. But instead of handshakes, hugs, and some priceless memories and friends, eight years had instead come down to nothing more than anger and lies. Somehow Burt couldn't stand the thought of leaving football—leaving the Giants—that way. So he did what Bill Parcells asked. He retired. The reason was simple. He had spent his whole life playing ball of one kind or another, and he didn't want to spend the rest of his life hating something he loved so much.

It didn't take long, however, for Burt to realize that he had made the wrong decision. That fall, when he watched the games on TV on Sunday, he could still feel everything inside him. The adrenaline. The intensity. He missed being around the guys. He realized that he missed everything about football. He realized that he wanted to be out on that field. During the fall of 1989, Jim Burt thought often about what Russell Warren had told him.

Jim, your back is as good as it's been since your operation. You should be playing.

Then he did some thinking of his own. *If my back is as good as it's been since my operation, then how come I'm not out there?* he asked himself. The answer, of course, was because the New York Giants didn't want him anymore. And if he couldn't play for the Giants, he didn't want to play at all. He had never really liked the idea of leaving home. He'd been born in Orchard Park, New York, where he played baseball, football, and hockey in high school. And except for his four years at the University of Miami, New York and New Jersey had been home for as long as he could remember. Besides, playing for another team meant uprooting Jimmy Jr., his first child, from his friends and finding a good school once the family got where they were going. And then there was the fact that Colleen would have to make friends all over again, too. On top of all that, in the fall of 1989, Colleen was pregnant with their second child. The baby was due right after Thanksgiving.

On the other hand, the way he left the Giants rankled Burt—big time. "The only thing I ever wanted in football was to leave on my terms," he said one day at the Taj. "I wanted to be in a position where I could say, 'Okay, I've done what I wanted to do, now it's time to leave.' With the Giants, I didn't leave on my terms." As September turned into October and the 1989 NFL season approached its halfway point, Jim Burt wasn't sure what to do or to think. He was confused. All he knew was that when he turned on the TV on Sunday, the one place in the world he wished he could be was on one of those football fields.

When the 49ers offer Jim Burt a job right before Halloween, Colleen Burt has a choice to make. She knows Jim misses football. And she's still furious—maybe even more than Jim is—at the way the Giants treated her husband. But she's pregnant. And if Jim signs with the 49ers, he's going to have to miss being in the delivery room like he was when Jimmy Jr. was born. The weekend the baby is due, the 49ers are playing on ABC's "Monday Night Football" in San Francisco. Colleen knows that it will be hard being apart at such an important and emotional time in their lives. Jim knows it, too. But both husband and wife also know what Russell Warren knew. Jim's back is as good as it's been for a long time. He should be playing football. Especially on that Monday night when the team the Niners are playing is the New York Giants.

On November 1, 1989, Jim Burt signs a one-year contract and becomes a backup nose tackle for the San Francisco 49ers.

On November 27, 1989, at 8:36 A.M. Eastern Standard Time, in a Bergen County, New Jersey, hospital, Colleen Burt gives birth to a baby girl, Ashlee Nicole. Colleen's labor lasts about two hours. She is on the phone with Jim almost the whole time.

Also on November 27, 1989, shortly after 9 P.M. Pacific Standard Time, in a football stadium 3,000 miles away, the San Francisco 49ers beat the New York Giants, 34–24, on "Monday Night Football." In the third quarter, the Giants are driving to tie the score when Jim Burt forces a fumble that San Francisco recovers. After the game, Burt roars into the locker room and pours chicken soup—part of the players' postgame meal—onto the floor in front of the defensive line's lockers. Then he showers, dresses, and heads to the airport and the red eye to New Jersey. Daddy is going home to see his baby girl.

Jim Burt has never forgiven Bill Parcells for the fact that he missed being there when Colleen had Ashlee. He says he will always remember how Parcells lied to him about his back. He remembers how things didn't have to end the way they did. He still thinks back to the times he told Parcells, *"When it's my time, tell me and I'll listen."* He remembers how he and Parcells used to be friends, and how these days they are the most bitter of enemies. What hurts the most, he says, is that it didn't have to be that way. It just didn't.

In his sleepless nights this week before the blood feud, Jim Burt also has been thinking about the promise he made to Bill Parcells during the good times in New York. The promise he never expected to have to keep. The promise he is now willing to do anything to keep.

If I ever go somewhere else, I'll haunt you. I'll do anything I can to beat you.

On the morning of the game, he has one thing left to try.

Ronnie Lott's gray Nissan Pathfinder hurtles toward Candlestick on Monday afternoon. Lott is on his way to the blood feud. He's not alone. This afternoon, hours before the biggest game of the season, Lott carries a passenger—a teammate who has never ridden with him to a home game before, and may never do so again. The two aren't close friends. They don't go bowling together or play golf together or have dinner together. In fact, the only thing they really do together is play football. But today Ronnie Lott and his passenger are as close as two men can be. Today they are more than teammates. They are kindred spirits, linked by one goal, one thought, one heartbeat. To both Ronnie Lott and Jim Burt, winning the blood feud is all that matters now.

It is everything.

Which is why, at their pregame meal this morning, Burt asked Lott if he could ride to the stadium with him later. He had a plan. He knew exactly what he was going to say.

Between the parking lot of the Airport Marriott, the hotel on the San Francisco peninsula where the Niners always stay the night before a home game, and the parking lot at Candlestick, Jim Burt and Ronnie Lott cover a wide range of subjects concerning the game they are about to play. One of the things they talk about is New York Giants' quarterback, Phil Simms. Jim Burt knows that what he is about to tell Lott about Simms will make Lott angry—the kind of deep, frothing anger that makes football players like Lott dangerous. Burt knows Lott will be angry about what he is going to say. That's why he's going to say it. He's taking no chances with this game. Burt scuffs the soles of his Nikes on the floorboard of the Pathfinder. Then he says what he's been waiting all day to say.

"When I was there, he always felt that he could throw the ball on you guys. He's always thought that."

Phil Simms and Ronnie Lott have been playing football against each other for nine years. And all that time, according to Jim Burt, Phil Simms has believed that he could challenge the 49er secondary—*Ronnie Lott's secondary*—anytime he wanted to and get away with it. *Anytime he wanted to.* Almost right away, Burt can see that his plan is working. By the way the conversation is going, he can tell that Lott is getting angry at what Phil Simms has been saying about him all these years. He can hear the anger in Ronnie's voice. And he can see it in his eyes. To Burt, Lott's eyes reflect the danger pumping through the heart of a warrior. *Don't mess with me*, the eyes say. *Don't even. . . .*

In the NFL, secrets last seconds. And so Ronnie Lott

Huey Lewis & the News handle the national anthem before the blood feud between the Giants and Niners. To the 49ers, Lewis is more than a celebrity fan. He's family.

Linebacker Keith DeLong flies at Giants' quarterback Phil Simms in the first quarter. Simms throws the ball away, and New York has to punt.

Jim Burt, a former Giant, is so wired for the blood feud he hasn't slept in three nights. Here, as New York drives deep in Niner territory in the second quarter, Burt whips The Faithful into a frenzy.

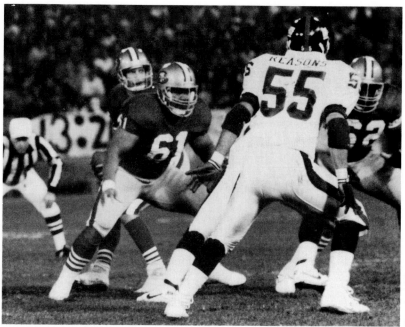

Just before halftime, Montana looks left toward the end zone for Jerry Rice. When a Giant safety runs to cover Rice, Montana hits John Taylor over the middle for what will be the winning score.

Simms and Ronnie Lott tangle after the Niners stop New York on fourth-down late in the game. Simms didn't know it, but Lott's fire had been stoked before the game by his old friend Burt.

Lawrence Taylor isn't Superman anymore, and the Giants have lost the blood feud. But LT is calm. He has a feeling the Giants will get another shot at the Niners this year.

George Seifert glowers at an official in the rematch against the Rams. Seifert is incorrigibly tense, but in Anaheim the pressure is worse because he knows that a win clinches the homefield advantage in the playoffs.

With the Rams beat and the Niners' playoff path secure, Matt Millen yuks it up on the sidelines. After the season, Millen jumps to the Redskins.

Dexter Carter suffers on the sidelines after his fumble costs San Francisco the Saints' game. Only six days before, the rookie had scored his first NFL touchdown.

From left to right: Harris Barton, Bubba Paris, Steve Young, and Jesse Sapolu wait out the final seconds of the win in Minnesota. It's the end of the regular season, and the whole team is exhausted. But the playoffs are next.

Jerry Rice's touchdown puts the Niners up on Washington in the playoffs.

Left: Less than three months after breaking his leg, Mike Sherrard scores against the Redskins. Right: After Michael Carter's touchdown in the final minute, Candlestick explodes. As usual, the Niners are making big plays when it counts. That's about to change.

Phil Simms (far left), hurt late in the regular season, watches the NFC Championship Game on crutches. Simms' replacement, Jeff Hostetler, helps New York win the game with his scrambling.

The Faithful swallow John Taylor and Brent Jones after Taylor's third-quarter score gives the Niners the lead. The mood at Candlestick is delirious. It won't last long.

Leonard Marshall's hit knocks Joe Montana out of the game. The Niners recover the fumble (left), but the Giants now have control of the game.

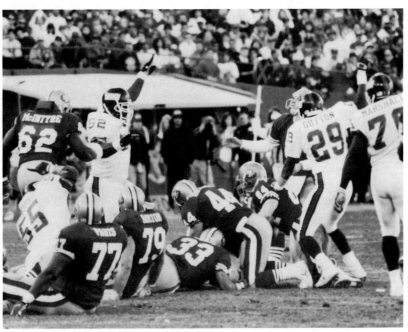

Roger Craig (33) fumbles and the dream is dead. The play ends a nightmare year for Craig, who, like Ronnie Lott, signs with the Raiders after the season.

has heard this kind of talk before. Being in the league as long as he has, he's heard things like Jim Burt has just told him from time to time. But now it's not just talk anymore. It's fact. Jim Burt said so. And Jim Burt was a Giant. Piloting the Pathfinder to Candlestick, Ronnie Lott thinks about what Phil Simms has been saying about him all these years.

He always felt he could throw the ball on you guys. He's always thought that.

To Lott, Simms's words have done the one thing that he cannot tolerate: They have challenged his honor. For Ronnie Lott, there is only one way he can react to an affront like this. He must defend himself.

At all costs.

After weeks of breathless hype, the game of the season has finally arrived. December third. Giants and Niners. "Monday Night Football" at Candlestick. The moon is full. The air is cold. The blood feud is about to commence. Up in the ABC booth, Frank Gifford is preparing what will be the largest television audience to ever watch a "Monday Night Football" game for the bloodletting to follow.

"Tonight," Gifford says, "one team will win, one team will lose. The loser will have dropped two in a row. The winner will be the best team in football tomorrow morning, and the favorite to win Super Bowl XXV. Who's the better team, you or me, baby?"

Slobberknockers. The blood feud is full of them. When New York has the ball. When the Niners have the ball. On punts. On kickoffs. All night. Nonstop. Only a few guys really know how to deliver slobberknockers. Guys who wake up hitting. Guys who dream about hitting. Guys who are supposed to be spending time with their kids or their wives or their girlfriends but are thinking instead about hitting. About slobberknockers. Hits that make a guy's mouth wrench open to spurt slobber. Sometimes, when a guy has just been slobberknocked, his mouthpiece pops out between his teeth through the bars of his face mask, and the slobber comes spitting out. Other times, the mouthpiece stays in and only the slobber comes out. Either way, the result is the same. Somebody gets their butt kicked.

John Madden talks about slobberknockers on CBS, but the blood feud is ABC's territory. And although Dan Dierdorf is like John Madden in a lot of ways, Madden is Madden. And on this night at Candlestick, Madden would be in heaven. There are slobberknockers everywhere. The first one comes on the fifth play of the game, when Niner Greg Cox rockets down the field on a San Francisco punt. Dave Meggett, the Giants' return man, catches the ball and cuts to his right when Cox explodes through two New York blockers. Like a stray dog fighting for the last scrap of meat at the back door of a restaurant, Cox rips into Meggett and bulls him to the ground. Meggett is flat on his back at Candlestick when Cox's teammates do to him what teammates often do when one of theirs has just delivered a slobberknocker. They jump in his face. They slap him on the helmet. They yell.

The blood feud is on.

Next series. New York ball. Rodney Hampton, the Giants' rookie running back, takes a pitchout and cuts left. Jim Burt slides down the line of scrimmage to make the tackle. As Hampton cuts up inside, Burt dives. Hampton's churning knee slams into the side of Burt's head. Both players go down. Burt gets up and doesn't know where he is. He wobbles toward the 49er bench. Sometimes, guys on offense give slobberknockers to guys on defense. Football is a crazy game.

Same series. Third and six from the 49er 30. From the shotgun, Simms hands off to Meggett, who tries to scoot outside. Charles Haley ditches his blocker and meets Meggett in the backfield. Six-five, 230 pounds against five-nine, 180 pounds. Meggett has no chance. Loss of four. Out of field goal range, the Giants have to punt.

In the beginning, the two teams are feeling each other out. On defense, the Giants are moving Lawrence Taylor all over the place trying to disrupt San Francisco's blocking patterns. One time Taylor lines up on the right side of the line. The next play, he's over on the left. One play, he's slashing in to get Joe Montana. On the next, he's retreating back in coverage. L. T. doesn't give out any slobberknockers, but the Giants are shutting down the explosive San Francisco offense. And since the Niners are stuffing New York, too, neither team is scoring any points. The blood feud is even. For now.

Just as Jamie Williams knew he would, Lawrence Taylor is challenging him as few opponents can. Just as Jamie had said during the week of the game, L. T. is still as good as linebackers come. *Fast, strong, and relentless.* But tonight, Superman is doing one other thing that Jamie knew he would to try to break his concentration. He is talking "mess." One of the first times L. T. talks mess to Jamie, it's a running play in the first quarter. Jamie has just driven Taylor out of the play sideways on a block.

"Fuck you, Jamie," Superman goads, his voice mixed with nonchalance and disgust. "Fuck you, Jamie."

Jamie grins at L. T.

"Don't cry, Superman," he says.

Then he walks back to the huddle. Later, after the game, Jamie will say that it was at this point, after this running play, when he decided it was time for Conan the Barbarian to take over for Spiderman. The forces of evil, he knew then, were going to stop at nothing to destroy the good people of the city. And, Jamie Williams knew, if he was going to help save the day, then drastic measures would be necessary. Because *the end must come.*

The first quarter ends with no score. The 49ers have had the ball three times. They have punted three times. The Giants have punted twice. Already, there have been

half a dozen wonderful defensive plays. And three slobberknockers.

Early in the second quarter, Phil Simms overthrows
wide receiver Lionel Manuel on third down and the
Giants have to punt. The Niners get the ball back on the
New York 38. The Giants don't deliver any slobberknockers, but with the help of a holding penalty on San
Francisco running back Tom Rathman, New York does
play defense well enough to stop the Niners on fourth
down at the Giant 26. Mike Cofer misses the field goal.
Still no score.

The Giants run three plays and punt. The 49ers run
three plays and punt. The Giants take over again on their
44. Running back Ottis Anderson takes a pitchout and
sweeps left for a gain of four. Simms finds tight end Mark
Bavaro over the middle for 23 yards. After two runs gain
three, Simms hits receiver Mark Ingram for eight and a
first down at the 49er 18. On third down, after Ottis Anderson hits the line twice, Simms rifles a pass for Rodney
Hampton at the 49er 10. The ball ricochets through
Hampton's hands—right to wide receiver Stephen
Baker, who catches the deflection and makes it down to
the San Francisco three. If Jim Burt had slept at all in the
past three days, he would have dreamed of this situation:
The Giants, three yards from the 49er end zone, the only
thing standing between them and six points is the Niner
defense. And him. This is what football is all about. Two
teams. One wants to get it in. The other wants keep it out.
Who wants it more?

On first down, Burt, linebacker Keith DeLong, and
defensive end Pierce Holt stuff Ottis Anderson on a run
up the middle. No gain. Simms misses Bavaro in the end
zone on second down. On third down from the three,
Ottis Anderson takes a handoff and starts off left tackle.
An avalanche of red and gold gushes toward him. The
first Niners to hit Anderson are Bill Romanowski, Keith

DeLong, and Michael Carter. Then Holt, Kevin Fagan, Matt Millen, and Dave Waymer help finish Ottis off after only a yard. It's not exactly a slobberknocker, but the Giants don't get into the end zone. On fourth down, though, New York does get a field goal and the early lead in the blood feud.

The Giants kick off. With 3:26 left in the first half, the 49ers take over on their 37. Roger Craig runs right for four yards. On second down, Montana throws too low for John Taylor up the right sideline. On third down, Montana takes the snap. Roger Craig flares out of the backfield to his right. The Giants' pass rush heaves toward Montana. Montana takes a quick drop and zips the ball by a charging Lawrence Taylor. Roger Craig catches the ball between two linebackers and runs for his life across the middle of the field. Craig outruns New York safety Myron Guyton and cuts up the left sideline in front of the San Francisco bench. His knees pumping like jackhammers, Craig chugs 31 yards to the Giant 28.

With 1:36 to go before the end of the half, the Niners come to the line on second and five at the Giant 23. Montana takes the snap and looks left. Jerry Rice is there, running a pattern toward the end zone. Montana cocks to throw. In the middle of the field, Giants safety Everson Walls sees Montana pump toward Rice. To Walls, it looks like the real thing, so he runs to cover Rice. But there's pressure up the middle, so Montana pulls the ball down and leaves the pocket. New York isn't rushing anyone from Montana's backside, so Niner left tackle Bubba Paris is just watching things. Bubba sees John Taylor bank his pattern sharply from right to left toward the middle of the end zone. Bubba can see that Taylor is open. Bubba looks back at Joe to see if he has noticed the same thing.

Taylor screams into the end zone. Giants' cornerback Mark Collins is right behind him. Joe sees Taylor. The opening is there. It's going to be close. Joe guns. The ball dives in low. Taylor slides to his knees and cups his arms to receive it. Collins lunges—and misses by inches. Taylor hugs a touchdown and spikes the ball. The Faithful go wild. The blood feud is theirs. They can feel it.

The second half is almost exactly like the first. Slobberknockers and punts, but no points. Late in the third quarter, the Giants have a first down on the San Francisco 35. Simms goes back to pass. Mark Bavaro lumbers upfield off the right side of the line. Simms spots Bavaro and throws. The Giants' tight end is six-foot-four, 245 pounds, but he's so tough that he plays heavier than that. Bavaro is a load, a cement mixer with hands like pillows. From his safety spot in the middle of the field, Ronnie Lott sees Simms throw, too. He breaks for the ball.

Four years ago, on another Monday night in the same year the Giants won the Super Bowl, Mark Bavaro did something that few players in the NFL can say they have done: He embarrassed Ronnie Lott. New York had the ball at midfield in a game it trailed 17–0 early but would come back to win, 21–17. The Giants were driving for one of their three second-half scores when Bavaro ran a route over the middle and Simms hit him with the ball. Like tonight, Lott saw the whole thing and kicked in the turbocharger. Most times, when Lott kicks in the turbo and delivers a hit, the guy crumples to the ground and doesn't get up for awhile. Nobody in football can deliver a slobberknocker like Ronnie Lott can. But on that December night in 1986, Mark Bavaro didn't go down when Ronnie Lott hit him. In fact, Bavaro carried Lott—and a passel of other Niners—almost 15 yards before finally going down.

Like Bavaro, Lott is as tough as a cement mixer. But tonight, courtesy of Jim Burt, Lott's engine has one thing Mark Bavaro's does not: a tank full of rocket fuel. Sandwiched between two Niner defenders, Bavaro reaches up for Simms's pass. Lott is on his way from the center of the field. The ball is overthrown, and, with Lott boring toward him, Bavaro is hung out to dry. Bavaro is falling, his right arm in the air, his body facing forward, as Lott unloads full force just under Bavaro's face mask. It's a major slobberknocker. Bavaro's head snaps back. He crumples to the ground. Then he gets up like nothing happened. Dave Waymer, however, does not. As Lott unloaded on Bavaro, Waymer converged on the ball and almost picked it off. As he hit the ground, though, Waymer's weight crunched down on his left wrist. He leaves the field wincing.

Up in the ABC booth, Dan Dierdorf and Frank Gifford put Lott's hit into perspective. "Ronnie Lott again sets the tone for this entire team," Dierdorf says. Gifford takes up the other side of the collision—Bavaro. "He'll be back over the middle tonight—perhaps looking for Ronnie Lott."

Both observations are correct.

Two plays later, the Giants have a third down at the San Francisco 35. Simms takes the snap and moves back in the pocket. From the left, Charles Haley explodes around Giants' tackle Doug Riesenberg. Up inside, Niner rookie Dennis Brown has lost his man, New York left guard Brian Williams, with a move to the outside. As Simms cocks to throw, both Haley and Brown hit him. Haley swipes at the ball and it comes loose. There is a scramble. When the officials get to the bottom of the pile, they give the ball to San Francisco. The Niner with the ball is Dave Waymer.

A damn football player.

On the fourth play of the fourth quarter, the Giants have a first down on their own 31. Simms finds Bavaro open in the middle of the field between three Niners. Lott thunders up from free safety to make another big hit

on the New York tight end. Bavaro goes down after a
gain of 14. But then, just like before, he gets up as if nothing happened. But something has happened. To Ronnie
Lott's right knee.

Soon after Lott's hit on Bavaro, the Giants have to
punt. The 49ers run four plays and have to punt. With
8:05 left in the game, the Giants have a first down near
midfield. Phil Simms drops back to pass. Before he can
even finish his drop, however, Kevin Fagan rumbles in
from his blind side and, just as Simms cocks his arm to
throw, smashes him in the back. The ball comes loose.
Ottis Anderson is just minding his own business, picking
up a blitz, when the football comes bouncing toward him.
Ottis grabs the ball and takes off. He gains 20. The Giants
have first down at the Niner 31. On the next play, Anderson ducks through the line and gains three. At the end of
the play, Ottis is going down in a pile of Niners. Lott sees
that Ottis will be down before he can get a hit in, so he lets
up. As Lott puts on his brakes, Kevin Fagan dives toward
Anderson. Fagan's helmet crashes into Lott's left knee.
At this moment, the Giants look like they have the luck. A
fumble by their quarterback has just turned into a big
play and a first down well into San Francisco territory.
Now, Ronnie Lott has to leave the game, limping. Both
knees are bad.

With seven minutes left in the game, the Giants have
the ball on the San Francisco nine. The score is still 7–3
Niners. But everyone at Candlestick knows one play
could change all that. On first down, Simms wants to
throw, but Michael Carter is up in his face so fast he has to
unload incomplete before he even has time to look for a
receiver. On second down, Simms throws for Stephen
Baker in the corner of the end zone. But cornerback Don
Griffin has Baker covered, so Simms launches out of
bounds, incomplete. Candlestick is buzzing. This—two
heavyweight football teams bashing each other to see

which is the best—is exactly what they have come to see. *Who wants it more, you or me, baby?*

On third and goal from the nine, Mark Bavaro rumbles off the line toward the end zone. Simms takes a quick drop, sees his tight end come open just across the goal line, and pumps a spiral toward him. Simms is sure the Giants have a touchdown. Bavaro is wide open. No one is around him. But there is someone. Someone he didn't see.

Just as the ball arrives, a hand reaches in and deflects it away from Bavaro. The hand of Ronnie Lott. With both of his knees sprained—one so badly that he won't play again until January—Lott had limped back into the Niner huddle before the snap. And, with the game on the line, he made a play that some guys couldn't make if they were healthy. Fourth down from the nine, less than four minutes left. The Giants have a choice. Kick an easy field goal and still trail 7–6, hoping the defense can stop the Niners and get the ball back in time to try for another score? Or go for a touchdown right now and either get the points for the win or nothing?

On the San Francisco sideline, Jim Burt stares across the field at Bill Parcells. Burt knows what Parcells is going to do on fourth down. *I know you, you sonuva bitch,* Burt thinks to himself. *I'm into your brain so deep it's scary. You don't want our offense to get the ball back. You want to win it right here. C'mon, call a play.* With 6:52 left in the game, Parcells sends the play into the New York huddle. Simms drops back and throws into the end zone for Lionel Manuel, who has juked and faked his way off the line into the end zone. Niner cornerback Darryl Pollard, however, doesn't bite on any of Manuel's fakes. Pollard deflects the pass away. Candlestick explodes. The chant of the Faithful is electric, a deafening, all-circuits roar that crackles down from the orange seats onto the field.

"DEE-FENSE! DEE-FENSE! DEE-FENSE!"

Down on the field, the Niners are celebrating, too. Dave Waymer jumps three feet into the air. Ronnie Lott, the adrenaline camouflaging the damage in his knees, jumps in the air and shoves his arms up into the night. Greg Cox, who played with the Giants last year, picks Darryl Pollard up by the waist. Pollard gives a high five to Pierce Holt. When Cox lets him down, Pollard sees Ronnie Lott charging toward him. Pollard thinks Lott wants to join him in an airborne high five, so he coils, jumps, and—Lott doesn't even see Pollard as he runs by, suckerpunching the air. Ronnie Lott doesn't see Darryl Pollard because the only person at Candlestick he can see right now is the quarterback of the New York Giants.

Jim Burt is probably the only person in the stadium at this moment who knows what has just happened. Who knows that Ronnie Lott has just exploded. Who knows that the rocket fuel he poured into Lott's tank on the ride to Candlestick has finally reached ignition temperature. The chemicals in the fuel are all there—the challenge Phil Simms has put to him—*he always felt he could throw the ball on you guys, he's always thought that*—the slobberknocker he delivered to Bavaro in the third quarter; the hit he put on Bavaro, when he hurt his right knee; the Ottis Anderson run when Kevin Fagan bashed into his left knee; the Giants, inside the Niner 10, driving to take the blood feud; the third-down pass he knocked away from Bavaro; the fourth-down ball Darryl Pollard batted away from Lionel Manuel. In one moment, in the north end zone at Candlestick, all of the volatile elements have smashed together inside Ronnie Lott. For Lott, the heat of the fusion is more than he can stand.

Suddenly, Lott is sprinting on two bad wheels up the field toward Phil Simms, who looks at Lott like a guy watching a car come at him while he's trying to make it across the crosswalk—*Is this guy gonna stop or what?* Lott puts the brakes on late and rams into Simms. Lott's gray face mask crashes into Simms's white face mask. Lott is barking at Simms. Later, Simms will say he was surprised more than anything else. He will say that it's never been like Lott to let his emotions get out of control. But with Lott up in his face, out of control is just what Simms decides Lott is right then. Later Simms will say he thought Lott was going to take a shot at him. That's why he snapped his chinstrap back up. For several moments, Simms and Lott square off, each barking and shoving at the other. Then the confrontation is over. For now.

On the last play of the game, the Giants have the ball at the San Francisco 27. New York can still win the blood feud with one play. Simms wants to throw, but nobody is open. Then the protection breaks down. Simms scrambles upfield to buy some time, but Kevin Fagan dives and catches him from behind. Sack. Game over. Face down on the cold turf at Candlestick, Simms explodes. Just like Ronnie Lott had on fourth down a few minutes ago. He is so frustrated he can't think. Ten years of losing games like this—10 years of losing games like this to the 49ers—have all been instantly distilled into a single time and place. Eating grass at Candlestick, Simms slams the ball into the ground. As it caroms crazily away, Simms gets up and goes looking for Ronnie Lott. He finds him near the Giants' bench.

Dozens of photographers, reporters, and players encircle them. The knot of people lurches and sways like a mob at a rock concert. At the center of the knot, the quarterback of the New York Giants is jawing at someone, the veins in his neck swollen with frustration and effort. The knot is too thick to see who Simms is yelling at. But there is no mistaking the words. They come quickly, a short, bitter blast fired from a smoking-hot weapon.

"I HAD FUCKING RESPECT FOR YOU," Simms snarls.

The knot of people turns, just enough to reveal that

Ronnie Lott is the one up in Simms's face. The knot turns again. From inside their helmets, Lott and Simms flash anger with their eyes. There's a detachment, a disconnectedness, in them that's frightening. They look like rabid dogs. Simms, however, is sparring with more than just his eyes. He has hold of Lott's jersey at the neck. As the knot lurches toward the locker rooms, Jim Burt, Simms's old teammate, joins the fray. Burt sees Simms. He sees Lott. He sees the way Simms is holding Lott's jersey. He does not like it. Because Ronnie Lott is his teammate. And because Phil Simms is his friend.

"HEY!" Burt yells. Simms doesn't let go.

"HEY!" Burt bellows again, banging Simms on the shoulder pad. This time, Simms lets go of Lott's jersey. But he ignores Burt and pushes to break away from the knot of people.

"HEY!" Burt yells. Simms turns and runs off into the crowd.

The 49er locker room is electric. Winning the blood feud has ignited something inside them. Something more potent than knowing that they are 11 and 1 and the best team in football right now. Winning the blood feud has squarely addressed something that has been loitering in the back of their minds since the start of training camp. A question has been answered—if only partially —that each player and coach has been doing his best not to talk or even think about: *Can we be as good as we were last year?*

Now that they have played the best team the NFL has to offer and come out on the right side of the score, the answer to the question is clear. And although they must still keep winning to earn the home-field advantage for the playoffs, San Francisco's win has given the team an important glimpse of who they are and where they are headed.

"From here on out, we can do anything we put our minds to," Charles Haley says, pulling his shoulder pads off over his head. In the blood feud, Haley was what coaches call a "force." He made five tackles, including the one on Meggett in the first quarter that knocked the Giants out of field-goal range. He had that sack on Simms in the third quarter, half a sack on the play in the fourth quarter when he knocked the ball from Simms and Dave Waymer recovered. And there were still other plays when the Giants could not figure out a way to keep him from making trouble. Sitting, still in his game pants, on the stool in front of his locker, Haley is talking about what winning has now given San Francisco.

"It's up to us," he says. "We can be whatever we want to be."

All night the battle had raged and no one knew how or when it would end. On one side there was good. On the other was evil. Sometimes, the battle got nasty. But in the end, good was better, and the day had been saved again. Fifteen minutes after the blood feud has ended, Jamie Williams stands with a towel around his waist, talking to a crowd of reporters. Spiderman tells them how this game meant more to him than beating the Giants and proving that the 49ers are the best team around. To him this game was personal because of the way the Giants had cut him in training camp earlier in his career.

Several minutes later, most of the reporters are gone when Williams turns around and sits down on his stool. His eyes are the same kind of eyes that had flashed out from inside the helmets of Ronnie Lott and Phil Simms in the knot of people near the Giants' bench. The blood feud is over, but Jamie Williams is still as pumped as if he was out there with L. T., who made only three tackles and, although he nearly got to Montana a few times, was largely neutralized in the blood feud.

"In the beginning, he was jumping around on me," Jamie says of Taylor. "He was trying to finesse me. When guys do that, sometimes it gives me trouble, because I don't know quite where he's going to be. I like it when guys take me on. When they take me on, I got 'em. L. T. started taking me on. And then he started talking at me. When he started talking, I knew I had him. I knew I was getting to him."

A reporter asks Williams if he still remembers what it felt like to be cut by the Giants. Spiderman stops dressing. He stares hard and cold right through the reporter.

"I'll never forget, man," he says. "I'll never forget the way they made me feel. *Never.* I hate those fucking Giants. I hate those fuckers."

Ronnie Lott sits hunched over on a table inside the trainer's room. His left knee, the one he hurt when Kevin Fagan crashed into him tackling Ottis Anderson in the fourth quarter, is stretched out in front of him, packed inside a brace. It's sprained badly—so badly that he'll leave Candlestick on crutches. Lott's right knee is also sprained, torqued the wrong way during his collision with Mark Bavaro a few plays before. It's throbbing almost as bad as the left one. A crowd of more than a dozen reporters loiters at the entrance to the trainer's room, which is off limits to the press. There's not much to see— or hear. For the longest time, Lott just sits there, staring down at his throbbing knees like they're old tree limbs with their bark gouged up by a chain saw. The reporters want to know what Lott has done to his knees. They want to ask him about the thundering slobberknocker he put on Mark Bavaro. But most of all, the writers want to know what happened out there in the knot of people near the Giants' bench. With Phil Simms.

Up the tunnel in the Giants' locker room, Phil Simms has just showered when the media horde presses in on him. Simms stands facing his locker. He has a towel around his waist. For a couple of minutes, the scene is the same. The reporters pepper him with questions. Simms dresses, staring silently at the back of his locker, trying to ignore the press. Finally, Simms knows the herd is not going to go away.

"All right," he snaps, turning around to squint into the lights of several television minicams, "let's do it."

The first topic is the fourth-down pass that Darryl Pollard knocked down in the end zone. A reporter asks Simms if the Giants were in the wrong formation on the play. Simms answers with his eyes locked blankly on the floor, the irritation in his every word. "There should have been another guy over there. It didn't make a difference. I was trying to throw it to Lionel, okay?"

Then a reporter asks what happened after the play, when Ronnie Lott charged over and got up in his face. Simms raises his eyes and glares at the reporter. Then his eyes fall back to the floor. "You play in this league twelve years," he mutters, "and you have to put up with this shit."

Simms takes a deep breath, letting his exasperation build, then lets it all out. Finally, he answers the question. "I ain't gonna tell you exactly what happened, but it was nothing."

"It looked like it got a little heated out there," a reporter says.

"Nah, it was nothing. Jim Burt just brought some of his friends, that's all."

Tomorrow, several newspapers will report that when Ronnie Lott charged into Simms, the 49er safety called the Giants' quarterback a "choker," according to a photographer who was on the sidelines. Tomorrow, both Lott and Simms will deny that claim. Tomorrow, Phil Simms will tell Frank Cooney of the *San Francisco Examiner*, "Believe me, if he had said that I wouldn't have taken it. It was just something like, 'We stopped you, we showed you.' It wasn't anything to remember."

But that's tomorrow. Tonight isn't over. Not yet.

A few minutes later, back in the Niner locker room, the crowd of reporters is still waiting to talk to Ronnie

Lott when there's a commotion by the trainer's room. Escorted by security guards, a stocky man with blond hair has slipped through a side door and walked over to the table where Lott is sitting. Phil Simms does most of the talking, in hushed tones that none of the reporters straining to hear him can make out. Except for when he looks up to see who is standing next to him, Lott doesn't look at Simms. He mumbles only once or twice. The expression in Lott's eyes reflects three emotions. The first two are exhaustion and pain from the throbbing in his knees. The third is embarrassment. After two or three minutes, Simms and Lott shake hands. Escorted by two security guards, Simms leaves. Lott remains seated, his damaged legs throbbing on the table in front of him. He is still staring at the floor.

In a few minutes, after Lott has struggled slowly into a pair of black designer jeans and a black sweater, Lindsy McLean fits him with a pair of crutches. Then Jimmy Warren leads Lott out through the mob of reporters into the tunnel. Someone asks Lott how his knees are. He stops and turns around.

"I actually sprained both my knees," he says, quietly. "I'm just going to have to take it day by day." Jimmy Warren puts a hand on Lott's shoulder. Lott swivels on his crutches and turns to leave. He stops himself after a step or two. He turns and looks back at the reporters.

"I'm too tired and too sore to talk right now," he says. "Thank you anyway."

A bead of sweat hangs from the tip of Jim Burt's nose. Half an hour after the blood feud, Burt is dressed in a red-and-black sweat jacket, jeans, and his white Nike high-tops. He's still woozy from his collision with Rodney Hampton's knee in the first quarter. Officially, he will be listed on the injury report with a concussion. It'll be another day and a half before he gets any real sleep. Tonight he'll be so wired from the game that he'll be up watching "SportsCenter" again. But just now Burt is at his locker trying to clear the cobwebs. He is also trying to tell a handful of reporters what winning the blood feud means to him and the 49ers. Earlier in the week Jim Burt had talked about the hate. Now he talks about the fear.

"A lot of the guys on that field tonight have dreamed about being professional athletes their whole lives," Burt says, wiping the sweat from his nose and forehead with his right hand. "I know I have. Four years in college, now 10 in the pros. Most people don't make it here. Once you make it, you want to be the best. Those guys are the best—one of the best—teams in the league right now. To me, this game felt like a championship game. There was so much emotion out there. Both teams wanted this game bad.

"This is a simple game. You either win or you lose. There's no in-between. And when you lose, there's nothing. It's the emptiest feeling in the world. I mean, when you're competing, when you put everything you have into something, when you go through training camp and bust your neck to get to these guys, to a game like this, and then to lose, it scares you. It scares you to think that all that work has gone into losing."

A drop of sweat formed and fell off the end of Jim Burt's nose. He looked away. Then he shivered.

After the newspaper reporters have gone back upstairs to write their stories, Pierce Holt sits alone in the San Francisco locker room. The blood feud ended more than an hour ago, and Holt is the last 49er at Candlestick. He rests his elbows on his knees. He stares down at the floor. He coughs. This morning, Holt woke up with a sore throat. If there hadn't been a game, he says, he'd have stayed home to rest. But there was a game. There was a blood feud. So he had to go. George Seifert says Holt is the kind of football player who uses up "an awful lot of energy" when he plays. Tonight, as Holt sits alone, exhausted and coughing after the blood feud, Seifert's words come to life.

"That was the hardest sonuvagun I've ever been involved in," Holt says, shaking his head at the floor. "It was a war. Losing a game like this is horrible. You go home and you go over every play trying to find that one thing that you could have done different. Losing a game like this makes it hard to sleep. You just lay there, running the plays over in your head. Over and over and over."

Pierce Holt coughs. He tiredly pulls a T-shirt over his head. He coughs again. Then he stands up and trudges slowly out into the tunnel toward the parking lot. The end has come.

Up the tunnel in the Giants' locker room, only one player is left. Dressed in his customary black ensemble—black turtleneck, black corduroy pants, and black loafers without socks—Lawrence Taylor is cornered by half a dozen New York television reporters just inside the door. The bright white lights of the minicams make Taylor squint as he quietly and automatically mouths the reasons why the Giants lost the blood feud. Tonight, for the second time in two years, Taylor's Giants have come to Candlestick to play the Niners on "Monday Night Football." And for the second time in two seasons, his Giants have lost. In the NFL, every loss is hard to take. And for the Giants, of course, losing to the Niners has always carried a little extra sting—especially after what happened last year. Lawrence Taylor is disappointed. It's all over his face.

But unlike last year, there is none of the devastation he felt when he hobbled up the ramp of the plane on crutches with a broken bone in his foot and the pain of another loss to the 49ers stabbing at his insides. Tonight in the blood feud, the Giants' defense held the NFL's most explosive offense to just seven points. New York forced San Francisco to punt nine times. The Giants never sacked Montana, but there were times when the world's greatest quarterback was running for his life. On several of those occasions, Montana was running from Superman.

They had come so close. Another inch or two and Mark Collins could have knocked down Montana's pass for Taylor in the end zone in the second quarter. Thrown a second sooner or a tad in the other direction, Phil Simms's third-down ball for Mark Bavaro in the fourth quarter would have been a touchdown—maybe the winning touchdown. But things didn't happen that way, and the Giants lost. In the NFL, there are no points awarded for almost winning. And there are no moral victories. You either win the game or you lose the game. Simple. Cold. Final. Lawrence Taylor knows this. And, for the umpteen-millionth time, he is saying that he knows this to some talking TV heads who are keeping him from getting on the bus for the airport and the red eye to Jersey.

But there is something different about L. T. tonight. The look on his face is different than the look on many of the other Giants' faces. He isn't angry, raw, and boasting of revenge in the playoffs as was Leonard Marshall, New York's relentless pass rusher.

"We'll be back, you can count on that," Marshall grunted. "I guarantee you the 49ers will remember the Giants."

As usual, Phil Simms was frustrated by the loss. But tonight it was clear he was as embarrassed as Ronnie Lott was by their confrontation on national television. Bill Parcells has already dealt with the reporters who are second-guessing his decision to throw on fourth down at the Niner three instead of kicking an easy field goal and leaving it up to his defense to get the ball back again. Parcells, who likes reporters even less than George Seifert does, couldn't have cared less what the hell a bunch of reporters thought.

But Lawrence Taylor, by comparison, doesn't look exhausted, disgusted, or broken by the effort and emotion of the blood feud. He is calm. Taylor slips into a black jacket and picks up his bag.

"Something tells me we'll meet again in January," he says quietly. Then the bright lights go out and Superman disappears around the corner.

Chapter 16

The Young and
the Restless

On the Friday after the blood feud, the Niners fly to Cincinnati. On Sunday, the Bengals are fired up. They play like it's the Super Bowl. They have San Francisco down in the fourth quarter. But the Niners still win on a field goal in overtime. San Francisco's record is 12 and 1, the best in the NFL. The Niners have already clinched their division, the NFC West, and are ahead of both the Giants and the Bears in the race to establish home-field advantage in the playoffs. With three weeks left in the regular season, San Francisco's climb up the mountain appears to be going perfectly. But for some Niners, things are as far from perfect as they can be.

On the Thursday night before the Bengals game, Chet Brooks could not believe what was happening. For weeks, Brooks had worked to get his knee ready for the blood feud. And then, two days before the game, George Seifert called him into the little room at the Taj and told him that he was going to miss the biggest game of the season. Brooks was not pleased, but he knew that there was still plenty of season left. Plenty of time for him to get back in shape and get out on the field and make some plays. So he set his sights on Cincinnati. He thought his knee would be ready by then for sure.

Besides, Brooks knew, the secondary was hurting. Ronnie Lott was still out with his bad knees, and the hard carpet at Riverfront wasn't going to help safety Johnny Jackson's ankle, which he had twisted against the Giants. With the secondary banged up, Brooks knew his boys needed him. And so, in practice on Wednesday and Thursday, he had shifted things into high gear. He tried to run a little harder, cut a little sharper, and jump a little higher. He was going to be ready for the Bengals. He was going to finish the season.

But when he looked down at his left knee on Thursday night, Brooks could not believe what he was seeing. His knee was swollen. It had filled up with blood. And there was more torn cartilage. Brooks didn't know these things at the time. He wouldn't know exactly what had gone wrong inside his knee until Monday. But Chet Brooks didn't need some fancy X-ray to tell him what was wrong with his knee. He knew what was wrong. He knew.

The elevator door opens and Chet Brooks shuffles in. His knee is heavily taped. He can barely bend it. Every step is painful. It's Saturday morning, and he is taking the elevator down to the lobby of the Omni Netherland Plaza hotel in downtown Cincinnati. He is dressed in a blue sweat suit. Headphones are plugged into both ears.

"You don't look so good," someone says when Brooks walks in. "What's wrong?"

"They don't know," Chet says, glumly, as he watches the numbers at the top of the elevator. "Two days of work and I go home and it blows up."

The elevator reaches the fourth floor. The doors open and an overweight man wearing a loud Hawaiian shirt and a straw hat barges in with three kids and two women. One woman looks like the man's wife. The other is either his mother or mother-in-law. Without seeing any obvious clues, the man identifies Brooks as a 49er. He does not notice that Brooks is in no mood for small talk.

"Practice, huh?" the man says in a loud, cheerful voice. "What time do you guys go to the stadium?"

Brooks glares at the man. He has that look on his face again. The one he had on the sidelines in Dallas. The one he had in the locker room at the Taj when George Seifert told him he wasn't going to play in the blood feud. Now Brooks has the look on his face because his knee is screwed up, he can't play against the Bengals, and he isn't going to practice today. With his knee throbbing and his season probably over, Chet Brooks glowers at the goof with the Hawaiian shirt and the happy attitude.

"About twelve-thirty," Brooks says, finally, his voice a fusion of anger and frustration. The elevator reaches the lobby. The doors open, and Brooks lurches forward to leave.

"Ninety-one, man," he mumbles to himself. "Ninety-one has to be better."

By Thursday, four days before the second Ram game in Anaheim in mid-December, San Francisco's other starting safety is also sick and tired of talking to reporters about the condition of his left knee. "I'm not talking," Ronnie Lott tells John Crumpacker of the *Examiner*. "I don't want to be bothered." The day before, Lott had told another reporter to call his 1-900-LOTT-LINE to find out the latest on his condition. When Richard Weiner of the *Peninsula Times Tribune* hung up, he knew about as much as he did before he spent $2 of company money. The message on Ronnie Lott's machine said that he was hoping to play against the Rams on Monday night, and that he had been using acupuncture to help heal his sprained knees.

By Thursday, however, things didn't look good for Lott and the Rams' game. That afternoon, according to the Niners' official injury spokesman, George Seifert, Lott had flown to Los Angeles to get a second opinion on his knee from "a doctor of his own choosing."

"It's professional, it's his career, and it's not unusual," Seifert said of Lott's trip to Southern California. A reporter then asked Seifert if Lott's injury, which the team was still calling a sprain, now involved torn ligaments. And if so, would surgery be necessary?

"You're inaccurate if you make [surgery] the imminent thing," Seifert answered, "because I don't think it is. But I'm not a doctor either. Right now that's about all I can really say about the situation."

As usual, reporters found two ways to interpret Seifert's obliqueness. First, there was the possibility that Ronnie Lott's knee was worse than anyone had thought. Lott might, in fact, need surgery and be out for the rest of the year. Or there was the chance that Seifert was just being Seifert. If reporters don't find out exactly what's wrong with Ronnie Lott's left knee, they can't put it in the paper. And if they can't put it in the paper, then the Rams won't know exactly what's wrong with Ronnie Lott's knee either.

"MAN, YOU PLAYIN' THAT TAPE GAME AGAIN?"

Defensive lineman Larry Roberts is yelling as he ambles toward the practice field at the Taj. It's early in the afternoon on Friday, 15 minutes before the coaches will come down out of their offices to start practice. Roberts is watching five 49ers take part in the most intense competition of the week. Joe Montana, Steve Young, and Steve Bono are playing for Team Tape. Jerry Rice and Roger Craig are today's amateur participants.

Three nights from now in Anaheim, the Niners will be playing to lock up the home-field advantage in the playoffs against the only team that has beaten them this season. Yesterday, one starting safety, Chet Brooks, had surgery on his left knee for the second time this season. The other starting safety, Ronnie Lott, flew to Los Angeles to see if he also will need knee surgery. The Niners should be intense. They are banged up on defense, and there is a pressure game ahead. They should be intense. Some of them are. But not for the Rams. Right now the Rams are three days away. And they have 15 minutes to play. Fifteen minutes is a very long time when the game is good. The Rams can wait.

Jerry Rice and Roger Craig showed up a few minutes ago. "The boys are here now," Rice had announced, an impish smile creasing his face.

"Look, Joe," Steve Bono said, "he's got his own tape."

Montana looked at Rice, who was cradling five rolls of tape in the crook of his left arm, like he was heading to the express lane at the store. Montana, however, was too busy lobbing rolls of tape to care that much right then. *Lob, miss, lob, miss.* Steve Young looked at Rice, too, but refused to debase himself by speaking to anyone who didn't play for Team Tape and, thus, was clearly outside the sacred circle of quarterbacks. Young went back to watching Montana. *Lob, miss, lob, miss.* That left it up to Bono, the lowest-paid member of Team Tape, to defend the honor of the circle. Bono watched Rice throw. He missed. Then he watched Roger Craig throw. Not even close.

"Amateur night at the Apollo," Bono said, trying his best to be condescending.

Jerry Rice put up another roll. It spun out of the top of the goal post like a putt lipping out of the cup.

"Shit," Rice snapped. "That was close."

"Try again, man," Roger Craig said. Rice did. He missed.

For the most part, the three quarterbacks ignored Rice and Craig—except when they saw a chance to make fun of them. This was easiest when Roger Craig was looping his wild launches in every direction up over his head. Every time Craig would lob a roll of tape, he would shriek with delight.

"*OOOOOAAAWWW . . . that was close.*" The throw might have missed by six or seven feet—most did—but Roger Craig still shrieked with delight as if he had almost put one in.

"AAOOOOOWWWW . . . that was close."

A couple of times, Craig wound up and heaved rolls of tape *behind* him. Still he shrieked.

"OOOOOAAAAWW . . . man that was close."

After awhile, though, Craig got bored and left to stretch his legs for practice. Jerry Rice didn't mind that at all. He didn't have to take turns anymore.

"Gonna make one today, boys," he announced, staring up at the goal post. "Got to make one *today*." Rice looked over at the quarterbacks. Steve Young was busy lobbing, Montana catching them as they fell. But, at the same time, Montana was watching every time Rice threw. *Lob, miss, lob, miss.*

Young was finished now, and it was Bono's turn. So Montana gave up the rolls of tape he was holding. Joe stood and watched as Rice missed by five feet with a loppy, off-balance toss. The next one got closer, but still missed. Then Rice wound up to lob one underhanded. He bent his legs and swung his right arm into motion. Just as he was ready to release the roll of tape, Montana skied into his face, his right arm outstretched like a six-ten center about to snuff some little guy's lay-up. Rice aborted his lob. Montana came down out of the air. Rice crinkled his mouth and looked exasperated. *Do you mind?* his face was saying. Montana grinned back at Rice. It was the All-American, apple-pie, I'm-going-to-Disneyland kind of look that one reporter who knows Joe says is partly an act so his teammates don't get jealous of him. But mostly, the reporter says, the look is real. Joe is real. A real Joe. Joe was grinning at Jerry Rice. *Of course I don't mind,* he was saying.

Montana sashayed in front of Rice back under the goal post where Steve Bono was throwing. Then it was Montana's turn. He threw and missed. Suddenly, Joe dropped his rolls of tape, picked up his helmet, and ran out onto the practice field. Jerry Rice, Steve Young, and Steve Bono did the same thing. Behind them, back by the locker room, George Seifert was walking across the artificial turf toward the two grass practice fields at the Taj. Play time was over. The Rams were important again.

Other teams such as the Falcons and Raiders have loud rock music blasting through their locker rooms. Not the Niners. Other teams laugh and whoop and goof off at practice. Not the Niners. The Niners are focused. The Niners are intense. They are a machine. A machine that when turned on knows only concentration and effort and intensity. The week of the Rams game, however, the machine starts to hum differently somehow. All of a sudden, the edge of tension and pressure, the precise purpose, the rigid relentlessness of weeks past are gone. Like they evaporated somewhere. Earlier in the season, Eddie DeBartolo had written his players a letter. In the letter, DeBartolo reminded everyone to lighten up a little, to have fun playing football. To some of the Niners, it was probably a new concept. But the week of the Rams game showed that many of them were learning. Even Harris Barton.

One day before practice, Barton was watching Joe Montana lob rolls of tape up at the top of the goal post. Usually, Barton is so intense, so deadly serious, that he looks like he's about to burst. He doesn't, but he looks like he could any minute. This afternoon, however, Barton watched Joe Montana lob a roll up, up—right into the tub. Steve Young and Steve Bono whooped and hollered, then—SSSMACK!—they slapped high fives with Joe. Watching from a distance, Barton smiled.

Harris Barton smiled.

What was happening? Only days from one of the more important games of the season and Harris Barton was smiling? Were the Niners cracking under the strain of it all? Was the NFL's most uptight team actually lightening up? One day during the week, Spencer Tillman, one of San Francisco's special teams' "Dogs of War,"

talked about the change. "I think a big part of it is the fact
that we can see the light at the end of the tunnel," Tillman
said. "All of the preseason goals that we set for ourselves
are starting to materialize in front of us. And everyone
understands now what it's going to take to actually realize
the dream. [The Super Bowl] isn't just an exercise in goal
setting anymore. It's not just something in our hearts and
minds. It's right out there on the field. We can all see and
feel the goal starting to come to fruition. And what that
does is justify everything we've done to get to this point.
All the extra work, the time. This thing is materializing.
The picture is coming into focus."

Someone told Spencer Tillman that Harris Barton
had smiled on the practice field. Tillman put his hand to
his chin. "Let me try to picture that," he said.

By Sunday afternoon, the picture is coming into
focus just as Spencer Tillman had said. The Niners may
be dinged and depleted, but at least now they know
where they are. This weekend both the Giants, NFC East
leaders at 11 and 3, and the Bears, NFC Central leaders
at 10 and 4, have lost. Until this season, the winners of the
three divisions in the National Football Conference—
East, Central, and West—were all guaranteed a week off
before their first playoff game. This season, that's
changed. In a bid to generate more TV money, the NFL
has added two more teams—and two games—to the
postseason tournament. Now the division winner with
the worst regular-season record has to play one of the two
new teams in the week that they previously would have
spent resting and healing before opening the playoffs.

But one other perk is at stake as the end of the regular
season approaches. The division winner with the best
record in the conference wins the right to play all of its
playoff games at home. With a win over the Rams on
Monday night, San Francisco will be 13 and 1. It means

that, even if the Niners lose the rest of their games and
the Giants win the rest of theirs—putting both clubs at 13
and 3 at the end of the regular season—the Niners will
hold the advantage over New York because of their win
in the blood feud. In the NFL, the home-field advantage
can mean the difference between standing on top of the
mountain with somebody else or alone. And in the NFL,
there can be only one.

As United charter flight 5073 touches down in Long
Beach late on Sunday afternoon, a burnt orange sun
strains to push through the clouds and smog that hang in
the fading winter light. After the plane lands, the players
file onto buses. Then, police officers on motorcycles es-
cort the buses out of the airport. As the buses slide toward
the 49ers' hotel in Anaheim, every member of the team
knows exactly what has to be done tomorrow night. They
all know exactly where they are.

They are at the end of the beginning.

And the beginning of the end.

At 3:45 Monday afternoon, two hours and 15 minutes
before the game, the buses rumble out of the hotel parking lot toward Anaheim Stadium. Jamie Williams and
Dexter Carter are sitting next to each other. Whenever
he's been able to, Jamie has tried to say something positive to Dexter before every game. He said it last week in
Cincinnati. He said it the week before that against the
Giants. Before that, he said it against the Rams, Tampa
Bay, Dallas, Green Bay—he's been saying it almost every
week for the whole season. Jamie has been saying it to
keep Carter positive. But he's also been saying it because
he knows it's true. Riding on the bus to Anaheim
Stadium, Jamie repeats what he's been telling Dexter
Carter all season.

"Man, I think tonight's the night. I think you're gonna
break one." Jamie is nodding his head at Dexter.

"Those jets, man. Those jets."

It's only a matter of time, Jamie tells the rookie, before those jets go to work on a defense. Only a matter of time.

Jamie Williams has been in Dexter Carter's corner all season. Williams was a rookie once, and so he knows how tough coming into the NFL out of college can be. He had to go through it alone. He had no one to help him get through being signed and cut by the Giants, signed and cut by the Cardinals, signed and cut by Tampa Bay. He had no one to help him stay strong and positive. And because he didn't have anybody telling him how dangerous getting down on himself can be in professional football, Jamie got down. It was a long time before he learned that he was only hurting himself. It was a long time before he crawled out of the black hole. This season, Jamie Williams decided that he was going to try to be for Dexter Carter the someone he himself never had.

Back in Rocklin, Jamie could see right away that Dexter could play. He could see that the guy had jets. And he could see that for a little guy, Dexter was tough and stubborn. But jets and toughness weren't what Jamie liked most about San Francisco's first-round draft pick. What he liked most was Dexter's attitude. "I like the way he approaches the game," Jamie said one day during the season. "He's a guy who can make ten mistakes, and he still stays up. He's still working, he's still listening to the coaches." Carter, Jamie could see right away, wasn't the kind of kid who got banged around on the field and then put his head down and pouted in the corner. Dexter wasn't like that at all. Dexter was gristly, like a three-day-old beard or a gravel road that's just been paved. He had a good head on his shoulders. And he had those jets.

Early in the season, Jamie gave Dexter a nickname. He named his rookie teammate after the one 49er Dexter reminded him of most—Jerry Rice. Rice's teammates used to call him "Fifi," after the puff of afro that was left after one trip to the hair salon early in his career. That name, however, was eventually forgotten. The nickname that stuck was "Flash." To Jamie Williams, Jerry Rice and Dexter Carter had one major thing in common. Jets. But Flash had been around a long time, and Dexter was just a kid.

Sometimes in practice, when Carter would catch a pass or take a handoff and explode 60 yards up the field just like he was trying to outrun the defense in a game, Jamie would yell, "KID FLASH!" Other times, when Dexter would come off the field after a kickoff return or a nice run in a game, Jamie would walk up and pat the rookie on the helmet and say, "That's my boy, Kid Flash."

Wherever he was, Williams took it upon himself to be Dexter Carter's personal cheering section. One day after practice, Dexter was at his locker getting dressed. He was in a hurry. He had to be somewhere, and he was late. Jamie Williams came over and asked Dexter if he had a quarter. Dexter told Jamie he couldn't think right now because he had somewhere to go and he was late. Jamie cocked his head sideways and a curious expression came over his face. Then he smiled.

"Kid Flash does *everything* fast," he said. Dexter stopped pulling on his jeans and looked up at Spider. Carter realized Jamie was giving him a compliment.

"Thanks, man," he said, slapping hands with Jamie. "Thanks a lot. 'Preciate it."

He was gone in two minutes.

John McVay is taking no chances. Neither is Allan Webb. Both McVay and Webb, the team's director of pro player personnel, are standing on the sidelines at Anaheim Stadium. It's an hour before kickoff, but already the two men are doing everything they can to bring victory and the home-field advantage in the playoffs to San Francisco tonight.

They have their lucky jackets on.

McVay's is a green, gold, and burgundy tweed. McVay's wife, Lee, can't stand the thing. Sometimes, when John puts on the coat to go to the stadium, Lee will ask her husband, "Are you going to put *that* thing on again?" John just smiles and puts it on. By McVay's count, the Niners have lost only twice in the time since he started wearing the coat in the middle of last season. With the home-field advantage at stake against the Rams, he's not about to stop being superstitious.

Allan Webb's lucky coat is more basic: a navy blue corduroy with black suede patches on the elbows. "I wear it on special occasions," Webb explains. "Monday nights, playoff games, games we need to win. I wore it against the Giants. Let's hope the magic works again."

On the other sidelines, Harry Edwards is also talking about tonight's game. But to the Doc, tonight's rematch with the Rams isn't about lucky coats or home-field advantage. For the Berkeley professor who grew up hard in Southend, this game has to do with what happened in the rain at Candlestick three weeks ago. "It's like this," Edwards says, folding his long arms tightly across his stomach. "Are you going to let somebody you hate kick your ass twice in one season?"

At the start of the game, the Rams look like they are the ones who are going to kick some ass. Less than two minutes into San Francisco's first drive down the field, 49er tight end Brent Jones slips over the middle and catches a Montana pass. At the Rams' 31, Jones gets knocked hard by safety Michael Stewart. As Jones flies forward, his body outstretched and completely off the ground, the Rams' Pat Terrell crashes in and hammers his helmet into Jones's, whose neck snaps sideways. He crumples to the ground, the ball comes loose, and L.A. recovers. Jones lies motionless on his back for several minutes. He spends the rest of the half sitting on the bench. It's sometime in the second half before he remembers that he's at a football game.

Although Brent Jones's concussion is only one of

three the 49ers will get against the Rams on the night, L.A.'s rough play doesn't look like it will be enough. In the first half, the 49ers have more of just about everything. Defense. Offense. Whatever. On the Niners' next series after Brent Jones gets his concussion, Mike Cofer drills a 23-yard field goal to put San Francisco up, 3–0. In the second quarter, a 15-play drive ends in a Tom Rathman touchdown run. Before the Rams finally score their own touchdown, Jerry Rice hauls in a Montana pass and streaks 60 yards for his first score in a month. At halftime, the Niners are up 16–7.

But mistakes keep the Rams in the game. In the second quarter, the Niners blow the conversion point after Rathman's touchdown when the snap for the kick goes bad. Later, after Jerry Rice scores his touchdown, Johnny Jackson picks off a Jim Everett pass deep in 49er territory. But a penalty against cornerback Don Griffin nullifies the play. Six plays later, Everett tosses a touchdown pass and the Rams are back in it 16–7. The mistakes continue in the second half. Rice catches a 13-yard pass from Montana for his second touchdown of the night, but the points are taken off the board when Rice is flagged for pushing off in the end zone. On the next series, the Rams are at the 49er 22 when Griffin picks off another Everett pass. But Griffin gets called for holding and L.A. ends up with a field goal. With almost the entire fourth quarter left to play, San Francisco leads 19–10. It's still a game.

The Niners have the ball, second and five from their own 26. Up in the press box, offensive coordinator Mike Holmgren looks over his play card. All Holmgren wants is the first down. Anything more is gravy. Holmgren finds the play he's looking for, 17 Weak O. It's a simple run to the left, with Tom Rathman out front blocking for Dexter Carter. Rathman's job on the play is to pull to his left and take out whoever gets in the way. Usually, it's a linebacker. Carter's job is to read the block and, depending on how Rathman does with the linebacker, cut the run up inside or take things out toward the sideline. Mike Holmgren sends the play down to the field—with one change. Jamie Williams goes in for Tom Rathman.

The Niners come to the line. As he crouches down into his stance, Dexter Carter thinks a last thought to himself. *Follow Jamie and read his block.* Jamie Williams lines up slot right, then goes in motion to the left. Montana takes the snap and hands the ball to Carter. As he heads to his left, the 49er blockers go to work. Jamie Williams pushes linebacker Mike Wilcher out toward the sidelines. Left guard Guy McIntyre explodes into Ram defensive end Mike Piel. When Piel crumples to the ground, McIntyre falls on him. Harris Barton pulls all the way from right tackle up into the hole and knocks out Michael Stewart. As Carter rockets up through the hole, there's one Ram who has a chance to get him. Linebacker Larry Kelm is picking his way through the falling bodies toward Carter. But before Kelm can get close enough, Bubba Paris, San Francisco's 300-plus-pound left tackle, throws himself on the ground in front of Kelm. It's not pretty, but Paris's flop seals Kelm away from Carter. There's now a huge crease in the L.A. defense for Kid Flash to run through.

Dexter is not thinking now. He's on autopilot, a computer programmed to execute instructions called 17 Weak O. Carter's computer has registered what Jamie Williams has done to the linebacker. He follows the program and cuts up hard inside. At the 49er 35, he slashes out toward the sidelines and then up the field. It's a footrace now. Up in the press box, Mike Holmgren sees Carter break into the open. Down on the field, Dexter is reacting. But up in the coaches' box, Mike Holmgren is thinking, *I just hope he's in good enough shape to make it to the end zone.*

The last 20 yards are the only time there's trouble. Two Rams have a shot. They're gaining. And the jets are almost out of fuel. At the 20, L.A. safety Vince Newsome swipes a right hand at Carter's back. Nothing but air. As he falls, Newsome claws a hand out at Carter's churning legs. He grazes Dexter's calf and then eats turf. Dexter stutter-steps but keeps going. Right before he crosses the goal line, Ram safety Jerry Gray reaches out for a piece of Dexter's jersey. Nothing but air. Kid Flash is in.

Out of breath, Carter coasts to a stop and points his gloved left hand out at the hundreds of Niner fans— many of whom have flown down into enemy territory from the Bay Area—in the back of the end zone. The Faithful are screaming, giving each other high fives and waving back at Carter, exploding madly in the afterglow of his jets. And the fact that Dexter Carter has just kicked the Rams' ass. Carter turns back toward the field. He's waited months for this moment. These last few weeks, in fact, he's been aching for this touchdown, this feeling. Now it's here. He *belongs*. At last. He's finally shown the guys that he can do what he has been telling everyone he could do if he got the chance. Use those jets. Now he wants to party. He wants to feel the guys slapping him on the back and on the helmet. He wants to hear them yelling his name. Maybe they will even pick him up and carry him off the field on their shoulders.

Jerry Rice is the first teammate to reach Carter at the back of the end zone. As Dexter holds his first touchdown ball, Rice gives Kid Flash a high five and a tap on the helmet. Jesse Sapolu is the next Niner to arrive. Sapolu picks Carter up at the waist and lifts him in the air. Dexter raises his right arm into the night. Back at the 49er bench, everyone gets in on the act. Ronnie Lott pats him on the helmet. Harry Sydney pounds him on the butt. Matt Millen offers a high five. Offensive line coach Bobb McKittrick, a tough ex-Marine who says the thing he is proudest of about himself is that he can endure pain better than just about anybody, gives Dexter a big hug. For several minutes on the sidelines, Jerry Rice stands talking to Joe Montana. Flash has been around. He's seen fast jets before. But now Flash has a huge smile on his face, and every few seconds he can be seen flailing his arms wildly. Sound effects are unnecessary. Anyone can see he is telling Joe about jets.

When he gets back to the bench after blocking on the point-after kick, Jamie Williams heads straight for Dexter, who's sitting by himself.

"That's my boy," Spider says to Kid Flash, offering his hand. "I told you you were gonna break one tonight."

It was only a matter of time.

The Niners have kicked ass and they know it. They've come into the Rams' front yard and delivered payback for that miserable loss in the rain. But more important than any payback, the Niners have just clinched the home-field advantage in the playoffs. Next month, when playoff time comes, they'll be playing at Candlestick for as long as they are around. In the visitors' locker room after the game, the players know they have just made an important surge up the mountain toward Tampa. "We don't want to go into Chicago, and we don't want to go into New York," Jamie Williams says to a handful of reporters. "Those are going to be hostile places. Plus, you've got the elements going against you. Playing at home—it means that if anybody wants to go to the Super Bowl, they have to go through San Francisco. I like those odds."

When he's through talking about the playoffs, Jamie addresses his favorite subject of the night. His boy, Kid Flash. "I told him before the game, 'This is the night you're gonna break one.' I knew he was going to do it one of these weeks. You could just see his work ethic in practice. He was ready to explode. Dexter is *baaad,* man. Did you see the way he took off? I'm tellin' ya, man. The guy's got jets. The guy's got jets."

"Is my hair straight?"
In the tunnel outside the locker room, Dexter Carter

peers into the lens of a television camera. He is patting his hair to make sure the ruts from his helmet have all been combed out so he can look his best when he goes on television.

"Is my hair straight?" he asks out loud. Someone tells him that he looks like a million bucks. The game ended 25 minutes ago, and Dexter already has explained his touchdown run half a dozen times. He looks like he could do it into next week, no problem. As he climbs up on a wooden box to meet the press, John McVay leans against a concrete wall on the opposite side of the corridor. His lucky tweed is folded over his left arm. McVay beams out over the knot of reporters pressing in on Carter. Contentment graces McVay's face as he listens to his club's top draft pick talk about the greatest night of his young career. He looks almost like a proud grandfather.

Tomorrow the Bay Area newspapers will be full of stories about Dexter Carter and his fantastic 74-yard touchdown run through the Southern California night. The stories will detail how 17 Weak O developed, second by second. They will describe how Dexter followed Jamie Williams out to the left, read his block, saw the crease, and kicked in the jets. The stories will quote Dexter as saying the run was his best since high school. They will point out that his 124 yards rushing is the most by a 49er rookie in nearly 20 years. In the *Chronicle*, Lowell Cohn will write how Carter "has the tight, small muscles of a middleweight fighter." Cohn will also quote Mike Holmgren, who says that although Carter is small and gets knocked around a little, ". . . his instincts are very good." In the *Examiner*, Frank Cooney will quote Dexter as saying, "I'm not here to be a backup my whole career. I'm working hard not to be a backup, but to start."

But starting for the Niners, Carter knows, is off in the future. On Monday night in Anaheim, the mob of reporters is now gone. Outside the stadium, the buses are idling, waiting to take the playoff-bound Niners to the airport for the flight back to San Francisco. In the visitors' locker room, Dexter is the last player left. He is saying how restless he has been the past few weeks, waiting and wondering when that first first touchdown was going to come. Although he's been aching to get that first one, he says, because the team kept winning it was all right with him if he never scored. And he says he's as satisfied as he can ever remember being after his first touchdown in the NFL.

"I've been waiting for this to happen for a long time," Kid Flash says, zipping up his bag. "It feels good, real good, to finally get that first one. I'm just going to try and enjoy it for as long as I can."

That will be exactly six days.

Dang.

The following Sunday, with 53 seconds left in the game against the Saints at Candlestick, the 49ers have the ball on the New Orleans 20. Within chip-shot distance of a field goal that could tie the game, Dexter Carter fumbles the ball and the Niners lose, 13–10. Six days ago, on Monday night against the Rams, Kid Flash turned up the jets and flew 74 yards into the night. Afterward, he had felt as satisfied as he ever had in his life. Now that all seems so long ago.   .

After the game, the media mob waits for Carter. The reporters stand packed in around a podium in the San Francisco Giants' clubhouse. Their mood is anxious and, in light of the 49ers' sudden, wrenching loss, oddly up-beat. As soon as Carter gets up behind the podium and begins to take questions, it's clear why. These mourners have come to the funeral to talk with the corpse about his tragedy. Carter speaks in a tired monotone. His answers are vague and evasive. This is definitely not Anaheim.

"As far as I know, I never had the ball," he says, answering one question. "When I watch the film, I'll see what kind of exchange it was. But regardless, we lost the ballgame. There were a lot of mistakes made out there, and who's at fault, I'm not saying. When I see the film, I'll see what happened. As of now, I know it was the exchange between me and the quarterback."

A television reporter says what everyone is thinking. "How do you feel as a rookie, a guy who's been counted on, to be involved in the play that a lot of people say cost the team the ball game?"

"They haven't been hostile or anything," Dexter says of his teammates. "Those kinds of things happen. I haven't heard one person say it's my fault. And I'm not putting the blame on me or the guy who gave me the ball—or tried to give me the ball or whatever. Those kinds of things happen."

Dexter Carter answers another couple of questions before he steps down from the podium in the interview room under Candlestick. He goes to his locker and begins to gather his things to leave. Tomorrow he'll watch the films and see that there was indeed a problem with the exchange with Steve Young at the New Orleans 20. He will see that Steve Young gave him the ball and he dropped it. Weeks from now, Dexter will look back on these last two weeks and realize that he's learned something. He will have learned that he can't get too high or too low or his head will be all messed up. He will have learned that thinking too much out on the field can often ruin a football player's concentration. Dexter will think about those things later. He'll even talk about them with Harry Sydney and Jamie Williams and Roger Craig. He will do all of those things later.

At his locker after he talks to the press early on a Sunday evening two days before Christmas, Dexter stuffs a comb and a mirror and a few other things in his bag. Then he pulls his jacket up tight around his neck. It's cold and windy outside. And he thinks he might be coming down with something.

Although Dexter Carter was unwilling to take the blame for the fumble that cost San Francisco the game, some of his 49er teammates were less than forgiving about what happened on the New Orleans 20. One Niner fumed, "Harry Sydney should have been in there. Sometimes, I don't know what the hell the coaches around here are thinking. They said they were going to rest [Sydney's] ankle [which was sprained two weeks ago in Cincinnati], but then they run the shit out of him on special teams. Then, when all we need is for somebody to take the handoff, run a couple of yards into the line and fall down, he's not in there. Does that make sense?"

For his part, Harry Sydney, a 31-year-old former schoolteacher from Kansas, doesn't want to get dragged into second-guessing the 49er coaches. But Sydney does have another theory. It concerns the lesson Dexter Carter will eventually learn from the last two weeks of his young career as a professional football player.

"You know what it'll do?" Sydney says. "It'll teach him to go with the flow. Don't get too high. Don't get too low. Stay even. That way, the road isn't so rocky. That's what this team is all about. We don't get too high or too low. We just keep moving. By keeping yourself mentally even, you're able to keep concentrating on the game, on what's up ahead. If you get too high, it affects you mentally. You think you have to make something happen all the time. This game is crazy enough. You don't need that added mental strain. Dexter will be fine. But right now, he's young. Dexter is a heckuva athlete. But sometimes I think Dexter thinks too much. He thinks too much instead of just going out there and reacting. He'll come along. He'll age. We all do—if we stay in this business."

"Don't you have enough?"
Matt Millen is growling. For days, a camera crew from NFL Films has been following the Niners around the Taj, filming just about everything. The Niners stretching in practice. The Niners throwing the ball in practice. The Niners catching the ball in practice. The Niners kicking the ball in practice. The Niners standing on the sidelines

during practice. Joe Montana, Steve Young, and Steve Bono lobbing rolls of tape up into the top of the goal posts before practice. Charles Haley and Harry Sydney playing dominoes between practices. The Niners sitting in front of their lockers. The Niners talking to the equipment manager. The Niners walking across the locker room. The Niners looking concerned. The coaches looking concerned. The crew from NFL Films has caught the Niners in almost every conceivable pose. On this afternoon a few days before the last regular-season game of the year, against the Vikings in Minnesota, Matt Millen is walking toward his locker when he notices the camera. It's practically in his face.

In a poll of the 49er beat writers conducted by Richard Weiner of the *Peninsula Times Tribune,* Matt Millen was voted the best interview on the team. The writers also voted the linebacker the funniest player on the team. Matt Millen will say anything to anybody. One day during the week of the blood feud, a reporter asked Millen what he thought of Charles Haley, who was on his way to leading the NFC in sacks and being voted the conference's Defensive Player of the Year by United Press International. That day, Millen leaned back against the stucco wall at the Taj and said the first thing that came into his head.

"What do I think of Charles right now?" Millen said, repeating the question as he often does. "Well, right about now, Charles is over at his locker, standing there with this big schlong hanging down in his shorts."

Everyone laughed. Nobody could believe he would say something like that. But then, if anybody could say something like that, it was Matt Millen. Matt Millen will say anything to anybody. Especially today. With the crew from NFL Films recording how he walks toward his locker, Millen glares right into the camera and growls.

"Don't you have enough?"

The camera keeps rolling.

NFL Films is getting ready for the Super Bowl. The crew has come to the Taj to shoot behind-the-scenes footage for a piece on the Niners' quest for history. The Niners themselves know full well that it's almost money time, that the playoffs are almost here. But there is one matter left to take care of before then. Getting past the Vikings at the Metrodome. NFL Films will be there to catch every snap.

Beating the Vikings, the Niners know, is going to be easier said than done. Minnesota has a lousy record and won't be in the playoffs. But the Vikings do have a defense that can bang an offense around better than a lot of teams in the league. And as it has been every game this season, San Francisco will be playing a team that thinks it's the Super Bowl. The Niners know that they will have to play better than they did against New Orleans, or they'll be heading into the playoffs with a two-game losing streak. And as John McVay said back in training camp, losing can be a difficult habit to break even for the best of teams. Lose a game, McVay said, and there is no telling what can happen. Lose two and. . . .

During the week, George Seifert tells reporters he is in somewhat of a quandary. Does he keep his best players in the game to beat the Vikings and build momentum for the playoffs but run the risk of having Joe Montana or Jerry Rice banged up right before the most important games of the year? Or would it be better to rest certain players so they'll be fresh for the playoffs and accept that the second-stringers who are out there might not be able to pull out a win? By the end of the week, Seifert has made a decision.

"I want to win the game," Seifert explains outside the locker room after practice. "I think we have to focus on doing what we have to do to win. And anything that develops from that, fine. You [also] go into the game and you want to play different players. We [have] that in our minds."

No one in the press corps is surprised to find Seifert sitting on the fence.

One-thirty Saturday afternoon in Minneapolis. The temperature outside is in the minus teens; with wind chill factored in, it's −60 degrees. There is snow everywhere. Inside the Metrodome, the Niners have finished the light workout they always have the day before a game and are headed back to their hotel. Down in the tunnel below the stadium, the players file into two buses. At the last minute, several players decide that they don't want to ride on the team bus. Jim Burt, Tom Rathman, and John Taylor are three of the half-dozen 49ers who pile into a courtesy van provided by the Hilton Metrodome hotel. Burt sits on Taylor's right. Rathman is squeezed onto a luggage rack directly across from them. More than a dozen people are crammed inside as the van lurches through the snow onto the freeway.

The driver says the ride back to the Hilton takes seven minutes. Jim Burt knows just how to spend the time. He taps Taylor on the shoulder. Soon, the nose tackle and the wide receiver are playing a game.

"One, two, three . . . one, two, three."

Rock, paper, scissors.

Tom Rathman watches his teammates, curiously. He's never played this game, and doesn't quite get it. Burt explains.

"At the count of three, you do one of three things. Put out a fist—the rock. Put out two fingers—scissors. Or you do like this—" Burt holds out his hand flat.

"That's paper," he says. "Scissors cut paper. Paper covers rock. Rock crushes scissors."

"Wanna play?" Burt asks Rathman, who nods yes.

"For a buck?" Burt adds, not asking really, but telling.

"Okay, man," Rathman says in his Nebraska Cornhusker drawl.

Almost the entire way back to the hotel, Burt, Rathman, and Taylor play rock, paper, scissors.

"One, two three . . . one, two three . . . one, two, three."

At one point, Burt erupts in laughter. Every time, when he's done counting three, John Taylor does the same thing. Puts out two fingers. Scissors. Burt has tried a little of everything. Paper, scissors, rock—then paper twice, then rock three times in a row. Taylor does scissors every time. Burt thinks this is hysterical.

"Whaddya doin'?" he quacks at Taylor.

Taylor looks right into Burt's eyes. His expression is matter of fact, serious, like a pool shark who knows he is about to sink the eight ball in the corner pocket.

"I'm comin' at ya, man," he tells Burt. "I'm comin' at ya. I'll tell ya right now what I'm gonna do every time."

Taylor holds out two fingers for Burt.

"I'm comin' right at ya, man" he says.

Tom Rathman drops out after a while. Burt and Taylor play all the way back to the hotel. Burt tries everything. Taylor does scissors. As the courtesy van pulls into the parking lot at the Hilton, Burt counts up the wins and losses. Burt takes most of Rathman's money. But John Taylor takes most of Burt's money. As Taylor steps down out of the van, Burt puts a hand on his shoulder.

"I'm comin' at ya, man," he says, mimicking Taylor. "I'm comin' at ya."

Burt laughs. Taylor looks back at Burt. His expression is almost blank. His eyebrows are raised. His eyes show all the confidence of a pool shark who knows he is about to sink the eight-ball in the corner pocket.

On Sunday, the most exciting thing that happens in the first half has nothing to do with the game. Of course, the crowd was stoked when Herschel Walker ran over Dave Waymer on his way to the end zone in the second quarter. But the biggest cheer came at halftime.

The Vikings had planned an exhibition featuring

dogs who catch frisbees. When it was his turn to show the crowd how fast he could run and how high he could jump and how well he could catch a frisbee, one dog trotted to the center of the field, bent down, and peed. Cheering and hollering erupted all over the Metrodome. It was a wash who got a bigger cheer, the dog or Herschel Walker, who plowed over Waymer for the score that put the Vikings up 10–0. Up in the press box, one reporter pointed out the irony that Viking fans were cheering louder for a dog than they were for Herschel Walker. Earlier in the season, *Sports Illustrated* ran a long feature on Minnesota's embattled running back, who had been traded from Dallas for five Vikings and seven Minnesota draft choices in October of 1989. The headline of the story: "I AM NOT A DOG."

In the first half, the Vikings and Niners both play like dogs. On the first play of the game, Viking receiver Cris Carter races by Niner corner Darryl Pollard on a post route down the middle. Minnesota quarterback Rich Gannon, who has the flu and is so weak he can hardly yell the signals loud enough for his teammates to hear, pumps the ball right over Carter's shoulder. It goes right through Carter's hands. The first half is like that for both teams. Passes are dropped. Balls are fumbled. By the end of the half, Joe Montana has completed only 10 of 20 passes for 88 yards. He's thrown an interception, and the Niners have fumbled twice. The Vikings lead, 10–0. It's the first time the 49ers haven't scored by halftime in more than a year.

And then the dog does his thing and the game starts for real. Steve Young goes in at quarterback, and the 49er offense begins to move the ball. On one drive, Young takes the team from the San Francisco 24 to the Minnesota 11. On third down, Young lofts a soft spiral into the end zone. It's an easy touchdown, but tight end Wesley Walls drops the ball and Mike Cofer has to kick a field goal.

Young saves his best for the fourth quarter. With a little more than half the fourth quarter left, Young takes the team down the field to the Minnesota 14. On the next play, he finds Jerry Rice in the end zone and the Niners lead 13–10. The Vikings are back in the lead 17–13 when Young brings the Niners up to the line on first down at the 49er 20 with 3:14 left on the clock.

On the first play of the drive, Young is sacked for a loss of three. Then everything clicks. Young hits Rice for 14, Taylor for 13, then Rice again for 11. A pass to running back Keith Henderson gains nine yards, and a toss to Jamie Williams picks up seven. After Young throws his only incompletion of the drive, he runs twice, first for three yards, then for two. With 36 seconds left, Young brings the Niners to the line at the Minnesota 34. Jerry Rice is split wide to the left. He's the decoy. John Taylor is split wide to the right. He's the one Steve Young will look for. At the snap of the ball, Rice runs a crossing route from left to right. On his way across the field, a Viking safety follows him. At the same time, John Taylor slants underneath toward the area of the field vacated by Rice. By the time Taylor reaches the left side of the field, he's all alone—the safety who is supposed to be covering him followed Rice instead. Young's pass is on the money at the 15 and Taylor outruns two Vikings into the end zone and the Niners have pulled out another win.

In the locker room, they look like they've been through a war. They have welts and bruises and cuts from the artificial turf. They are exhausted. Charles Haley is so tired he asks Harry Edwards to pull his shoulder pads off over his head for him. When the job is done, Haley slumps back on a folding chair in front of his locker. He sits there for a long time.

Most of the players say the game was like every other they've played this season. The other team's record was not as good as theirs, and they didn't really have the kind of talent the Niners have, but they played their best. They played on emotion. They played over their heads as if it were the Super Bowl. At the Metrodome, it had almost worked. The Vikings had almost upset the world champs. Like so many times in the past, the Niners had been down. But right at the end, when it was either make a play and win or let the other team make a play and lose, they had made the play when they had to and the other team didn't. Sometimes it seemed like it had always been that way. Sometimes it seemed like it would always be that way.

Twenty minutes after he scored the winning touchdown, John Taylor stands alone in a corner of the visitors' locker room at the Metrodome. He is pulling on a turtleneck. There are no reporters around him. Not one. At the locker next to Taylor's, at least a dozen reporters are in a semicircle around Jerry Rice. Rice's nine catches gave him 100 for the season. Only three other receivers in the history of professional football have ever caught that many passes in one season. Clearly, Rice's feat is historic. But why does no journalist talk to John Taylor, who, along with Steve Young, is really the hero of this day? Every writer in the league knows why. John Taylor doesn't talk. He just doesn't.

Most believe the receiver's silence dates back to 1988, when, right before the first game of the season, the NFL suspended Taylor for violating the league's substance abuse policy. Supposedly, the newspapers broke the story the same day Taylor's parents were in town from New Jersey. Presumably, Taylor thought the timing of the story was bad. Either that or it was insensitive or inaccurate. No one really knows for sure. Except the man with the scissors.

A few lockers away, Steve Young stood answering questions for almost half an hour. Sweat dripped from his face. Red and pink welts from the artificial turf rose like loaves of fresh bread on his back and sides. The reporters came and went in shifts. Young would start out with half a dozen reporters clustered close around him, and he would answer all of their questions. Then, one by one, the reporters would get their quotes and leave. There would be just two or three left when Young would reach for the strap of his bag as if he was leaving. But then more reporters would drift over and he would feel obliged to answer their questions.

Young had played wonderfully in his half of work. He completed 15 of 24 passes for 205 yards and two touchdowns. The Niners had scored all 20 of their points with Young at quarterback—17 of them had come in the fourth quarter when the game was on the line. With his own team tired and flat, Steve Young had played hard and inspired his teammates just like Joe Montana does.

That man again.

Standing in the locker room at the Metrodome, Steve Young knew that unless a miracle took place in the next two weeks, he had just played in his last football game of the season. Steve Young knew that when the Niners opened the playoffs in early January, he was going to be where it seems he has been all four years he has spent in San Francisco. On the sidelines, wig-wagging the plays in to Joe Montana. Being second-string has always been difficult for Young. Even after making the clutch throw that beat the Vikings.

"I'd like to be a regular quarterback, and to do that you've got to do those kinds of things at the end of a game," Young says matter-of-factly of his pass to John Taylor.

Young pauses for quite a while, thinking. Of what it means to make plays when it counts. Of the four years he's spent pretending to be an NFL quarterback in practice and then watching Joe Montana enhance his legend on Sundays. Of the prospect that, after playing only the second half today and all of last week's game against the Saints, his season is probably over. Finally, a reporter breaks the silence and asks Young what happens now that the season is over and the playoffs are around the corner. Young sighs and lifts his eyes out over the empty-ing Niner locker room. Like every one of his teammates, he knows exactly what's going to happen next week. The players get three days off.

Three whole days.

Chapter 17

Playoffs: Washington

*T*he week started with the tree.

The eucalyptus tree grows outside the fence at one edge of the Taj. It's big. Tall, with branches that are fat and strong. The tree is so tall and strong, in fact, that from almost anywhere in the tree, someone can sit down and look over the fence and see what's going on out on the practice fields. On Tuesday morning the week before the Redskins game, George Seifert decides that he does not like the eucalyptus tree that grows outside the fence at the Taj. Not at playoff time. Only four days before the divisional playoff game against Washington at Candlestick, the 49ers' head coach spotted someone in the branches of the tree watching his team practice. George Seifert knew then that drastic measures were necessary to protect the peace.

That afternoon, Seifert closed practice to all members of the media for the rest of the week. In the past, Seifert and Bill Walsh before him had occasionally locked visiting reporters out of practice. But not since the NFC Championship Game at the end of the 1984 season were local reporters not allowed inside the gray, metal gates to watch the Niners work out. After practice on Tuesday afternoon, Seifert gave the reasons for his decision.

"There was somebody in that tree this morning watching practice," he said. "Swear to God. Absolute swear to God. . . . I'm just showing you the type of environment we live in. It's a war. . . . Things could get out. I jest about them, but they can. We've had a couple instances this season that people knew things they shouldn't have known. We're closing practice not necessarily [just] to the media. We're closing practice to everybody. We just want to have it as secure as we can."

In the days before the game, the airspace above the Taj was crowded with reporters trying to infiltrate Seifert's blockade. The Fuji blimp flew over on Wednesday. The following afternoon, a San Jose television station rented a helicopter and hovered over the Taj for the last 15 minutes of the Niners' practice. The helicopter was so close to the field, George Seifert said later, that he "could have probably hit it with a football." On Thursday, the press tried some ingenious ground tactics. Before the 49ers called the Santa Clara police to shoo them off, a television reporter and camera operator from a Washington, D.C., television station were filming practice from the overpass on the other side of the Taj from where the eucalyptus tree grows. The team was trying to protect the peace. The reporters were doing their best to ruin it. The battle was on as it had always been. Except now, the stakes were as high as they could be. The playoffs were finally here.

Friday morning is overcast and cool. Perfect weather for the men of Team Tape. Before the Niners' playoff-game walk-through, Joe Montana, Steve Young, and Steve Bono are lobbing rolls of tape up at the open end of the portable yellow goal post at the Taj. Because it's playoff time, the quarterbacks have an audience. Mike Holmgren has been through already, talking style and trajectory with Joe Montana. Jerry Rice and Roger Craig stopped by. They stood watching for a minute, giggling the whole time. No one thought to ask them what they were giggling about. Mostly because Jerry Rice and Roger Craig are always giggling about something.

Just now, Spencer Tillman and Jesse Sapolu are

standing off to the side of the goal posts watching their three quarterbacks toss tape into the air. Also on hand are several members of the CBS crew that will be broadcasting the game at Candlestick tomorrow. When Joe Montana tosses and misses, the roll of tape hits the ground and begins swerving along the ground toward the crew from CBS. Steve Young bounces over to retrieve it.

"What are you guys doing?" one of the CBS guys asks Young. "We got a big game tomorrow."

Young looks up at the guy. He's insulted.

"No," Young says. "No. This is regulation play here."

It's Young's turn to throw now. He lobs. He misses. As Young's second throw misses, CBS's Pat O'Brien walks up. O'Brien is dressed in a green trench coat, bleached black jeans, black cowboy boots, and a white-and-black striped oxford buttoned up at the neck. His John Lennon glasses are tinted green to match his trench coat. O'Brien watches Steve Young throw two rolls of tape. Both tosses are way off.

"I'll put up $100 to whoever makes it first," O'Brien says loudly enough so the quarterbacks can hear. Joe Montana is throwing now. He looks over at O'Brien and grins. He throws. A miss. Again. No good.

"When's the last time you made it?" O'Brien asks.

"Yesterday," Montana answers, lobbing another roll of tape—a miss.

"In that case, let's make it $500." The voice is Dick Stockton's. Stockton will do the play-by-play commentary for CBS.

Joe Montana has a few rolls left. He looks over at Stockton. He smiles.

"We made one yesterday and the guy wouldn't pay," Montana says.

Stockton is firm. "Five hundred."

Montana throws. The roll climbs right over the top of the goal post, falling down the other side. Steve Young catches it quietly. Montana looks at Young. He thinks he's made it. Young sees the expectant look on Joe's face. He holds the roll of tape up for Joe to see.

"Oh," Montana says, deflated. "I didn't see it come down."

"Oh, no," Pat O'Brien says.

It's Steve Young's turn now. He throws. A miss. Another throw. Another miss. George Seifert is on his way out of the locker room toward the field. Steve Young has one roll of tape left.

"Last chance," O'Brien says.

Young throws. He misses. As Young picks up his helmet and runs off to join his teammates at practice, Pat O'Brien walks over to Dick Stockton.

"Five hundred?" O'Brien says, arching his eyebrows behind the John Lennon glasses.

"Pat O'Brien, ladies and gentlemen," Stockton announces heartily, turning around and pointing at O'Brien as if he's introducing him at his own roast. Then Stockton walks out onto the field to watch practice.

Back in September, the first time Washington came to Candlestick, the Niners got ahead early. This forced the Redskins, a team that likes to run the ball, to pass and play catch-up. They couldn't do it, and San Francisco won easily 26–13. In the NFL, smart teams don't change what they do best, especially in the playoffs. At Candlestick on Saturday, the Niners and Redskins will both try to do the same things they tried to do in their first meeting, in second game of the regular season. The Niners want to pass and put up points early and force the Redskins to play catch-up. The Redskins want to get out in front so they can eat up the clock with their running game—and keep Joe Montana and the explosive Niner offense off the field.

On Saturday, the Redskins start the game just like they want to. The Niners get the ball first. San Francisco runs three plays and punts. The Redskins get the ball on their 26. After a run for no gain and an incomplete pass, Washington quarterback Mark Rypien finds receiver Ricky Sanders open in a seam over the middle for a gain of 15 and a first down. From the Washington 41, running back Earnest Byner barrels off right tackle and gains four yards. On second down, Rypien hits receiver Gary Clark for a gain of 11 and another first down. The Redskins are moving. On the next play, Byner escapes around right end for 16 yards. After Charles Haley slices in to hit Byner for a loss, Rypien brings Washington to the line on second down at the San Francisco 31. Art Monk, Washington's ageless wide receiver, is split wide to the right. Rypien takes the snap and drops deep in the pocket. Monk drives 49er cornerback Darryl Pollard up the field. Monk fakes a cut to the outside. When Pollard bites on the fake, Monk steams upfield past him. Rypien's pass is on the money at the goal line, and with less than six minutes gone in the first quarter, Washington is up 7–0. It was easy. Candlestick is silent. The Faithful are not sure what to think.

The Niners open their next drive at their own 26. On first down, Montana hits Brent Jones for 12 yards. Then, from the 38, Montana finds Jerry Rice over the middle for a gain of 11. At the end of the play, Washington cornerback Darrell Green bear hugs Rice from behind. Green picks Flash up, then slams him into the ground head first. The refs call Green for unnecessary roughness, and the 15-yard penalty gives the Niners a first down at the Redskin 36.

Montana drops back to pass. He cocks his arm to throw to the right, but Brent Jones is covered. So is Roger Craig, who has flared out of the backfield. Joe brings the ball down, steps away from the pressure, and looks for Jerry Rice over the middle. But Charles Mann, a six-foot-six, 270-pound defensive lineman, is right in Montana's face. Joe pulls the ball down again and takes off to his left.

There is one receiver he hasn't checked yet. John Taylor had lined up slot left to the inside of Rice. Taylor ran a flare toward the sidelines. When Montana got in trouble and started scrambling to his side of the field, Taylor broke his route off and slid upfield. When Washington cornerback Martin Mayhew slipped, Taylor was wide open along the sidelines. On the run to his left, Montana lets fly. Taylor pulls the ball in and is out of bounds at the Washington 14. Five plays later, Jesse Sapolu and Guy McIntyre carve a hole in the Washington line and Tom Rathman's one-yard touchdown run ties the game at 7–7. The Faithful go nuts. This is more like it.

On the next series, the Redskins drive down the field and kick a field goal to lead 10–7. The Niners get the ball back on their 20. Seven plays later, San Francisco comes to the line on first down at the Washington 34. It's time for some schoolyard football.

It was almost midnight on Thursday back at the Taj. George Seifert had already gone home. Lynn Stiles, who coaches San Francisco's tight ends and special teams, was fighting sleep himself. His eyes were so blurry, in fact, that he could barely make out the film of the Redskins he was watching. Just before he went home that night, Lynn Stiles got an idea. Stiles scribbled a play down on a piece of paper and left it on Seifert's desk. Later Stiles would say that his play was "like one of those sixth-grade plays you draw up in the sand." Every once in a while, Stiles will draw up a play and leave it for Seifert to look over. Most of the time, though, the plays don't make it into the game plan. Lynn Stiles was as surprised as anyone when his play went up on the board and into the game plan on Friday, the day before the game.

Why not? Stiles thought to himself. *It's a good play.*

In Washington territory on Saturday, Montana takes the snap and hands the ball to Harry Sydney. Sydney runs to the right, trying to sell the Redskins—especially free safety Todd Bowles—that the play is a run. As Sydney sweeps right, Bowles charges toward the line of scrimmage. This is exactly what Lynn Stiles was hoping he would do. With Bowles coming up to play the run, Redskin strong safety Alvin Walton is stuck covering Brent Jones, the 49er tight end, one-on-one up the field. Jones is six-four. Alvin Walton is six feet. It's a clear mismatch—the part of Lynn Stiles's play that George Seifert liked best. The play is working perfectly until one of the Redskins barges through the line and gets in Harry Sydney's face.

Before he's ready to, Sydney pulls the ball down and lets fly for Jones deep up the right sideline. Jones has Walton beat by three steps when Harry Sydney lets go of the ball. But Sydney's pass, rushed because of the pressure, looks more like a punt than a pass. It takes so long for the ball to float down the field that Walton has time to recover. Walton is all over Brent Jones as the ball arrives at the Washington nine. Both players sky up to get it, but Jones makes the catch and falls to the ground. First and goal at the Redskin six. Three plays later, Joe Montana threads a pass through a handful of Redskins to Jerry Rice in the back of the end zone and the Niners are up 14–10. The fireworks are just starting.

Washington gets the ball back and can't go anywhere. After the Redskins punt, Montana brings the Niners to the line on first down deep in San Francisco territory. Before the snap, Roger Craig goes in motion out of the backfield to the right. Montana takes the snap. Craig slashes up the right sideline. Before Montana can finish his drop, Redskin defensive tackle Darryl Grant storms by Niner guard Guy McIntyre. Montana pulls the ball down and flushes out of the pocket to his right. Running out of field, Montana sees Craig running behind Alvin Walton downfield. Craig is open, but it's going to take a perfect pass to get the ball over Walton and still allow

Craig enough room to make the catch and keep his feet in-bounds. Montana throws on the run. The ball is a spiral that climbs over Walton and then drops into Craig's waiting hands in front of the 49er bench. *A perfect pass.*

After Harry Sydney runs off left tackle for three yards, Montana looks right for Brent Jones, who's slipped off the line behind rookie Redskin linebacker Andre Collins. Collins has Jones covered fairly well. But just as the pass arrives, Collins turns his head to look back for the ball. His timing is bad, and the ball whizzes past his head. Brent Jones tucks it away and takes off up the sideline. Alvin Walton drags him down 47 yards later. With a first down at the Washington seven, the Niners are looking to score again and put the Redskins in a hole. They have just the play—and the player—to do it.

Mike Sherrard was hanging around his room at the Airport Marriott on Friday night when the phone rang. It was George Seifert, who told Sherrard that he was going to activate him from the injured-reserve list for the game. Sherrard had been practicing for several weeks. He'd been running and cutting and catching full speed, and his ankle felt good. Two and a half months ago, after he broke his fibula against the Browns at Candlestick, Dr. Michael Dillingham put a three-and-a-half-inch metal plate and six screws into Mike Sherrard's leg. While reporters were waiting for the retirement announcement they were sure was forthcoming after the receiver's third broken leg, Sherrard confidently marked San Francisco's first playoff game as the date he wanted to be ready to come back. Sherrard's rehabilitation had gone better than anyone expected, and he was out of his cast and in the hydrotherapy pool at the Taj in no time. Now at Candlestick against the Redskins in the playoffs, the indomitable receiver is ready to play football again.

On second down at the Washington eight, Mike Sherrard lines up tight on the left side of the line. John Taylor is split wide to the right. Taylor will run a crossing route to Sherrard's side of the field. Sherrard will filter underneath in the area Taylor has vacated. Montana takes the snap, and Sherrard works his way to the right just behind the line of scrimmage. A Redskin linebacker has the chance to knock Sherrard down within the five-yard area where it's legal to bump a receiver. The Redskin decides to let Sherrard go—a bad decision. Joe Montana looks up and sees Sherrard running all alone at the six. Joe flips Sherrard the ball, who catches it and looks upfield. What Mike Sherrard sees makes his eyes widen as big as saucers. There is nothing but end zone. Sherrard lopes in for six and a 20–10 49er lead. Running out of the back of the end zone, Sherrard launches the ball into the stands. Later he will say he had never thrown the ball into the stands like that after scoring a touchdown. But, he would add, after all he had been through it seemed like the perfect thing to do.

Right before the end of the half, the Niners are trying to put up another score when Harris Barton, San Francisco's right guard, hurts a shoulder. After the game, Barton will be in so much pain he can't even lift his arm to spray on deodorant without wincing in agony. Against the Redskins, Barton will suck it up and play the whole second half. But with the second quarter almost over, Barton walks off the field and into the locker room for treatment. A young guard named Ricky Siglar enters the game. With 34 seconds left in the half, Montana drops back to pass. James Geathers, a Washington defensive lineman, bulls into Ricky Siglar, who lets the Redskin slide off his block. Siglar thinks Jesse Sapolu will pick up the charging lineman before he gets to Montana. But nobody is between Ricky Siglar and Joe.

Geathers hits Montana high in the numbers just as Joe

lets the ball go downfield. The six-foot-seven, 290-pound Redskin drives Montana to the turf, landing squarely on the quarterback's chest. Montana rolls quickly over onto his elbows and knees. Joe's head is buried in the grass. He's trying to breathe.

Joe Montana comes out of the game, and Steve Young takes the last snap of the first half. Joe is okay. Geathers had just knocked the wind out of him. When Joe jogs into the locker room, he is already grinning. But the next time that Joe will have to come out of the game after a hit this season, he will need help just walking.

If the first half belonged to the Niner offense, the second half was an entirely different story. In the third quarter, Washington was at the San Francisco seven trying to score and get back in the game when Mark Rypien threw for Art Monk in the corner of the end zone. Johnny Jackson leaped in front of Monk and came down with an interception that halted the drive. Later, on Washington's first possession of the fourth quarter, Rypien let fly for the Niner end zone again, this time for Ricky Sanders. When Sanders slipped making his break for the end zone, the only player even near the ball was Darryl Pollard. Another Redskin drive was dead.

On the scoreboard, the game was already over when Charles Haley thundered through the line and hit Rypien just as he threw late in the fourth quarter. Rypien's arm had already started forward when Haley hit him. The ball squirted up into the air and wobbled into the gloved hands of Michael Carter, who somehow managed to chug his 326 pounds into the end zone 61 yards away. As Carter lumbered through the end zone, his taped right arm thrust high into the air, Candlestick came unglued. The Faithful threw paper. They waved their arms. They gave each other high fives. They spilled beer on one another. And they chanted, more than 65,000 voices raised as one.

"THREE-PEAT!!!   THREE-PEAT!!!   THREE-PEAT!!!"

It was like old times. The playoffs were at hand, and the Niners had come through again.

The Faithful stood and yelled for a long time as the players left the field. They cheered for Mike Sherrard, whose first catch in 11 weeks was a touchdown. They cheered for Ronnie Lott, who had four tackles in his first game back since hurting his knees on Monday night early in December. And they cheered for Michael Carter, who had scored the first touchdown of his seven-year career in the NFL. But after awhile, there was no one left to cheer for, so the Faithful headed for the exits. The only thing left to do was go home and wait to see who would be coming to Candlestick next week.

On Sunday, the New York Giants played the Chicago Bears at the Meadowlands in the NFC's other divisional playoff game. The Bears couldn't do anything on offense, and the Giants could do just about anything they wanted. New York crunched Chicago 31–3. The Faithful knew who was coming to Candlestick. The team that had sworn it would take its revenge for losing the blood feud.

Chapter 18

War of the Worlds

On that Wednesday afternoon, the first reports were sketchy, the details not always consistent. But the main message was clear. U.S. war planes had attacked Baghdad, the capital of Iraq. Saddam Hussein was not bluffing. Neither was George Bush. There was war in the Persian Gulf.

At the Taj, Dr. Harry Edwards had been prepared for war for weeks. One morning back in December, after San Francisco had won the blood feud and it was clear that the Niners were headed for the playoffs around the time of the United Nations' deadline for Iraq to withdraw its army from Kuwait, Edwards had approached George Seifert.

"George, I've got to have fifteen minutes today," Edwards said. "This war is something I think we should deal with as a team. I think the guys ought to know what's coming down the pike."

Later that day, the players and coaches gathered in a large meeting room downstairs. Harry Edwards told them that if war broke out in the Middle East, it was "going to be a tremendous goddamn distraction" during a time when they would hopefully be getting ready for a playoff game. He told them that because professional football was a "high-intensity business," they must begin bracing to handle being confronted with the war "in every single situation, in every set of circumstances." And he told them the most important thing of all. That with the world either waiting for the first bombs to drop or waiting for the bombs to stop dropping, a football game "becomes next to irrelevant."

"But," Edwards emphasized, "we cannot feel that way. Because, 30 years from now, the United States will still be doing business with Iraq, because Iraq has oil and the United States needs oil. It's as simple as that. In 30 years, we will not want to look back and see where we did not take care of business because we were distracted by a temporal though extraordinarily significant event that we can neither influence nor become involved in in any direct way. We must not let that happen. We must get our business done."

Harry Edwards was right. As soon as the reports from Baghdad started to come in, the 49ers were grilled on their thoughts about what the war in the Gulf would mean to the coming conflict at Candlestick. It was a war between two worlds. One was deadly. The other was just deadly serious. The players were as patient and as expressive as they could be. Mostly, though, they tried to stay out of the cross fire.

"There's no doubt I have the anxieties the rest of the people have," said Jesse Sapolu, whose brother-in-law was serving on a U.S. Navy ship that fuels F-15 fighter-jets in the Persian Gulf. "But I have to go out and do my job, and that's play center for the 49ers."

Steve Young compared the eerie feeling he felt inside when he imagined people dying in Baghdad to the way he felt after the earthquake hit San Francisco and part of the Bay Bridge collapsed in October 1989. Although he admitted he was troubled by the morality of war, Young added that he did not believe "America should stop working. People shouldn't lock their doors, crawl in bed, pull the covers up around their heads, and turn the alarm clock off until it's over," he said. "We should go on with our lives."

For Dave Waymer, the whole complicated situation was simple. He was a football player, not a politician. When the reporters turned on their tape recorders and pointed their cameras at him, Waymer drew a parallel between the war in one world and the war in his. "Just like those guys have their own fight on their minds, their own war, we have one too on a smaller scale," he said. "We have to keep our focus. [There aren't] live bullets [in our war,] but if we get beat, we're dead."

It was the only thing a damn football player could say.

Other players chose not to deal with the war at all. When it was their turn before the media, Joe Montana, Roger Craig, and Tom Rathman all stepped up on the box outside the locker room at the Taj and started their interviews by saying they didn't want to answer any questions about the war. So the reporters asked them why they didn't want to answer questions about the war.

Perhaps it was fitting that it was Harry Edwards who put the war between worlds in the sharpest perspective. On Thursday afternoon, Edwards was standing outside the lobby at the entrance to the Taj. Holding court for more than a dozen reporters, Edwards talked about how he had been trying to prevent the war in the Persian Gulf from becoming a tremendous goddamn distraction to the San Francisco 49ers.

"Here our basic focus has been that, irrespective of the war, we must go on with the business that we have chosen, which is football. That normalcy, that continuity, is very critical right now.

"I pointed out to the guys that, 'You're the team of the decade not because somebody voted it like a beauty contest,'" Edwards boomed in his lecture-hall baritone, "'but because every playoff season, bread is still baked, shoes are still made, the sun still rises in the East and sets in the West, and the 49ers kick ass during playoff time. That's normal in American society, and that is what we must be about.'"

While the Gulf war was throwing lives into chaos, everything seemed as normal as it always had for Joe Montana. On Tuesday, for the second year in a row, the

Niner quarterback was named the Male Athlete of the Year by the Associated Press. In the voting, Montana edged out Nolan Ryan, the 43-year-old Texas Rangers' pitcher who notched his 5,000th strikeout and sixth no-hitter of his career in 1990, and Wayne Gretzky, who owns most of the scoring records in the National Hockey League. Joe was on a roll.

The week before, AP had named Montana the Most Valuable Player in the NFL—for the second year in a row. In 1990, Montana completed 61.7 percent of his passes, best in the NFC. He also threw for 26 touchdowns and set a 49er team record with 3,944 yards passing. Joe was in the shower at the Taj after practice when Dexter Carter congratulated him.

"Oh, I don't know," Joe said. "I guess I'll take it."

It wasn't that Montana didn't appreciate or want the award. He almost felt like he didn't deserve it. He knew he certainly hadn't had a year like the year before, when he set an NFL record for the highest quarterback rating ever, 112.4. In 1990, Montana's quarterback rating, 89.0, was his lowest since 1981, the year he became the starter in San Francisco. And he threw 16 interceptions, his most ever. Montana wondered if he hadn't won MVP because his team posted the best record in the league, 14 and 2. Besides, Joe knew there were plenty of other quarterbacks who had put up bigger numbers. In Houston, Warren Moon threw for 4,689 yards and 33 touchdowns. In Buffalo, Jim Kelly led the NFL in passing. Philadelphia's Randall Cunningham ranked fifth in passing, and ran for almost 1,000 yards. Even Jay Schroeder, the much-maligned quarterback of the L.A. Raiders, had a higher rating than Joe Montana. Joe was absolutely right. There were other guys who had the numbers to be MVP.

Then Joe carved up the Redskins and it was clear there was nothing wrong with AP's choice. The images from the Niners' playoff win were a graphic Montana highlight film. The quick scamble to the left and the per-

fect pass on the run to John Taylor along the sideline.
The daring bullet into traffic that Jerry Rice caught for a
score at the back of the end zone. The escape from a col-
lapsing pocket and the perfect throw on the dead run
over the linebacker to Roger Craig. And the quick drop
and touch pass by the linebacker's head to Brent Jones.
Against the Redskins, Joe Montana made plays that redefined possibilities.

Again.

"Montana threw some balls that simply *couldn't* get
there," Redskin cornerback Darrell Green said after the
game. "And yet they did."

As the Niners worked to get ready for the Giants, one
other memory from the Redskin game lingered in the
minds of the members of the offensive line. It was not
something they talked about openly, but if pressed, they
admitted they were all thinking the same thing. They did
not want Joe to take another hit like the one he took
against Washington. They did not want to see Joe like
that again—down on the ground, his cleats clawing the
grass, his lungs gasping for air. No—NO! That was not
the way they were supposed to let the other team treat
Joe. That was not the way they were going to get to
Tampa.

Jim Burt sits on the wooden bench outside the locker
room at the Taj. It's almost noon on Saturday. The game
is tomorrow. Burt has big bags under his eyes again. He
didn't sleep last night. He was wired. He tossed and
turned. He was thinking—but trying not to think—about
what it will feel like if the Giants win on Sunday. It might
happen, he says, because the Giants have a good team.
How will it feel—no. He won't think about it. He won't let
himself. They can't get to him. Not again. But it won't go
away. The Giants won't go away. The Giants are here.
They're waiting. Just like he is. For the game. He thinks
about it. He lets himself.

What will it feel like to go back home to New Jersey with his tail between his legs because the Giants beat the 49ers and went to Tampa to play in the Super Bowl? He knows how it will feel. Sick. No lie. It'll be down there, slinking around in his insides, eating him away, making him hollow, empty, like somebody has gone in and ripped out his insides just like the Giants did when they got rid of him. There it is. Yes, there it is. That's what it comes down to. Eight years he gave the Giants, and they treated him like shit at the end. They couldn't even tell him straight. They waffled and danced around the subject. *Jim, we don't think you should play anymore. Your back, you know. Those sons of bitches,* he thinks. Parcells. He thinks about Parcells. Not for very long. He won't waste his time.

He thinks about the guys. He knows the guys. Simms. L.T. Leonard Marshall. And Bart. He knows Bart the best. Bart is still his best friend. Not on Sunday, though. Because Bart wants the same thing he does. And only one team can win the war and go to the Super Bowl. *The Super Bowl.* That's why they play the game. *The Show.* They all want to get to The Show. *The Super Bowl.* Sonuvabitch. He's thinking again. The Giants can't win. They can't. It's not right. But they might. They have a good team. Don't think about it. Just play the game.

Might as well think about it. Can't sleep.

Jim Burt was thinking about the blood feud last night, too. About how upset Colleen was before the game. They were on their way to the Taj one day, and Colleen was going on about how Parcells had kicked him off the team three days before training camp and he had to go all the way out to San Francisco to play football and so he couldn't be there in the delivery room when she had Ashlee. Colleen was going on about how low it was of Parcells to treat him like that after he had played hard all those years—played hurt, played sore, played well. None of it mattered to that pig Parcells. Colleen was crying now. *Jimmy*, she said in the car, *I always hope you're healthy, but this week what I hope even more*—she clenched her fist and gritted her teeth, her voice was flashing stronger through her crying—*I want you guys to win the game. I can't stand the Giants. I want you guys to win the game.* Jimmy had never seen Colleen cry like that.

Jimmy was laughing. It was the Monday of the blood feud. He was at the Marriott. Colleen was on the phone. She was intense, competitive. That wasn't like her. *You get those guys fired up,* she was saying, *'cause I can't stand the Giants. You get those guys fired up. Do anything you have to.* Jimmy was laughing. He couldn't believe his wife.

"My wife is not a competitive person," he would say later. "She doesn't even want me to play football, because she's afraid I'm gonna get hurt. Most of the time, she couldn't care less about the games. She thinks I'm a psycho 'cause I get so wound up about football. And here she is givin' *me* a pep talk the day of the game."

Back on that Monday night, when the moon was full and the air was cold, Colleen Burt got what she wanted. The Niners won the blood feud. But not by much. And that game doesn't count for anything now. What counts now is this game. This war.

"The Giants have a good team," Jim Burt says, sitting on the wooden bench outside the locker room at the Taj. "They might beat us."

He looks out across the empty practice fields. A breeze flicks the leaves on the eucalyptus tree outside the fence in the distance.

"It's gonna come down to a three-point game," he says, after awhile. "If we lose, we go home, and the Giants go to the Super Bowl."

The Giants go to the Super Bowl. The words linger like poison. *The Giants go to the Super Bowl.* Jimmy reaches down and picks some mud and grass from his Nikes. He tosses the clump gently onto the grass past the sidewalk.

He hunches forward and rests his elbows on his knees.
He covers his eyes with his hands.

He feels sick.

The Giants are different this time. Phil Simms is not
the quarterback. Back in December, two weeks after the
Giants lost at Candlestick, Simms went back to pass
against the Bills and hurt his ankle at the Meadowlands.
After the game, Bill Parcells said his quarterback had suffered a "very, very severe sprain of the midfoot." Parcells
originally guessed that after surgery, Phil Simms would
be able to play in the Super Bowl if the Giants made it that
far. Five days before the renewal of the blood feud, however, the Giants' coach gives in to the obvious. Phil
Simms's foot is worse than anyone had expected it to be.
He will watch the war on crutches. So it's up to Jeff Hostetler.

Jeff Hostetler has been with the Giants for seven seasons. For the first four, he didn't throw a single pass.
About the only time he touched the field was when the
Giants were trying a field goal or kicking an extra point
after a touchdown. Jeff Hostetler was the holder. But because Phil Simms got hurt, Hostetler is now the starting
quarterback. Lanky and stubborn, he is every bit the
competitor Simms is. In fact, at one point early in his
career, Hostetler wanted on the field so badly that he
asked the coaches to let him play on special teams. For
awhile, they did. Hostetler, Dave Waymer says a few days
before the game, "is the kind of guy who isn't afraid to
buckle up and go after guys."

There's even one thing Hostetler—"Hoss" to his
teammates—can do that Phil Simms cannot do even
when he isn't on crutches: scramble. Against the Bears,
Hoss threw for two touchdowns and ran for a third. The
Niners know the defense they played in the blood feud is
not going to work this time.

"It's a different game now than when we played them

with Simms," George Seifert said a few days before the game. "They've added a dimension with his ablity to run."

On Saturday night, Bill Parcells gathered the New York Giants in a room at the Airport Westin hotel in San Francisco. His remarks that evening included a brief discussion of office equipment. The 49ers, Parcells told the Giants, had already set up shop in Tampa, where the Super Bowl was being played a week from tomorrow's NFC Championship Game. Telephones, fax machines, file cabinets—even team pennants—had all been installed on the order of Eddie DeBartolo Jr. Everything was ready and waiting for the time when the mighty Niners would arrive to battle for another Super Bowl crown.

As usual, Parcells did not mince words. He made sure that his players knew that he did not appreciate the arrogance of the 49ers. He made it clear that if the 49ers assumed they were going to beat the Giants, then perhaps it was time for the Giants to make the Niners pay for their mistake. For the team that still burned from the blood feud, Parcells' words added only more gasoline to the flames.

It wasn't until the morning of the game that Paul Tagliabue, commissioner of the NFL, decided that the league's two championship games would be played as planned. All week the league had been prepared to cancel the games—and the Super Bowl—if the war in the Persian Gulf went badly. On Thursday, Joe Browne, the NFL's vice-president for communications, issued a statement by Tagliabue.

"We have tremendous respect for the bravery and achievements of the nation's military forces in the Middle East. We recognize the importance of achieving the goals established by President Bush and the United Nations. We also recognize that the American people will not be paralyzed by the events in the Middle East or allow the fabric of daily life to be destroyed.

"We thus expect to play Sunday's Conference Championship Games and the Super Bowl as scheduled. We will obviously continue to follow events in the Middle East and take those into account as we approach kick-off."

The next day, Browne said that, although the league fully expected to hold the games as planned, "we're prepared to go as late as Sunday morning" before making a final decision. Paul Tagliabue would make the call.

On Sunday morning, hours before kickoff in Buffalo, where the Bills and Raiders were playing to see who was going to represent the AFC in the Super Bowl, the news from the Gulf was disturbing. Both the city of Dhahran and Riyadh, the capital of Saudia Arabia, were under missile attack. Bad weather over much of Iraq and Kuwait was forcing the Allies to cancel most bombing operations. And in his first broadcast message since the start of the war, Saddam Hussein said on Radio Baghdad that Iraq had used only a fraction of its military power thus far. When Iraq put forth its full military might, Hussein claimed, the Allies would suffer heavy casualties. Despite the grim news, Paul Tagliabue made his call. The football games would be played. By the time the Giants and Niners took the field at Candlestick, Buffalo had battered L.A., 51–3. The Bills were going to Tampa. They would have an opponent in about four hours.

Matt Bahr kicks off for the Giants to start the game. Spencer Tillman takes the ball back to the San Francisco 26. On first down, Joe Montana wants to hit John Taylor over the middle. But Lawrence Taylor beats Bubba Paris on Joe's back side, and Leonard Marshall, New York's six-foot-three, 285-pound left end, bulls past tackle Steve Wallace on his right, and Montana has to pump the ball into the ground. After completions to Tom Rathman,

Mike Sherrard, and Brent Jones, the Niners have a first down on the New York 48. Roger Craig knifes ahead for four yards. On second down, Montana looks for John Taylor on a slant from the left. The ball is behind Taylor, who jumps, makes the catch, and falls to the ground. Although television replays clearly show that Taylor loses control of the ball before he hits the ground, officials rule that the whistle blew Taylor down and the play is thus ineligible for review by instant replay. The gift is a San Francisco first down on the Giants' 30. The Niners, however, can't go anywhere, and Mike Cofer kicks a field goal.

When the Giants get the ball, it isn't long before Jeff Hostetler's scrambling begins to hurt San Francisco. On third and 13 from the Giant 17, Hostetler drops back to throw. But all of his receivers are covered, and the pocket collapses, so he flushes to his right. On the run, Hoss guns a strike to Giant receiver Mark Ingram for a gain of 20. The Giants move the ball into 49er territory exactly the way they want to. Hostetler to tight end Mark Bavaro for seven. Dave Meggett on a run for five. Hostetler to Ingram for nine. A run off right tackle for two. Dink here. Dink there. Move the chains. Control the line. Shorten the game. On third and eight at the San Francisco 35, the Niners make their first costly mistake of the game. Hostetler is throwing for Ingram up the right side of the field. As the ball arrives, Darryl Pollard nudges Ingram in the back, and swipes at the ball with his left hand. A late flag calls Pollard for pass interference. Up in the CBS booth, John Madden says it's a ticky-tack call. Perhaps it is. But the Giants have a first down on the Niner 30. Two plays later, however, the Giants give the gift right back.

On first down at the 49er 11, Meggett takes a pitch and sweeps to the right. Fullback Maurice Carthon lumbers through the line into the end zone. When Meggett throws, Carthon has linebacker Matt Millen beat by three steps. Meggett's ball is perfect. But Carthon can't handle it. It should have been six. Three plays later, the Giants settle for a field goal. Soon after, the first quarter ends. The war is tied.

The teams trade punts to start the second quarter. With 9:32 left before halftime, the Giants start a drive at their own 20. Ottis Anderson rumbles for three. Then Meggett bashes for four. On third and three from the New York 27, Hostetler drops back to pass. Meggett is running a "scat": He lines up in the backfield and, after the snap, waits for his line to make a hole. Wherever the hole is, Meggett goes. This time, the hole is between 49er left end Larry Roberts, rushing from the outside, and nose tackle Dennis Brown in the middle of the field. Meggett fills the hole and looks back for the ball. But Hostetler has pulled the ball down and is almost running up his back. Meggett turns back upfield and blasts into a 49er as Hostetler lunges to the 31. First down, Giants.

New York grinds the ball down the field. Hostetler to Ingram for nine. Ottis Anderson over the top for a first down. Hostetler to Bavaro for 13 and a first down. Ottis off right tackle for two. When Dennis Brown shoves his hands up under the chin of Giants' guard Eric Moore, the referees tack on five more yards to Anderson's run. The Giants are rolling. First down at the San Francisco 39. Meggett takes a pitch and bangs left for eight. Maurice Carthon chugs off right tackle for six. Hostetler flips to Bavaro for three. At the 49er 22, Kevin Fagan slams into Ottis Anderson and the Giants lose two. It's third down now, and with 1:10 left in the half, the Giants call time. The play will be a pass into the end zone. It will be broken up by Darryl Pollard. Matt Bahr's 42-yard field goal puts the Giants up 6–3. One minute shows on the clock after Dexter Carter takes Bahr's kickoff back to the San Francisco 34. The Niners still have three time-outs.

On first down, Jerry Rice gets loose up the right side and Montana's throw is there for a gain of 19 into New

York territory. Joe drops back on second down. When nobody gets open right away, Montana takes off up the middle. He slides down at the Giant 41 and calls San Francisco's first time-out. On second down, the officials make their presence known once again. Just after Montana releases a flare to the left sideline for Roger Craig, New York's Eric Dorsey hits Joe below the knees from behind. The personal foul call tacks on 15 yards to the five Roger Craig gained before he ran out of bounds. The Niners now have a first down on the Giant 21. Twenty-one seconds are left. Time to take a shot at the end zone.

As Montana fades to throw, Leonard Marshall screams by Bubba Paris to the inside. Bubba lurches toward Marshall—and whiffs. Montana has to eat the ball and take a second time-out. The sack puts the ball back at the Giant 29. The Niners need a few yards to put Mike Cofer back in field-goal range. After the time-out, Roger Craig takes a flare and goes out of bounds after a gain of three. With 13 seconds left, Craig gets open over the middle. Montana finds him and Craig goes down at the 18. Montana calls San Francisco's last time-out. Just before the half ends, Mike Cofer ties the war at 6–6. The race to Tampa is still a dead heat.

The Giants get the first shot of the second half. But Charles Haley sacks Hostetler on third down near midfield and the Giants have to give up the ball. New York's punter, Sean Landeta, launches the ball deep into the shadowed end of the field. John Taylor makes the catch at the San Francisco eight, but has nowhere to go. Five Giants have him trapped. Taylor changes direction and heads back to the left. He finds a wall of Niners to run behind. Thirty-one yards later, Landeta forces Taylor out of bounds.

On first down, Montana slides away from center. John Taylor runs an out pattern up the left side. Montana sees him break open and launches a spiral. Everson Walls, the

Giant corner covering Taylor, has always been a defensive back willing to gamble to make a big play. As Montana's pass hurtles toward J.T., Walls thinks he has the angle to pick it off. If he's wrong, there's no one behind him and John Taylor will have been the one who made the big play. Everson Walls will be toast. It will not be the first time that has happened to him at Candlestick.

Nine years ago, Walls was covering Dwight Clark in the back of the end zone when Montana sailed a pass that Clark caught with his fingertips to beat Walls's Dallas Cowboys by one point for the NFC Championship. Down in the tunnel this morning before the game, the Niners had Clark, who now works in the 49er front office, hang around outside the Giants' locker room—just to give Walls something to think about before he went on the field. Walls got famous as the guy Dwight Clark burned that winter day at Candlestick nine years ago. That could all change on this winter day if Walls picks off Montana right now.

As Taylor jumps for the ball at the New York 44, Walls strikes. He's wrong. He doesn't have the angle. Taylor hugs the ball and takes off up the sidelines. Safety Myron Guyton is the only Giant who has a shot at Taylor. At the five, Guyton lunges for Taylor's feet. No dice. Touchdown, Niners. The Faithful are delirious. Bring on the Bills. But there's plenty of war still to be fought. And the fighting is about to take its most primitive form.

An eye for an eye.

Early in the fourth quarter, the Giants have second down on their 39 when Jim Burt rips off the line toward Jeff Hostetler. Burt bulls by his friend, center Bart Oates, and Giant guard Eric Moore slides over to help Oates block Burt. As Hostetler steps up to throw, Burt squeezes between Oates and Moore. Burt dives at about the same time Moore pushes him. Burt hits Hostetler just above the left knee as Hoss gets rid of the ball. The pass is good

for 14 yards into San Francisco territory. But Jeff Hostetler isn't getting up. He's on the ground in agony, his
face mask buried in the grass. The Giants are livid. Burt
used to be one of them. But now he's the enemy—a
Niner—and he's just taken their quarterback out of the
game on a cheap shot. The whole Giants' bench is yelling
at Burt. Many of their words are obscene.

Later, Burt said he recognized the familiar voices.
Leonard Marshall. Pepper. Parcells. And L.T. He heard
L.T. clearly.

"IF THAT'S THE WAY YOU WANT TO PLAY
IT," Superman bellowed from the sidelines, "OKAY.
SOMEBODY ELSE IS GONNA LOSE A QUARTER-
BACK!"

When the play was over and Hostetler was on the
ground, Burt walked to the New York huddle to explain
that he'd been pushed, that he hadn't gone for Hoss's
knees on purpose. No one would talk to him. Even Bart.
Bart would talk to him later—Bart would tell Jimmy that
he knew it wasn't a cheap shot, that he and Eric Moore
had pushed him—but right then, in the white heat of the
war, even Bart gave Burt the silent treatment. Jimmy got
mad, and used some of his own obscenities.

After awhile, Hoss got up and limped off the field.
Matt Cavanaugh, New York's second backup quarterback, went into the game. After three plays, the Giants
punted. It was time for somebody else to lose a quarterback.

With 10:07 left in the game, Joe Montana took the
snap from Jesse Sapolu and dropped back to throw on
third down. On Montana's blind side, Leonard Marshall
put on an inside move and then shot around Bubba Paris
to the outside. Marshall's move, though, threw him off
balance, and he fell to the turf in the 49er backfield. Tom
Rathman had stayed in to block on that side. When Marshall fell, Rathman drifted over and fell over the top of

Marshall. Rathman, though, didn't want to get called for holding, so he quickly slid off Marshall, who scrambled to his feet and headed for Joe Montana. Down the field, the Giants had all three 49er receivers covered. Montana stood in the pocket waiting for someone to get open. But when he felt Marshall coming toward him, Joe left the pocket and headed for the sidelines. While Marshall was coming from Montana's blind side, Lawrence Taylor was boring toward Joe from the middle of the field. Running to his right, Montana stutter-stepped to a halt, then backed up. L.T. charged by him. But just as Montana set himself to throw, Leonard Marshall unloaded.

The ball caromed forward out of Joe Montana's hand. It was in the air for six yards before it hit the ground. Mark Collins of the Giants dove on it first, but Collins rolled over and the ball was still on the ground. Steve Wallace, San Francisco's right tackle, screamed forward and dove over Collins for the ball. One of the referees shouted twice in quick staccato. "RED BALL! RED BALL!"

The Niners still had the ball. But they did not have Joe. Not anymore.

Montana was on his hands and knees back at the 17. As he had cocked to throw seconds before, Leonard Marshall lowered his helmet right into the letters stitched in white on Joe's back. As the two players fell, Marshall wrapped his right arm around Montana's throwing hand. Joe's hand was pinned between his helmet and the ground when Leonard Marshall smashed them both into the grass.

Steve Young was the first one to leave the sidelines. In fact, Steve Wallace had barely finished recovering Montana's fumble when Young sprinted off the sidelines and kneeled at Joe's side. Young knew something was wrong with Joe. But exactly what would come later after the game. There was still almost the entire fourth quarter to play. And someone had to win the war.

Joe Montana was on his back for a long time out on the field at Candlestick. After Steve Young got there, both 49er team physicians, Michael Dillingham and James Klint, ran onto the field to find out where he hurt. A few minutes later, after Montana had wobbled to his feet and was back on the sidelines, the report from the Niner bench was that Joe hurt everywhere. So did most of Candlestick.

On fourth down, the Niners punt. When the Giants come to the line on first down at the New York 38, the quarterback is Jeff Hostetler. He isn't even limping anymore. After Ottis Anderson bounces off right tackle for a gain of three, Hostetler drops back to pass. Kevin Fagan blows into the Giant backfield, forcing Hoss out of the pocket to the left. Just before Hostetler runs out of bounds, a 49er dives and falls hard on his right side. Linebacker Bill Romanowski comes out of the game to have a trainer look at him. The Giants need a yard for a first down. Ottis Anderson gets the call. Michael Carter hits Ottis for a loss, and the punting unit comes onto the field.

As the two teams settle in over the ball on fourth down at the New York 46, Gary Reasons, the upback in the Giants punt formation, sees a hole—an open gap—between the 49er who is lined up over center and the other Niner who stands out at the edge of the line. From the films, Reasons knows that number 53, Bill Romanowski, is the Niner who is supposed to be in that gap. Bill Parcells has already given Reasons the option to call a fake punt. When Reasons sees that San Francisco only has 10 men on the field, he calls the signals quickly. On the 49er bench, assistant trainer Fred Tedeschi spots the problem too late.

"Bill's out," Tedeschi says to Lynn Stiles, the special teams coach.

"Bill who?" Stiles asks.

"Bill Romanowski."

Stiles frantically tries to send Keena Turner into the game. But Gary Reasons already has the ball and is headed hell-bent over the middle. Reasons is going to score but for John Taylor, who cuts the linebacker to the ground at the San Francisco 24. Four plays later, Matt Bahr kicks the Giants to within a point, 13–12. The clock shows 5:47 left. Joe Montana is still slumped on the Niner bench, his head full of cobwebs, his body sore from the pain Leonard Marshall gave him. Steve Young will have to take things to the end.

On first down, Young hands off to Roger Craig, who tucks the ball in his left arm and heads into the line. Pepper Johnson, a Giant linebacker, hits Craig first, but not hard enough to bring him down. While Johnson hangs onto Craig's left ankle, Leonard Marshall spears into Craig's left arm with his shoulder. The ball comes loose. When the officials pry the bodies off the pile, Bubba Paris has the ball for San Francisco. On second down, Brent Jones gets open over the middle. Steve Young's first— and only—pass of the game is a rope and the Niners have a first down near midfield. There is 4:29 left to play.

For the Giants' defense, Jones's play has changed everything. With the Niners driving, they are not going to concentrate on stopping San Francisco now. They want to take the ball away. When the Giants' defense is back in its huddle, Pepper Johnson leans in and says what every one of his teammates is thinking.

"If you ever make another play in your life, make it now."

Now is coming. Twice.

Roger Craig runs the ball on the next three plays. He gains six up the middle, then five around right end. On first down at the New York 40, Craig is supposed to run a trap play to the left, between the blocks of Harris Barton, who will have pulled over into the hole from right guard, and Jesse Sapolu, who is supposed to handle Giant nose tackle Erik Howard. But as Craig hits the line, Howard is handling Sapolu. Beaten, the 49er center is pushing

Howard to the ground. Falling, Howard stuffs his torso in front of Roger Craig. Howard nudges at the ball with his helmet. It comes loose. Lawrence Taylor picks the fumble out of the air and falls on the ground at the New York 43. There is 2:36 left in the game. All the Giants need is a field goal.

On first down, Charles Haley and Pierce Holt flush Jeff Hostetler out of the pocket to the right. On the dead run near the Giant bench, Hostetler fires upfield for Mark Bavaro. Bavaro makes the catch in front of Niner linebacker Michael Walter at the San Francisco 42. Bavaro makes it down to the 38 by the time two 49ers can drag him down. After the two-minute warning stops the clock, Ottis Anderson tries to run left. But Kevin Fagan blows by his man and Ottis loses four. With 1:17 left, Jeff Hostetler takes the snap and rolls out to his right. Wide receiver Stephen Baker has driven Darryl Pollard up the field, then curled back at the sideline in front of the Giant bench. On the run, Hostetler throws another strike. Baker falls out of bounds at the San Francisco 29. With third and one and 1:10 left on the clock, the Giants call time. The war is a chess match now. The Giants need a few more yards for Matt Bahr. The Niners need to hold them right where they are. The side that wins the battle will probably win the war.

Ottis Anderson gets the first down after the time out. The ball is at the 27 now. The Giants call time again. Twelve seconds are left on the clock. The Giants run another play. Hostetler keeps it over center and gains a yard. A little closer for Matt Bahr. The Giants call their last time out. Matt Bahr runs onto the field. The Niners call time. Their only chance now is to block the kick. Four seconds are left on the clock. Jim Burt was right. It's going to come down to a three-point game.

Spencer Tillman got closest. Tillman had lined up on the far right of the formation next to Dave Waymer and Michael Walter. Tillman's assignment called for him to scream in from the outside, diving at the last moment in a bid to block the kick. But when the ball was snapped and the two lines thundered together at the 24-yard line, Tillman saw a trench open in the middle of all the bodies, so he knifed behind his two teammates. He was already in the air when Matt Bahr's foot thumped into the ball. He was just starting to come down when the ball climbed above his straining fingers.

The Niner locker room was quiet, except for a CBS crew rustling nervously with its equipment. It had taken the crew an entire Saturday to set up everything. But they had to be ready when the Niners beat the Giants. They had to have a photogenic backdrop to present the George S. Halas Trophy to the champions of the National Football Conference. CBS was ready, but the George S. Halas Trophy was being presented up the tunnel, to the coach in the visitors' locker room.

George Seifert spoke to the Niners before he went on CBS and graciously complimented the Giants on the great effort that had earned them a trip to Tampa. Seifert told his Niners that, although they had not gotten the job done they had set out to do, they still had plenty of which to be proud. They had won more games than any other football team in the league. And they had won those games playing through more pressure than any other team in the league. They had been expected to win. And now that they had lost, there would be people who would call them failures. But, George Seifert said, they were not failures. They just had to suck this thing up and play harder next year.

Roger Craig didn't hear a word George Seifert said. He was in the ozone. He couldn't even replay the fumble in his mind. There was no tape to watch. The ball was there and then it was gone. There. Gone. It was simple. Like black and white. Or win and lose. That's why it hurt so much. It was so simple. It was a trap play. A trap play is as basic as a football or a pair of cleats. Take the handoff and hit the hole. Against the Giants, though, it wasn't that easy. Against the Giants, it was there and it was gone.

Five months ago, after Craig had fumbled against the Seahawks at Candlestick in the last game of the pre-season, reporters had waited in front of his locker. They wanted to ask him about his fumble. But Roger left that night. He didn't want to talk to anybody. He just wanted to get the season started and everything would be all right. It always had been. He ran his hills in the off-season so he could take the punishment. He put himself through that hell so he could batter his way through anything that anybody brought to him out on the field. Except this season. This year was his worst. First he was dropping the ball in preseason. Then he got hurt in Houston—he was never the same after Houston. And then there was today. He didn't need hills to get him into shape to tuck the ball and hit the hole.

Outside, the field at Candlestick is empty. A winter breeze blows garbage across the grass. Inside the Niner locker room, reporters wait for Roger Craig. For almost 15 minutes, they mill in front of his locker. Finally, he appears. He has already taken a shower. He has a towel around his waist as he squeezes through the crowd.

"Why is everybody here?" Roger Craig innocently asks. He pulls his pants from a hanger and bends over to put them on. He bumps into one of the reporters, the pack is that close.

"Sorry," the reporter says.

"I'm sorry, too," Roger Craig answers.

He answers the questions—the ones he can. The one all of the reporters want to know about is the one he has the most trouble with. *What happened out there?*

"I thought I had the ball," Craig says softly, rubbing cream into his hands. For a long time, none of the reporters says anything to Roger Craig. Finally, it's Craig himself who breaks the silence.

"This is tough, real tough. I've just got to live with what I did."

There was really nothing more to say.

Harry Sydney was dressing at the locker next to Roger Craig. Sydney was talking about what he was planning to do now there were no more football games left to play. He was going to be nothing but a full-time dad for a few weeks. He was going to coach a little T-ball with his boys. He was going to chill out and let his body heal. It would be awhile, Harry Sydney said, before he would start working out to get ready for next season. Sydney pulled on his pants. He was halfway done zipping them up when he stopped.

"It's weird," he said, looking blankly down at his feet. "You dream a dream for three years, and then it's over. It's just over."

The players drifted in quietly the next morning. One by one, they arrived at the Taj, took physicals, met with their position coaches, and cleaned out their lockers. At 10 o'clock, George Seifert addressed his team for the last time. His words were directed at next year, next season. Because there was nothing left to say about the last one.

Until yesterday, they had a dream. For six months, they carried the dream inside them, each one harboring a little piece, holding it close, always holding it close, as they pushed and pushed up the side of the mountain. They never once put the dream down to rest, because they were afraid that if they put it down they wouldn't be able to pick it up again. They all knew that they were going to get one chance to make the dream come true. Only one chance to do something that no one had ever done before. And they didn't want to blow it. So they pushed and dreamed.

Back in Rocklin, every one of them had known that this was how it might end. They might lose. Losing was possible. Losing is always possible. They all knew that.

But yesterday at Candlestick wasn't possible. None of them could ever have imagined that what happened yesterday could happen to them. Yesterday, they lost everything. They lost Joe. They lost the ball. They lost the game. They lost the dream.

Last night, when they went to bed, they were all thinking the same thing. *How could it have happened?* They had the game won. It was theirs. All they had to do was hold onto the ball for a little while longer and they would be getting ready to go to Tampa right now. Bring on the Bills. Instead, they were getting ready to go home. Home to think about how close they had gotten to the top of the mountain.

In the days, the weeks, the months ahead, they would have plenty of time to think about how close they had come to making their dream come true. And about how close they had come to achieving what no one had ever achieved before. But the day after they lost everything, all they were thinking about was that their dream was gone. They had given it to the Giants.

As they walked out into the morning sun to their cars, the players carried cardboard boxes. The boxes were full of cleats and T-shirts and pictures of their wives, girlfriends, kids, and dogs. When they talked, their voices were soft and uncertain, as if they had been asked to recite a poem that they hadn't quite memorized yet. They weren't sure what to think or how to feel. They were all trying to understand where the dream had gone. For six months, the dream had been with them, living and breathing, just like one of their teammates. Now it was dead, and they were all grieving for their loss. Some were doing better than others. Jim Burt was one who was not doing well at all.

Does that look like a cheap shot to you? Huh? Does that look like a cheap shot?

Jim Burt is hunched on the edge of a chair in the quarterbacks' meeting room downstairs at the Taj, watching tape of his hit on Jeff Hostetler in the fourth quarter of yesterday's game. Burt is almost in a panic. After the game yesterday, Lawrence Taylor did a television interview in which he said that the Giants felt Burt's hit on their quarterback "was a cheap shot." But Superman didn't stop there. He had something else to say.

"That's the way Burt plays," Taylor had said. "He goes for the knees."

Burt can't believe L.T. would say that about him. When L.T. was suspended for drugs a few years back, who was there to help him? Jimmy was. When Hoss was on the sidelines all those years, frustrated out of his mind playing behind Phil Simms, who was there to help him? Jimmy was. Years ago, when the Giants were nothing, who was the long-shot nose tackle who sweated and bled to help make them into something? Jimmy was. Now those same guys that he had sweated with and bled with and gone to war with were calling Jimmy the worst kind of football player there is. A dirty football player who goes for the knees. Burt cues up the play again.

"Okay," he says, riveted to the screen at the front of the small room, "I rip the center. I rip by Bart. I'm coming in low—there, look. Moore pushes me—Moore pushes me in my back. I'm diving in low and he pushes me—there. Where'd I hit him? Right in the thigh. Right in the thigh. Is that a cheap shot? No way. Not even close."

That morning at the Taj, Jimmy goes through it again and again and again. He hits Hoss. Hoss goes down. He can't let go. Maybe he never will.

Sitting outside on a brick bench at the front of the Taj, Jesse Sapolu is munching on a cheeseburger. Sapolu is doing about as well as Jim Burt is. "When people get depressed, they eat all the fat food they can," Jesse says, taking a bite of his burger.

Sapolu knows that the vultures are already circling. According to the press, the Niner dynasty died yesterday at Candlestick. Today, at the Taj, it's time for reporters to start picking the corpse clean. The newspapers are already burying Bubba Paris alive for the game he had against Leonard Marshall. Bubba, the reporters have been writing for most of the last half of the season, is too fat to be any good as San Francisco's left tackle. Leonard Marshall broke a bone in Joe Montana's hand and proved that point. The knock on the offensive line all season was that it wasn't opening holes for the running game. Against the Giants, the Niners gained only 30 yards on nine carries. That performance has revived discussion of big changes in the line. But blocking is only one of the uncertainties facing San Francisco as the off-season begins.

The Plan B list has to be done by the end of the month, and rumor has it that some big names will be left unprotected. Roger Craig and Ronnie Lott are at the top of the list. Craig will be 30 by the time training camp starts in July. Can Craig come back from his worst season and the disaster against the Giants? Ronnie Lott will be 32 in a few months. How much does the Ultimate Warrior have left? The doctors say that the broken bone in Joe Montana's hand will be healed by spring. Joe has a four-year contract. He says he wants to finish it. Where does that leave Steve Young, whose contract is up in a few days? Will Chet Brooks's knee ever be strong enough for him to play like the Assassin again? Can Dexter Carter learn to catch punts? Will Jim Burt be back next year? Will Matt Millen? What about Dave Waymer? Most of those Niners are older than 30. Almost half the team is.

There are also rumors of changes in the front office. One scenario has Carmen Policy moving to the Bay Area to take over the presidency of the team from Eddie DeBartolo. The Prince was not happy after the loss to the Giants—he was so mad, in fact, that he slammed his hand into something and broke a bone. Supposedly, after the shattering disappointment against the Giants, the Prince is determined to take a more active role in the operation of his football team. Even Dr. Harry Edwards is going to need some time to heal from what happened at Candlestick.

"We gave it away," Edwards says the morning after the game, shaking his head tiredly. *"We gave it away.* That's what hurts." Edwards is leaving soon for his house on the California coast. He needs to get away from things so he can start working on the chemistry of next year's team. His job will not be easy. Because this season has ended exactly the way it began. So many questions. So few answers.

Spencer Tillman didn't sleep much last night. He kept watching himself. The picture in his mind was always the same. He would knife behind the line and launch into the air toward Matt Bahr. He would fly and fly and fly. But he never flew high enough.

On the way to his car in the parking lot at the Taj the morning after the game, Tillman stops to talk about the end of the dream. "We're all very disappointed," he says, softly. "It wasn't just one year of effort, it was three years' worth of effort that went into yesterday. I think the healing process has begun, though. We've accepted the fact that it did happen. We're all looking forward to coming back and trying again."

Spencer Tillman squints up into the sun. He slides his sunglasses down over his eyes. "This is the way life goes. Life is a series of beginnings and endings. Sometimes, endings aren't the most pleasant of situations. But it's how you handle those situations that determines your relative success or failure in life. If we can learn from this setback, this doesn't have to be an end. It can be a beginning."

As Spencer Tillman got in his car and drove away from the Taj, there was no way to know which one it was. No one would know that until next season. When the hurt was gone and it would be time to dream again.

Epilogue

Roger Craig's fumble and the shattering loss to the Giants provoked a series of changes inside the San Francisco organization. Several weeks after the NFC Championship game, Eddie DeBartolo Jr., George Seifert, and Carmen Policy held a press conference at the Taj, which included sparkling wine and hors d'oeuvres for the press. Several announcements were made that afternoon. Carmen Policy was the team's new president, replacing DeBartolo. Policy would soon be moving from Youngstown, Ohio, to the Bay Area. Seifert, meanwhile, had been given a raise and a two-year extension on his contract. And, finally, there was going to be a new team logo.

For nearly two weeks, the Faithful had raged over San Francisco's decision to leave Ronnie Lott unprotected under Plan B. It didn't seem to matter much that Roger Craig, Matt Millen, Chet Brooks, Jim Burt, Dave Waymer, and other Niner veterans had also been put on Plan B. What mattered to the Faithful was that their team—their Niners—was giving up on a proud warrior who had spent a decade sacrificing his body for them. The Faithful were also upset over the matter of Lott's contract. Back in November, as their quest for the Super Bowl was gathering wins and momentum, the Niners had offered Lott a lucrative three-year package. Less than two months later, however, after the dream died at Candlestick, the team was reportedly asking Lott to take a big cut in pay to come back for only one more season. To the Faithful, that kind of treatment was unconscionable. But so was the new logo.

When San Francisco's new helmet design debuted at the press conference in mid-February, the reaction was immediate. People hated it. Bay Area columnists called it "dorky" and "dumb." A big design firm in Los Angeles had come up with the new helmet, on which the letters "SF"—which had graced the Niners' helmets since the 1960s—was being eliminated in favor of a clean, modern look consisting simply of the word "49ers." A short time later, after thousands of calls from angry Faithful and a torrent of negative press coverage, the 49ers quietly issued a one-page fax that announced that the team was going back to its old helmets.

Spencer Tillman was right.

When Roger Craig fumbled against the Giants to keep the Niners out of the Super Bowl, it didn't have to be an end. But what Tillman didn't know was how painful beginning again would be.

Lott was the first to leave. After a decade as a 49er, Lott signed with the Los Angeles Raiders late in March, more than two months after the New York Giants beat the Buffalo Bills in Super Bowl XXV. Matt Millen and Roger Craig were the next Niners to leave. Millen, an anchor on the 49er defense that had ranked third in the NFL in 1990, signed with the Washington Redskins. Roger Craig followed Lott to the Raiders on April 1.

By late spring, when the Niners held minicamp at the Taj, it was clear that San Francisco was not the same team that had lost to the Giants. The looks on the players' faces showed the same promise and the same hopes of achievement that they had only a few months before. But the faces themselves were so different. In addition to the departures of Lott, Millen, and Craig, players like Keena Turner, Eric Wright, and Mike Wilson had all retired. Joe Montana was now the only member left from San

Francisco's first world championship team back in 1981. In the veterans' places were the eight new players San Francisco had signed under Plan B, a host of anxious rookies culled from the college draft, and a batch of eager free agents looking to hook on with the four-time world champions.

But while Ted Washington and Ricky Watters and Sheldon Canley were getting ready for their first season in professional football, some of the surviving veterans from the loss to the Giants were still trying to get over the last one.

On the Tuesday after Leonard Marshall smashed him into the grass at Candlestick, Joe Montana had two metal screws inserted into his right hand. By the time mini-camp arrived, Joe's broken bone had healed and he was throwing the football again.

So was Steve Young, who had recently decided to sign a new contract and stay with the one-heartbeat team for two more years. In San Francisco, Young had waited four years for a chance to play. After the Giants' game, trade rumors surfaced. One report had San Francisco offering Young to the New England Patriots in exchange for the number one pick in the NFL draft. But for the great-great-great-great grandson of Brigham Young, leaving the Niners was the last thing he wanted to have happen. To Young, his situation was simple. He wanted to be the starting quarterback for the 49ers, and the 49ers wanted him to be their starting quarterback—wanted him so badly that they were willing to pay him more than $4 million. If the team wanted him that much, Young decided, he would wait a little longer.

Chet Brooks was not as fortunate. Following the loss to the Giants, Brooks returned to Dallas. He was deter-mined to work his way back from injured reserve, where he had languished for the final two months of the season. To get his knee back in shape for football, Brooks ran hard on the bumpy field at Carter High School, and he pumped iron in the Carter weight room. It had been a long time since he had hit anybody, and Brooks wanted to get out there on the football field again. He wanted to prove to the coaches that he could still get the job done at safety.

But when minicamp arrived, Brooks's tenuous situation had only worsened. During the Plan-B period, San Francisco had signed several defensive backs. Then, early in May, the Niners were blunt with Brooks: His knee was not in football shape. Brooks didn't agree. Nevertheless, John McVay also informed Brooks that in the event another team became interested in his services, the 49ers would gladly release him.

As Brooks drove away from the Taj in a rental car early in May, it did not look like he was going to be a 49er very much longer.

The same also could be said of Jim Burt, who at 31 had reached the point in his career where a combination of age, injuries, and young blood at his position was threatening to halt his love affair with football. After the loss to the Giants, Burt flew home to New Jersey. He watched the Super Bowl on television. At first, with the bitterness of the loss to his old team roiling inside him, Burt rooted for the Bills. But then when Buffalo got ahead in Tampa and some of the Bills' players started to showboat, Burt decided that Buffalo didn't have good people so he went back to rooting for Bart and L.T. and Hoss.

The Giants beat the Bills 20–19 to become champions of the NFL. Jimmy swallowed hard and started thinking about next season. There was a chance he would need to have surgery on his shoulder. He had hurt it working out with Bart Oates back before training camp. He'd played with the injury all year. It had limited his movement, and he wanted to get it taken care of. Soon, Burt started working out again.

But like Chet Brooks, he was not sure if he would be a 49er when next season rolled around.

For three 49ers whose futures seemed more secure, the off-season was more productive. Dexter Carter married Sheryl Ridgeway and took a honeymoon cruise. Jamie Williams played with his dogs—three Akita purebreds—and took a college history course. Then there was Jesse Sapolu.

In the middle of all the turmoil that followed the loss to New York, Sapolu returned to Southern California and quickly got down to the business of figuring out where the dream had gone. It didn't take him long to realize that he was thinking almost the same thing Spencer Tillman was. "I live in L.A. and all I've been hearing is, 'What are you going to do now that you don't have Ronnie and Roger,'" Sapolu told reporters at minicamp. "I can't answer that. I think it's an exciting opportunity. It's like when George stepped in. A lot of guys will be motivated to try to prove we can win without those great players in the same way we tried to prove we could win without Bill Walsh."

After a season of tension, a season in which they had given every bit of effort they had in them and then on a painful January afternoon found out that it simply was not enough to make their dream come true, the Niners were back to where they started.

They had great expectations.

Acknowledgments

My dream began with three people. My wife, Annette, helped me see that dreams don't come true unless the dreamer has the courage to claim them. Jennifer Bern Basye at Prima was willing to let me try. And Jerry Walker, the public-relations director of the San Francisco 49ers, let me in. Without a ticket into the show, I had nothing. Without Walker, I had no ticket. I am deeply indebted to him.

In the end, my deepest feelings are for the people who took the time to share who they are and how they got there. I'll never forget the time I spent with Chet Brooks, Jim Burt, Dexter Carter, Harry Edwards, Jesse Sapolu, Harry Sydney, Spencer Tillman, Jamie Williams, and Steve Young. These class acts were willing to give a new guy with an idea a chance. I also have special feelings for John McVay, who treated me with respect.

I'm especially grateful to two people who made my five months in the Bay Area much easier than they might otherwise have been. Sam Skinner, a respected journalist long before I was even born, introduced me to Carmen Policy and Harry Edwards. Without such introductions, I would never have gained critical insights into the business of professional football and the internal operation of the 49ers. I thank Sam for his patience with a rookie, for advice that was not always taken, and for reminding me on every possible occasion that John Fourcade is the greatest quarterback in the world. I thank Jeff Bayer of the *Foster City Islander* not only for many of the photographs that grace this book, but also for getting as excited about this project as if it were his own. To Bayer's children, Alabama and Sabrina, ruff!

Although I benefited from the work of several reporters during the five months I spent in the Bay Area, I'm especially grateful to Richard Weiner, who covers the Niners for the *Peninsula Times Tribune.*

I would also be remiss if I didn't acknowledge the valuable assistance of Rodney Knox, Darla Maeda, and Dave Rahn of the public-relations staff.

Finally, thanks also go to my grandparents, Frederick and Charlotte Rother, who gave me a place to work when I needed one.

Dennis Pottenger
Sacramento, California
May 1991

Index